POLITICS IN BLACK AND WHITE

POLITICS IN BLACK AND WHITE

RACE AND POWER IN LOS ANGELES

Raphael J. Sonenshein

PRINCETON UNIVERSITY PRESS

PRINCETON, NEW JERSEY

LIBRARY OF CONGRESS CATALOGING-IN-PUBLICATION DATA

SONENSHEIN, RAPHAEL.

POLITICS IN BLACK AND WHITE : RACE AND POWER IN LOS ANGELES /

RAPHAEL J. SONENSHEIN.

P.   CM.

INCLUDES BIBLIOGRAPHICAL REFERENCES AND INDEX.

ISBN 0-691-02548-7 (PBK.)

1. LOS ANGELES (CALIF.)—POLITICS AND GOVERNMENT.   2. AFRO-

AMERICANS—CALIFORNIA—LOS ANGELES—POLITICS AND GOVERNMENT.

3. LOS ANGELES (CALIF.)—RACE RELATIONS.   I. TITLE.

F869.L857S66   1993

979.4′94053—DC20   92-33249

THIS BOOK HAS BEEN COMPOSED IN LINOTRON JANSON

PRINCETON UNIVERSITY PRESS BOOKS ARE PRINTED ON ACID-FREE PAPER
AND MEET THE GUIDELINES FOR PERMANENCE AND DURABILITY OF THE
COMMITTEE ON PRODUCTION GUIDELINES FOR BOOK LONGEVITY OF THE
COUNCIL ON LIBRARY RESOURCES

PRINTED IN THE UNITED STATES OF AMERICA

3 5 7 9 10 8 6 4

TO THREE GENERATIONS OF

WOMEN IN MY LIFE

CRS, PA, JMAS, and ACAS

CONTENTS

ILLUSTRATIONS

Maps

Photo sections follow pages 66 and 226

TABLES

PREFACE

TWICE in the last three decades, Los Angeles has dramatically shown the pain of American race relations in outbursts of shocking violence. In 1965 Watts became a symbol of a new racial polarization, and in 1992 a nation looked on in fearful fascination as violence wracked South Central Los Angeles. These dramatic and urgent events justly command our attention.

But Los Angeles has another part of the story to tell—one deeply intertwined with the events of 1965 and 1992. It is the struggle to form coalitions across racial lines. Racial violence brings to the fore in the sharpest possible way some enduring questions: Are interracial alliances compatible with the political assertion of minorities? Can whites and minorities find common ground?

The preliminary evidence is mixed. Alongside the Los Angeles violence, we have witnessed a small jump in "crossover" Black politics. In 1989, David Dinkins was elected New York City's first Black mayor, L. Douglas Wilder of Virginia became the first African-American ever elected a state governor, and largely white New Haven and Seattle elected Black mayors. Urban violence and crossover politics seem to be opposites, but both are part and parcel of the paradoxical shape of race in the United States.

Biracial politics lie at the heart of the American political system. Since the early 1960s racial issues have structured party coalitions, and race underlies many apparently nonracial issues (Carmines and Stimson 1989; Edsall and Edsall 1991). To understand why parties succeed and fail, we must understand how interracial coalitions rise and fall. We can unravel the puzzles of U.S. politics only by breaking into the delicate world of race relations.

Since the rise of urban racial polarization in the mid-1960s, the pessimism about biracial politics presented in Carmichael and Hamilton's classic *Black Power* (1967) has been prevalent. Carmichael and Hamilton argued that liberal ideology provided a weak foundation for coalition; only self-interest could be trusted.

I argue in this book that biracial coalitions between African-Americans and white liberals have been prematurely declared dead. And since biracial politics are still alive, I explore how biracial coalitions work—why they rise and why they fall. Even as coalitions arise phoenixlike from the ashes of civil violence, the fondest hopes for interracial alliances often run up against the limits of racial bridge building.

This is a new look at interracial politics—one that aims both to make a theoretical contribution to the study of interracial politics and to have practical implications for the choices people make in the political arena. In that sense, it is intended to be accessible both to scholars and to a more general audience.

As other minorities flex their political muscles, they search for coalition partners and ask many of the same questions that Blacks and whites have asked over the years. There may even be good reasons not to pursue coalitions—but the best choices will be made when the Black-white experience has been fully understood.

I argue that three factors are crucial to the formation of biracial coalitions: ideology, interest, and leadership. The necessary factor is shared ideology. Without common liberal beliefs, biracial alliances are unlikely to form. In racial matters, pure interest is unlikely to be sufficient to form long-lasting alliances. Racial attitudes go to the heart of how Americans think about politics. Objective interests may help people choose alliances in other areas, but are unlikely to overcome deeply held racial feelings.

But beliefs are not enough. Conflicts of interest between Blacks and white liberals can jeopardize biracial coalitions, as Carmichael and Hamilton argued. At the same time, alliances of interest based on a shared desire for political power can be powerful forces for coalition. Leadership—particularly the long-term ties between Black and white activists—helps ideological coalitions bridge the hazards of interest conflict or build on interest alignment.

My discussion of the last factor—leadership—draws on Barbara Hinckley's (1981) important critique of traditional coalition theory. Hinckley argued that while coalitions are indeed subject to the objective factors of ideology and self-interest, the human dimension of how elites learn to trust each other is too often overlooked. In the long term, she contended, the coalition that has already formed on the basis of elite trust is likely to continue. Therefore coalitions must be studied over time at both the elite and mass levels.

In particular, I explore the evolution of biracial politics in Los Angeles, the second-largest city in the United States. With a population less than 18 percent African-American, Los Angeles has been the site for an extraordinary level of minority power, behind its Black mayor, Tom Bradley. The key to this political success has been a durable alliance between Blacks and white liberals in general, and Blacks and Jews in particular. Over time the coalition has offered a major role to the business community and has expanded to include Latinos and Asian-Americans.

For many years, Los Angeles has illustrated the viability of biracial politics (and more specifically of Black-Jewish coalitions). But this model of western interracial politics has been largely overlooked. Much closer attention has been paid to the sad history of interracial conflict in New York City and Chicago. By bringing Los Angeles and its prototypically western experience into the debate, we can devise more general approaches to biracial politics. Now that Los Angeles is in the public mind again, the violence of 1992 may overshadow the important lessons that its racial history offers.

My analysis of Los Angeles biracial politics confirms the importance of elite interracial networks. In this sense, it overlaps with the social-psychological literature on racial interaction, which indicates that the setting in which people of different races interact has a major impact on the success of race relations (e.g., Norvell and Worchel 1981). How do these small-group insights hold up in the much larger world of big-city coalition politics?

The Los Angeles experience casts a sharp light on New York City. It is, after all, a mystery why the nation's most liberal city has had such vituperative race relations. The approach offered in this book may help provide some answers.

In both interests and leadership, New York City and Los Angeles stand worlds apart. I contend that a direct conflict of interest existed between Blacks and white liberals in New York City, while in Los Angeles they had common interests. In Los Angeles a strong biracial leadership network exploited that shared interest, while in New York City leaders failed to carry their communities across racial lines. Understanding this history is essential to the efforts of activists in both cities seeking to deal with the difficult years to come.

In exploring the evolution of the Los Angeles coalition, I have used a variety of research methods. I reviewed the archives of local African-American newspapers for the years 1960–1963; interviewed elite activists, including Mayor Bradley; studied city hiring patterns and commission appointments; conducted original voting analysis of elections involving Black factions; collected voting data by council district over a 35-year period; and examined public and private opinion polls.

In pursuit of the evolutionary perspective, I have followed an immersion strategy. I have read hundreds of newspaper articles on microfilm from the *Los Angeles Times* and the Black-owned *Los Angeles Sentinel* and *California Eagle*. The *Sentinel* and the *Eagle* were particularly useful for the period preceding the 1965 Watts riot, marked by the *Times*'s neglect of the African-American community. I have drawn on campaign expenditure reports and voting returns for a wide range of city, county, and state elections.

I conducted a series of open-ended interviews with political activists and government officials. In addition, I co-conducted another twenty interviews with Alan Saltzstein for a study on federal aid to Los Angeles (Saltzstein, Sonenshein, and Ostrow 1986). I accompanied Mayor Bradley on a day in South Central Los Angeles and recorded an interview with him.

I supplemented the council district analysis with polling information. I obtained full reports of *Los Angeles Times* polls. In addition, the private polling firm of Fairbank, Maullin, and Associates made available to me a series of unpublished polls that provided a wealth of detail on the city's groups.

I explored Black factions through the analysis of three elections—one for state senate, two for state assembly—in which factional lines emerged. These elections are explored in Chapter Eight, and combine elite interviews with an analysis of the vote by social status.

I also drew on fifteen years of personal experience in Los Angeles biracial politics. I grew up in New Jersey. From across the Hudson River, I witnessed both the rise and the decline of the liberal Lindsay administration in New York City. By the time I left the East Coast in 1974, I had been thoroughly immersed in the general belief that biracial coalitions were an outdated feature of an unrealistically optimistic civil rights movement.

Upon my arrival in Los Angeles, I was interested to discover that a new biracial coalition, led by the city's Black mayor, Tom Bradley, was just in the process of consolidating the power it had won the year before. I became deeply curious about the origins, dynamics, and prospects of this western-style biracial coalition. How could its existence be reconciled with all that had surrounded me on the East Coast? As an intern in the mayor's office and later as a deputy to a Bradley ally on the city council, I had the opportunity to explore these questions.

Soon I was hired as press secretary for several political campaigns within the Los Angeles Black community—Democratic primaries for state legislative posts. The candidates represented two great factions of the Los Angeles Black community, one headed by Mayor Bradley, and the other by his long-time rival, Mervyn Dymally.

I began to wonder if these factions had something important to do with the biracial coalition. My research eventually led me to establish such a linkage. The biracial coalition was more than an alliance between masses; at the crucial level of leadership, it grew out of factions within the Black and white communities.

For the last fifteen years, I have tried to make sense out of what I found—both to understand race in Los Angeles through a broader understanding of biracial politics and to see how the western experience can expand our existing notions of interracial coalitions. The broadest purpose of this study is to show that a wider theory of biracial coalitions than has yet been presented can comfortably accommodate the experiences of both the newer western communities and the eastern and midwestern cities. In spite of the racial chasm, there are valuable lessons to be learned about the path across the divide.

Structure of the Book

Part One explores the background of Los Angeles coalition politics. The first chapter examines the literature on biracial politics, and sets out a theory of interracial coalitions. The second chapter places Los Angeles minority politics in the setting of an entrepreneurial western metropolis where minorities were neither seen nor heard—but in which there were surprising openings for Black economic advancement. The third chapter traces the extraordinary success of Black politics in the early 1960s and the victories it won without substantial coalition.

In Part Two, I show how the Black and white liberal movements came together in Bradley's 1963 election to the Los Angeles city council. How this district-sized coalition expanded into a dominant citywide regime is illustrated over the course of several chapters. Part Two concludes with Bradley's election to the mayoralty in 1973 and the expansion of the Bradley faction in local Black politics.

Part Three explores the political and economic changes wrought by the biracial regime, and the rise and fall of its political support. Has biracialism prevented change, and how stable has cross-racial politics been? Strains in the ruling regime since 1985 are explored. Finally, I examine the impact of the Rodney King case and the Los Angeles riots on Los Angeles coalition politics.

Part Four discusses the wider implications of the Los Angeles case. Why did biracial politics succeed politically in Los Angeles but not in New York City, where there are more Blacks and more white liberals? Are multiracial alliances among African-Americans, Latinos, Asian-Americans, and liberal whites viable in the Los Angeles of the 1990s? Finally, what does the exploration of the western biracial experience and the dynamics of biracial coalitions tell us about a theory and practice of biracial politics?

—*October 1, 1992*
Santa Monica, California

ACKNOWLEDGMENTS

A T EVERY STAGE of its development, this book has been helped
along by generous colleagues, friends, and family. Early encour-
agement from Dale Rogers Marshall got me started and Rufus
Browning provided ongoing support. Dean Mann, former editor of the
Western Political Quarterly, helped me find the path of my own thinking.
John Mollenkopf and Bruce Cain read the entire manuscript, and their
comments were immensely helpful.

I have been fortunate to have wonderful colleagues and staff at California
State University, Fullerton—friends who have been willing to listen to my
Los Angeles spiel again and again. Alan Saltzstein has read everything,
including the roughest drafts, and has provided the friendliest of guidance
and feedback. He was also a marvelous collaborator on parts of the research.
J. Owens Smith challenged me to think theoretically, and Billy Vaughn
provided sage advice. Stuart Ross helped me locate grant support. To my
students at Fullerton, UC Irvine, and UCLA, who have listened in class to
much of this book, I am deeply grateful. Phil Harris, Heidi Overturf, and
especially Corecia Davis made major contributions as research assistants.

The bulk of the research was completed with the help of a one-year grant
from the John Randolph Haynes and Dora Haynes Foundation. The
Haynes Foundation and its executive director, Diane Cornwell, truly believed in the project, and their confidence helped more than they know. I
was also helped again and again by Los Angeles city employees, particularly Hynda Rudd and Rob Freeman of the City Archives and Tom Hasse
of the City Clerk Election Division.

Susan Pinkus of the *Los Angeles Times Poll* provided valuable information
on short notice, and I was greatly helped by Richard Maullin, a private
polltaker who shared a number of his surveys with me. I was fortunate to
have the cooperation of numerous political activists and public officials,
including Mayor Bradley, who agreed to be interviewed. Of course, they
bear no responsibility for the conclusions presented here.

Princeton University Press has been a superb partner in this enterprise.
From Gail Ullman, who first showed great interest in my proposal, to
Malcolm DeBevoise, who carried it to completion, and Jenn Mathews,
who fielded my numerous desperate calls, dealing with the Press has been a
pleasure. Lyn Grossman edited the copy with great care, and Jane Low
handled the editorial production of the book with a soft touch but firm
deadlines.

My parents Israel and Celia instilled in me a love of politics and a passion for justice. I am deeply grateful for all they gave me. Their spirits live on in this book.

I have had the good fortune to be inspired not only by my parents but by two other great people. Paul Ylvisaker brought me into urban politics more than twenty years ago and until his most untimely death in 1992 was both mentor and friend. Paul showed me that the thoughtful life should be lived as well as observed. Maxine Waters hired me off the street to work in Los Angeles campaigns. She took the time to teach me as much as I could learn and showed me that politics and social change can be both inspired and inspiring. My gratitude to both is unbounded.

My brothers Linc and David have been both friends and models of a scholarship and humanity I greatly admire. The Dropouts showed that in softball as in politics, the best coalitions are built on trust, experience, and the will to win. Herman DeBose has shared my love for the politics of Los Angeles. Joe Hertzberg spent hours and hours helping my voting data to make sense; without his help, it would have been hopeless. He treated my work as carefully as his own. John Youngman heroically restored the book manuscript from apparent extinction by a rampaging computer virus. Ken Cole was always a fount of support and friendship; he was both helpful critic and thoughtful contributor. Alexis Nehemkis and Barbara Mitchell buoyed me always with their enthusiasm and interest. My deepest and fondest gratitude belongs to my wife Phyllis and my daughters Julia Mary and Anna Cecelia, who during the writing of this book, treated me as sane when the evidence was all the other way. Phyllis was there from the beginning, wisely editing, listening and suggesting, and full of confidence. For this loving help in the face of my obsession, I am truly thankful.

PART ONE

BACKGROUND

ONE

OVERVIEW: BIRACIAL COALITION POLITICS

[W]e believe that political relations are based on self-interest:
benefits to be gained and losses to be avoided. For the most
part, man's politics is determined by his evaluation of material
good and evil. Politics results from a conflict of interests, not
of consciences.
(Carmichael and Hamilton 1967:75)

Liberals on race issues are very different from conservatives,
and ideology has an important influence on the nature
and outcome of the minority struggle for access
to local government.
(Browning, Marshall, and Tabb 1984:248)

T HE DEBATE over biracial coalition politics has been an enduring and intensely argued one. Should minorities go it alone and bargain with the larger society, or do they need to form alliances to counter their minority status? And if they make alliances, with whom should they link their fate?

More specifically, the relationship between African-Americans and white liberals, once widely admired, has been a source of bitter division since the conclusion of the civil rights movement and the rise of a more independent and assertive Black politics.

The movement to end racial segregation in the South in the 1950s and 1960s gave rise to a broad, powerful, and successful biracial coalition linking Blacks, liberal whites, and organized labor. The civil rights movement planted the seeds for an optimistic view of biracial coalitions based on goodwill and liberal ideology. It established the belief that ideology alone could be a firm basis for a productive biracial coalition. Moral overtones permeated the coalition, and remain central features of today's liberal politics.

Following the historic March on Washington in 1963, the main objectives of the civil rights movement were enacted into law. The Civil Rights Act of 1964 ended racial segregation in public accommodations, and the Voting Rights Act of 1965 brought Blacks into the southern political system. A new federal program to end poverty was enacted in 1965, along with major initiatives in education and health care. With the completion of this agenda and the rise of racial conflict in the North, strains among coalition members grew.

In their 1967 book, *Black Power*, Carmichael and Hamilton argued that Blacks could not depend on white allies, no matter how liberal. Since "politics results from a conflict of interests, not of consciences," white liberals were not very different from other whites, and would desert the Black cause if their own interests were threatened. Carmichael and Hamilton proposed that *interest*, not ideology, provided the most solid basis for an effective biracial coalition. Whites would have at most a supporting role in a Black-led movement for equality.

Bitter struggles between African-American and white mayoral candidates in Gary, Cleveland, Newark, and other cities cast further doubt on the prospects for interracial politics. Racial polarization meant that victory depended on the ability of the Black community to outmobilize the white community (O'Laughlin and Berg 1977). While even in the most polarized cities, white liberal support provided the winning edge for Black mayoral candidates (Cole 1974; Pettigrew 1971; Ransom 1987), the main focus was on racial polarization.

To some, the broad implication of this evidence was that the independent Black movement—a phenomenon that brought Blacks positively and enthusiastically into the system—must inevitably create white antagonism and racial polarization. Black political assertiveness was widely thought to be incompatible with biracial coalition politics.

Such pessimistic views of interracial politics have great practical consequences. Political analysis affects political strategy. African-Americans might feel it advantageous to avoid white liberal support and search for a new type of biracial alliance—or forgo such alliances entirely. Black activists might conclude that the only political hope lies in a coalition of non-white minorities against a united white community.

The question of interracial politics is highly relevant to those who are neither Black nor white. Just as the African-American struggle has influenced the struggle of other minorities, the Black-white coalition experience—positive and negative—is likely to affect current debates over multiracial alliances. As newly assertive minorities gain in numbers, these considerations are likely to be highly significant. The same questions need to be answered, the same pitfalls seen and surmounted. Latinos and Asian-Americans might decide that white liberals are unreliable and ineffective partners.

With the death of biracial coalitions so widely assumed, new alternatives were suggested. Some called for "independent power politics," with a unified Black community bargaining with the larger society (Holloway 1968). Henry (1980) found that despite significant obstacles, Black-Latino relations had some potential for a strong coalition. Others promoted a class alliance between Blacks and white workers (Hahn and Almy 1971; Davidson 1972), which had been specifically mentioned by Carmichael and Hamilton as meeting their criteria for biracial coalitions.

Jesse Jackson's 1984 and 1988 presidential campaigns combined the various alternatives into a "rainbow coalition." A progressive alliance of color and class would unite minorities and disadvantaged whites. It would be unlike the liberal coalition, in which Jews and other white liberals played a prominent part. Whites would play the subordinate, supportive role outlined by Carmichael and Hamilton.

The various alternatives fell short of their promise. Reexamination of voting data cast doubt on the presumed racial liberalism of working-class whites (Murray and Vedlitz 1978; Halley, Acock, and Greene 1976). The Jackson campaigns did not build a majority within the Democratic party. Those whites who supported Jackson were generally not from the working classes, but were educated liberals (Plissner and Mitofsky 1988). Yet few scholars were led to a general reassessment of the role of liberal biracial coalitions—a task this book seeks to carry out.

The dominant pessimism about Black-liberal alliances may have been deepened by the settings in which they have been studied. Eastern and midwestern cities have dominated the debate to the exclusion of the western experience.

The "polarization model," in which Blacks and whites are highly opposed and in which victory is due to the greater unity and mobilization of Black voters, is predominant in eastern and midwestern cities with large African-American populations, strong competing ethnic communities, remnants of party organizations, and high levels of white racial animosity. Studies of these localized settings have often been the basis for broad national generalizations.

Levine (1974:45), for example, considered polarization the key to understanding racial politics. On the basis of research in Gary and Cleveland, he predicted that interracial elite alliances ("consociations") would be exceptionally unlikely to form: "Observers of American urban politics should not be overly optimistic about the chances of consociational regimes developing in our cities in the near future . . . racial antipathy in most municipalities tends to create too many centrifugal forces for consociations to persist."

The same pessimistic conclusion emerged from Eisinger's (1976) examination of Milwaukee, where attitudes of Blacks and whites were so polarized that elite biracial coalitions seemed out of the question. In another study, Eisinger (1983) argued that Black mayors have a difficult time forming a constituency among the white middle class. Kleppner (1985) found that racial polarization was the central axis of Chicago politics.

Perhaps the most significant generalizations have come from the experience of New York City. As the spiritual home of American liberalism, New

York City was the site of the progressive John Lindsay regime (1965–1973). Strains between the city's Black and Jewish communities soon undermined the Lindsay administration. The Lindsay coalition eventually gave way to more conservative political alliances, with little minority or liberal representation (Mollenkopf 1990a).

Because of New York City's historical liberalism and massive communications role, the breakdown of its liberal coalition led to dire conclusions. New York City has been a beacon of doom for those interested in biracial coalitions and specifically in Black-Jewish relations. The assumption seems to be that if biracial liberalism can't make it in New York City, it can't make it anywhere. (The election of Black mayor David Dinkins in 1989 has thus far failed to lift the city's persisting gloom about race relations.)

But a view from the other coast suggests a different conclusion: that biracial coalitions between Blacks and white liberals have been prematurely declared dead. A more complete model of biracial politics has eluded us because of the omission of the western experience—where the role of interracial coalitions can be neither ignored nor discounted. In the western states, and especially in California, there are smaller Black populations, fewer competing ethnic groups with an established power base, reform political cultures, and lower levels of white prejudice. Mollenkopf (1990a) has shown how political reform in the West facilitated the evolution of minority politics.

If white liberals are viable allies for Black politics, the western setting might offer both a greater need and a greater opportunity for cross-racial alliance. The result could be a "crossover model," in which Black unity is supplemented by major linkages to white liberal support.

In 1984, Browning, Marshall, and Tabb published *Protest Is Not Enough*, a pathbreaking study of minority incorporation in ten northern California cities. They found considerable, if varying improvement in the level of minority power between 1960 and 1980. They attributed minority political success to a combination of African-American numbers and mobilization and white liberal support. Their research unmistakably challenged the dominant pessimism about liberal biracial coalitions.

Protest Is Not Enough was open to challenge because it was limited to cities in northern California. The San Francisco Bay Area is unusually liberal; therefore it could be an anomaly, even in the West. The largest city studied was San Francisco (sixteenth in the nation), where a strong biracial coalition did not form. The most powerful and enduring coalition was found in Berkeley, an atypically liberal city with a population of only 103,000. *Protest Is Not Enough* needed to be tested in more conservative, more populous areas of the West.

The case of Los Angeles is therefore particularly significant. As the second-largest U.S. city and as the metropolis of conservative southern

California, Los Angeles offers an important test of the model. Despite a Black population that has never exceeded 18 percent, Los Angeles has experienced a very high degree of minority incorporation and biracial coalition politics. Since 1963, African-Americans have controlled 20 percent of the city council seats and have held the mayoralty since 1973. Latinos have gained increasing incorporation in recent years.

The vehicle for minority incorporation has been a tightly knit coalition of Blacks and white liberals of which Latinos and Asian-Americans have become increasingly important members. In its levels of minority incorporation and biracial coalition, Los Angeles most closely resembles the Berkeley of *Protest Is Not Enough*. This evidence confirms the existence of a valid western element in an expanded national model of biracial coalition politics.

Dynamics of Biracial Coalitions

If, indeed, biracial coalitions are not completely dead, we must begin to analyze their origins and dynamics. How do coalitions between Blacks and white liberals form, and why? Why do they fail to form, and why do existing coalitions break down? Can a theory of biracial coalitions apply throughout the country, and not only in specific regions?

While the debate over biracial coalitions is highly political and pragmatic, it is also an argument over a theory of biracial coalitions. One side sees interest as the glue of coalitions, viewing biracial coalitions as, at best, short-lived tactical compromises between self-centered groups. The other camp focuses on the role of ideology, emphasizing the enduring and solid character of biracial coalitions based on common beliefs.

Ideology—specifically, racial ideology—is a set of beliefs that deeply affects political opinions. Ideology shapes opinion, even at the expense of immediate self-interest. Interest is quite different. The realities of competition and advantage suggest the best strategy—maximization of advancement regardless of philosophy. This division reflects the debate over Black-liberal coalitions: goodwill versus practical calculation.

An active scholarly debate on racial issues divides along roughly the same lines. One school of thought suggests that racial conflict can be understood as a realistic power struggle between groups. As whites identify with other whites in the face of a Black challenge, they protect their group interests through racial hostility (Giles and Evans 1986; Giles and Gatlin 1980). In this view, political actions are affected by the political situation of individuals and groups.

Carmichael and Hamilton's focus on interest complements this view of racial politics and is directly related to traditional coalition theory. Based on "rational choice" models, Downs (1957) and Riker (1961) tried to understand political events on the basis of perceptions of self-interest by political actors. They hoped to free scholars from sentimental notions about how coalitions form, and focus instead on the cold calculation of coalition politics. This "economic" interpretation of coalition behavior has attained wide currency.

A contrasting view holds that preexisting racial attitudes deeply influence perception of racial issues; in this sense, racial politics is inherently ideological. Regardless of the political situation and their specific interests, some whites are more racially liberal than others, and their attitudes shape their political actions (Kinder and Sanders 1987; Kinder and Sears 1981). The emphasis on white attitudes fits well with Browning, Marshall, and Tabb's (1984) approach.

The crossover model has much in common with "ideological distance" theories of coalition formation, which suggest that coalitions form not on the basis of cold self-interest but on the grounds of shared ideology. The most likely coalition to form is the one between groups close in ideology even when another alliance might be more advantageous. A study of European parliaments found this to be the dominant mode of party coalitions in a wide variety of settings (Browne and Dreijaminis 1982).

Thus the study of biracial electoral coalitions between Blacks and white liberals can be seen as a test case in a more general debate about the roots of racial conflict and cooperation.

Both polarization and crossover theories leave much unexplained. How is it that biracial coalitions rise and fall? Neither the polarization nor the crossover studies address the dynamics of biracial coalitions. Polarization theory assumes the impossibility or uselessness of such coalitions. Why explore how they work? Crossover theory tends to assume that there will be a positive relationship between white liberalism and minority politics. Without exploring dynamics, we may miss the key point: coalitions are possible, but not inevitable.

Most studies on either side do not consider the ups and downs of a particular biracial relationship in one city. Mollenkopf's (1990a) study of the "rollback" of minority gains in New York City suggests the importance of exploring the dimension of time. The popularity of opinion surveys makes a longer-range perspective less likely. By contrast, the dimension of time allows more general conclusions to be drawn, even from a single-city case study. And things do change over time, sometimes quite dramatically—a fact that is hard to miss in the Los Angeles of 1992.

For help in these areas, we can turn to the work of Barbara Hinckley. In her critique of coalition theory, Hinckley (1981) noted that the single game played at one time is the focus of most coalition research. She suggested that the critical variable of time is wrongly excluded:

[I]n sharp contrast, real political games occur in time. They occur as one of an experienced or expected series, where players know each other and expect to meet and play again. . . . Bargaining is shaped by historical alliances. Deception is constrained by the risk of retaliation. . . . The single-game situation, then, deliberately excludes the temporal context within which political activity occurs. (66)

While conscious of interest and ideology, coalition partners operate within a human framework:

[W]ith both a past and a future, players may reason that a stable coalition will bring the greatest return and prefer to stay with a past partner, despite present resource distribution, to maximize returns over all games. Thus in any one game in a series, the past choice of partner may be the best predictor of present coalition formation. (68)

Hinckley noted that trust garnered over time is a critical factor in coalition behavior: "a player, faced with uncertainty and many other things to do, seeks a trustworthy partner as the quickest, easiest, surest way to maximize a share of returns. Likewise, historical memory, repetition of the game—all suggest who is to be trusted" (74). The historical view of coalition suggests that time, experience, and the actual environment of the game independently affect coalition behavior. Coalitions arise out of the very human tendency to seek out the familiar and the comfortable.

Hinckley's theory requires close attention to elite interactions. According to Eisinger (1976:3), "the relationships among groups, both organized and unorganized, in political enterprises are forged ultimately by elites or leaders." The level of rational calculation implied by coalition has been expressed by Hinckley (1981:5): "To form a coalition, both partners must be aware that they could gain more by working together than by working alone." That is the language of the activist, not the mass.

Hinckley did not specifically address interracial politics. Are there particular dynamics involved in leadership alliances across racial lines? Political scientists have not generally addressed this question, but social psychologists have. Some literature on racial interaction suggests the importance of equal status among the individuals involved and participation in a common activity. I show in this book that the Los Angeles biracial coalition was an alliance of leaders with shared philosophies and equal status engaged in a common activity—the search for political power. In the context of shared political interests, the combination was extremely potent.

This study therefore can be seen as joining together Hinckley's view of coalitions and some insights from the social-psychological literature on interracial elites in order to suggest an approach to the study of biracial coalitions.

I contend that the success of a biracial electoral coalition between Blacks and white liberals depends primarily on ideology, but with crucial roles for interest and leadership. Racial attitudes structure political choices (Carmines and Stimson 1982, 1989). A racial conservative is highly unlikely to join a biracial coalition, especially if one of the coalition's explicit goals is African-American political incorporation. Shifting interests are unlikely to shake that basic view of the world.

Despite the great variety of political situations from city to city, the white base for Black politics seems to be highly consistent. Those whites who have supported Black mayoral candidates have tended to be young, Democratic, well educated, liberal on social issues, and sympathetic to political reform. Jews have been disproportionately represented among those who have voted for Black candidates (Cole 1974; Pettigrew 1971; Ransom 1987).

Where race is an issue, common economic interest is unlikely to override racial hostility. Davidson's (1972) study of Houston, for instance, argued that economics would eventually unite Blacks and poor whites in a class-based radical coalition. However, in the face of Black candidacies, this class alliance collapsed in many southern settings (Murray and Vedlitz 1978). Eisinger's (1976) study of Milwaukee, a city with a large white working-class population, concluded that racial attitudes were so polarized that leaders had limited freedom to create a durable biracial coalition.

One elite context in which economic interest may override racial attitudes is in the close relationship between Black mayors and white business leaders. Despite their conservatism, white corporate figures have played prominent roles in Black incorporation regimes, and their interests have been advanced (Stone 1988; Eisinger 1983; Erie 1980). The important interaction between Black mayors and white corporate figures, which will be further explored in this study, is quite different from the relationship between Blacks and white liberals. While the two white groups—downtown business and white liberals—are frequently treated interchangeably by scholars, they often strongly oppose each other.

While racial liberalism is necessary for the creation of a biracial coalition, it is not sufficient. Biracial coalitions between Blacks and white liberals are viable on ideological grounds, but they are not inevitable. Like most political coalitions, biracial coalitions are influenced by interest. The interests of white liberals may conflict with Black interests. Interest alliance, or at least the absence of interest conflict, is a condition required for a strong biracial coalition.

Interests are, however, neither completely objective nor inflexible. Leaders and organizers have an impact on how group interests are perceived. The prospects for biracial coalitions depend significantly on the willingness and ability of Black and white leaders to create and sustain such coalitions. In racial matters, leaders will find it easier to overcome interest conflicts among ideological allies than to create an interest alliance among ideological foes.

Before completing the picture, however, we need to look more closely at the roots of biracial coalitions in the African-American community itself.

Black Factions and the Origins of Biracial Coalitions

While divisions among whites have been highlighted in studies of interracial politics, the Black community has been portrayed as relatively monolithic. As Eisinger (1976:6) has written,

> In short, there is justification for viewing black urban populations as constitut-
> ing racial political communities, distinctive from white political communities
> and capable of independent and cohesive action. In order to understand the
> implications of this view, however, one must, first, break away from the con-
> ventional historical interpretation of the black role in urban politics and sec-
> ond, overcome the resistance of those who insist on stressing the heterogeneity
> of the black community and its inability to resolve internal tensions in order to
> present a united racial front.

This "unitary" view was an important advance over earlier conceptions that undermined the self-determination of the African-American community. The election of Black mayors with consistently solid Black support has testified to racial solidarity. With this unity in place and recognized, there is little reason to overlook Black factional divisions and their possible role both in Black empowerment and biracial coalitions.

We know that coalitions are built by leaders. The question then becomes, *which* leaders? One key to the origins of biracial coalitions may lie in factions within the African-American community. Black factional divisions are central factors in the development of biracial coalitions for Black empowerment. The movement for Black empowerment was not only a shift in power between Blacks and whites; it also marked an important change in power relations within the Black community. This inner structure becomes obscured as the coalition draws wider support. It is only by carefully studying coalitions over time that the factional element emerges.

Just as some whites are more likely than others to participate in a biracial coalition for Black empowerment, some Blacks are more likely than other Blacks to join. The divisions are hardly noticeable at the mass level when Black candidates oppose white candidates. They are far more visible at the elite level, and at both the mass and elite levels when Black candidates face each other.

Virtually no attention has been devoted to the important role of Black factions in biracial coalitions. Social differences among Blacks have seemed interesting largely in the search for an elusive middle-class Black conservatism. It has long been known that there are significant class differences among Blacks. In fact, the gap may be growing (W. Wilson 1978). The belief that middle-class Blacks are more conservative than poorer Blacks, however, has been generally discredited. There is much greater agreement among Blacks of all classes than conservatives had hoped. At every income level, Blacks are more liberal than whites. On a number of issues, middle-class Blacks are more liberal than poor Blacks (Welch and Combs 1985; Jennings 1982).

But the question remains, Do internal Black divisions have some political consequences? The unitary view may still obscure the political reality of the Black community (Jackson 1987; Parent and Stekler 1985). It is hard to observe biracial coalitions without noting that especially at the leadership level such coalitions arise from some elements of the Black community and not from the community as a whole.

Biracial coalitions for Black empowerment have often collided with traditional Democratic party organizations. African-American mayoral candidates have generally run as reformers in the face of party opposition (Tryman 1974; Preston 1990). The Black politicians most likely to be allied with traditional party organizations tend to represent working-class Black districts, while those who seek to build reform alliances around Black empowerment generally come from upwardly mobile or middle-class and professional communities. The second group is also more likely to challenge the political party system.

The examples are legion. Richard Hatcher took on the county Democratic machine and its Black allies to win the mayoralty of Gary. Harold Washington's struggle with the Chicago machine and Black politicians still within its embrace played a central role in Black empowerment in Chicago, as well as in its failure after Washington's death (Starks and Preston 1990). Newark's Kenneth Gibson, a middle-class Black civil engineer, had to overcome the power of Black party regulars to win the mayoralty (Sonenshein 1971).

In Philadelphia, the election of Wilson Goode marked a transition from a traditional, party-based Black leadership to a more professional, broadly based cadre (Keiser 1990). Indeed, when Jesse Jackson ran for president in 1984 against the wishes of many party leaders, his original base of support came from middle-class Blacks (Reed 1986).

It makes sense that this segment of the Black community would also be more amenable to alliance with liberal white reformers. At the intimate level of social contact, interracial relationships tend to flower when people of equal status meet in an atmosphere of equality (Jeffries and Ransford

1969). Upwardly mobile Blacks and liberal, educated whites are the most likely to form a strong elite tie. The same Blacks who might be most willing to take on established party politicians would also be best situated to work with white reformers. In this way, Black power and biracial politics during the era of Black empowerment can be seen as potentially complementary.

Los Angeles

Los Angeles is the prototypical western metropolis—a city of the twentieth century, built by entrepreneurial visionaries on a path quite different from that of eastern and midwestern cities. The twin concepts of boom and reform that underlie the experience of Sun Belt cities have characterized the spectacular growth of Los Angeles.

The setting for Los Angeles minority politics developed out of the "entrepreneurial political economy" of many Sun Belt cities. In Elkin's (1987:61) definition,

> all entrepreneurial cities have in common a relatively unimpeded alliance at work composed of public officials and local businessmen, an alliance that is able to shape the workings of city political institutions so as to foster economic growth. In each, moreover, electoral politics is organized so that businessmen play an important role, and urban bureaucracies are adept at organizing their domains so that they are neither dominated by elected officials nor in the service of local businessmen.

The long tradition of nonpartisanship in California cities helped ensure that party organizations would play a minimal role in city politics. The result was a boomtown with undeveloped politics. This combination served the political and economic interests of the dominant white Protestant establishment. The city they created was dominated by a sort of conservative reform ideology. It was only when minorities expressed their aspirations in the language of reform that they won a share of citywide political power.

This study will help correct the general inattention to Los Angeles in urban studies. While there has been considerable writing about the culture and lifestyle of Los Angeles, few books have been produced on Los Angeles politics. By comparison, New York City and Chicago politics have been the subjects of books too numerous to list.

Historical studies are available on Black, Jewish, Latino, and Asian-American Los Angeles and will be discussed frequently in the chapters to follow (e.g., Klein and Schiesl 1990). While each ethnic community of Los Angeles has been extensively studied by historians, there has been little attempt to trace interethnic and interracial political relationships (for a recent exception, see Erie, Brackman, and Ingram [1992]).

Within the last several years, there has been a renewed interest in Los Angeles—for the first time since Bradley's election and, before that, the 1965 Watts riot. Another burst of attention is likely to accompany the 1992 violence. Yet the focus has been only marginally on biracial coalition. Los Angeles's multiracial population has captured national attention, and the city is seen as the wave of America's future. Reiff (1991) and Davis (1991) are among those exploring the shape of the new Los Angeles beyond Black and white.

There are growing numbers of studies of Asian-Americans and Latinos in Los Angeles. Yet studies of "rainbow Los Angeles" address the city's remarkable biracial experience only in passing, as a stage barely relevant to a changing city. That essential piece of history continues to be missed or minimized—an oversight comparable to writing about Chicago without discussing the political machine.

Tom Bradley has received some attention, but largely in a biographical vein (Robinson 1976; Galm 1984; Payne and Ratzan 1986). Patterson (1967, 1969) explored Bradley's 1963 council election, while several scholars examined the bitter biracial 1969 and 1973 mayoral campaigns between Bradley and Sam Yorty (Hahn and Almy 1971; Maullin 1971; Halley, Acock, and Greene 1976; Hahn, Klingman, and Pachon 1976).

A major research challenge has been to trace ideological lines in Los Angeles politics over a thirty-five-year period. Maps 1.1, 1.2, and 1.3 show city council districts in 1965, 1972, and 1986, respectively. After 1971, the city redistricted on the basis of equal population, not registration. In 1972, the council created a Latino majority district, the Fourteenth, by including territory from the Ninth District. In 1986, the council set the stage for a second Latino seat by moving the First District from the Valley to the East Side. The Second District was thereupon moved out into the near Valley. Table 1.1 shows the racial and ethnic distribution of all fifteen council districts under the 1986 plan.

While some districts have moved over the years, certain patterns have remained stable. The African-American districts have been the Eighth, Ninth, and Tenth. Other districts with large Black populations are the Fifteenth, which includes Watts, and the biracial Sixth District.

The East Side is the site for the main Latino population. The Fourteenth District includes Boyle Heights and other Latino areas, and the current First District is overwhelmingly Latino. The Seventh District, in the Valley, is now the site of an increasing Latino population.

The Valley districts are separated from the rest of the city by the Santa Monica Mountains. The main Valley districts are the Twelfth, the Third, the Seventh, and until 1986, the First. The West Side communities, also largely white, are the Fifth and the Eleventh.

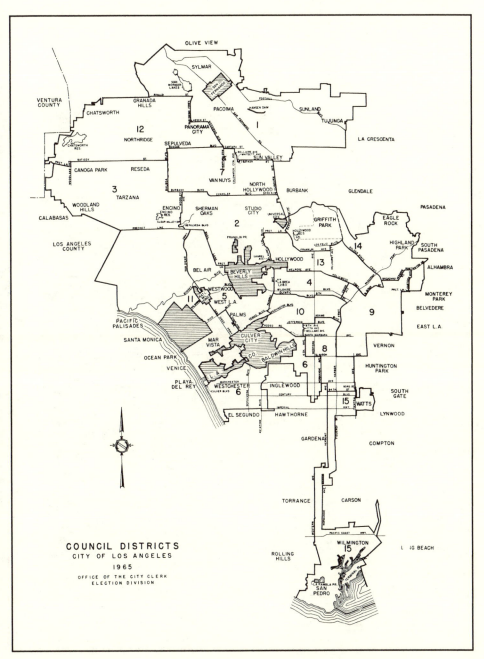

Map 1.1 City of Los Angeles by Council District, 1965

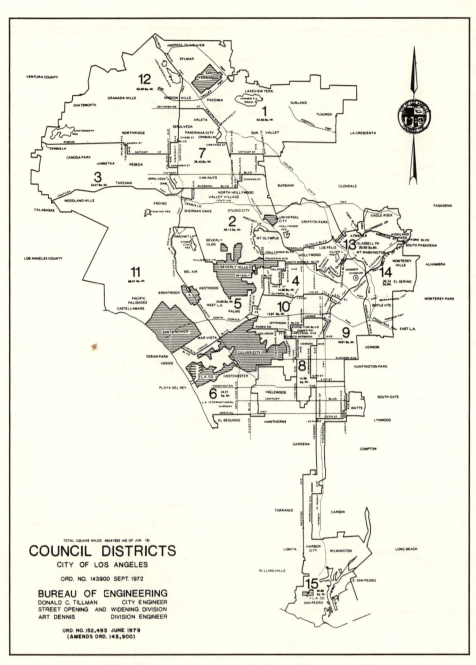

Map 1.2 City of Los Angeles by Council District, 1972

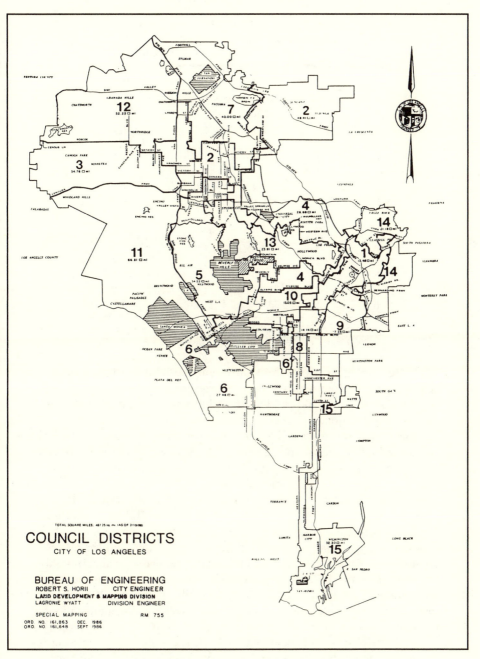

Map 1.3 City of Los Angeles by Council District, 1986

TABLE 1.1
Racial and Ethnic Composition
of City Council Districts, 1986 (percent)

	White	Latino	Black	Asian-American
1st	14.4	69.1	2.1	13.5
2d	74.7	17.1	2.6	4.2
3d	82.6	11.3	1.5	3.5
4th	53.8	26.1	5.1	13.1
5th	87.6	5.1	2.6	3.5
6th	44.7	15.8	33.5	5.2
7th	42.5	43.8	8.9	3.7
8th	6.4	21.1	67.5	5.2
9th	5.9	36.4	56.2	1.9
10th	21.8	22.0	43.7	11.9
11th	82.5	9.7	1.4	5.2
12th	83.1	9.0	1.7	4.9
13th	60.2	23.0	4.5	10.1
14th	21.1	69.4	1.6	7.2
15th	35.5	33.9	23.8	6.2

Source: Selected Demographic Data for Los Angeles City Council
Districts, Final Lines (1986), City of Los Angeles.

The remaining districts, the Fourth and the Thirteenth, are heterogeneous midcity communities. The Thirteenth is home to Hollywood;
along with the Tenth and the Fourth, it has a major share of the Asian-
American population.

I found that the most stable and homogeneous city council districts
provide a highly consistent base for analysis. Four of the city's fifteen
districts have been closely examined. They will appear often in the book,
almost as geographical dramatic characters.

These districts represent four diverse poles of the city. Two are largely
white and affluent; two are poor and working class (see Tables 1.2 and 1.3).
Of the less affluent districts, one is Black, and one is Latino. Of the white
districts, one has a large Jewish and liberal population, and the other is
dominated by white conservatives. The four districts have remained roughly
the same since the 1972 city reapportionment and are the most homogeneous for each group. Three have been generally stable since 1964; two of
these have been stable since the 1950s. Their composition allows a long-
term analysis of ethnic, racial, and ideological divisions within the city.

The Fifth District is known as the "Jewish district." Its population is
around 30 percent Jewish (in a city 7 percent Jewish). Fairfax Boulevard is
the center of the older Jewish community. The Fifth District has one of the
highest levels of education in the city.

TABLE 1.2
Racial and Ethnic Composition
of Four Key Council Districts, 1980 (percent)

		White	Black	Latino
5th	White liberal/Jewish	77.8	7.7	9.5
8th	Black	5.8	73.0	18.7
12th	White conservative	83.1	1.7	10.0
14th	Latino/white moderate	17.2	1.0	74.4

Source: City of Los Angeles Planning Department.
Note: Percentages do not total 100 because of omitted categories.

The Eighth District has been the "Black district." Central Avenue, the historical base of the Black community, runs through a corner of the Eighth—a poor and working-class community.

The Twelfth District, in the San Fernando Valley, is a white suburban district, created in 1964. The Jewish population is smaller (though growing). As in the Fifth, income and education are at high levels.

Finally, the Fourteenth District is a "Latino district." Drawn by the city council in 1972 to create a Latino seat, the district has a Latino majority, heavily concentrated in the southern side of the district. Of the four districts, the Fourteenth is the most difficult to analyze. A large share of the voting population is white, concentrated in the northern portion of the district. While most of the district's Latinos are Democrats, a strong base of white Republicans registers at high levels. Thus estimates of the Fourteenth

TABLE 1.3
Socioeconomic Indicators in Four Key Council Districts, 1980

		Income ($)	College Education (%)	Postgraduate Education (%)
5th	White liberal/Jewish	29,098	26.8	31.7
8th	Black	13,062	22.1	6.0
12th	White conservative	31,308	28.2	23.1
14th	Latino/moderate white	16,199	14.1	7.6
Citywide		21,714	22.2	17.4

Source: City analysis of 1980 census data.
Note: Income is mean household income; College Education is the percentage of those age eighteen and older with college education; Postgraduate Education is the percentage of those age eighteen and older with postgraduate education.

District's vote will likely underestimate Latino liberalism. Conversely, the socioeconomic portrait in Table 1.3 undoubtedly overestimates Latino economic status.

Factors in Biracial Coalitions

The following propositions on biracial coalitions will be explored in this study:

1. The primary basis for political coalitions between Blacks and whites is *ideological*. Minority mobilization and liberal ideology are the cornerstones of any interracial coalition pursuing minority incorporation.

2. The existence of white liberal support for racial liberalism is insufficient to guarantee the creation of a successful interracial coalition. The prospects for interracial coalitions are deeply influenced by *interest* alliance or conflict. Leaders can help structure the impact of interest.

3. Interracial *leadership* ties arise out of factional divisions within the Black and white communities. These factional ties underlie elite links based on trust and equal political status.

Taken together, the conditions for biracial coalitions are most auspicious when the ideological affinity between Blacks and white liberals is enhanced by both mutual interest and long-standing trust among leaders. To understand such leadership ties, it is necessary to look within the Black and white communities. Such coalitions are likely to be far stronger than alliances based on the shifting sands of self-interest in the absence of ideological affinity. They are also likely to be much stronger than coalitions based on goodwill alone. Goodwill alone is not enough, but neither is cold self-interest.

TWO

MINORITIES IN THE ENTREPRENEURIAL CITY:

1781–1960

O N SEPTEMBER 4, 1781, a band of Mexican settlers sponsored by the Spanish Empire founded a village they named el pueblo de Nuestra Señora la Reina de Los Angeles. They had been directed by California's governor, Felipe de Neve, to find a spot on southern California's coastal plain (Fogelson 1967:7). Among the twenty-two adults were two Blacks, seven "mulattoes," one "half-breed" and nine "Indians" (Bond 1936:2). Blacks, and persons of mixed Black and white ancestry, were soon outnumbered by Mexican settlers; in the 1790 census, the city's first, the total population of 141 included only 22 persons of mixed Black and white ancestry (DeGraaf 1970). Blacks are presumed to have assimilated into the larger Mexican society that dominated the city (Bond 1936:4), and the Black involvement in the founding of the city was forgotten for many generations.

African-Americans arrived after Americans gained control of California in 1850. The first U.S. census of Los Angeles County (1850) reported 12 Blacks and 1,598 whites (including Mexicans). Most of the Blacks were probably servants indentured to white families; only one lived on his own (Bond 1936:6). The Black population grew slowly, from twelve in 1850, to sixty-six in 1860 and ninety-three in 1870; in 1870, the city's population was only 1.6 percent Black (see Table 2.1).

Economic Participation

A remarkable feature of Black Los Angeles emerged early: the ability of Blacks to acquire property and to convert it into wealth. Despite state limits on African-American political equality, there were no barriers to the acquisition of property. In 1856, for example, the local courts freed Biddy Mason, a Black slave who had been rescued from the south. She acquired land in the center of the city that eventually made her and her descendants wealthy (Bond 1936:12–13). Thus there were significant economic opportunities for the small Black community. These chances became even greater as white Americans began to dominate the city and aimed it toward economic boom.

As Los Angeles grew, midwestern white Protestants made up a large part

TABLE 2.1

Black Population of Los Angeles, 1850–1900

	Total Population (N)	Black Population (N)	Black Share (%)
1850[a]	1,610	12	0.7
1860	4,385	66	1.5
1870	5,728	93	1.6
1880	11,183	102	0.9
1890	50,395	1,258	2.5
1900	102,479	2,131	2.1

Sources: Census data; Bond 1936:12–13.

[a]County of Los Angeles. All others are City of Los Angeles.

of the in-migration, but there was also a major influx of Blacks. The modern Black community traces its roots to the land boom of the late 1800s (DeGraaf 1970:327). The new city was now more open to Blacks than ever before, as racial prejudices were overwhelmed by the consuming desire to build a great city (Bond 1936:11). In a city about to take off, labor was short, land was plentiful and cheap, and the future was filled with promise.

In bustling Los Angeles, Blacks were even able to win some political recognition. In the late 1890s, for instance, Black agitation led Mayor Meredith P. Snyder to appoint one Black police officer and one Black fireman, "an act which, it is reputed, gave Los Angeles the distinction of being the first American city to have Negroes so employed" (Bond 1936:13).

In the three decades after 1880, the Black population increased from 102 to 7,599 (see Tables 2.1 and 2.2). Until around 1915, Blacks lived wherever they could afford, and many bought property—some of which they later resold to developers for large profits. By the 1880s, the Los Angeles schools

TABLE 2.2

Black Population of Los Angeles, 1910–1970

	Total Population (N)	Black Population (N)	Black Share (%)
1910	319,198	7,599	2.4
1920	576,673	15,579	2.7
1930	1,238,048	38,894	3.1
1940	1,504,277	63,774	4.2
1950	1,970,358	171,209	8.7
1960	2,479,015	334,916	13.5
1970	2,816,061	503,606	17.9

Source: Census data.

had been desegregated, and racial tensions were low (DeGraaf 1970:329). The great promise of Los Angeles was advertised widely among the nation's Blacks, and Black migration grew.

On February 12, 1909, the *Los Angeles Times* devoted six full pages to a glowing description of the local Black community. Laudatory articles appeared on the business and professional successes of local Blacks. Robert Owens, a grandson of freed slave Biddy Mason, was described in an admiring profile as "the wealthiest Negro capitalist in Los Angeles": "In 1890 he read an advertisement in the morning Times for the sale of a lot and cottage on South Hill Street, between Seventh and Eighth Streets, and he and his mother bought the property for $7,500, selling it to local investors in 1905 for $75,000. Their Spring-Street property could not be bought for a quarter of a million dollars."

In a growing entrepreneurial city, Blacks were participating in the system by which wealth was being accumulated at a remarkable rate, through real estate, "the mother lode of society's system of wealth" (Smith 1987:4). By this standard, early Los Angeles provided some tenuous ladders for Black upward mobility.

In 1900, 34 percent of Los Angeles Blacks lived in owner-occupied homes, a remarkable figure for the time, far in excess of homeowning rates for Mexicans or Japanese, close to that for whites, and far beyond the level enjoyed by Blacks in other cities (Bond 1936:22; DeGraaf 1970). It should be noted, however, that Black-owned homes often had many occupants; there was a high degree of homeownership, but a smaller number of homeowners (Bond 1936:22).

Homeownership helped counterbalance low occupational status. As late as 1960, an estimated 95 percent of the city's refuse workers, 80 percent of its street maintenance workers, and 95 percent of its custodians were Black (*Eagle*, 7 April 1960). Some of the most important and socially prominent Blacks held government jobs as janitors. While Blacks still had low occupational status, locked into laborer and service jobs, property ownership allowed them to accumulate some wealth (DeGraaf 1970).

In a study of Jacksonville, Florida, Stacey (1972) found that Blacks who had the opportunity to own their own homes were significantly less alienated and were much more likely to participate in political and community affairs. As we will see, a small but mobilized and confident Los Angeles Black community, led by an effective Black middle class, was able to win an extraordinary level of political power in the 1970s.

Despite its Spanish and Mexican origins, the city in its early days was substantially more hospitable to Blacks (and Jews) than to Mexican-Americans and certainly more hospitable than it was to either Japanese- or Chinese-Americans: "In an era when Chinese were being excluded from jobs and driven from cities, the small and relatively inconspicuous Negro population appears to have enjoyed a lessening of racial tension and a considerable degree of acceptance" (DeGraaf 1970:329).

Los Angeles had originally been a Mexican territory, and even after the U.S. takeover, the Spanish influence remained very strong. But with the influx of white midwesterners, the Mexican-American population became less and less significant. Once it had been a sign of status for white Americans to marry into leading Spanish families. By 1876, all the Mexican elements had been shorn from the city's civic celebrations (Singleton 1976).

Los Angeles's Mexican-American community was far worse off economically than were Blacks. A 1920 church study documented the horrible living conditions of Mexican-American workers. Many lived in substandard housing in the center of the city (Oxnam 1920). A comparison of homeownership rates showed the disparity between a struggling but hopeful Black community and a desperately poor and often hopeless Mexican-American population.

By the twentieth century, the city's Mexican-American population was dominated by laborers, whose status was uncertain at best. Upward mobility from generation to generation was virtually nonexistent (Romo 1977). Mexicans living in Los Angeles could be deported when the labor market became saturated and reimported when workers were needed. In 1931, massive deportations of the city's Mexican residents began; the process continued for a decade and depleted the community (Miranda 1990). Not until after World War II, and the return of Mexican-American war veterans, were more substantial community roots formed.

Chinese-Americans and Japanese-Americans were also outcasts in the Los Angeles community, as far back as the 1880s. California was a hotbed of anti-Asian sentiment, where laws severely limited immigration and prevented Japanese residents from owning property and even from passing it to their naturalized children. Hostility culminated in the notorious incarceration of Japanese-Americans in 1942.

With the decline of Chinese immigration to California after the passage of the Chinese Exclusion Act of 1882, Japanese migration to Los Angeles increased until the passage of restrictive immigration laws in 1920. Between 1900 and 1930, the Japanese-American population of Los Angeles County grew from an estimated 1,200 persons to 35,390 (Modell 1977:18). For a time, Japanese-Americans did well in Los Angeles, a city whose economic structure was "highly encouraging to newcomers as ambitious and hard working as the Japanese" (ibid.:24), and created numerous niches for an ethnic subeconomy parallel to the city's main economy (ibid.:26–27).

But anti-Japanese sentiment, the heir to the long tradition of anti-Asian feeling in California, threw the gains of Los Angeles Japanese-Americans into turmoil when on February 19, 1942, President Franklin D. Roosevelt issued Executive Order 9066, authorizing the internment of thousands of Japanese-Americans in California and other western states. The internment had a devastating impact on Japanese-Americans, who lost property and hope for full membership in the wider community—perhaps contributing to their low profile for many years to come in Los Angeles politics. The property could be replaced and regenerated, but the confidence necessary to engage in effective political work was not as amenable to rebuilding.

Jews came to the city as early as 1845, while California was still a Mexican territory. They were successful traders, aided by their willingness to learn Spanish (Vorspan and Gartner 1970). A Jewish community formed in the 1850s, just after the U.S. takeover. A small merchant class and communal institutions formed roots. By the 1870 census, Jews numbered at least 330, 5.76 percent of the local population (Stern 1976).

From the earliest days of U.S. rule, Jews played an active role in local politics. A Jew was elected to the first city council in 1850. Other Jews were later elected to the council, and one was elected both county treasurer and supervisor in 1865. The largely Democratic Jewish vote was considered crucial in the 1868 presidential election, and the Republicans devoted substantial effort to wooing Jews. The high Jewish literacy rate suggests that Jewish voters represented a higher share of the electorate than of the population (Stern 1981).

Jews continued to win local offices. John Jones, one of eight Jews elected to the city council between 1850 and 1875, was chosen president of the council in 1870 (Caper and Stern 1984). In 1878, the Jewish politician Bernard Cohn served briefly as mayor pro tem, and was nominated for mayor by the People's Party. Cohn lost the election but was reelected to the council. In 1900 a Jewish mayoral candidate, Herman Silver, ran on the Republican ticket and lost (Stern 1980).

By the 1880s Jews were among the most prosperous and accepted members of the community. Their share of the population fell as the city grew, but their absolute numbers continued to rise. In 1880, they represented 4.47 percent of the population, held a disproportionate share of white-collar jobs, and were nearly dominant in the dry goods and clothing businesses (Gelfand 1979a).

Economically successful and politically prominent, Jews were a stabilizing force in the community: "The community was rough, lawless, untutored in government. The Jews were peaceable, intelligent, literate. They were needed in early government, and filled a vacuum which lasted until a later surge of immigration from the Midwest and the East changed the ethnic and civic complexion of the community" (Vorspan and Gartner 1970:18).

Of the various Los Angeles minorities, Blacks and Jews had the greatest opportunity to put down roots in the new world of Los Angeles. This may have had something to do with their ability eventually to join together into a dominant political coalition. When they did, they were less likely to face well-organized competition from other safely rooted minority groups—in contrast to eastern cities, with their highly mobilized and settled blocs of Irish, Italians, and other immigrant groups. This situation, of course, changed dramatically in later years: the 1990 census revealed Latinos to be the largest minority group in the city, and Latinos and Asian-Americans became far more politically assertive than before.

The boomtown atmosphere of Los Angeles provided important economic opportunities for the early Black community. But the puritanical conservatism of the city's leadership severely constrained the long-term prospects for all minorities. The large migration from the Midwest changed Los Angeles from a frontier city open to diversity into an economic powerhouse with a narrow civic culture.

The midwestern newcomers had their own view of an ordered, homogeneous community. They sought to build a new type of metropolis, freed from the ethnic, heterogeneous influences of eastern and midwestern cities: "the people of Los Angeles desired the size but not the character of a modern metropolis . . . to combine the spirit of the good community with the substance of the great metropolis" (Fogelson 1967:191). Is it any wonder that a city so consciously designed to differ from New York City and Chicago would, in time, generate its own brand of minority politics?

Fueled by a militant Protestant clergy, this new group had become nearly a ruling elite by 1920: "in 1900 Los Angeles was about as much a native, white anglo-saxon Protestant city as existed anywhere in the United States for its size" (Gelfand 1981:31). With their high mobilization and unity, white Protestants controlled most of the public offices (Singleton 1979). The new atmosphere was puritanical and ethnocentric. As Fogelson (1967:198) noted,

> Unfortunately, the white majority so subordinated and segregated the colored minorities—though, admittedly, not each group in the same way or to the same degree—that they were completely frustrated. . . . These immigrants were not the least capable of their countrymen. Among them were many Mexican mestizos from active towns, semi-skilled Russian Jews and Northern Italians, ambitious American Negroes from northern metropolises, and young Japanese educated in their island's modern cities.

The civic culture and eventually the local economy became increasingly hostile to Blacks and other minorities. The dominant conservative philosophy was augmented by the migration of southern whites to the city after 1910. By now, the increased size of the Black community made it potentially threatening. The southern whites were particularly hostile to Blacks, but the white Protestants also sought to preserve their "small town" city.

The result was the development of restrictions on Blacks and other minorities, cutting them off from the next stages of the city's system of generating wealth.

One of the first signs of trouble came in 1914, when the southern white migrants helped create a whites-only jitney bus system, so that they would not have to ride public transportation with Blacks. After a great effort, the Black community was able to get the jitney buses outlawed, but substantial white hostility had emerged (DeGraaf 1970; Bond 1936).

In a sense, an alliance developed between the conservative reformers who dominated the city and the southern whites who later came to it. Working together, these groups saw to it that Blacks did not build on their modest beginnings, but would ultimately fall behind. The 1911 and 1925 city charters, which drastically limited the ability of elected officials to control the city government, further reduced the incentives for the development of party organization—which might have provided some modest incorporation for minorities.

One of the few exceptions to this hegemony came in 1925, when the city's voters approved district elections for city council. The measure was heavily backed by union organizations, and its passage shocked the city's leaders. The reactionary and anti-labor *Los Angeles Times* had campaigned strongly against it. Conservative reformers were outraged and filed an unsuccessful lawsuit to invalidate the vote; one writer argued that the voters must have been confused (Dykstra 1925). But two years later a new vote was taken to eliminate district elections, and it failed overwhelmingly. District elections were later to have great significance for biracial politics—which should come as no surprise to today's students of minority representation.

The most important change was the growing, organized white resistance to Blacks, Mexican-Americans, and Japanese-Americans, buying homes in white neighborhoods. The main tools were restrictive convenants and block agreements. The first bound individual homeowners not to sell their property to a minority family, while the second pledged whole neighborhoods. These documents were backed by the courts and bolstered by white intimidation. Whites even brought suits to remove Black families from homes they had bought and were currently occupying on the ground that a restrictive covenant retroactively made the sale illegal (Bond 1936).

Housing restrictions were instrumental in creating the first Black ghetto in Los Angeles (DeGraaf 1970). By shutting off housing in other areas, Los Angeles deprived Blacks of their chance to free up new housing for poorer Blacks while building an even stronger middle class. When thousands of Blacks moved into the city of Watts, it quickly incorporated into Los Angeles in 1926, thereby preventing a Black-dominated local government.

Los Angeles African-Americans fiercely resisted housing segregation. When Blacks moved into new neighborhoods, other Blacks would occasionally defend them from white attack by force of arms. Black realtors developed ingenious blockbusting techniques, thereby integrating some neighborhoods (Bond 1936). Blacks organized politically in the Negro Forum to agitate for equality (Unrau 1970).

Housing discrimination was a devastating blow to Black economic prospects in Los Angeles. The high level of Black homeownership made victory on this front essential. Los Angeles became the nation's leading center for legal challenges to restrictive covenants, and in 1948 the U.S. Supreme Court finally declared them unconstitutional.

In dynamic Los Angeles, growth was moving quickly out of the central city into suburban areas. It was here that the new opportunities for wealth were being created, but successful attempts were made to exclude Blacks. When Blacks tried to buy homes or start communities in Santa Monica, Huntington Beach, Lomita, and Manhattan Beach, they were driven off by angry whites (DeGraaf 1970:348).

Even so, Los Angeles African-Americans were distinctive in the higher level of economic progress they enjoyed compared to Blacks in other cities. Despite restrictive covenants, they slipped into new communities, creating middle-class enclaves to the west of the central city. The city was growing so quickly that many white homeowners wanted desperately to break their restrictive covenants and sell to Blacks at inflated prices (Bond 1936). The persistence and growth of a Black middle class beyond the scale of other cities continued, if at a more constrained level than before.

But it was really World War II that broke the downward cycle and regenerated the Los Angeles Black community. The economic changes caused by the war economy set off an explosion of Black migration and generated high hopes for social change. While some of these hopes were fulfilled, major new problems arose as well.

Wartime mobilization transformed Los Angeles into a technical and industrial metropolis. Los Angeles became a major site for military construction. Aircraft and shipbuilding were sustained by massive military contracts, and required a steady flow of skilled labor. The federal government defined Los Angeles as an area of extreme labor shortage, and relocated thousands of workers to the city.

Los Angeles Blacks had generally been kept from skilled industrial jobs—by both job discrimination and the generally low level of industry. But now the nation desperately needed their labor. The internment of Japanese-Americans in 1942 removed a major competitor for jobs and housing. Tens of thousands of Mexican immigrants had been deported to Mexico just before the war. Much of the labor force was in uniform—as many as 150,000 men from the area. Moreover, federal contracts meant that employers would have to follow national antidiscrimination rules.

Even so, it took a strong political effort by local Blacks to win jobs in the war industries. Nationwide, Blacks organized in the "Double V" movement—victory overseas and victory at home. This less well known campaign foreshadowed the great civil rights crusade of the 1950s (Dalfiume 1968). The movement was particularly successful in Los Angeles because of the strong bargaining position of African-Americans and outstanding leadership. The Negro Victory Committee, headed by Reverend Clayton Russell and working closely with the middle-class NAACP, utilized direct action techniques. Mass rallies of as many as a thousand Blacks and marches on the offices of public agencies won concessions. Between 1942 and 1945, the Negro Victory Committee achieved one victory after another and greatly improved Black prospects in employment (Anderson 1980; Unrau 1971).

In 1942, the iron grip of racial discrimination was finally broken—at least for the duration of the war. Under great pressure from Black labor leader A. Philip Randolph, President Roosevelt issued an executive order forbidding racial discrimination in the defense plants. In the spring, the Southern Pacific Railroad began importing southern Blacks at a rate of three hundred to four hundred a day (Unrau 1971:18). In June 1943 nearly twelve thousand Blacks entered the city; comparable waves came in July and August (Smith 1978). Many of the migrants went to Watts (Unrau 1971; Anderson 1980).

But these thousands of Blacks were coming into a city that restricted them to a ghetto in the central city, hemmed in by housing segregation. A major housing crisis developed almost immediately. Poor Blacks moved into the abandoned Little Tokyo area, creating dangerous overcrowding and scandalous health conditions. The occupancy rate in the Central Avenue area was over 98 percent; middle-class Blacks were now cut off from escape and pushed together with much poorer Blacks in the central city (Sandoval 1973:52).

City authorities provided little help. The deputy mayor blamed the problem on excessive Black migration. Public housing officials severely restricted new construction, and used a quota to limit Blacks to less than 6 percent of these units—even though Blacks comprised 64 percent of the waiting list (Sandoval 1973:61). Until near the end of the war, persistent Black efforts to change the situation were successfully resisted. A conservative local electorate offered little sympathy; challenger Norris Poulson defeated incumbent mayor Fletcher Bowron in 1953, in part by opposing measures to create public housing.

In the face of all these troubles, Blacks made significant gains during the war years and became a major group in the city. While in 1940 Blacks had comprised 3.1 percent of the population, they constituted 8.7 percent in 1950 and 13.5 percent in 1960. Despite the housing crisis, the reputation among Blacks that Los Angeles was a good city kept the migration going.

The wartime situation was exceptional in that necessity required the system to include Blacks in the generation of employment income. With low labor competition, Blacks were able to reduce racial discrimination in the workplace. Between 1940 and 1950 Los Angeles Blacks made significantly larger occupational gains than did Blacks in other cities (Sandoval 1973:91). But they were slow to generate new wealth because of the persistence of housing restrictions.

Postwar Los Angeles disappointed and frustrated the aroused expectations of Blacks. The end of the labor shortage became the vehicle for restoring the old rules. Japanese-Americans released from internment obviously wanted to regain their homes and jobs. Returning soldiers clogged the labor force. Mexican workers were imported to Los Angeles once again; by 1950, they outnumbered Blacks. The postwar era allowed for the first time in decades the development of a stable Latino community. The key element was the return of Latino war veterans with aspirations for incorporation into the bustling postwar world. The city was returning to minority competition for unskilled jobs, while whites gained most of the skilled jobs.

Discriminatory rules were reimposed, and skilled jobs were once again harder for African-Americans to obtain. The lack of public transportation kept Blacks from access to suburban jobs (Smith 1978). The rise of conservative anticommunism encouraged the restoration of white hegemony. Politically, the strong bargaining position of wartime Blacks was eliminated. The Negro Victory Committee collapsed soon after the war, in the face of Reverend Russell's ill-fated campaign for public office and aggressive federal investigations of his organization (Unrau 1971; Anderson 1980).

Between 1950 and 1960, Blacks lost some of the occupational gains they had won during the war (Sandoval 1973:130). But they were able steadily to erode the ghetto boundaries as mobile whites moved to the suburbs. The U.S. Supreme Court ended restrictive covenants in 1948, and it became much easier for middle-class Blacks to move to the West Side.

Victory on the housing front ironically helped establish the basis for a long-term class conflict among Blacks; the homeowning, upwardly mobile sector was able to enlarge its western enclaves, while the poorer central city fell farther behind in economic and educational terms. But even the economic gains of middle-class Blacks were shaky; Sandoval (1973) found a remarkably high degree of unemployment even in the West Side Black neighborhoods.

By 1960 Los Angeles Blacks were in a mixed position. Their socioeconomic status persistently exceeded that of Blacks in other cities. But they were falling farther and farther behind the economic gains of Los Angeles whites, as the system of accumulating wealth kept moving out of their reach. Between 1940 and 1960, "the quality of the black experience in the city actually declined vis a vis white standards during the twenty-year period. . . . Blacks in Los Angeles were less likely to compare themselves to other Blacks farther away than to whites in their own community" (Sandoval 1973:133).

Political Representation

In 1960 Los Angeles was one of the most backward cities in the nation in African-American political representation. Los Angeles Blacks had yet to elect a city council member or a congress person. Their only political representative at any level was State Assemblyman Augustus Hawkins. In 1934 Democrat Hawkins had defeated the only previous Black elected official, Republican Assemblyman Fred Roberts. All three city council districts with large Black populations were without a Black representative.

The homogeneous reform culture of Los Angeles was strongly inhospitable to minority political representation. Blacks had achieved some economic successes, but these had not been translated into any sort of political power. Mexican-Americans had already attained public office in Los Angeles through the election of Edward Roybal in the Ninth Council District in 1949. Roybal was elected through a multiracial coalition of Latinos, liberal Jews, and Blacks (Regalado 1988a).

The Jewish community had flexed its muscles in the Fifth District, electing Rosalind Weiner (later Wyman) in 1953. But as Roybal later recalled, minority and liberal voices in the council were muted (Regalado 1988a). Even this small minority representation was largely excluded from the dominant social, political, and economic culture of the city. Despite their economic mobility, Jews found themselves excluded from the civic culture—both as Jews and as holders of a liberalism that found little expression in Los Angeles. After 1900, "Jews no longer appeared as municipal candidates. . . . The free participation of early years was considerably pinched" (Vorspan and Gartner 1970:136–38).

Lack of minority and liberal representation had important policy consequences. City hall was insulated from changes in U.S. society, and could pursue a small-town conservatism of fiscal stringency, strong support for the forces of order, and reluctance to participate in federal social programs. The combination of downtown business and the conservative *Los Angeles Times* was a potent power structure, which restricted political debate. With the backing of the police bureaucracy, this tightly knit leadership could hold back the hands of time.

Wilson and Banfield (1963) have noted that in modern cities, public employees have developed high levels of political power in the gap left by the decline of party organizations. They have contrasted the Chicago machine's power over the bureaucracy to the political stratum's relative weakness in Los Angeles. Thus, the reform culture allowed public bureaucracies effectively to resist the political control of any winning coalition.

The Los Angeles Police Department (LAPD) represents one of the most extreme cases of bureaucratic independence, even in the context of reformed city government. And it has been the most persistent source of dissatisfaction among Los Angeles's minority groups. Bringing the LAPD under civilian control eventually became one of the great challenges of the Bradley regime.

After William Parker became chief in 1950, the LAPD developed the ability to insulate itself completely from political oversight. The department ultimately developed an independent political power base, which it used to restrict the city's politics (Woods 1973). In time, the LAPD became one of the city's main roadblocks to social change, resisting the rise to power of minorities and liberals. While the downtown business community made its peace with the biracial alliance, the LAPD never did. The city leadership fully backed the police. A Black police officer recalled:

> We felt that it was one big system, and we were confronted by this racist system. We knew that this unwritten policy—that blacks couldn't work with whites and we could only work certain places—it had to be supported all the way up the chain of command including the Chief of Police. And so who do you appeal to in a system like that? And so we didn't feel that we had any support anywhere, even in the city government. [Chief Parker] really ran the city. (Brewer interview)

The LAPD would oppose and undermine any challenger to an incumbent mayor. If the challenger won, the Department would attempt to co-opt the new mayor, whereupon the next challenger would be the enemy. This pattern was followed for both Norris Poulson and Sam Yorty. Parker had perceived each as a threat. Even though Poulson was a moderate conservative backed by much of the civic leadership in his 1953 mayoral bid, he recalled that he was closely watched by the Department during his campaign against Mayor Fletcher Bowron: "I later found that I was followed, 'bugged,' and checked, on the theory that I might be working with certain groups wanting to overhaul the Police Department and dispose of Chief Parker" (Poulson 1966:174).

Poulson's camp suspected that the Parker forces were quietly helping Bowron. He also mentioned a specific incident: "I was once approached in the Hotel Mayflower by an active police detective in plainclothes to ask me what I would do about the Police Department if elected. I just casually reached over and touched a microphone which I detected pushing out from his shirt" (ibid.:190).

But when Poulson ran for reelection in 1961 against Yorty, the police treated Yorty as the danger. Like Poulson in 1953, Yorty had promised to hold the LAPD more accountable. Shortly after Yorty's election, he met privately with Parker and never again said a harsh word against the Department.

The strength and unaccountability of the police department both reflected and symbolized the political weakness of the minority and progressive communities in Los Angeles. Black activists were acutely aware of the political gains being made by Blacks in other cities. An *Eagle* editorial (10 November 1960) noted that in St. Louis, Blacks had elected seven of the twenty-eight council members, and that even Nashville, Tennessee, had elected two Black city officials. Another *Eagle* editorial (15 December 1960) indicated that "Los Angeles is one of the most laggard big cities in the nation when it comes to entrusting public offices to Negroes."

In light of the later weakness of New York City's Black politics, it is ironic to find Los Angeles Black newspapers in 1960 bemoaning how much better Blacks were doing in New York. The *Eagle*, for instance, concluded that "the Negro proportion of Los Angeles' population is about the same as that of New York's. We needn't take time to point out the vast difference between the influence of Negroes in New York and our influence in Los Angeles" (*Eagle*, 4 May 1960).

New York City had elected its first Black alderman in 1917 (Lewinson 1974:56–57). By contrast, Los Angeles Black political exclusion matched the pattern found for the same era in the ten northern California communities studied by Browning, Marshall, and Tabb (1984).

Why were Blacks so far behind in Los Angeles politics? The city had opened some limited economic opportunities to minority groups, albeit less than those available to the dominant group. But the social and political design of the city left little room for the upward political mobility of minorities.

One could foresee an ambivalence in the Los Angeles Black community about the growth culture, dominated by business, that has influenced and at times dominated Los Angeles as strongly as political machines have ruled Chicago and other cities. That ambivalence continues today: Los Angeles Blacks have mixed feelings about both downtown redevelopment and white-led slow-growth movements. Like political machines on the East Coast and in the Midwest, booming growth in a new city created new opportunities for Blacks. But like political parties, the system that supported this growth allowed little room for independent Black political power and for the further consolidation of Black economic gains.

The growth metropolis opened some doors, but closed others. There were no political party organizations to recruit precinct captains and mobilize minority voters. The doctrines of homogeneity and conservative reform left little incentive for elite groups to incorporate new groups through balanced tickets.

City leaders used blatant gerrymandering to fragment the Black vote (and just as dramatically divided Latino communities). The conservative Los Angeles reform philosophy proclaimed it improper to set up Black districts, but did not prevent city leaders from purposely crippling Black political power. An analysis by the *Eagle* (10 November 1960) showed that as far back as the 1930s, the city divided up Black districts that went naturally north-south and joined them to adjacent West Side white areas. When restrictive covenants ended in 1948 and Black westward mobility increased, the city then drew the lines north-south to prevent the creation of Black majority districts. A system that in the name of reform both refused to acknowledge the need for minority representation and at the same time acted to forestall it was breathtakingly hypocritical.

Gerrymandering made it hard for Blacks to take advantage of the one great opening the system offered: district election of council members. In fact, were it not for the anomaly of district elections, Blacks might never have overcome the barriers to representation in Los Angeles. But with a growing population and a city council divided into fifteen geographical areas, Blacks would inevitably attain some political power.

The particular configuration of Los Angeles helped shape its Black community. Until the rise of biracial politics in the 1960s, Los Angeles had become a city in which minority people were neither seen nor heard. Obviously this setting contrasts sharply with eastern and midwestern cities, where party organizations acted, however imperfectly, to bring minority groups at least a modicum of political recognition.

In Los Angeles conservative whites managed to exclude minorities and white liberals from influence through a combination of economic and political leadership. This power elite turned the freewheeling, multiethnic city of the late 1800s into a western outpost for midwestern conservatism. At the same time, the city contained unusual openings for minority economic development. These western configurations influenced the Black search for equality and for alliance.

Open growth helped allow the formation of a substantial Black middle class and upwardly mobile working class. That development fostered the development of class politics within the Black community, but also created high expectations for Black life in the city. The unusual circumstances of western Black life led to various anomalies, such as a high proportion of Black homeownership but little political incorporation. The results were a strong Black middle class and a hunger for political incorporation. These factors played a major role in the eventual formation of the city's biracial coalition.

Jews and other minorities were also excluded from the civic culture, and thereby became potential allies for Blacks. This isolation contrasts most markedly with the case of New York City, where various groups, particularly Jews, found their own partial political incorporation long before the rise of the independent Black movement (see Chapter Fourteen).

It is not surprising that a foundation for multiethnic politics developed in Los Angeles. Modern Los Angeles had never been a melting pot; *everybody* who differed from the white conservative model was excluded. Therefore, a Los Angeles-style melting pot had to be created politically.

While Los Angeles Blacks faced disheartening political exclusion, they did not have to compete with organized ethnic groups, as in many eastern and midwestern cities. Sadly, Latinos and Asians-Americans faced many roadblocks to political power. There was no political machine. Thus, the eventual leadership of the progressive movement in Los Angeles flowed in the direction of the Black community.

For a minority challenge to succeed, a way would have to be found to frame it within the political culture of reform that dominated the city's life. It was ultimately the juncture of liberalism, minority assertion, and political reform that provided the needed formula.

THREE

FIRST VICTORIES: 1960–1963

BETWEEN 1960 and 1963, the Los Angeles African-American community obtained a major beachhead in city politics. From a position of complete exclusion, it gained significant representation on the city council and joined a new mayoral coalition. These achievements depended in largest part on Black unity and mobilization, with only a secondary role for biracial coalition politics.

By 1960 Los Angeles Blacks had reason to hope for political change. The 1960 census, released in March 1961, revealed a big jump in Black population, to nearly half a million people. Blacks now comprised 13.7 percent of the city's population, compared to 8.9 percent in 1950 and 4.2 percent in 1940.

Encouraged by the national civil rights movement, Blacks concentrated on winning political power. The de facto residential segregation that limited Black social mobility created a political opportunity in three council districts: the Eighth, Ninth, and Tenth. Three-quarters of the Negro population resided in 14 percent of the city's census tracts, where they constituted over one-half of the population of each tract (Patterson 1967:50). In fact, the steady out-migration of Blacks from the central city due to the ending of restrictive covenants concerned some Black strategists seeking to build a Black political base (Patterson 1967). But since most of the upwardly mobile Blacks were moving into the Tenth District, mobility actually enlarged the Black political foundation.

The Reapportionment Battles

Change was in the air. The state legislature had begun its own decennial reapportionment based on the 1960 census. Now dominated by Democrats, the legislature could undo the weakening of Black legislative districts created by the Republican reapportionment of 1951 (Hardy 1955). The reapportionment process was in the hands of two Los Angeles Democrats, Jesse Unruh and Augustus Hawkins. Hawkins was the only Black elected official representing a Los Angeles constituency.

The city reapportionment process followed a wholly different set of rules from that of the state. Every four years, Los Angeles was required by charter to draw districts equal in voter registration, not population. This provision helped the growing middle-class areas in the San Fernando Valley, which seemed always to be on the verge of adding another district. Unlike the state Democrats, the Los Angeles city council was almost completely unreceptive to arguments for minority representation.

Influencing the state and city reapportionments became a crucial task for Los Angeles Blacks. The Black newspapers, the *Sentinel* and the *Eagle*, led a communitywide effort to advance Black representation through the Committee for Representative Government (CRG).

The representation movement was independent of Democratic party leadership and established Los Angeles Blacks as a self-directed force with a unified agenda. Heavily supportive of the CRG, the *Sentinel*'s editorials castigated Unruh and even Hawkins for their resistance to the "two-four" plan, intended to create two Congressional and four Assembly seats for Blacks. Such a plan would have cut into Hawkins's own Sixty-fifth Assembly District; his main priority was to create a heavily Black congressional seat for himself. Hawkins's self-interest therefore required the concentration of a large number of Black voters in one district rather than several districts.

The Democratic party's interest required splitting the heavily Democratic Black community among a range of Democratic districts. Heavily Black districts would have helped the Republicans by making white Democratic seats marginal. Part of the maturation process going on in the Los Angeles Black community was the realization that Black interests did not necessarily coincide with those of either the Democratic party leadership or Hawkins. A similar process is going on today in the Los Angeles Latino community as it contests redistricting plans at the city and county levels.

Ultimately the reapportionment plan had to be approved by the state legislature, and incumbent protection was a major priority. The issue made strange bedfellows. While the state Republican party, interested in discomfiting Democratic incumbents, backed the CRG plan, many Democratic leaders opposed it (*Sentinel*, 25 May 1961). The Republic intervention has a contemporary feel; national Republicans in the 1990s have tried to help minority challenges that will weaken incumbent Democrats. The final agreement was a "one-two" plan, for one Congressional and two Assembly seats for Blacks.

The city reapportionment was more disappointing. In 1960, the council presented a map of proposed new council districts, which managed to preserve incumbents and prevent any near-majority Black districts (*Eagle*, 6 October 1960). The Black neighborhoods were divided into five districts; only the Eighth District had a Black majority. There was talk of moving the Tenth District from the inner city out to the Valley.

Despite widespread resistance from Blacks, the council adopted the plan, and Mayor Norris Poulson allowed it to become law without his signature. Even several liberal council members joined the majority. The only voice raised consistently and vociferously in opposition was that of Latino councilman Edward Roybal. The council passed the plan in the second week of November. The *Eagle* (1 December 1960) attacked Poulson for failing to veto the law and for his suggestion that the city adopt some elements of an at-large council system, which would have further disadvantaged minorities.

The 1961 Mayoral Election and Its Aftermath

The sense of Black isolation reinforced the need for independent action. The growing sense of Black political independence emerged dramatically in the 1961 mayoral election. Blacks defied both major wings of the Democratic party to join Sam Yorty's insurgent mayoral coalition.

In 1961 Mayor Poulson ran for reelection against maverick Democrat Yorty. Poulson was a moderate Republican, heavily favored by the downtown business establishment and the conservative *Los Angeles Times*. Yorty was a former state assemblyman, a leftist turned reactionary, and by then a renegade Democrat. He had blasted liberal Democrats at their 1956 state convention when they would not endorse him for the U.S. Senate. Yorty had rejected the 1960 presidential nominee of the Democratic party, John F. Kennedy, as too liberal and endorsed Republican Richard Nixon. He published a leaflet: *I Cannot Take Kennedy.*

Among Democrats, Yorty was a pariah. Both the regular and reform wings of the party detested him. Mayo (1964:330) suggested that " . . . Yorty had so thoroughly antagonized the leadership of the Democratic party of California by his actions in 1956 and 1960 that the only chance for reviving his political life lay in a campaign for a nonpartisan office."

Poulson had the support of the leadership of both parties, the leading newspaper, and the business community, along with a large campaign treasury and the incumbency. He had the support of both feuding wings of the Democratic party. But Yorty beat him.

Yorty forged an unlikely coalition of Valley homeowners and inner-city minority groups. He assured Valley residents that he would end the trash collection system that required the use of two garbage cans and the annoying separation of trash. According to Poulson, Nixon helped Yorty in the Valley, in gratitude for Yorty's help against Kennedy in 1960. Poulson retaliated by refusing to support fellow-Republican Nixon against Pat Brown for governor the next year (Poulson 1966:431).

Yorty told Blacks and Latinos that he would fight police brutality and appoint minorities to city commissions. Poulson was vulnerable in minority communities. Tom Bradley said that "there was a feeling that Mayor Poulson was not sensitive to, nor responsive to, the problems of the black community. There was fertile ground that could be plowed by any candidate, and Yorty made the best of that" (Galm 1984:99).

As early as 1960, the *Eagle* (18 August 1960) had argued that it was time for Mayor Poulson to leave office, and suggested that he was being kept in power by "reactionaries" who feared the election of a liberal Democrat. In fact, Poulson had intended to leave office, and was talked into staying by a group of business and civic leaders (Mayo 1964).

The *Eagle* sarcastically linked Poulson with the local myths about the founding of the city: "that these Founding Fathers were noble Spanish Dons who came here with a built-in vision of a great city that would someday birth the Los Angeles Times and elect Norris Poulson mayor" (8 September 1960). When no liberal candidate entered the race, the *Eagle* was less certain that Poulson should be defeated (26 January 1961), but did encourage Blacks to be the swing voters between Poulson and Yorty (13 April 1961). While the *Sentinel* ultimately endorsed Poulson (30 March 1961), the *Eagle* went with Yorty (18 May 1961).

Just before the general election, there was a tense confrontation between police and Blacks in Griffith Park. Yorty said that, if elected, he would "school" Police Chief William Parker, implying that if Parker failed to stem police brutality, he would be fired. This position was popular among many Blacks and Latinos.

Blacks acted strategically in the election, ignoring the counsel of both wings of the Democratic party and the city's establishment. An examination of the three districts with the largest Black population (the Eighth, Ninth, and Tenth) suggests the impact of the Black vote. Yorty gained a net 20,587 votes in the three districts between the primary and the general elections. His citywide margin over Poulson was 15,725 votes. A contemporary analysis showed that Blacks were only one pillar of Yorty's victory (Bureau of Governmental Research 1961). But Black activists firmly believed that Black votes had been the key (*Sentinel*, 8 June, 24 July 1961), greatly increasing the confidence and expectations of the Black community.

Shortly after the election, Yorty said that the police were unfair to minorities and attributed his victory to minority support (*Eagle*, 8 June 1961). The *Eagle* (15 June 1961) called on Yorty to deliver a "New Deal" for Blacks at city hall. Poulson (1966:441) said that his defeat came on the "East Side," a euphemism for minority areas. In his words,

> To add to our troubles, on Memorial Day there was a minor race riot in Griffith Park. Some Negroes who insisted on riding the merry-go-round, encouraged by a few drinks, resisted arrest, and, of course, that made headlines in the Negro districts. That would have been good campaign strategy on the part of [the] opposition as the Negroes loved to say, "police brutality."

In some ways, Yorty delivered. Publicly committed to major changes in city policy, and to breaking the hold of the city establishment, Yorty increased the number of African-Americans on the mayor's staff and on city commissions (Ainsworth 1966). He appointed some Blacks to key city commissions. At the symbolic level, Yorty insisted that the 1961 celebration of the founding of Los Angeles include recognition of the Black role in that event. When the issue could not be resolved, that year's party was canceled (Ainsworth 1966; *Eagle*, 24 August, 31 August 1961).

On the other hand, Yorty immediately backed down on his promises to pressure Chief Parker and in other ways showed his lack of enthusiasm for Black political assertiveness. After a mysterious postelection talk with Parker, Yorty gave the police whatever they wanted. There was much speculation that Parker had collected some personal material on Yorty (Bradley interview). Never again did Yorty say a word against police misconduct, and he characterized all such charges as communist-inspired.

Council Elections

Emboldened by Yorty's victory, Blacks turned enthusiastically to council elections. One seat was already open. Tenth District councilman Charles Navarro had been elected city controller on the May ballot. Navarro had narrowly defeated Black challengers in 1957 and 1959, and, according to the *Sentinel*, had seen "the handwriting on the wall" (12 January 1961). A *Sentinel* writer argued even before the election that it was time to elect a Black council member in the Tenth; community unity would be needed to elect a candidate and keep the council from moving the district out into the Valley (25 May 1961).

Black activists began to lobby the city council, which would fill Navarro's seat by an interim appointment. Obviously the appointee would have a significant advantage as the incumbent in the scheduled 1963 council election. There was still some pressure within the council to fill the Valley's need for a new seat by moving the Tenth District.

At times the arguments the council members used to avoid a Black appointment were as ingenious as they were disingenuous. For instance, when the council was besieged by Black applicants, some members floated the idea that a Black appointment would distress the other Black candidates. The major Black contenders immediately sent a letter to the council denying this suggestion and repeating the call for a Black appointment; the *Eagle* blasted the "alibi" being used by the council to avoid its responsibility (15 June 1961).

Mayor Yorty, newly elected with minority support, urged the council to make a Black appointment. Of the council members, only Latino Ed Roybal and Jewish liberal Rosalind Wyman openly spoke on behalf of a Black appointment (*Eagle*, 10 August 1961). Thirty-one applicants, including seventeen Blacks, sent letters to the council committee. Tom Bradley, a recently retired Black police lieutenant, submitted a petition with hundreds of signatures on his behalf (Terry interview).

Bradley and his boyhood friend, Frank Terry, developed a campaign capitalizing on Bradley's reputation and accomplishments. They set up a Committee for the Appointment of Tom Bradley filled with prominent supporters. Terry organized a letter-writing campaign to the council. As he recalled:

[Bradley's] background was tremendous. He had all this involvement with groups and organizations. He was very much involved in his fraternity and law clubs and alumni associations. This guy was the best qualified of any name I had heard. So I made that a campaign theme for him and I devised a card that would ask people to write in and endorse Tom Bradley for the 10th district, using as a tag "the Best Qualified." (Terry interview)

Terry's committee hoped to be present as Bradley's cheering section when the decision was made, but the council had other plans: "We planned for the hearings in the council on a Friday morning. What they really did was make the appointment late Thursday afternoon . . . when that happened, of course, it was just like a bombshell" (ibid.).

The council committee had already decided on Joe Hollingsworth, a white Republican businessman. Under heavy pressure from Roybal, the committee added the name of George Thomas, the Black director of the County Human Relations Commission. The whole council then voted eight-six to appoint Hollingsworth over Thomas. Gordon Hahn, whose Eighth District had the largest Black population, voted against Hollingsworth, but quietly supported the majority on a crucial procedural motion. This was not ignored by the *Eagle* (31 August 1961). Councilman Ransom Callicott, whose Thirteenth District was nearly 30 percent Black, voted for Hollingsworth. The mayor signed the ordinance. The regime seemed intent on preventing Black representation.

The African-American community was in an uproar; there was "a wave of indignation" (*Sentinel* 31 August 1961). Rallied by the Reverend H. Hartford Brookins, a dynamic young leader newly arrived from Wichita, Kansas, and pastor of the elite First African Methodist Episcopal Church, political activists began meeting the next day. Many Blacks were furious at Yorty, feeling that he had been lukewarm in his support for the Black appointment. Terry recalled bitterly: "Yorty, the Mayor, the great champion of the Black appointment, couldn't be reached. He was incommunicado. Rumor had it that he was in a yacht on Catalina Harbor, where he couldn't be reached. So the appointment of Hollingsworth was made" (Terry interview).

The group that met under Brookins's leadership adopted the strategy of recalling Hollingsworth, a plan requiring 6,718 valid signatures on petitions (Patterson 1969). A massive program was undertaken to gather signatures in the Black community. A recall organization quietly backed by Bradley and headed by Black activists Brookins, Terry, Warren Hollier, and

Geri Scott Smith coordinated the signature gathering. Bradley's role was, in Terry's words, "like he typically is, low profile. . . . We needed resources and he helped us in making contacts. He took no leadership role; H. H. Brookins was the front man" (Terry interview). Black community groups and individuals were prominent among financial backers of the recall, and donations were frequently announced in the *Sentinel* and *Eagle*.

Terry characterized the period as one of deep change:

> It was the first awakening in a long time of the Black community, in terms of trying to rally them around an issue, and this kind of political action. And it wasn't easy. When we started, a lot of people were opposed to us. We looked like a bunch of, at best, zealots, and, at worst, a bunch of crazies who were trying to disturb and tear up everything. (Terry interview)

Brookins added rhetorical fire to the movement. He charged that "inside the city of Los Angeles are devils and demagogues who would plot to keep minority groups from being represented in city government" (*Sentinel*, 25 January 1962), and said that failure to get enough signatures would be "abject humiliation" (ibid.). In six months, the committee gathered 7,630 signatures, but 3,032 were ruled invalid (Patterson 1969). Though anticipated by the organizers, the rejection by the city clerk set off another community mobilization. Terry remembered Brookins's response: "It was the most dramatic thing. The TV cameras were there and he said this was a double-cross and he accused them of trying to defeat the people's will. It aroused, for the first time, the community. When I went back to the headquarters, the phones were ringing off the hook, people saying, 'give me a petition'" (Terry interview).

In the ten-day supplemental period authorized by law, the group gathered another 5,320 signatures, well over the requirement (Patterson 1969). Excited about the petitions and certain of their validity, Brookins and Terry designed a community convention to nominate a Black candidate to run against Hollingsworth in the recall election. The idea took hold. The rules gave delegate votes to community groups representing a wide range of interests. All candidates were required to sign a pledge that they would support the convention's choice (Patterson 1969). Bradley's allies had great influence at the convention (Terry interview).

The historic convention was held on April 28, 1962, at the Alexandria Hotel, just before the petitions were handed in to the city clerk. Brookins's name was placed in nomination, but he refused. Bradley won the nomination and could now run as the Black community's "official" representative. A *Sentinel* columnist suggested that if "[s]ome misguided member of our community lets himself be paid into filing in order to split the Negro vote, we should run over him with a steam roller" (10 May 1962).

In the midst of the gathering Black enthusiasm, the city clerk, astoundingly, ruled the recall invalid because of an alleged technical flaw in the petition forms—a flaw he had only then noticed. An attempt to overturn this decision in the State Court of Appeals was denied.

This latest city tactic only increased the agitation in the Tenth District. At a breakfast meeting, Bradley and Brookins were joined by the Reverend Martin Luther King, Jr., to discuss what to do next. In early August, the recall committee closed shop, having received and spent over $10,000. African-American activists began to plan for a Black candidacy in the 1963 council race against Hollingsworth.

While the recall failed to remove Hollingsworth, it may have saved the Tenth District for the African-American community. Throughout the controversy, there had been repeated calls on the council to move the Tenth District out to the growing San Fernando Valley. A similar tactic had prevented a Black majority from forming in the Seventh District several years earlier (*Eagle*, 5 October 1961). The appointment of the unknown Hollingsworth raised suspicion that he was meant to be a transition to ease the shift to the Valley. The pressure exerted by the recall made it all but impossible to displace the district.

During this quiet period in the struggle to win in the Tenth District, a vacancy developed in the neighboring Ninth District. Edward Roybal, the council's only minority member, resigned to run successfully for Congress in 1962. The district was about evenly divided between Blacks and Latinos, but had generally been known as "the Hispanic district." Once again, the council was faced with a decision—whom to appoint to fill the seat until the 1963 elections. What happened next had a great influence on the development of Black and Latino representation at city hall for the next two decades.

The Hollingsworth fiasco was on everybody's mind. The council was faced with two strong candidates, one Black and one Latino. Gilbert Lindsay, a Black former janitor and then deputy to county supervisor Kenneth Hahn, announced his intention to seek the seat. Mayor Yorty, mindful of his links to the Latino community, hoped to keep the seat in Latino hands. Yorty supported his aide, Richard Tafoya, Roybal's first cousin. Council members, by now hostile to Yorty and anxious not to further alienate Blacks, were inclined to support Lindsay. Yorty and Roybal hoped for a delay until the spring elections. Some Black activists speculated that it would be easier for the council to appoint a Black to replace an Hispanic in the Ninth than to replace a white in the Tenth.

Ironically, the frustrated movement for Black representation in the Tenth may have led the council to make a Black appointment in the Ninth. A former councilman later recalled, "The Hispanic community had Ed Roybal. I thought it was time we had a Black" (*Herald-Examiner*, 1 December 1985). In fact, the Lindsay appointment set off a period of twenty-three years in which Latinos had no elected officials at city hall.

White council members from Black districts, feeling the heat, took the lead in pushing the Lindsay appointment. Beleaguered Tenth District Councilman Hollingsworth nominated Lindsay, and pushed through a key procedural motion to accelerate the selection (*Los Angeles Times*, 29 January 1963). He was backed by Gordon Hahn, whose Eighth District council seat was also likely to be contested by a Black candidate. Lindsay was appointed on January 28, 1963, becoming the city's first Black officeholder.

An outraged Yorty charged that the council had gone back on a "deal" to delay the appointment. Tafoya said the council was "crazed with power" (*Los Angeles Times*, 29 January 1963). But the Black leadership was pleased and began to agitate for a united vote behind Lindsay, who would face Tafoya in 1963. A Black-Latino struggle was shaping up, as ascendant Blacks sought to hold onto their one seat—itself the only seat Latinos had ever won. A particular irony of this battle was that Roybal had been the main opponent of the council's various plans to prevent Black council representation.

Black candidates now lined up to run against Gordon Hahn in the Eighth District. The best known was Billy Mills, who had the backing of most Black elected officials and community leaders. There were other Black candidates—one endorsed by Roybal, another endorsed by Yorty. Seeing the demographic trends, Hahn stepped down from his seat. The Eighth was now open.

Thus, as the 1963 municipal elections approached, Blacks were certain to win in the Eighth, Bradley was challenging an unelected appointee in the Tenth, and Lindsay was defending a brief incumbency in the Ninth. The Committee for Representative Government now turned its attention from redistricting to politicking. It presented a plan for winning all three seats at a December public meeting at the Mt. Zion Baptist Church; the plan included demographic and voting analyses of all three districts (*Eagle*, 27 December 1962). In those days, demographic data on council districts were hard to find and were the subject of intense political debate. The CRG estimated that the Eighth was 54 percent Black; the Ninth, 39.8 percent Black; and the Tenth, 34.4 percent Black. Mexican-Americans made up 33.5 percent of the Ninth, and Asian-Americans made up 14.3 percent of the Tenth (*Eagle*, 3 January 1963).

Mayor Yorty was backing his own slate of council candidates to settle his many scores with council incumbents. At the last minute, he endorsed Bradley over Hollingsworth. Perhaps he was taking some advice from the *Eagle*'s political writer, who had suggested that the mayor endorse at least two Black candidates, since "after two years in office, it would be the colossal understatement of the year to say that Sam Yorty's popularity in the Negro community is waning" (3 January 1963).

While Yorty continued to back Tafoya in the Ninth, he supported his ally Everette Porter in the Eighth against Mills. Porter was hardly the Black community's choice; as Yorty's appointee to the Police Commission, he had attacked the NAACP for its criticisms of Police Chief Parker (*Eagle*, 21 March 1963).

The council meanwhile provided more fuel for the fire of African-American mobilization. In January 1963, a council committee headed by Hollingsworth quietly killed a fair housing ordinance. The *Eagle* prominently displayed the story and highlighted Bradley's stinging criticism of the council action (24 January 1963).

The *Eagle* and the *Sentinel* illustrate the unified effort that emerged in the struggle to win the three seats. Virtually every week, the *Eagle* ran an editorial and a column, "Body Politic," commenting on the campaigns, along with extensive news coverage of the races. The newspapers openly challenged the Black community. For instance, an *Eagle* editorial stated: "We have the best opportunity we have ever had to crack the racial barrier in the city council. We must make the most of it" (3 January 1963). Shortly after Lindsay's appointment, another *Eagle* editorial exhorted: "It's time to put up or shut up" (31 January 1963). The *Sentinel* commented: "[I]f we do not get a Negro in Council now, somebody had better pack up and move back to the farms" (22 August 1962).

The papers provided a forum for discussing political strategy. The general theme was the need to unify around a single Black candidate in each district and to mobilize the vote. When several Black candidates appeared in the Eighth district, the *Eagle* commented: "We stand on the threshold of success. Selfish ambition and desire for personal advancement should not be permitted to abort the victories that lie within our grasp" (10 January 1963).

The *Eagle* was particularly intent on getting Black voters to prioritize their participation. In the Tenth District, where a community convention had chosen Bradley as its candidate, the stakes were the highest. With only two candidates in the race, there would be no runoff. Therefore, Blacks needed to be sure to vote or provide volunteer help for Bradley (*Eagle*, 14 February 1963). The *Eagle* ran one or two photographs of Bradley in each issue until the election. An *Eagle* editorial blasted Gilbert Lindsay, discussing rumors that he was repaying Hollingsworth's help in gaining the council appointment by diluting his own support for Bradley (28 February 1963). A final preelection editorial called for a massive turnout (28 March 1963).

On the following Tuesday, Bradley was elected in the Tenth District, and runoff elections were set for May 28 in the Eighth and Ninth districts. Bradley's surprisingly easy victory made him the first Black elected by the voters to city office. Bradley won by collecting the overwhelming share of a highly mobilized Black vote, and by breaking even or better in many white neighborhoods (Patterson 1969).

Bradley's hard-earned victory in a multiracial district set off much more euphoria in the Black community than had Lindsay's appointment. An *Eagle* editorial saw it as the culmination of a long struggle for representation that had begun in the 1930s. The writer was particularly impressed by Bradley's cross-racial coalition: "We can't go it alone. We can find allies" (11 April 1963). Publisher Loren Miller wrote: "Los Angeles Negroes came of political age last week," and noted accurately that the citywide press had still not noticed the significance of events within the Black community (ibid). The *Los Angeles Times* ignored the grass-roots effort that elected Bradley and instead noted Yorty's role, suggesting that the "election of Thomas Bradley in the 10th district over Hollingsworth gives Yorty a little more strength in the council" (4 April 1963). Yorty had endorsed Bradley on the Sunday before the election as part of his strategy to take on virtually all council incumbents; his help would have been inconsequential in a district where his own popularity was fast fading.

On May 28, Blacks completed their sweep with the elections of Mills and Lindsay. Lindsay's race was the closest. Bradley's key aide, Warren Hollier, had gone over to the Lindsay campaign to map out precincts (*Eagle*, 16 May 1963). Ultimately the greater unity and mobilization of the Black vote outweighed the strong Latino population base (Patterson 1969).

The blatant injustice of the regime's exclusion of Blacks had led to a disciplined, effective political response from a minority community. Black political activist Willard Murray commented, "I always say that the probability is that if they hadn't gotten into that recall thing, that we would have wound up with one councilman. But that recall thing just got everybody stirred up" (Murray interview). Once stirred up, the Los Angeles Black community was able to hold its ground; the same three seats remained in African-American hands thirty years later.

The 1963 council victories demonstrated that an organized and united Black community could overcome the indifference and hostility of city leaders to win political representation. Blacks in Los Angeles might be few in number and divided along class lines, but they had made their presence known and their impact felt. Despite pressure from Democratic party leaders and from city hall, Black activists pursued their community interest in an independent, self-directed fashion. These dramatic events lend support to Anderson's (1980:1) view of Los Angeles:

> The conventional wisdom shared by most social scientists up until the turbulent 1960's was that black communities throughout the United States were totally dependent upon the dominant white community for leadership and direction. Closer examination of the situation suggests that there were Black community organizational networks which whites either were not aware of or were reluctant to publicly recognize.

The Role of Biracial Alliances

The initial path to power forged in the council elections established that Los Angeles Blacks were extremely effective in the independent exercise of political power. While white liberals, Latinos, and others played supportive roles along the way, the initiation, direction, and momentum came from the Black community itself. (The major role of white liberals in Bradley's campaign will be explored in the next chapter.) Led by active community members and goaded by the Black press, Blacks generated an impressive level of unity and mobilization. A foundation of community mobilization—"a hefty infusion of Black Power" (Holloway 1968:547)—had translated demographic potential into political representation.

But Blacks and liberal reformers were fighting their own battles largely in isolation. Liberals fought against the Unruh machine in the Democratic party, while Blacks struggled to make the Los Angeles city government open its doors. During this period, Blacks won initial incorporation largely without biracial coalition. At the same time, a strong liberal reform movement was developing in the city.

Beginning in the 1950s, the California Democratic Council (CDC) arose to pursue a liberal agenda within the fragmented Democratic party. The organization was inspired in California, and under other names in other states, by the 1952 presidential campaign of Adlai Stevenson. The CDC ultimately became the vehicle for educated, middle-class liberals to become a force in state politics.

In the absence of an organized Democratic party in city politics, the CDC could have a substantial impact. As one Los Angeles CDC activist recalled, "In our minds, we *were* the party" (Weiner interview). As party reformers, they spoke the language of Los Angeles reform, but as liberals they intended to offer a new progressive vision.

The CDC's strongest base was in southern California. In Los Angeles, CDC chapters were found in West Side assembly districts with large Jewish populations and near universities. The highest level of CDC membership was in the Sixty-first Assembly District, which had the highest concentration of Jewish families in Los Angeles county; "other areas with large numbers of CDC members were similarly heavily Jewish" (Wilson 1962). Wilson found similar patterns of reform club membership in New York City and Chicago. The CDC represented one way to express the Jewish liberalism that the Los Angeles civic culture had so effectively repressed. As the Jewish community had grown and become identified with specific areas of the city, its general exclusion from civic leadership had become more aggravating.

The Jewish migration to Los Angeles had continued, and increased after

1930. In 1946, an estimated 168,000 Jews lived in the city. Between 1945 and 1948, 66,000 Jews came to Los Angeles. The Jewish community was steadily moving from its early base in the central city and East Side to the West Side and the near parts of the San Fernando Valley. By 1965, 120,000 Jews lived in the Valley (Vorspan and Gartner 1970:242, 225, 276). This mobile Jewish community, with its middle-class base, was therefore some-what different from the less affluent and mobile Jews of New York City.

Reform liberals seemed to offer the potential for a new civic model and a coalition of excluded minorities in the homogeneous city political system. In particular, a coalition between Blacks and white liberals based on shared ideology and a desire for incorporation seemed natural. Los Angeles Blacks, Jews, and Latinos had voted similarly in the 1960 presidential election (Dawidowicz and Goldstein 1963:35–37). All three groups were heavily Democratic. There were significant efforts to work together in such areas as equal housing. But as late as 1962, such a coalition had yet to develop into a key aspect of the Black struggle for political incorporation.

Several obstacles stood in the way of coalition. Overcoming them was the key to the creation of the ruling citywide coalition. This early era, though, provides an important insight into how Blacks and white liberals can be out of step with each other at certain stages of political development.

From the standpoint of Blacks, there had always been a strong suspicion of white allies. Blacks had been alone for a long time in Los Angeles, and had learned to be distrustful. In Los Angeles, this alienation was especially pronounced among the poor and the working class. During World War II, white civic organizations interested in race relations were largely ineffective in reaching Black-defined goals. Often civic peace was more important than changing deep-rooted city policies that disadvantaged Blacks (Unrau 1971). Even white council members with Black constituencies voted against mea-sures to ensure the appointment of the first Black council member in 1961.

The progressive Congress of Industrial Organizations (CIO) was more closely tied to the Black movement than any other union, but this linkage was highly controversial among Blacks. Debates arose over working with the CIO in language that foreshadowed the Black Power arguments of the 1960s (Unrau 1971). Furthermore, there were already tensions between Blacks and Jews over Jewish leadership of minority organizations and the role of Jewish businesses in Black neighborhoods (Vorspan and Gartner 1970:244).

Wilson (1962) found in 1960–1961 that minorities played only a very small role in the reform movements in New York City, Los Angeles, and Chicago. In Los Angeles, the white middle-class style of the CDC alienated potential minority members. The CDC had few Blacks in key positions, and few Black CDC clubs existed. Blacks rarely sought to use the CDC as a vehicle; there were few office opportunities, "because of the manner in which district lines are drawn" (Wilson 1962:279).

But the trouble lay deeper, in a philosophical struggle over progressivism. Does equality mean Black officeholding? Blacks clearly thought so. But intellectual, white middle-class reformers, while attuned to the struggle for civil rights, were slower to make the connection to Black empowerment. As Wilson (1962:80) noted,

> In all three cities, amateur club leaders have been disheartened by their attempts to bring Negroes into the movement. Except for a handful with an intellectual orientation or a professional background, most potential Negro leaders seem (to the amateur Democrat) to be primarily interested either in the conventional rewards of the professional politician or in "racist" slogans and extreme positions. Few seem to share the white liberal's concern for "integration" and "equal opportunity" or the white reformer's desire to "democratize" the party.

Wilson (1962:284–85) argued that when the Committee for Representative Government sought to expand Black representation, the CDC offered only minimal assistance. While Wilson's argument may have been a bit exaggerated, it was echoed by a Los Angeles activist in 1962. Writing in the *CDC Bulletin*, William B. Jones (1962) argued that despite its ideological liberalism, the CDC had done far too little to assist Black empowerment. Presaging the Black Power argument, Jones called for African-Americans to approach the CDC with their own interests in mind rather than falling for the CDC's liberalism as a substitute for power sharing. Jones suggested that the CDC needed Blacks as much as Blacks needed the CDC.

The election of Sam Yorty to the mayoralty in 1961 offered an example of how Blacks and white reformers could be on opposite sides. Yorty made a direct appeal for Black support, offering incorporation into his regime and civilian control of the police. Feeling alienated from the incumbent Poulson regime, Blacks helped provide Yorty's margin of victory.

Yorty was anathema to the CDC liberals. He had stormed out of the 1956 CDC state convention when he was denied the preprimary endorsement for the U.S. Senate. He blasted the CDC from then on, and the CDC people considered him to be a fraudulent demagogue. The CDC activists worked hard to keep Yorty out of city hall, even helping the Republican Poulson.

The struggle between liberal reformers and Black activists to develop a shared agenda was discussed by Greenstone and Peterson (1973) in their study of the War on Poverty in New York City, Los Angeles, Chicago, and Philadelphia. They discussed the relationship between "black factional interests" and "community conservationists," the latter representing the most liberal and participatory white reformers. While these white reformers were enthusiastic about participation in the Community Action Program (CAP) by poor and minority people, they

> differed from Black Power advocates because they were concerned that the program consistently adhere to participatory and constitutional principles. They opposed limiting employment in CAP agencies to Black Power advocates, for this would make political beliefs relevant for public employment and reintroduce patronage practices into local politics. (123–24)

On the other hand, Black activists were highly suspicious of any sort of coalition with whites, fearing that any sharing of power for practical ends would compromise the integrity of the Black movement.

The 1957 school board elections showed the distance between white liberal and minority communities. In that year, liberals scored a dramatic breakthrough, winning control of the Board of Education in citywide elections. Before 1978, school board members were chosen at large, and conservative slates had dominated the elections. The board members investigated the loyalty of teachers, and even removed the UN Educational, Scientific and Cultural Organization (UNESCO) from the city schools.

In 1957 a pair of liberal candidates, Ralph Richardson and Mary Tinglof, challenged two of the leading conservative board members, Ruth Cole and Edith Stafford, respectively. Both were backed by the progressive Committee for Better Schools (*Los Angeles Times*, 30 May 1957). Despite the *Los Angeles Times*'s strong support for the conservative candidates, both liberals won. Richardson won in the primary, and Tinglof won in the runoff.

The liberal candidates did best in the white liberal/Jewish Fifth Council District; Richardson, in particular, won by a two-to-one margin. Their other areas of strength were in the San Fernando Valley, soon to become the city's bastion of conservatism. By contrast, the conservative candidates did very well in the African-American Eighth Council District. In the biracial Tenth District, Richardson won, and Tinglof lost. In short, the schools became the site for early mobilization by white liberals on the West Side and even in the Valley but did not attract much interest from other groups.

But in Los Angeles the failure of the pragmatic alliance with Yorty to ensure citywide accountability to the Black community showed the limitations of independent power politics. In a city less than one-fifth Black, three council members could not reverse the insensitivity of the police or the budgetary policies of city hall. Yorty's early betrayal of Black objectives showed how easily pragmatic politics could turn into political exploitation of an isolated minority. At some point, Blacks would need to forge a durable, trusting biracial alliance if these patterns were to be challenged and reversed.

Thus, while there were solid grounds for an alliance between Blacks and white liberals in Los Angeles—ideological affinity and a mutual exclusion from the civic culture—there were significant forces keeping them apart. Without alliance, neither would be able to attain citywide power. In a western city dominated by a conservative regime, such an alliance became a necessity. Each side would have to make some adjustments for such a coalition to arise and prosper. Alliance still lay in the future.

PART TWO

THE ROAD TO POWER

FOUR

THE ROOTS OF BIRACIAL POLITICS:

THE TENTH DISTRICT

T HE FORMATION of a winning biracial coalition in Los Angeles represented the flowing together of two broad and powerful movements for social change—that of Blacks for political representation and that of liberal whites for political reform. By the early 1960s, the Los Angeles Black community, built around strong political leadership and unity, had mobilized to express its political potential. These were also critical years in the growth of a white liberal reform movement—destined to become the key partner of Blacks in Los Angeles politics.

There were significant obstacles to interracial coalitions. Class and ideological differences had the potential to keep the movements apart. But while in other cities these obstacles limited Black candidacies, the Los Angeles Black and white liberal reform movements came together around the election of a Black candidate to office, and laid the groundwork for the citywide biracial coalition that took over the city government ten years later.

The Tenth District, seedbed of the biracial alliance, was both the center of Black upward mobility and the site of major reform activity among white liberals. While it had long been one of the three main districts of Black population (along with the Eighth and Ninth), the Tenth differed from the other two districts in the class composition of the Black community.

One of the distinguishing features of the Los Angeles Black experience has been the growth of a substantial Black middle class. From early times, a higher percentage of Blacks owned homes in Los Angeles than in other cities. The pattern in Los Angeles has been for more successful Blacks to move westward, out of the Central Avenue area into the Baldwin Hills, Santa Barbara, Exposition and West Adams neighborhoods. As early as the 1920s, Blacks leaving the central city moved to the area bordered by Arlington, Adams, Jefferson, and Western avenues (Bond 1936:48). By the 1960's these blocks fell within the borders of the Tenth District.

As Blacks continued to migrate to Los Angeles after World War II, more Blacks moved westward, out of the core city. Between 1960 and 1963, the African-American percentage of the Tenth District increased from 38 percent to nearly 47 percent (Patterson 1969:171–72).

In 1960, the citywide median income was $5,324, compared to $3,618 for Blacks. But in the Tenth District, some Blacks lived in the exclusive Baldwin Hills section, where median income exceeded $12,000 (Patterson 1969; Sandoval 1973). Many Tenth District Blacks lived in areas with median income ranging from $5,500 to $6,500 (Patterson 1969:172), hardly wealthy but above the city median and well above the median for Blacks.

The Tenth District was better educated than the inner city. As early as 1940, Black education clearly divided along geographical lines, with the lowest levels in Watts and the highest in the West Side areas. In 1950, median school years completed were 12.0 in West Adams and Santa Barbara, approximately the city median. Central Avenue was at 8.9 years of schooling; Watts, at 9.2. By 1960, the middle-class areas had stayed at the same level, while the central areas had declined (Sandoval 1973:109–12).

The Tenth became the home and emerging base of the African-American lower-middle and middle classes in Los Angeles. Many poor Blacks lived in the Tenth. But with their greater resources and education, upwardly mobile Blacks could be expected to set the tenor of the district. The belief in individual upward mobility and the pursuit of "status goals," (Wilson 1960) such as the abolition of restrictive covenants in housing, might take precedence over the working-class concerns of the Blacks in the Eighth and Ninth districts.

The strength of the Black middle class and its physical separation from the center city created social and political factionalism among local Blacks— and a crisis of leadership. In a 1967 interview, Tom Bradley recalled that

> the natural development which occurred was as the influx of new residents came to Los Angeles, that they occupied the older sections of town, and those that formerly lived there moved west, and this resulted in a sort of vaccuum of leadership. . . . There was no established leadership, no long term or grass roots kind of stability in the community and this has presented one of the difficulties of organizing and molding and shaping of the community. (DeGraaf 1967:7)

The Tenth District inevitably became a base for the political expression of upwardly mobile Blacks. Black candidates had run for the council seat in each election of the previous decade. More oriented to upward mobility and to links with liberal whites, these Blacks differed markedly in political approach from the residents of the central city.

In the Eighth and Ninth districts, Black politics was dominated by the California version of traditional Democratic politics: the machine operated by white assemblyman Jesse Unruh, later in alliance with Black assemblyman Mervyn Dymally. With its ties to organized labor, the Unruh-Dymally combine slated candidates, shared funds, and managed campaigns, using direct mail, slate cards, and sample ballots marked with favored candidates. The Unruh-Dymally style in the Black community was Black oriented and directed toward traditional Democratic goals. Over time

Dymally was able to build a group of Black assembly members and state senators who owed their election to him.

The Dymally approach was much less appealing in the upwardly mobile Tenth District. As the Black middle class expanded, its political style resisted the working-class orientation of the Dymally forces. These class-based differences in political approach underlay the rift that eventually developed in the Black community between the Bradley "reformers" and the Dymally "regulars." (See Chapter Eight for the battles between Black candidates backed by Bradley and those backed by Dymally.)

The West Side faction was led by Tom Bradley. The competition started early. Willard Murray, one of Dymally's earliest allies, said, "We, meaning Dymally and I and our little group, were lobbying for George Thomas [for the 1961 council appointment sought by Bradley]" (Murray interview). Thomas had been endorsed by Unruh, and Bradley was backed by the California Democratic Council (CDC) (*Eagle*, 18 May 1961). Robert Farrell, elected to the city council from the Eighth District in 1974, was once an aide to the "regular" Black councilman Billy Mills of the Eighth and then became an aide to Mayor Bradley. Farrell had therefore worked both sides of the street during his career and saw the differences: "[In the Tenth,] it's more diverse patterns of resources and political centers as opposed to South Los Angeles, homogeneous black, working-class, church-based. In my perspective, the difference between the integrated community and the homogeneous community. It's cotton socks vs. silk stockings" (Farrell interview).

The Tenth District was also the center of Los Angeles political reform. With its large Jewish population, and lively CDC clubs (some Black, some white, some mixed), the district was a hotbed of activism in the early 1960s. The Tenth District was an extraordinary conjunction of several assembly and congressional districts in which liberal reformers were dominant (Weiner interview). The constituencies of Congresspersons Edward Roybal and James Roosevelt and Assembly member Charles Warren—all strong liberals—overlapped.

There was, according to a leading liberal organizer, "a tremendous convergence of that 30th congressional district that Roybal had just formed and the 10th council district . . . the largest single ethnic group in the 10th was probably the Jewish community on the west side. Certainly the number of registered voters was the largest" (Weiner interview). One way to visualize the role of the Tenth Council District is to look at a map of three districts: the heavily Black Eighth, the largely Jewish and liberal Fifth, and the biracial Tenth (see Map 1.1). The Tenth appears as a bridge between two worlds. And back then, portions of today's Jewish Fifth District were still within the Tenth District.

The white liberals who lived in or near the Tenth District were extremely hostile toward the Dymally-Unruh forces—the regulars in the Democratic party. They were the core of the CDC movement. CDC liberals sought to take the party leftward and out of the hands of their archenemy, Unruh. In statewide Democratic politics, the Unruh-Dymally forces acted as the "moderates," in strong opposition to the mostly white reformers, or "liberals," from more educated areas. This factional struggle, heightened during the Vietnam War, tore the California Democrats apart (Tuttle 1975).

The liberal reformers were apt allies for the Black activists in the Tenth District. A number of white liberals helped Blacks buy homes in the West Side areas. They helped Black friends evade restrictive covenants and hostile neighbors by buying homes, and then transferring title (Payne and Ratzan 1986:50–51).

Impelled by political idealism, liberal activists were put off by the pragmatism of the regular Black party activists (Wilson 1962). A prominent CDC activist noted that "the Dymally approach was more self-promotion, less a cause; more self versus a movement" (Weiner interview). For their part, the Dymally forces disliked the white liberals with whom their Black factional opponents were working. Willard Murray, Dymally's Black ally, saw the Black liberals as "too left wing" and too oriented toward "race-mixing" (Murray interview).

The two movements came together in 1963 around Tom Bradley's candidacy for the city council. The foundation of Bradley's candidacy was laid in the Black community between 1961 and 1962. This was the vanguard campaign of the Los Angeles Black community. But even in that early phase, white liberals were involved, and in the more open 1963 council campaign a full-scale biracial coalition developed. The long campaign to elect Tom Bradley to the city council represented a slow evolution from a Black community effort to a fully biracial coalition. It began with ferment in the Black community and ended in the formation of a biracial coalition.

Up until the failure of the recall campaign against Hollingsworth, the struggle had been largely conducted within the Black community. Some liberal whites and Asian-Americans were involved even at the early stages of organization. During the recall, the *Eagle* noted that "white and Japanese residents were just as ready to sign as Negroes" (30 November 1961). But Blacks provided the leadership and grass-roots strength of the recall. Once the recall failed, the Black organizers reached out across racial lines to create a fully biracial campaign.

A major factor in the forging of a Black-liberal link was the presence of a Black candidate with an affinity for biracial coalition politics and with a record of involvement in both Black and reform causes. Bradley acted both as a bridge between African-American and white activists and as a political symbol for the biracial movement. His personal style and background suited the development of a "crossover" approach to racial politics.

Bradley's own life signified the Black movement from the poverty-stricken central city to the West Side. Born in 1917, the son of Texas sharecroppers, Bradley came to Los Angeles with his family at the age of seven. The Bradley family lived in the Central Avenue area. They were extremely poor, and attended the New Hope Baptist Church—not one of the elite churches. A boyhood friend recalled, "They were poorer than a lot of folks were poor" (Terry interview). Bradley's father left the family when Bradley was young, and his mother worked as a domestic in white homes. Bradley's mother relied on him to make financial decisions for the family (Robinson 1976).

A studious and quiet youngster, Bradley did not run with the other kids, including a much rougher contemporary named Jackie Robinson (Robinson 1976). A boyhood friend remembered Bradley as "tall, kind of withdrawn, not outgoing or gregarious" (Terry interview). He was an excellent academic student and an exceptional athlete in track and football.

When he was ready to go to high school, Bradley went to some lengths to transfer to Los Angeles Polytechnic High School, a predominantly white school with a better academic program than the largely Black school in his neighborhood. In explaining his decision years later to a *Los Angeles Times* (28 June 1973) sportswriter, Bradley revealed his self-directed plan for upward mobility: "It was clear that I had to dissociate myself from those who didn't have ambition and those who would turn to illegal activity. I went to Poly High rather than Jefferson, where I actually lived, for the purpose of a clean break, to try to find some new identification, new associates."

At Poly High, Bradley was in both a racial and an economic minority. He was one of about one hundred blacks out of fifteen hundred students, and had almost no decent clothes to wear. Despite these difficulties, he was elected student body president in 1937 (Galm 1984). Bradley played football and ran track at Poly, making all-city as a tackle and setting the city record in the 440-yard dash.

After graduating from high school, Bradley entered the University of California, Los Angeles on a track scholarship in 1937. Located in white, middle-class Westwood, UCLA was an excellent school with a diverse student body. Once again, Bradley was isolated, one of about one hundred Blacks out of about thirteen thousand students. He became active in the Black fraternity Kappa Alpha Psi, eventually becoming a national officer. In 1940, Bradley left UCLA without his degree, married Ethel Arnold (from a family more affluent and socially prominent in the African-American community than his own) and joined the Los Angeles Police Department.

The department was highly segregated and promotions of Black officers were extremely limited. Like most of the Black officers, Bradley was assigned to juvenile and vice work in the Black community. Bradley eventually organized a new community relations unit for the department, and was assigned to a precinct in the West Side Tenth District. He and his family moved into the largely white Leimert Park area, where they were met with some hostility. A white friend had to buy the home for them (Littwin 1981). Bradley and his wife joined the elite First A.M.E. Church, headed by a dynamic young minister named H. H. Brookins.

Through his new job, an extremely unusual one for a Black Los Angeles policeman, Bradley met many of the local Jewish merchants and civic activists in the Tenth District (Robinson 1976). He also rose to the rank of lieutenant, only the second Black to reach that level. Studying at night, he obtained a law degree from Southwestern Law School.

Bradley's career made him a well-known figure in the Black community, even as his successes removed him physically from his central city roots. His name and picture appeared frequently in the *Sentinel*, in articles noting his police work and referring to his previous scholastic and athletic achievements. When he qualified for his pension in 1961, Bradley quit the force to go into law practice.

Bradley's "up from poverty" story became a staple of his political career. Its metaphors proved appealing to both Blacks and whites. Bradley's isolation in a white world, his role as a pioneer entering uncharted territory, and his extraordinary academic, professional, and athletic achievements made him a suitable subject for symbolic recognition. His life became a metaphor for individual Black upward mobility in the face of great odds. But it could also obscure the conditions of those Blacks unlikely to rise up as well. The symbol of individual achievement helped predict that provision of opportunity would be a greater preoccupation of Bradley's progressive politics than redistribution of wealth.

In the 1950s Bradley became a liberal activist. He joined the Democratic Minority Conference, a multiethnic group that aimed to increase Black and Latino representation in government. He also joined the CDC movement. Wilson (1962), perhaps incorrectly, assessed these two groups as being at odds. Weiner said that "many, if not most of the people in the DMC were also members of the CDC" (Weiner interview). Certainly Bradley was able to bridge the two groups.

The liberal reformist CDC was becoming increasingly powerful in California politics, but had a very weak presence in the Black community (Wilson 1962; Jones 1962). Bradley and his Tenth District associates were among the few Blacks to join up with this liberal group; the regular Black politicians were on the other side. Willard Murray, a Black regular, derided Bradley's choice of allies: "It always seemed where everybody was, Tom put himself on the other side" (Murray interview). In a 1967 interview, Bradley strongly defended the "progressive," "liberal" approach of the CDC

(DeGraaf 1967). Bradley later explained his feelings on party factions in greater detail:

> I believed in a kind of openness and full opportunity to participate in the direction of the party. But shortly after I became involved, Jesse Unruh came to power and he was determined that the party was to be built in his image. And if you didn't agree with everything he wanted you were on the outs with him, and that's what happened. I was on the outside of the Unruh regulars. . . . I can't remember any other politicians who were in my side of the party. (Bradley interview)

Unruh's intervention at first limited Bradley's national involvement:

> When John F. Kennedy ran for office in 1960, Jess would not permit me to participate in that campaign. I couldn't get in, no matter what I did. So I went directly to John F. Kennedy and told him what the situation was, told him I was available and wanted to help. And he put me in touch with Ted Kennedy, who was in charge of the western region of the campaign. And that's how I was able to get into and participate in the 1960 election of John F. Kennedy. (ibid.)

Bradley soon became president of the biracial Leimert Park Democratic Club, a CDC affiliate. Black and white members of the Leimert Park and other CDC clubs became Bradley's most enduring loyalists and comprised the inner circle of his campaign organization (Sonenshein 1984).

Bradley's ties to the CDC brought him a base of support independent of Unruh. Bradley said that Unruh "did not have a hold on the leadership CDC members living in the Tenth District, the western end of the district along Adams, both north and south. In the Black community in the district I had the strongest following, so he did not have a great influence there" (Bradley interview).

Bradley's work as a police officer and as a liberal political activist gave him access to the non-Black community. He was especially close to liberal Jewish CDC activists and such liberal labor unions as the United Auto Workers. As he recalled, "The coalition effort began as a result of my involvement in CDC. Out of that experience, I gained a group of friends throughout the city" (ibid.). Through his own activism he recruited one of his closest liberal allies, Maurice Weiner. Weiner first met Bradley in 1962 when they were both helping Latino congressional candidate Edward Roybal: "One day a very tall black man walks in and offers to walk precincts. Everyone else in the office knew him. At that point he was fully involved in Democratic clubs. People told me, 'That's Tom Bradley'" (Weiner interview).

Bradley recruited Weiner to help in his council campaign, and later Weiner became a key link to a wide range of liberal groups. It was Weiner's job to bring along the organized CDC structure—the club activists from within and outside the district. In fact, Weiner was able to translate much of the precinct structure he had used in the Roybal campaign in 1962 to Bradley's 1963 race (ibid.).

With the failure of the recall in 1962, the Bradley forces turned to the 1963 municipal elections and a direct challenge to the incumbent, Hollingsworth. While Blacks represented the largest single group in the district, they fell well short of a majority.

After the 1962 nominating convention chose Bradley, an attempt was made to develop a fully biracial effort. Weiner recalled that he

> received a call from Tom Bradley asking if I would join him and a group of people at a meeting at the real estate office of Victor Nickerson. And Ruth Abraham, who was a big leader in the CDC, was asked which of the clubs and which of the club leaders might be available. Warren Hollier, who had good contacts with the Black community, was asked that. I was asked in terms of people and groups that had helped in the Roybal campaign. (Weiner interview)

The campaign had two main elements: the recall group and the CDC clubs. The recall organization, coordinated by Warren Hollier and Frank Terry, was dominated by African-Americans. The CDC effort was biracial. There were about twelve highly active CDC clubs: a big West Side bloc of Jewish clubs, an effort on the South Side by the largely Black New Frontier Club, and a biracial base in the Wilton Place, Leimert Park, and Queen Anne clubs (Weiner interview).

Organizationally, the campaign was highly integrated. Black activists Brookins, Terry, and Hollier were central figures. The campaign manager was Teddy Muller, who was white, and Weiner was the precinct coordinator. Ruth Abraham and other Jewish CDC activists played key roles in decisionmaking. But Bradley's friend Terry also saw a subtlety in Bradley's handling of his interracial campaign: "I'll tell you about Tom. A large part of the campaign was over on Western Avenue and essentially in the black community. But at that time the 10th District had a sizable Oriental community and the majority, of course, was white. Now he didn't abuse you or misuse you, but he just didn't bring it all together in one bowl of soup" (Terry interview).

According to Patterson (1969), the campaign had two different, but overlapping themes. One was the notion of Black representation, especially within the Black community. In a modified form, the notion of Black representation was also appealing to whites. The Reverend Brookins promoted larger issues of community concern, such as the right of the people of the district to select their own representatives rather than having one imposed by city hall.

This two-track approach helps explain why a biracial coalition may seem to mean different things to Blacks and whites. As Downs (1957) suggested in his study of party strategy, parties use different appeals to the convinced and to the less convinced. A party is likely to seem different to each group. White liberals often saw Bradley's success in somewhat different terms than did Blacks. Whites saw Bradley as a symbol of racial harmony, while Blacks saw him as a symbol of racial assertion (Sonenshein 1984).

In the election, Bradley solidly defeated Hollingsworth. Patterson's (1969) detailed analysis by census tract reveals that Bradley won overwhelmingly in the Black community and made a very credible showing outside it. The lack of white polarization against the Black candidate reflected first of all the biracial nature of Bradley's organization and the liberalism of the Tenth District. But timing mattered, too. These events took place at the height of the civil rights movement and before the 1965 Watts riot. For many of those involved, the campaign to elect Bradley grew directly out of the civil rights movement.

Tenth District biracial politics built a linkage between two overlapping movements: one among Blacks for representation and another among whites for liberalism. (Surprisingly, Patterson's excellent analysis of the Tenth District campaign omits any mention of the ideological importance of white liberalism. He implies that whites supported the Black candidate in order to protest against the city council's unfairness to the district.)

Only a minority of Black activists, generally within the Tenth District, were drawn to link themselves with the liberal wing of the California Democratic party. On the white side, biracial politics grew out of a group of liberals who were active in the multiracial Tenth District or in the CDC outside the district. Unlike more isolated white liberals who had little contact with Blacks, these white activists worked closely with Blacks as equals in the CDC and in various civil rights and civil liberties organizations. They were early converts to the movement for Black representation, which to them overlapped with the biracial civil rights movement, rather than conflicting with it.

Thus at its roots Los Angeles biracial politics was a result of joint efforts under African-American leadership behind a Black candidate by a relatively small group of Black and white reformers, linked by ideology and opposition to dominant party forces. This small biracial group of mavericks was much more suited than the regulars to eventually seize control of city hall in a city permeated by the style and ideology of reform.

A number of factors combined to make the Tenth District a good nest for biracial politics. First, the district system of council elections allowed the coalition to evolve gently and quietly. Second, there were enough activist Blacks to lead the coalition. White liberals in the Tenth came along behind Black leadership, reducing Black fears of having their struggle co-opted.

This alliance, and the extraordinary level of Black council representation, could not have occurred without the district system of council elections. In a rigidly nonpartisan system, with no party ladder of opportunity, and in the face of a conservative white majority, the district system facilitated minority success. The upset victory won by progressive forces in the 1925 charter reform was echoing almost four decades later.

The emerging biracial leadership had been branded by the fire of electoral politics. In other cities, the Black-reform alliance came together around the antipoverty program and its calls for citizen participation (Greenstone and Peterson 1973). When it came time to seek electoral power, these coalitions were less prepared than the one in Los Angeles, which had already learned important political lessons. The Tenth District was an excellent training ground both for building elite links and for appealing to mass audiences.

New York City illustrates the point. There was little electoral linkage between the rising Black movement and white liberal reformers. The connection finally arose in the antipoverty battles of the mid-1960s, but these efforts ultimately became a diversion from electoral strategy (Hamilton 1979). For many activists in New York City, being on the outside dealing with federally funded agencies was absorbing politics.

The later success of the Bradley coalition in attaining citywide power should not obscure the essential facts about the 1963 council coup. In all three districts, the independent Black movement for political representation succeeded largely because of Black numbers, unity, and organization. Following the campaigns in the Black newspapers shows the high priority the battles commanded among Blacks.

Even in the biracial Tenth, where Bradley's campaign mixed themes of Black recognition with biracial appeals, Patterson (1969:182–83) concluded that "no matter how well cloaked in acceptable phraseology the ideological rationales of the movement were, the underlying motive was the same— that of the achievement of recognition through Negro representation." But the linkage to whites made a significant difference in the outcome. And the biracial linkage was to be far more significant in the future struggle to win citywide power. The three council seats, while very important, were not enough to alter city policy under the volatile Yorty regime. When it came time to seek citywide power, it was the biracialism of the Tenth District that gained the leading role.

By 1963 a new biracial factional coalition had formed in the Tenth District of Los Angeles, without close ties to the dominant regular forces in the Democratic party. While Yorty had originally backed Bradley, they quickly became rivals. The members of this incipient coalition would go on to endorse James Roosevelt's losing mayoral campaign against Yorty in 1965 and eventually help Tom Bradley seek the mayoralty in 1969 and 1973.

Theoretically, the basis for a Black-Latino alliance could be envisioned in

Los Angeles. But Latinos were not present at the creation of the ultimate winning coalition. Latinos were not a major constituency in the Tenth District; in fact, they were desperately trying to hold back the tide of Black political mobilization to preserve their only island of power in the Ninth District. Hinckley's (1981) view that elite trust earned over time is a crucial factor in the development of a political coalition suggests that Latinos were latecomers to an important political relationship, which developed instead between Blacks and white liberals.

History might have been different had Edward Roybal, so similar to Bradley in style and political base, stayed in city politics. In fact, his 1949 council campaign had much in common with Bradley's first victory. As Roybal recalled:

> We registered Hispanics in our district, in all the Boyle Heights area. We registered 17,000 people. Of those, 13,500 were Hispanics. Then when we went to the polls on election day, we got those 13,500 out and of the 17,000 we got 97% out to the polls. I got the support of the Anglo and other communities with the coalition of Hispanics and Jews in my district, and also the Blacks in the housing projects. (Regalado 1988a)

But with Roybal's move to Congress, the elite ties between minority politics and white liberalism moved quickly and easily into the Black movement surrounding Tom Bradley. Maurice Weiner, who had directed Roybal's precinct operation, simply folded that effort into the Bradley council campaign. After Roybal, no Latino politician with major crossover appeal arose to build on the base he had developed. And the Ninth District seat, the foundation of Latino city politics, was lost.

In the Tenth District, Black and white liberal activists worked together day by day, developing an understanding of each other's abilities and personalities. This experience, shared over time, greatly strengthened the network's later ability to resolve conflicts and organize citywide politics. Joint membership in an array of liberal groups gave a common focus to interracial efforts in and around the Tenth District. It also reflected a theory of interracial contacts, which was studied after the Watts riot a few years later. Those whites, regardless of ideology, who worked closely with Blacks in equal, voluntary social settings were the most sympathetic to Black protest (Jeffries and Ransford 1969).

A key activist remembered the interracial aspect:

> Working together is the surest way of avoiding misunderstandings and serious disagreements and collisions. Perhaps it was enough that all of us who were involved in both the Roybal and Bradley campaigns had the same objective, the same goal, supported the same person. I think the fact that we had this easy mixing of people with different backgrounds helped us to avoid a lot of errors

that other political campaigns may make just because they don't know and they don't have the people who know the differences among people. Everyone felt that we were accomplishing something important. (Weiner interview)

At a stage of the civil rights movement when the election of Black candidates had not yet become an accepted goal, this biracial network had already transformed the Black candidacy into a shared symbol of progressive politics. The debate between liberal reformers and Black activists on Black representation was absent in the Tenth District, where the common goal of political victory emerged. Earlier than in most parts of the country, the transition from civil rights to political empowerment had been accepted as valid and idealistic.

The 1963 council election provided invaluable electoral and organizational experience for the progressive network. The later success of the liberal coalition was greatly aided by the presence and resolution of the same issues that later arose citywide: maintaining Black support while pursuing biracialism, organizing at the grass-roots level, and keeping the crusading spirit alive while becoming politically pragmatic.

There was a great deal happening in the minority and liberal communities of Los Angeles in the early 1960s. But despite the remarkable ability of Blacks to use the ballot to win power and forge coalitions, the larger body politic paid little attention to these efforts. Blacks were invisible still, especially in such citywide media outlets as the *Los Angeles Times* (Johnson, Sears, and McConahay 1971). Other than the 1963 election results, there was very little coverage of the crucial council races in the *Los Angeles Times*. It is supremely ironic that Los Angeles Blacks succeeded admirably with the ballot, as whites had often advised, but were still ignored. It took massive civil violence to unmistakably express Black concerns and command the full attention of the city.

The newly elected Los Angeles school board meets on July 1, 1957, after stunning victories by two liberals over conservative candidates. The liberal winners, Ralph Richardson and Mary Tinglof, are the second and third from the left. (Herald Examiner Collection, Los Angeles Public Library.)

City councilman Edward Roybal, the city's first Latino elected official, first victorious in 1949 in the Ninth District. (Daily News, Department of Special Collections, University Research Library, UCLA.)

Rosalind Weiner (later Wyman), just elected to the city council in the Fifth District, 1953. (Daily News, Department of Special Collections, University Research Library, UCLA.)

Sam Yorty celebrates his upset victory over incumbent Mayor Norris Poulson at his city hall inauguration, July 1, 1961. (Los Angeles Times, Department of Special Collections, University Research Library, UCLA.)

Mayor Sam Yorty joins Police Chief William Parker (left) on a tour of the Police Academy, c. 1962. (Sam Yorty Collection, City Clerk's Office, Los Angeles City Archives.)

Joined by his wife, Congressman James Roosevelt concedes his defeat at the hands of Mayor Sam Yorty, April 7, 1965. (Los Angeles Times, Department of Special Collections, University Research Library, UCLA.)

Smoke rises from a burning building during the Watts uprising, Avalon Boulevard, between 107th and 108th streets, August 1965. (Los Angeles Times, Department of Special Collections, University Research Library, UCLA. Photo by George R. Fry, Jr.)

Street scene at 103rd Street, near Wilmington Avenue, during the Watts uprising, August 1965. (Los Angeles Times, Department of Special Collections, University Research Library, UCLA. Photo by Larry Sharkey.)

Tom Bradley debates Sam Yorty (left) on May 8, 1973, at the Tarzana Chamber of Commerce, moderated by Ross Porter (center). (Herald Examiner Collection, Los Angeles Public Library.)

Mayoral candidate Tom Bradley campaigns in Jewish neighborhoods along Fairfax Boulevard, May 25, 1973. (Los Angeles Times, Department of Special Collections, University Research Library, UCLA.)

Tom Bradley, his wife Ethel, and their daughters Phyllis and Lorraine celebrate Bradley's 1973 mayoral victory. (Herald Examiner Collection, Los Angeles Public Library.)

George Takei, a television actor well known for his role as Mr. Sulu in *Star Trek*, and a leading Asian-American political activist, shown in September 1973 when he made a strong challenge in a special election to succeed Bradley in the Tenth Council District. (Herald Examiner Collection, Los Angeles Public Library.)

Mayor Bradley congratulates David Cunningham and his family after Cunningham's election in 1973 to fill Bradley's vacant seat in the Tenth Council District. (Herald Examiner Collection, Los Angeles Public Library.)

FIVE

RACE, IDEOLOGY, AND THE FORMATION
OF A NEW CITYWIDE COALITION

THE EVENTS discussed so far occurred outside the glare of city-wide politics. In Los Angeles, with its low salience of politics and pursuit of the "good life," out of sight could often mean out of mind (Carney 1964). African-Americans had gained a major beachhead in political representation, and had even forged a winning biracial coalition in the Tenth District. These events had made barely a dent on the larger life of the city.

But that neglect was about to end. Race and ideology went rapidly from the back burner of city politics to the heart of city life. In the process the city became far more racially polarized, but Blacks also developed the capacity to compete for a share of citywide power.

Between 1964 and 1966, the fault lines of Los Angeles politics shifted. In the process, a new and durable pattern of political cleavage, based on race and ideology, began to dominate city politics. New coalitions formed around these fault lines and competed for city power. The alliances and conflicts that arose in those years remain central to the city's politics twenty-five years later, as they have been in national politics (Edsall and Edsall 1991; Carmines and Stimson 1989).

During this period, a statewide referendum on an open-housing law, the federal antipoverty program, citywide elections, and the Watts uprising all reflected a twofold division: a racial conflict between Blacks and whites, and an ideological conflict among whites. The Watts protest of 1965 is, of course, the best known of these conflicts. But Watts fell right in the middle of a number of crucial political changes. To a great degree, the city became divided between Black assertiveness, moderately supported by white liberals, and white reaction. The growing and ambivalent Latino community was caught in the middle.

Even before Watts, major changes had been occurring in the city, drawing Blacks and white reformers into common activity. A linkage of ideology and interest was growing. As this juncture emerged, the biracial Tenth District network was in the best possible position to lead it. When the two groups united against their common enemy—Yorty and his conservative coalition—success became possible.

Yorty's alliance with the Black community had shown signs of fraying not long after the 1961 election. Yorty's opportunistic coalition could not hold beyond its protest against the Establishment. From the very start, Yorty was whipsawed by the gap in interest and ideology between racial minorities in the central city and conservative white homeowners in the San Fernando Valley. Without a unifying ideology, the Yorty regime desperately sought to paper over these inherent differences. Without shared beliefs, it was an increasingly difficult thing to carry off.

Perhaps more important, given the pragmatic nature of the alliance, was the numerical strength of the Valley whites. After World War II, the Valley was the main growth area of the city. Until 1971, city council districts were reapportioned every four years on the basis of voter registration, not population. As a middle-class area with many homeowners, the Valley had high voter registration. By this standard, the Valley was consistently underrepresented, and districts were moved into the Valley in 1952, 1956, and 1964 (*Los Angeles Newsletter* 1 October 1960, 4 July 1964).

Blacks had won some political clout with the 1963 council elections. When the council considered its quadrennial reapportionment in 1964, the Valley was once again entitled to a new district. The three Black council members were all in undersized districts, ripe for plucking. The council instead moved the Twelfth District, with a smaller Black population, far out into the northwest valley. Black councilman Lindsay was given the highly desirable downtown area, gaining access to campaign donations from the big companies who did business there (*Los Angeles Newsletter*, 4 July 1964).

But Yorty's conservative beliefs and the growing importance of the Valley made it inevitable that his coalition would sacrifice Blacks on the altars of political expediency and ideological consistency. Shortly after his election, Yorty met with Police Chief Parker. As Tom Bradley described it,

> He did threaten Sam Yorty. One day Parker sent a message over with a package. And they showed that to Yorty and told him he wanted him to shut up and stop criticizing the chief and laid out all of these bits of information that they had gathered on him. And we never again heard Yorty criticize Chief Parker. It was well known around City Hall. From that day forward, the day he threw that package on the desk, that was it and it shut him up. (Bradley interview)

White reformers already detested Yorty, so it was a matter of Blacks' developing the same intense dislike. In time, Blacks and white reformers were clearly understood to be the main excluded groups under the Yorty regime. As racial issues rose to citywide importance, the support of racial liberals became increasingly important to Black political success.

Proposition 14 and Antipoverty Politics

In 1964, a statewide ballot proposition illuminated the racial polarization that was soon to dominate California and the nation. Proposition 14 was intended to repeal the Rumford Fair Housing Act, which prevented racial discrimination in the sale of homes. The ballot measure passed with two-thirds of the statewide vote, although it was later declared unconstitutional by the U.S. Supreme Court.

Wolfinger and Greenstein (1968) found that the white vote against Proposition 14 followed a new pattern, which was later to become very familiar to students of urban political coalitions. Educated, liberal Democratic whites voted no. Three-quarters of Jewish voters opposed the measure.

Beverly Hills, with its large Jewish population, divided down the middle, while virtually every other community in Los Angeles County (except Compton, with a 40 percent Black population) passed it with heavy majorities. Remarkably, affluent and all-white Beverly Hills was not far away from Compton's vote (50.1 percent for, versus 41.6 percent for in Compton). Because of their large Jewish or Black populations, Wolfinger and Greenstein classified these as "deviant" cases.

Browning, Marshall, and Tabb (1984) considered Proposition 14 to be an excellent way of measuring white support for minority interests. They found a wide variety of white voting patterns on Proposition 14 in the ten cities they studied. The highest level of anti–Proposition 14 voting occurred in Berkeley, where a strong biracial coalition eventually developed. Berkeley went against Proposition 14 with 64.9 percent, compared to 43.5 percent in Los Angeles. In general, Wolfinger and Greenstein found that there was much greater support for Proposition 14 in southern than in northern California. In historical perspective, it makes the later winning of minority incorporation in Los Angeles seem all the more remarkable.

Closer examination of the Proposition 14 vote indicates the new shape of city politics. (Unfortunately, a council district breakdown was not available for statewide elections in that year.) A contemporary analysis of state assembly districts in Los Angeles showed that white San Fernando Valley districts overwhelmingly favored Proposition 14 and that Black districts were heavily against it; Jewish and Mexican-American districts were divided (*Los Angeles Newsletter*, 2 January 1965).

State records show that the assembly districts with the largest Black populations, the Fifty-third and Fifty-fifth, voted overwhelmingly against Proposition 14. White districts, whether Republican or Democratic, voted for the measure in the range of 65–75 percent. Virtually all Republican districts voted heavily for the measure. But there were a number of other assembly districts, particularly on the Jewish liberal West Side, that split on the proposition. While they were still far from the Black position, this vote placed them about twenty-five points away from other whites.

The districts represented in Congress by James Roosevelt and Edward Roybal were crucial in the development of the Bradley coalition. In the previous chapter, we saw that the Tenth District contained elements of both constituencies. These areas and the assembly district represented by

Charles Warren were hotbeds of liberal reform and minority activism. This was the "melting pot" out of which the Bradley coalition emerged. And these areas went against the flow on Proposition 14, generally opposing it or breaking even.

As we will see later, it is striking how stable this pattern became. In election after election, the white liberal, and particularly the Jewish, neighborhoods of Los Angeles differed in a major way from other white districts, and the Black community represented the principal bloc on the Left.

The passage of Proposition 14 showed that the next stage of racial politics would not simply mean the maintenance of the Kennedy-Johnson Democratic coalition. New types of urban coalitions would be required. As the *Sentinel* noted after the passage of Proposition 14, "Ironically, however, thousands of Californians who supported President Johnson—himself a strong civil rights advocate—proved to be racial 'hypocrites' by voting for Proposition 14, the insidious initiative" (5 November 1964).

While Johnson swept the city and county of Los Angeles, so did Proposition 14 (see Table 5.1). Los Angeles was by no means a racially liberal city in 1964. While the Democratic presidential candidate did exceptionally well, Los Angeles joined southern California in strong support of Proposition 14. The road to winning citywide minority power would be a long and difficult one.

The same year witnessed an important conflict in the city council over police-minority relations. Council members Bradley and Wyman introduced a motion to explore these tensions but were persistently rebuffed by two conservative members, John C. Holland of the Fourteenth District and Karl L. Rundberg of the Eleventh District (*Los Angeles Herald-Examiner*, 6 June 1964; *Sentinel*, 12 November 1964). The high hopes of 1963 were running up against the reality of white racial conservatism in Los Angeles.

Greenstone and Peterson's (1973) study of the federal antipoverty program in four cities showed the growth of an ideological alliance in local politics between racial minorities and white reformers. Both sought to increase "citizen participation" and both opposed the existing, mostly party elites. The Community Action Program (CAP), with its call for participation in the allocation of antipoverty funds, supported the conflict between liberal and conservative or moderate local coalitions.

TABLE 5.1

Democratic Presidential Vote and Proposition 14 Vote
in City and County of Los Angeles, 1964 (percent)

	Johnson Vote	No on Proposition 14
City of Los Angeles	64.5	43.5
County of Los Angeles	57.5	32.6

Greenstone and Peterson found that antipoverty politics in Los Angeles were very different from those in New York City, Chicago, and Philadelphia. In the other three cities, incumbent moderate leaders sought to co-opt or even support the liberal coalitions, using sophisticated tactics to fend off challenges to their own leadership. Only in Los Angeles, the western city, was the mayor openly hostile to the program and a direct enemy of the liberal participation coalition. In fact, the far more open opposition of the incumbent regime in Los Angeles helped further cement relations between Blacks and white reformers.

Yorty and the council conservatives refused actively to pursue federal antipoverty funds, fearing federal interference and the cost to the city of matching shares. Bringing resources to inner-city neighborhoods was not high on their agenda anyway. When major federal funds were committed in 1965, Yorty was not enthusiastic and the city received a surprisingly small share (Saltzstein, Sonenshein, and Ostrow 1986). Yorty's liberal opponents began to demand that he more actively chase federal funds to fight poverty. The liberal position was far less clear in the other cities, where sophisticated mayors actively sought federal funds and played off groups against one another.

The political leaders of Los Angeles were largely unresponsive to federal initiatives, despite increased availability of federal funds. The city's grants process prior to 1973 was highly decentralized, episodic, inefficient, and uncoordinated. Individual departments became aware of grants, made their own contacts with federal agencies, and prepared their own proposals (Rogers interview). The Office of the Mayor and the council were frequently unaware of grant applications by departments and hence had little control over resulting programs. Many grants were not pursued, although the city was eligible for them (ibid.).

Federal officials tried unsuccessfully to give money to Los Angeles. Dr. Emma McFarlin was sent by the U.S. Department of Housing and Urban Development to offer funds to Los Angeles after the Watts riots. She found little enthusiasm among local elected officials. Los Angeles had a poor reputation among federal bureaucrats. The quality of its applications was uneven, and federal officials were uncertain whether the proposals bore significant support of elected officials or merely reflected departmental priorities (McFarlin interview).

Consequently, Los Angeles received less federal money than did comparable cities. Greenstone and Peterson (1973:276) claimed that Los Angeles lost millions of dollars as a result of conflicts among Yorty, community residents, and federal officials over the administration of War on Poverty funds in the late 1960s. The lack of mayoral influence, allegedly stemming from the weakness of the office, limited Yorty's ability to forge the necessary compromises.

There was another crucial difference between Los Angeles and the other three cities. Only in Los Angeles had the Black-liberal alliance already transformed itself into an electoral, pragmatic alliance able to contest and win elections. While there was a certain ambivalence between the goals of Black political power and liberal reform, both embodied in the antipoverty program, the connection between Black politics and liberal ideology had already been forged in the Tenth District of Los Angeles.

The challenging coalition included three liberal congress members: James Roosevelt and Augustus Hawkins of Los Angeles, and Adam Clayton Powell (D-N.Y.), who controlled the OEO pursestrings. Local critics were led by the Reverend H. H. Brookins, a close ally of Tom Bradley. Despite his unpopularity in the Black community, Yorty continued to work closely with Black council members Mills and Lindsay, and shared control of the antipoverty program with them:

> [W]hen Councilman Mills, one of Yorty's black allies, proposed that the poverty area residents vote for their representatives, Yorty accepted the election procedure. . . . Yorty accepted the proposal partly, it appears, because of Mills' political difficulties in a heavily black district. The councilman's earlier support of Yorty when the mayor opposed any community participation had aroused criticism in his district. . . . (Greenstone and Peterson 1973)

Bradley was not tied to the Mills and Lindsay faction, referring to them later as "part of the clique at city hall" (Galm 1984). In addition to their cooperation with Yorty, Mills and Lindsay were close to Bradley's rival Jesse Unruh. Bradley recalled, "Billy Mills was very friendly with all of the Jesse Unruh people. Gil Lindsay had been independently elected, so he didn't have to join, but he did have a cordial relationship with Jess . . . and when I ran for chairman of the county committee, it was the Unruh forces in control and Billy Mills and Gil Lindsay were with them" (Bradley interview).

Greenstone and Peterson have argued that Yorty's opposition to the program transcended his own political interests, that it was fundamentally ideological:

> In understanding Yorty's motivations, however, it is important to note that his opposition to participation continued well into the middle of 1965. . . . It then continued, even after the end of the 1964–1965 fiscal year, leaving Los Angeles without more than the barest minimum in poverty funds. Had he simply embraced *symbolic* participation early in the dispute, in the way that his alliance with Mills later required, Yorty would certainly have placed himself in a stronger political position in minority group communities without obviously endangering his white support. (160–61, emphasis in original)

Los Angeles antipoverty politics were so bitter that the Reverend Martin Luther King, Jr., came to Los Angeles in 1965 to call on the city to increase the representation of minority and poor people on the antipoverty board. By general agreement, the 1965 municipal elections would help determine which local coalition would control the agency.

The 1965 City Elections

The 1965 mayoral election was the first electoral battle between the dominant Yorty regime and the emerging progressive coalition. Within the Democratic party, the CDC and the regular factions saw the race as a clear struggle for control. Governor Edmund G. Brown, Sr., had joined the CDC side, and therefore backed the mayoral candidacy of Congressman James Roosevelt. Once Brown had intervened, the Unruh forces joined Yorty, even though he had been a party maverick (*Los Angeles Newsletter*, 16 January 1965). As a party outsider, Yorty won the endorsement of the *Los Angeles Herald-Examiner*, in an editorial entitled "Will the Party Take Over?" (25 March 1965).

The Roosevelt forces were allied with Councilwoman Wyman and her husband, Democratic leader Eugene Wyman, both among Yorty's bitterest enemies. Bradley and Wyman were close allies in the council; as Bradley said, "We had a very friendly relationship and were in agreement on most issues" (Bradley interview). Hawkins and Bradley were the only major Black politicians to back Roosevelt. The other Black politicians all lined up with Yorty and the Unruh forces now behind him. As Willard Murray said, "We supported Yorty against Roosevelt, we being myself, Dymally, Lindsay, Rev. [F. Douglas] Ferrell. If you want to talk about factionalism, I think that's when it began, because Hawkins and Bradley supported Roosevelt" (Murray interview).

The same alliances had emerged in the 1964 Alan Cranston–Pierre Salinger Democratic senatorial primary. Murray said:

> We wanted to have a united front [of Black elected officials] so we called all of them together and talked about the Senate race and agreed that it would be nice if we were together. Everyone wound up supporting Pierre Salinger, with the exception of Tom Bradley, and Hawkins had already committed to Cranston. CDC was with Cranston and the regulars were with Pierre Salinger. (ibid.)

To the winner of these conflicts would go citywide power, including control of the antipoverty program. Congressman Hawkins had already succeeded in cutting Mills and Lindsay out of key aspects of the antipoverty operation (*Los Angeles Newsletter*, 15 May 1965). As a sidelight to the mayoral race, Yorty intended to defeat Wyman in the Fifth District to show his power over the council. One observer saw the Yorty-Wyman and Yorty-Roosevelt battles as a struggle between "established downtown interests and the wealthy insurgents in Beverly Hills" (*Los Angeles Newsletter*, 16 January 1965). The downtown versus West Side power struggle continued to influence Los Angeles politics for years to come (Davis 1991).

Despite Yorty's support from most Black politicians, his appeal to Black voters had waned considerably. Roosevelt campaigned heavily in Black neighborhoods, charging that Yorty had neglected Blacks. A white reform candidate was now directly appealing to the Black constituency.

Roosevelt noted the city's refusal to do anything with Wrigley Field, given to the city in exchange for the land that became Dodger Stadium (*Sentinel*, 4 March 1965). He publicized the fact that Yorty had used city funds to pay his dues to the Jonathan Club, which excluded Blacks (*Sentinel*, 25 March 1965). Rev. Martin Luther King, Jr., visited the city several times in 1964 and 1965, lending his prestige to the reform coalition and indirectly to the Roosevelt campaign (*Sentinel*, 11 March 1965).

The *Sentinel* gave substantial space to person-on-the-street interviews, in which Blacks were asked if they would vote for Yorty. A large number said they would not. On February 18, the *Sentinel* printed an editorial that strongly criticized Black politicians for backing Yorty, saying they were "out of touch" with the Black community. On April 1, the paper endorsed Roosevelt, charging that Yorty had "fooled the Negro community."

Willard Murray, who was organizing Black support for Yorty, saw the problem: "He had not a good reputation in the Black community. They had some polls done and he was getting 17% of the Black community. So we put together this operation, we wanted him getting 35% of the Black vote" (Murray interview).

On election day, Yorty crushed Roosevelt by 57.9 percent to 36.5 percent, winning in most areas of the city. In addition, Wyman was badly defeated in the Fifth District, creating a heady sense of vindication for the Yorty regime. Yorty had proved that he no longer needed Black support. The *Sentinel* reported that in many Black precincts, Yorty had lost by two to one (8 April 1965).

Roosevelt's strongest areas were the three Black council districts, the Eighth, Ninth, and Tenth. In fact, the Black districts joined the largely Jewish Fifth District in backing Roosevelt. At the mass base, a biracial alliance was forming. The new Twelfth District in the northwestern Valley displayed its conservative leanings with a strong showing for Yorty (see Table 5.2).

Wyman's defeat revealed class conflict in the Jewish community as much as it showed Yorty's popularity. While Wyman was indeed swept away, Roosevelt carried the Fifth against Yorty. A contemporary analysis noted that the wealthy Wymans had moved from the middle-class and working-class Fairfax area to exclusive Bel Air (*Los Angeles Newsletter*, 29 May 1965).

TABLE 5.2

Mayoral Vote in Three Key Council Districts, 1965
(percent)

		Yorty	*Roosevelt*
5th	White liberal/Jewish	47.2	48.0
8th	Black	34.8	59.9
12th	White conservative	71.1	19.5

Source: City Archives.

In Chapter Eight, we will see that in 1975 the Fifth District council election continued the pattern.

In the general election, however, the Reverend James Jones, an African-American, won election to the school board over conservative Marion Miller. In contrast to the 1957 school board races, the racial and ideological lines that would soon dominate the city emerged. Table 5.3 shows the vote for the two school candidates in three key districts. Jones crushed Miller in the Black district, and won by a two-to-one margin in the white liberal Fifth. The white conservative Twelfth District, newly created in 1964, was 25 points more pro-Miller than the white liberal district.

The 1965 elections gave Yorty the confidence to challenge Governor Brown in the 1966 Democratic primary for governor. Yorty now had full control of the antipoverty program (*Los Angeles Newsletter*, 17 July 1965) and the confidence to pursue his conservative agenda. With the antipoverty program out of reach as a political vehicle, Blacks and their white allies had to return to an electoral focus. It would be necessary to dislodge the mayor. This was yet another important development; without control over the federal program, progressives were not diverted from the electoral goal.

Opposition continued to grow within the Black community. The reform faction consistently struggled with the antipoverty board. In July, the Rev-

TABLE 5.3

Vote for School Board Candidates in
General Election, 1965 (percent)

		Jones	*Miller*
5th	White liberal/Jewish	63.5	32.9
8th	Black	80.0	17.6
12th	White conservative	41.2	57.0

Source: Same as Table 5.2.

erend Brookins bitterly attacked the board; his position was again backed by the Reverend Martin Luther King, Jr. (*Sentinel*, 15 July 1965). Relations between Blacks and the police continued to be extremely tense and hostile, and Councilman Bradley repeated his unsuccessful calls for the formation of a Human Relations Commission (Galm 1984). By this time, even Mills and Lindsay spoke critically of the police. Bradley recalled that on police issues, the Black members of the council were usually isolated:

> Generally, only the three Black council representatives, Lindsay, Mills and I were willing to speak out and be critical of Chief Parker. We got, I suppose you might say, quiet encouragement occasionally, but nobody was willing to come out. Parker was in the heyday of his power, and the council members, if not in agreement with him, were afraid of him and wouldn't challenge him. (Bradley interview)

But within the police department, the outside pressure so unfamiliar to the organization had begun to have an impact. Black officer Jesse Brewer remembered: "I think the department was beginning to feel the pressure from the city council. And so things were gradually getting better. A few things were happening—people got different assignments, people got promoted" (Brewer interview).

Watts and Its Aftermath — Protest and Cleavages

It was in this setting—a newly enhanced conservative regime facing a bitter, excluded Black community in tentative alliance with white reformers— that Marquette Frye was stopped.

At 7:00 P.M., on Wednesday, August 11, 1965, California Highway Patrol (CHP) officer Lee W. Minikus arrested Marquette Frye, a twenty-one-year-old Black man, on suspicion of drunk driving in the heart of Black Los Angeles. Through a remarkable series of events, this routine arrest turned into the first major race riot of the 1960s.

At first, Frye and the officer were jocular. A crowd gathered, friendly at first, as Minikus and his backups prepared to have Frye's car towed. Frye lived only one block away, and his mother, hearing of the arrest, remonstrated with the officer to allow Frye's brother to drive the car home. The discussion soon turned ugly, and by 7:23 PM all three members of the Frye family had been hustled into a CHP vehicle. The growing crowd objected vehemently to the arrests.

As the officers were withdrawing from the scene, someone apparently spit on the back of one of them. Using very questionable judgment, the enraged officer and his partner waded into the crowd to find the assailant.

The officer grabbed a young woman wearing a barber's smock resembling a maternity dress, and with great force, dragged her to a police vehicle. To the increasingly agitated crowd, the police had brutalized a pregnant Black woman. As the officers hurriedly left the scene, rocks began to fly. Soon, young men in the crowd began to attack passing vehicles with rocks and bottles. The riot was under way. On that Wednesday night, violence continued until after midnight. (Much of this narrative account comes from Conot 1967.)

At 2:00 P.M. the next day, Black community leaders called a meeting at Athens Park to cool down the young people. To the consternation of the meeting's organizers, who had hoped to have a frank exchange of views with the potential protesters, many television and print reporters attended. Quiet negotiation was therefore out of the question. The meeting was proceeding reasonably well until a young African-American man ran up, grabbed the microphone, and—as the television cameras rolled—said:

> I was down on Avalon last night, and we the Negro people have got completely fed up! They not going to fight down here no more. You know where they going? They're after the Whiteys! They going to congregate. They don't care! They going out to Inglewood, Playa del Rey, and everywhere else the white man supposed to stay. They going to do the white man in tonight. And I'm going to tell you . . . (Conot 1967:15)

Although the leaders grabbed back the microphone and beseeched the television stations not to use the footage, it was broadcast that night. By Thursday evening, violence had broken out again, and it continued on Friday morning. General looting had begun by midmorning, and fire fighters were driven off by snipers and by people throwing missiles at them (McCone 1965:17–18). At 5 P.M., the lieutenant governor, in the absence of a traveling Governor Brown, called out the National Guard.

Friday was the roughest night. Violence continued all over the area, and a number of deaths occurred. By Saturday, the lieutenant governor had ordered an 8 P.M. curfew over an area of 46.5 square miles (McCone 1965:20). The rioting subsided by Sunday, and the curfew was lifted on Tuesday.

The final toll of the Watts uprising was staggering. Thirty-one Black people were killed, along with three whites—one fire fighter, one deputy sheriff, and one Long Beach police officer. A total of 1,032 people were injured, and 3,438 adults and 514 juveniles were arrested. Property damage was estimated at $40 million (McCone 1965:23–24).

The indifference with which white Los Angeles had viewed the Black community was shattered in one week of violence. Suddenly local, national, and even international attention focused on the city. From virtually nowhere, race had become the number one issue in city politics. The mayor,

Police Chief Parker, and Black and liberal leaders all competed to interpret the riot. Even the *Los Angeles Times*, which had until then virtually ignored the Black community, won a Pulitzer Prize for its riot coverage.

In the short run, the riot was an unqualified disaster for biracial politics, creating a durable and powerful backlash among whites and Latinos. But Blacks saw things differently. A survey taken after the riot (Sears and McConahay 1973:160–63) indicated that they were optimistic about the effects of the violence on white attitudes. Forty-two percent of the sample thought the riots would make whites more attentive and sympathetic to the problems of Blacks. Very few suggested that a white backlash would result from the disorders. There was strong sentiment among Blacks for a police review board and for the removal of Chief Parker (*Los Angeles Newsletter*, 21 August 1965).

In the same survey, an exploration of white and Latino attitudes showed this Black optimism to be unjustified. Large majorities of both groups were profoundly affronted by the violence and expressed strong support for the police. Few thought the riot would improve race relations. Both groups expressed substantial personal fear of attack by Blacks (Sears and Mc-Conahay 1973:164–66). The clearest racial polarization was evident in evaluations of Chief Parker (see Table 5.4).

Some Latino activists expressed resentment at the great attention being paid to Blacks in the wake of the riot, especially in the allocation of anti-poverty funds. The obvious lack of Latino political influence was remarkable considering that Latinos outnumbered Blacks in the county (*Los Angeles Newsletter*, 28 August 1965).

A survey of whites in six Los Angeles communities was generally consistent with these results (Morris and Jeffries 1970). Whites living in the districts closest to Black population concentrations were the least sympathetic. The majority of the whites were unsympathetic to the riot, although a substantial minority held liberal views, showing at least moderate sympathy for Black grievances (485–86). Over half were quite fearful, and nearly one-third had considered obtaining firearms for personal protection. Over

TABLE 5.4
Evaluations of Chief William Parker, 1965
(percent of group)

	Blacks	*Whites*	*Latinos*
Favorable	10	79	74
Unfavorable	76	15	15

Source: Sears and McConahay 1973:59, 165.

Note: Percentages do not total 100 because of omitted categories.

70 percent felt that the riots had hurt the Black cause and would polarize the races. Paradoxically, nearly 80 percent thought that whites would now be more aware of Black problems. The majority supported the police and their handling of the riot.

Jews responded differently from other whites and expressed much more support for the Black drive for equality (549). Further, the authors found that voluntary social contact was most related to white sympathy for Blacks. This finding underlines the importance of the shared activism in liberal reform politics for Blacks and whites in the Tenth District.

The riot gave Yorty a way to appeal to his already conservative base. He could harvest great support from the violence by highlighting Black protest tactics. Bollens and Geyer (1973:154) concluded that

> the major beneficiary of the Watts riots, in a political sense, was the Little Giant of City Hall. Yorty's staunch law and order position was exactly what many voters wanted to see. His political fortunes rose markedly during and after the riot period. . . . Yorty had emerged from the ashes of Watts with a new image—an enforcer of laws and anything but a coddler of criminals.

The violence also helped Yorty with the downtown business community. The president of the Los Angeles Chamber of Commerce sent Yorty a bound volume of letters from individual members of the Chamber, all praising the mayor and Chief Parker. Letter after letter congratulated them on restoring law and order (Yorty Collection, City Archives).

But the Watts riot and its aftermath also solidified a movement for Black political representation at the citywide level. It was clearer than ever before that Blacks needed more power at city hall. Scoble (1967:672) suggested that "Negro politics in Los Angeles now seems at a pause. The political/governmental aggregate has been expanded rather dramatically, but it is not providing particularly visible nor effective leadership." With Yorty in full control of the antipoverty program, Blacks did not have the option of wielding power without mobilizing votes, as they did in New York City. There, the 1965 upset election of reformer John Lindsay allowed the "participation coalition" to achieve victory in the antipoverty struggle (Greenstone and Peterson 1973).

The riot pushed along the movement toward Black unity, crossing class boundaries. Sears and McConahay (1973) found that one of the main outcomes of the riot was a much more positive self-evaluation among Blacks. Surveys showed that virtually all Black elected officials (and some white liberals as well) received high levels of support from Blacks. The riots made Black politicians, even the regulars tied to Yorty, more prominent as spokespersons.

The rebellion had involved a wide cross-section of Blacks. The Sears and McConahay (1973:13) survey of riot participation disproved the McCone

Commission's "riffraff" theory of about 10,000 drifters, estimating that "between 31,000 and 35,000 adults in the Curfew Zone were active as rioters at some time during the week-long upheaval. About double this number, between 64,000 and 72,000 persons, were involved as close spectators." The survey further showed that the riot involved the mainstream of the Black community, especially young and well-educated African-American males.

Bradley emerged as the most outspoken and vociferous critic of Chief Parker and the police role in the Black community. With Wyman's defeat, Bradley also became the chief liberal spokesperson against Yorty (*Los Angeles Newsletter*, 18 September 1965). Indeed, Bradley became a major citywide figure, and his office received numerous calls for help from people outside his district (Moore interview; Galm 1984). Bradley was increasingly involved in public confrontations with the police chief. With his intimate knowledge of the department, Bradley could raise questions. As Bradley noted, "When I challenged him on certain statements he had made as to the cause of the Watts riots and challenged him when he described the area of Watts as reaching all the way to Crenshaw and Adams, he resented that one of his former minions would publicly challenge him on anything" (Bradley interview). The distinction Bradley was making was between the central city and the midcity area of Black upward mobility. It suggested how little Parker knew about the social complexities of the Los Angeles Black community.

According to a fellow Black police officer, Bradley was a particular thorn in the LAPD's side: "From the very time he became a council person, he became a threat. Because he made it very clear, vocally, that he didn't agree with the department's philosophy or policies. Tom was usually the opposition. He was the one who got up at the council and asked very interesting questions. They were fearful of him" (Brewer interview).

The riot had the further effect of solidifying Black opposition to Yorty. Yorty had, after all, received many Black votes in 1965, and Dymally and Mills had felt safe in backing him. After the riot, Blacks placed Yorty only barely higher than the hated Parker. Yorty and Parker were explicitly hostile in their postriot comments, and the message was received in the Black community:

Yorty on the National Guard
What a difference between these fine young men and the people they were sent to control! (Bollens and Geyer 1973:154)

Yorty on the Causes of the Riot
For some time there has existed a world-wide subversive campaign to stigmatize all police as brutal. The cry of police brutality has been shouted in cities all over the world by communists, dupes, and demagogues, irrespective of the

facts. Such a campaign has been ingloriously pushed here in Los Angeles. (Sears and McConahay 1973:155)

Parker on the Riot

. . . a rebellion of a gang of Negro hoodlums who had no real purpose except rebellion and destruction. (ibid.:150)

Parker on the Rioters

. . . monkeys in a zoo . . . we're on top and they're on the bottom. (ibid.:151)

Parker on Black Leaders

[They] seem to think that if Parker can be destroyed officially, then they will have no trouble in imposing their will upon the police of America, and that's what it amounts to, because nobody else will dare stand up. (Fogelson 1967:126)

Bradley and his liberal allies were now more in tune with the concerns in the Black community than were the "regular" Black politicians allied with Unruh and Yorty. A subtle shift had taken place, in which those Blacks representing upwardly mobile areas were speaking in tones most likely to appeal to the Black masses. The formula now included opposition to Yorty as well as to Parker.

The riots unified and mobilized the Black community in the direction of citywide power. They also energized liberal reformers, who sought to create a more socially active city government. Liberals had been out of power when the riot took place. In no sense was the riot a rebellion against entrenched liberalism, and therefore it provided little ground for conflict between the two movements.

Liberal politicians were not the main targets of the protests; in fact, a number of liberal politicians were perceived very positively even by those arrested during the riots (Sears and McConahay 1973). Liberals had an agenda for meeting the challenge of racial unrest. The situation in New York City only three years later was vastly different. There, Black mobilization took place against a school bureaucracy heavily staffed by liberal whites. Thus the grass-roots protest was aimed at established liberalism.

The Los Angeles liberal agenda involved the use of federal funds to aid the central city. Without disrupting the tax base of the city, an infusion of federal support (which seemed very likely at the height of the Great Society) could solve problems while being politically palatable. For the next several years, liberals called for an increased city effort to obtain federal funds. The riot provided an even more compelling argument for this agenda. If Piven and Cloward (1971) were correct in arguing that urban violence led to increased federal money, Watts may have advanced the local liberal agenda.

Even in the wake of the riot, council conservatives were extremely reluctant to apply for available federal funds, partly on ideological grounds. They were even reluctant to seek federal money to demolish buildings damaged in the riot (*Los Angeles Newsletter*, 25 September and 9 October 1965). In addition, conservatives attacked plans for downtown redevelopment heavily favored by Blacks and white liberals. (*Los Angeles Newsletter*, 27 November 1965)

The Watts riot focused public attention on the social needs of the city and the mayor's lack of leadership. At the start of the violence, Yorty was out of town campaigning for higher office and saw no pressing need to return (Conot 1967:202).

Yorty denied that he was unfair to the Black community or that he had been derelict in staying in San Francisco to make a speech when the violence was under way. In a handwritten memo found by researcher Corecia Davis in the Yorty Collection (City Archives), Yorty apparently directed an aide to:

> Tell Otis C. [presumably *Los Angeles Times* publisher Otis Chandler] he does not know about our continuous contacts with Negroes thru staff. . . . It is groups who publicly demand to see me and come down with appts [appointments] that I don't see. I even sat down with CORE [Congress of Racial Equality]. . . . Chief Parker has had a series of unpublicized meetings—once two hours with Brookins who requested Chief not to let the conference be made known.

The note—which seemed to draw on information supplied by Chief Parker—was accompanied by a memo to the mayor from the city administrative officer, C. Erwin Piper, blaming the Communist party for public attacks on Yorty and Parker (ibid., 16 August 1965). Finally the package included a four-page report on Brookins, which referred to him as "Subject" and discussed notices of his activities in various media. The source of the report on Brookins is unknown.

Yorty's public feud with Senators Robert Kennedy and Abraham Ribicoff during Senate hearings on the riots highlighted both his lack of concern for the poor and his perception that there was little he could do about the problems of the city (Bollens and Geyer 1973: 135).

Ribicoff saw Los Angeles as ill equipped to handle the upcoming flood of federal funds:

> I believe that there will be federal programs initiated in the next two years that will really put America on the road to start doing something about the cities of America.

> That means the cities are going to have to be in a position to take advantage of these programs. I would say as I have listened to you, and if it is the Charter it is no reflection on you personally, that one city that won't be able to take advan-

tage of these programs will be Los Angeles because you are not organized to do
so. (Ruchelman 1969:316)

Bradley and the other council liberals saw Watts as an opportunity to
forge a consensus for more direct social and economic action by the city. For
the liberal faction on the council, federal grants represented a way to finance
social programs without diverting basic funds from the city budget. The
availability of federal aid became a major rhetorical argument in favor of
social change.

As chairman of the council's State, Federal, and County Affairs Committee, Bradley became a leading advocate of an expanded city grants effort.
He often challenged Yorty to be more aggressive in the search for federal
and state funds. In 1971, the council set up the Board of Grants Administration (BGA) to coordinate the city's grant-seeking effort. Federal officials
objected to the original format of the board, which excluded Mayor Yorty.
Eventually the board was set up (over Yorty's veto) with three council
members, the mayor, and the City Administrative Officer.

The BGA acted as a significant centralizing force in city government. For
the first time, city departments, such as the LAPD and the Community
Redevelopment Agency, were required to pass through a review process
conducted by elected officials and their staffs. This constituted a significant
restraint on freewheeling by city bureaucrats (Bruce 1974). It helped pro-
fessionalize the city council by familiarizing at least some of its members
with the nature of the grants process. The chief legislative analyst's office
was ordered by the council to actively seek federal funds for the city and
began to keep records of grants "victories" on a large board in its offices.

In addition, the protest had the greatest single impact until the election of
a new liberal coalition in 1973 on the police department. According to Jesse
Brewer:

> Everything opened up for blacks [in the department] after the riots. There was
> a dramatic change in the attitude. The department went for a retreat up in
> Arrowhead, and there were attempts to sensitize police officers, especially the
> upper staff. So the department did start to open up. And I made lieutenant in
> 1967, and went out to Venice, and then I got selected to be on the Chief's staff.
> (Brewer interview)

The shifting pattern of city politics accords with the ten northern California cities studied by Browning, Marshall, and Tabb (1984). The rise of
federal programs, Black protest activity, and the formation of Black-liberal
linkages occurred in those cities that developed Black political incorporation. The establishment was conservative, and there had been strong resistance to these developments.

But the whole group of western cities, including Los Angeles, represented a different experience from that of eastern and midwestern cities. In the East and Midwest, incumbent regimes were not as conservative, often representing a type of labor-based, interest-group liberalism. The Black communities shared some incorporation through party organizations. As a result, the continued development of Black-liberal coalitions was shaped by the western experience.

The shared "out" status of Blacks and white liberals created the political basis for cooperation. An elite link from the Tenth District created the trust and leadership. The next stage, aiming at citywide power, would rest on the ability of this coalition to extend its alliance throughout a racially and ideologically polarized city.

SIX

THE 1969 MAYORAL CRUSADE

THE SHADOW of the Watts riot and of a nation polarized by race and ideology rested heavily over Tom Bradley's 1969 campaign to unseat Mayor Sam Yorty.

The United States had changed profoundly in the four years since Watts. Race and ideology were now at the forefront of intense national debates. A wave of big-city riots occurred between 1965 and 1968. Antiwar students protested in violent incidents at Columbia University and at the 1968 Chicago convention of the Democratic party. Martin Luther King, Jr., and Robert F. Kennedy were killed within months of each other in 1968. With the broad reach of television, Americans communally witnessed the disorders and reacted with racial and ideological polarization.

In this agitated setting, African-Americans began to run as mayoral candidates in cities with large Black populations. In 1967 Richard Hatcher of Gary and Carl Stokes of Cleveland were elected mayors in extremely bitter, racially polarized elections. In the same year, major riots broke out in Detroit and Newark. Blacks were clearly moving toward an independent political position and in the process were generating a furious white backlash. Black mayoral candidates received low shares of the white vote: 19 percent for Stokes, 15 percent for Hatcher, 18–19 percent for Richard Austin in Detroit, 23 percent for Maynard Jackson in Atlanta, and 16–17 percent for Kenneth Gibson in Newark (Hahn, Klingman, and Pachon 1976:508).

In California, where voters had in 1964 passed a statewide initiative against open housing, conservative Republican Ronald Reagan defeated Governor Edmund G. Brown, Sr., in 1966. Reagan drew on Democratic voters disillusioned with the "breakdown of law and order." Brown had been weakened in the Democratic primary by Sam Yorty's challenge and lost to Reagan by over a million votes. In the 1968 presidential election, conservatives Richard Nixon and George Wallace used the law and order theme to win a combined 56 percent of the presidential vote. Wallace shocked the nation by winning thousands of Democratic primary votes in northern industrial states and by taking a stunning 13.5 percent of the general election ballots.

In Los Angeles, the winds of change were channeled into the cleavages already carved out by the Watts riot: the conservative Yorty administration and its council allies against the alliance of Blacks and white liberals. Latinos were in the middle. These coalition lines had already appeared in the antipoverty program controversy and in the 1965 mayoral election.

Much had happened in Los Angeles since the Watts riot. The immediate wave of public attention to Blacks subsided soon after the violence and the publication of government reports. Johnson, Sears, and McConahay (1971) reported that local media coverage of Blacks declined to preriot levels; the reporting that did occur focused mainly on "antisocial acts" by Blacks. The seeds of racial polarization planted in the aftermath of the riot were therefore supplemented by the nature of media coverage of the Black community.

The debate between the liberal forces and the Yorty administration centered on police conduct and federal aid. Blacks saw that in order to influence police practices, it would be necessary to win a share of citywide power. In the commission form of government, only a mayor could appoint members of the police commission and only the police commission could supervise the police. But winning power would require a remarkable biracial coalition in a period of intense racial polarization. The same challenge blocked the search for the abundant federal aid available in the wake of the riots.

The battle for citywide power continued to transform the Black struggle for equality in Los Angeles. It thrust forward the faction of the African-American community located in the West Side neighborhoods. Alienated from the Yorty regime, these Blacks had been the first to pursue the citywide goal independent of the existing regime. Citywide ambitions also forced Blacks to consider biracial coalition options. The two were related. It was generally the upwardly mobile Black sector that pursued coalition with liberal whites, a strategy that moved to the forefront with Bradley's attempt to win the mayoralty.

Persistent attempts would be made to incorporate Latinos into this coalition, but it was to be a long, frustrating process. As often as cooperation, conflict appeared between Los Angeles Blacks and Latinos over antipoverty programs, the Watts riot, police practices, and Sam Yorty. The overall belief that Blacks and Latinos would be good partners persisted and eventually bore fruit, but only after the 1969 election.

The Mayoral Campaign

In 1968 Councilman Bradley decided to challenge Yorty for mayor in the 1969 election. As the representative of the Tenth District, the site of Black upward mobility, and as a highly involved CDC activist, Bradley was in a good position to solidify the linkage between Blacks and white liberal reformers. This alliance had already been tested in the Tenth District.

The overall campaign strategy called for construction of a three-sided coalition. As Richard Maullin (1971:42), a Bradley strategist, wrote,

"Bradley and his managers began the campaign in January with a strategy based on justifiable expectations of massive black support, as well as several ideological assumptions about the fittingness of a coalition incorporating blacks and Jews, liberal gentiles and Mexican-Americans."

The 1970 census figures would show that the ethnic composition of the city had changed substantially in ten years (see Table 6.l). But the overall dominance of white *voters* remained a crucial element of electoral strategy. It still does more than two decades later.

White liberals gained a new prominence in the Bradley coalition as it expanded citywide. In the Tenth District council campaign, white liberals had supplemented a Black-run grass-roots effort. In 1969, white liberals played a coequal role. The biracial leadership of the campaign came from Bradley's Tenth District CDC associates. The deputy manager of the campaign, Anton Calleia, said that "without the west side Jewish liberals, we simply *had* no campaign" (Calleia interview). Maurice Weiner said: "The most significant portion of the white component in Bradley's mayoralty campaign was Jewish, just as the most significant portion in the council campaign was Jewish" (Weiner interview).

Weiner, who had been precinct coordinator in the council campaign, served as campaign manager and chief strategist. Robert Farrell, who was a young Black community organizer in the mayoral campaign, remembered that "in 1969 it was Maury who was the key aide and the top deputy, the advisor, the confidant . . . who built on the bridges that Bradley had in place by service and involvement in activities. Maury was the first set of brains in the operation, other than the candidate himself" (Farrell interview).

Weiner established a decentralized campaign structure based on grass-roots liberal community organizations. The structure grew directly out of the Tenth District experience. The 1963 council coalition, in Weiner's view, "formed the nucleus for what six years later was this truly overwhelming coalition of forces in the mayoralty campaign" (Weiner interview).

Don Rothenberg, in charge of a portion of the field operations, said:

TABLE 6.1
Racial and Ethnic Composition
of Los Angeles, 1960 and 1970
(percent)

	1960	1970
White	71.9	59.0
Black	13.8	17.7
Latino	10.7	18.3
Other	3.6	5.0

Source: City of Los Angeles figures.

"Those CDC clubs which were really well-grounded in their community and had a membership in their district played a major role in those communities" (Rothenberg interview). Left-liberal activists, many from the antiwar Eugene McCarthy presidential campaign, came from out of town.

A steering committee composed of long-time Tenth District activists and chaired by African-American lawyer Sam Williams still made the key decisions, even designing in-house the television ads for the primary. Rothenberg recalled: "It was a committee on large decisions, certainly on media, certainly on whether to welcome or encourage or allow outsiders from outside the state to come in. And how funds should be spent. What were the major themes. What kind of countermeasures would we take to the opposition's campaign" (Rothenberg interview).

In the African-American community, a massive mobilization program was directed by Warren Hollier, a Black businessman who had been a key participant in the council campaign and then served as Bradley's council deputy. Like the 1963 council campaign, this effort was communitywide, involving Black media, the highly organized Black churches led by H. H. Brookins (by then a bishop), and a network of young Black activists.

It was assumed that virtually every Black vote would go to Bradley. Therefore the Bradley team relied on a registration and get-out-the-vote plan fueled by massive local publicity. In a sense they were repeating the 1963 council campaign, with Hollier handling the Black mobilization and Weiner reaching out to liberal whites. The difference was that whites were now a much larger share of the population, and especially of the electorate.

Despite the inevitable segmentation of the campaign, there was an atmosphere of extraordinary unity and purpose. Of all the eras of Bradley's career, the 1969 defeat is remembered most warmly by Bradley's activists. Rothenberg recalled: "It was a crusade for many, many people and the feeling that we were making history was stronger than any stand that Bradley took on specific issues" (Rothenberg interview).

The 1969 primary was hardly a professional operation. Weiner, for instance, had never run a campaign before he was appointed Bradley's campaign manager. Largely for financial reasons, the campaign relied more on published polls than on private ones. Despite substantial strategic leadership from the policy committee, it was more a movement and crusade than an organized political campaign.

Rothenberg estimated that the campaign had "some 15,000 volunteers. . . . We had people who came from literally every walk of life, from unemployed persons in Watts to Hollywood stars" (Rothenberg interview). The future leaders of the Waxman-Berman machine on the heavily Jewish West Side worked as volunteers in the campaign. The local media underestimated the campaign's strength during the primary; Bradley was not favored to finish among the top two candidates. After all, Bradley's informal precampaign surveys had shown him to be known to only 7 percent of the city's voters (Weiner interview).

The results were indeed surprising. Bradley had finished first in a crowded field with 42 percent of the vote. With 26 percent, Mayor Yorty placed a distant second. The better-known Republican Congressman Alphonso Bell and newscaster Baxter Ward were far behind. With 8 more percentage points, Bradley would have won election outright.

Not surprisingly, Bradley had a solid base in the Black community and had made substantial inroads into white liberal West Los Angeles. Yorty and Ward were strongest in the San Fernando Valley. Liberal Republican Bell was most successful in the affluent coastal areas contained within his congressional district (McPhail 1971).

By demographic group, Bradley outpolled Yorty overwhelmingly among Blacks and substantially among Jews. An internal Bradley campaign survey (Maullin 1971) showed Bradley trouncing Yorty among Jews (52 percent to 18 percent). Among Mexican-Americans, Bradley barely led Yorty (34 percent to 30 percent). Among white Gentiles, Yorty led Bradley by almost the same slight margin (32 percent to 27 percent).

By key council district, the primary vote showed Bradley's strengths and weaknesses (see Table 6.2). He was far ahead of all three main opponents in the Black council district, and had twice as much support as any other candidate in the liberal Jewish Fifth District. He was, however, winning only a quarter of the vote in the white conservative area. His overall problem was that Ward was a conservative and Bell was a moderate. It would be difficult to create a combination of the losing candidates' votes for the challenger in the runoff.

The question for the general election between Bradley and Yorty, then, was the viability of a coalition among Blacks, Jews and other liberal whites, and Latinos. Bradley needed to *increase* his showing among Jews and Latinos in order to avoid the feared white backlash. The campaign that followed placed intense strains on the emerging citywide biracial coalition as it sought to adapt to an unforeseen series of Yorty charges. And unlike the Tenth District campaign, this experiment would be conducted in the full

TABLE 6.2

Mayoral Vote in Primary in Three Key Council Districts, 1969 (percent)

		Bell	Bradley	Ward	Yorty
5th	White liberal/Jewish	16.5	43.7	14.6	21.5
8th	Black	2.4	81.0	3.3	7.7
12th	White conservative	17.2	25.6	25.1	28.2

Source: City Archives.

glare of local and national publicity against a ruthless and effective opponent.

Having done so well in the primary, the Bradley forces began to generate more organizational coherence. Bradley's strong showing made him the focus of national media attention. According to Weiner, increased visibility made possible changes in the nature of the organization: "In the runoff, the whole effort became more professional. Once Tom had won the primary, there was considerably more money available. Locally here there was a massive transfusion into the campaign, largely for media" (Weiner interview).

In 1969, Bradley received his first major contributions from Max Palevsky, a wealthy Jewish liberal activist, and from Marc Boyar, a Democratic Party fundraiser. Boyar "helped to organize the fund raising for Tom. He came on in a modest way at the end of the primary and then with Tom's enormous victory in the primary, he came on all the way" (Weiner interview). Boyar contributed a $25,000 loan, and the campaign borrowed another $10,000 from Palevsky, toward Bradley's total of just over $1 million (City Campaign Finance Reports).

As the Bradley organization pulled itself into shape, Yorty worked to separate the liberal activists of the Bradley coalition from the more moderate mass base of voters. Among Jews and Latinos, Yorty hastened to portray the Bradley organization as a liberal/leftist cabal unrepresentative of Jewish and Latino voters.

Yorty even hoped to make inroads into Bradley's African-American support. Black politicians allied with Jesse Unruh were less than enthusiastic about Bradley's campaign. Councilman Gilbert Lindsay stayed neutral during the primary (*Los Angeles Times*, 3 April 1969), and even in the runoff was lukewarm (*Los Angeles Times*, 22 April 1969). Yorty hired Black activist Willard Murray, an ally of the Dymally-Unruh faction, to help him in the Black community.

On primary election night, Yorty charged that the Bradley forces were a team of "radical Democrats and the bloc Negro vote" (*Los Angeles Time*, 2 April 1969)—almost a caricature of the biracial coalition. The simple theme that the emerging biracial coalition was not liberal or moderate but radical would be extremely damaging in the midst of Black and student protests nationwide. Student strikes at California universities and colleges emphasized the point.

In striving to prevent a liberal biracial coalition from arising, Yorty reminded Jews of Black-Jewish conflict in New York City's 1968 school strike and of increasing crime in the Fairfax area. He suggested to Latinos, whom he had carefully cultivated for years, that a Black mayor would ignore their interests.

Yorty connected the moderate Bradley with Black militants. He charged

Bradley with being antipolice and asserted that thousands of police officers would resign if Bradley were to be elected. Ironically, Yorty's 1961 opponent, Mayor Norris Poulson, had charged that the Police Commission would resign if the insurgent Yorty were elected (BGR 1961). As the leader of the liberal forces calling for increased police accountability, Bradley was vulnerable to comparison with Yorty's unquestioning support of the police.

Yorty directly exploited white fears. His campaign ran ads in the real estate section of Valley newspapers showing Bradley's picture with the caption "Will Your City Be Safe with This Man?" The Yorty campaign also used a variety of undercover projects to tap into white fears. Rothenberg said that

> four or five days before the general election I got a call from an individual in the Black community who said that Yorty's campaign had offered him $5,000 to do what amounted to dirty tricks and he would consider turning down the offer if we could come up with more money . . . clearly we were not going to outbid. The following Saturday, two days later, a parade in open convertibles went through the Valley with Black persons . . . giving the fist and carrying bumper strips [saying] "Black is beautiful," "Bradley for Mayor," etc. (Rothenberg interview)

Yorty brought to the fore the conflict between Los Angeles progressives and the LAPD. Feelings ran high between the Bradley people and the police. Jesse Brewer, one of the department's highest-ranking Black officers, was assigned as part of an all-Black detail to guard Bradley:

> I don't know why he [the Chief] would select me and my unit because we were community relations; there were other people who normally did that who were white. Tom was almost hated by rank and file white officers because he was the person who made the department toe the line in some areas and was very critical of their operations, some of the shootings, for example. (Brewer interview)

Brewer found that white police officers were antagonistic to African-American officers protecting Bradley:

> In our role as security, we ran into hostilities at different places with white officers. I'll never forget, we were in the Valley. And we had parked our cars on some private property because that was the most convenient thing to do to make sure we were close to him at all times. And some white officers recognized us and said, "Okay you guys, you have to move your car." There was no camaraderie, no professional interaction. They were very hostile. (ibid.)

The plan to paint the Bradley forces as leftist took on new life when Yorty revealed that campaign aide Rothenberg had once been a member of the Communist party (*Los Angeles Times*, 23 April 1969). The charge was devastating. Yorty drew a picture of Rothenberg as one of the campaign's top leaders—and as typical of its leftist influence, which Yorty also linked to Weiner (*Los Angeles Times*, 24 April 1969). The attacks on Rothenberg, who was a popular figure within the campaign, stunned the organization.

Yorty's strategy created a major dilemma for the enthusiastic Bradley crusaders. With their sky-high morale, they found it hard to see that they themselves were being made into one of the central issues of the campaign. This might help explain the difficulty the Bradley people had in responding to Yorty's charges.

In effect, Bradley hardly responded at all, taking a "high road" approach, assuming that the voters would see through Yorty's demagoguery. Bradley continued to portray himself as a reform-minded liberal who would be a more competent and able mayor than the mercurial Yorty. After Yorty's attacks began, the moderate Bell endorsed Bradley and the *Los Angeles Times* strongly backed the Black challenger in an editorial blasting Yorty (27 May 1969). Bradley's dignified response was therefore helpful in gaining some "establishment" support and a base in the affluent coastal region.

Ultimately, the Bradley campaign never addressed the questions of crime and civil disorder so much on the minds of Los Angeles voters (Wilson and Wilde 1969). In addition, Bradley courageously refused to dismiss Rothenberg, arguing that his Communist party membership was a thing of the past.

In retrospect, Bradley's stance has been seen as a major tactical error, but Bradley's response grew out of the nature of his evolving coalition. Bradley's campaign had unleashed a movement that would someday coalesce into a governing coalition. At this point, it was a wildly enthusiastic and passionately liberal mass of crusaders with some organization at the top, who saw their candidate as clearly the best choice for the voters.

In those days, the law and order issue was fairly new, and among many liberals, it was seen as nothing more than a code word for racism. White liberals and Blacks had great difficulty developing a popular position on crime that would not seem to embrace anti-Black views. Yet crime was a central issue to the voters.

As Maullin (1971) noted, the 1969 campaigners failed to take advantage of Bradley's police experience for ideological reasons. In some ways, Bradley's police background could have been a liability within the organization; even in 1963, one Black community leader hesitated to back Bradley for the city council because Bradley had been a police officer (Galm 1984). Thus, Yorty's strategy to split the Bradley organization from the potential Bradley mass coalition had a lever on which to work.

Not cognizant of Yorty's comeback victory in 1961, some of the younger activists may have failed to see the standard Yorty strategy—to stun the front-runner with a series of effective, unanswered charges late in the campaign. Few recalled how effectively Yorty had weakened Mayor Poulson in 1961 by calling attention to Poulson's loss of his voice due to illness; Yorty frequently challenged him to debates. Positive poll results right up until the election may have lulled the campaigners into feeling that the charges need not be answered (Maullin 1971). Back then, no one knew, as we do today, that polls can be deceptive in biracial contests. Now we would allocate all undecided voters to the white candidate, and no lead short of a rock-solid majority would be considered remotely safe for the first-time Black candidate (Pettigrew 1988).

When the election results came in, Bradley had suffered a devastating and wholly unexpected defeat at Yorty's hands. Yorty finished with 53 percent of the vote to Bradley's 47 percent. As in 1961, Yorty had made a remarkable comeback between the primary and general elections against a favored candidate. Table 6.3 indicates the huge jump in Yorty's vote, compared to Bradley's more moderate increase.

The 1969 and 1973 mayoral elections generated a wealth of survey and voting analysis. The three-way coalition of Blacks, liberal whites, and Latinos had not come together. Jewish support for Bradley was moderate, but Latinos had turned to Yorty in numbers indistinguishable from those among whites.

The overall city turnout was a record 76 percent. All groups turned out at high levels, with Blacks at the highest (Halley 1974). According to an internal Bradley campaign document, the shifts to Yorty among whites, Jews, and Latinos (see Table 6.4) were devastating.

Bradley's only real non-Black base was among Jews. Jews were twenty points more pro-Bradley than either white Gentiles or Latinos. But even among Jews, he suffered significant erosion. To the great disappointment of the Bradley campaign, Latinos voted much as did white Gentiles in both the primary and general elections (Pettigrew 1971).

Within groups, some interesting patterns emerged. Maller, who found a

TABLE 6.3
Mayoral Vote in Primary and General Election, 1969

	N	%	Points Gained	Votes Gained
Yorty				
Primary	186,174	26		
General election	449,572	53	27	263,398
Bradley				
Primary	298,336	42	5	96,336
General election	394,364	47		

Source: Analysis of data from City Clerk, Election Division.

TABLE 6.4
Yorty Vote among Selected Groups in Primary
and General Election, 1969 (percent)

	Primary	*General Election*	*Shift*
Jews	18	48	30
White Gentiles	32	68	36
Latinos	30	67	37

Source: Maullin 1971:48.

higher level of Jewish voting for Bradley than did the internal Bradley poll, indicated that Jews were divided by social class:

> In those areas where most of the Jews are in their 40's and up, have incomes under $15,000 a year, are not college graduates and are affiliated with Orthodox synagogues and Zionist organizations, Bradley received 50 to 60 percent of the vote. In those areas where most of the Jews have family incomes of $15,000 to $20,000 and up, are college graduates, are in their 30's and 40's and are affiliated with Reform temples and Jewish "human rights" organizations, the vote for Bradley was 80 to 90 percent. (1971:162)

Hahn and Almy (1971) found the reverse pattern among Latinos. Bradley's support among Latinos declined as the social class of the neighborhood increased. The data suggested that Bradley was most preferred by Blacks, middle- to upper-status Jews, and poorer Latinos. He would need to gain the support of more whites, a wider array of Jews, and upwardly mobile Latinos. The data may also reflect the fact that better-off Latinos live in neighborhoods with more whites. But Pettigrew (1971) also found that a majority of Latinos voted for Yorty.

Bradley's strongest base, of course, was the Black community. However, he also "received approximately fifty percent of the vote in the high occupational and income status portions of west Los Angeles and the Santa Monica Mountains [in both elections] though the area is fifteen miles . . . from the nearest black concentration" (McPhail 1971:749). McPhail noted that "this high status area is separated by buffer zones of lower status white communities from Negro concentrations . . . a middle and lower status non-Negro block is aligned against a high status white–low status Negro vote" (753).

This observation should remind the reader of the survey of white response to the Watts riot. Whites in transitional areas were more fearful of Black violence and less sympathetic to Black grievances than those whites in high-status areas physically separated from Black neighborhoods. The importance of membership with Blacks in voluntary associations was suggested as an important way to overcome potential racial fears (Jeffries and

Ransford 1969). The Bradley organization in 1969 was a model of the effort to bring races together in a common cause. But in 1969 biracial unity was more successful as an internal organizational mechanism than as a public vehicle for electoral success.

In the Fairfax neighborhood, for instance, some elderly Jews fearful of crime were drawn into Yorty's embrace (Wilson and Wilde 1969). Their personal interests were, in their minds, directly threatened. Even so, Jews were much more inclined than white Gentiles to vote for Bradley. Clearly that provided hope for a future Bradley campaign.

Similar patterns appeared in the key council districts—the Fifth, the Eighth and the Twelfth. (The Latino Fourteenth was not created until three years later.) Table 6.5 indicates the vote in the runoff for Bradley and Yorty. The Jewish liberal Fifth was twenty points more pro-Bradley than the white conservative Twelfth.

The high-turnout anti-Bradley vote coming from the San Fernando Valley reveals the critical role of conservative racial ideology in the 1969 election. The overwhelming vote for Yorty in the northwest San Fernando Valley Twelfth District helped turn the tide for the mayor. There are very few transitional neighborhoods in the largely white San Fernando Valley because, with the exception of Pacoima, there are very few Blacks there. One might expect that, in the absence of direct racial threats, Valley whites would have been somewhat less amenable to Yorty's appeal than more directly threatened Fairfax Jews. The opposite was true: Valley whites were enthusiastic, mobilized listeners to Yorty's message.

Sears and Kinder's (1971) survey of Valley voters revealed that direct racial threats had little to do with Yorty voting. Rather, whites expressed more "symbolic" concerns, such as their dislike of the breakdown of law and order and decreased respect for authority in society. This ideological view accorded closely with likelihood to vote for Yorty.

Jeffries and Ransford (1972) developed a measure known as Troubled American Beliefs (TAB) to assess conservative ideology about social order, and found that it independently predicted a major share of the Yorty vote. A separate measure of racial prejudice also had independent predictive value.

TABLE 6.5
Mayoral Vote in General Election
in Three Key Council Districts, 1969 (percent)

		Bradley	Yorty
5th	White liberal/Jewish	50.7	47.8
8th	Black	86.2	12.2
12th	White conservative	30.6	68.3

Source: City Clerk, Election Division.

Together they overwhelmed any "normal" campaign issues. Yorty's campaign interacted with social values and racial prejudice to mobilize an enormous Valley bloc for the mayor.

Liberal ideology mattered a great deal among those Jews whose social class placed them in a position to avoid direct racial threats. Many Latinos were in a sort of lower-class coalition with Blacks. One might argue that in 1969, there was an ideological coalition linking Blacks and white liberals and a class coalition linking Blacks and poor Latinos. But there was not yet a majority.

Other Ballot Issues

The mayoral race did not stand by itself. In 1969, the city's voters also divided along racial and ideological lines over taxation and education. Signs of a strong conservative constituency appeared in the April primary, when city voters resoundingly defeated three tax and bond measures for city schools and the junior college district. In the May runoff, conservative insurgents defeated two incumbent liberal school board members, and conservatives took a five-two majority on the newly created junior college board.

Evidently, there was more at stake than the biracial mayoral race. How should tax money be raised and allocated? In the face of imminent decisions on school busing, what should be the direction of the Board of Education? In 1969 the Los Angeles electorate turned to the right, clearly and unmistakably. Yorty's campaign, the presence of tax measures, and the specter of school busing surely interacted to evoke that sentiment.

The nonmayoral elections illuminate a central point: the election of a Black mayor is only the most visible aspect of the struggle for minority incorporation. The control of other city institutions and the authority to raise revenue to support them are crucial to the ability of a minority-progressive regime to deliver benefits once in power.

The three educational measures lost in the April primary because conservatives were not only unified but more highly mobilized than minorities and white liberals. Table 6.6 indicates the vote on the three propositions in the three key council districts. The totals shown are the proportions of those at the polls who actually voted on these less newsworthy measures. It is a crucial test of intensity.

The white conservative voters were solidly antitax, while the Black and white liberal areas were ambivalent—more protax than the community as a whole but unsure. More striking, however, is the degree of mobilization. Virtually every white conservative who went to the polls (nineteen out of twenty) voted on all three ballot measures, even though they were far less

TABLE 6.6
Vote for Educational Revenue Measures
in Three Key Council Districts, 1969 (percent)

		Yes	No	Total
		Proposition A		
5th	White liberal/Jewish	47.0	41.7	88.7
8th	Black	40.8	31.6	72.4
12th	White conservative	38.6	57.1	95.7
		Proposition B		
5th	White liberal/Jewish	43.4	44.8	88.2
8th	Black	37.0	35.7	72.7
12th	White conservative	33.2	62.3	95.5
		Proposition C		
5th	White liberal/Jewish	44.9	41.1	86.0
8th	Black	34.3	32.8	67.1
12th	White conservative	36.7	57.4	94.1

Source: Analysis of data in City Archives.

Note: Proposition A was for city school bonds; Proposition B was for a city school tax; Proposition C was for a junior college tax.

publicized than the mayoral race. White liberals were somewhat less likely to vote on these measures, and Black voters were even less likely to do so. Only two-thirds of Black voters cast ballots on the junior college tax.

An important lesson—to be learned years later—was that while white conservatives could someday be defeated in the highly visible mayoral race, they could exert great power over city policy through electoral vetoes of less noticed revenue measures. And while they might someday be demobilized in mayoral battles, they might be highly energetic in fighting tax measures.

In the May runoff, conservative victories in two school board races and a near-victory in the third showed that city politics were overlapping with school politics—a potentially serious problem for the Bradley coalition. The insulation of divisive school politics from city hall had been one of the great advantages of the biracial coalition in Los Angeles, in stark contrast to New York City. Two incumbent liberal members were defeated, and a liberal incumbent barely survived. For the first time since 1957, liberal control of the schools was in danger.

In the two white districts, a Black candidate (Jones) ran behind a white liberal (Docter), while Docter trailed Jones among Blacks (see Table 6.7). To win citywide power, Bradley would have do even better than Jones among

TABLE 6.7
School Board Races by Key Council District, 1969 (percent)

		Jones	*Newman*[a]	*Total*
5th	White liberal/Jewish	46.5	42.8	89.3
8th	Black	74.6	12.5	87.1
12th	White conservative	30.8	62.8	93.6
		Docter	*Martin*[a]	*Total*
5th	White liberal/Jewish	54.5	33.3	87.8
8th	Black	64.8	24.0	88.8
12th	White conservative	36.3	56.6	92.9
		Richardson	*Ferraro*[a]	*Total*
5th	White liberal/Jewish	52.0	37.7	89.7
8th	Black	60.3	20.0	80.3
12th	White conservative	32.7	61.2	93.9

Source: Same as Table 6.6.
[a]Conservative candidate.

Blacks and much better than Jones among whites. And while the differences were less pronounced than in the revenue measures, white conservatives again outmobilized white liberals and Blacks on the school board ballot.

Hahn and Almy's (1971) examination of these races indicated that Latinos were more supportive of liberal educational candidates and propositions than they had been of Bradley. Oddly, then, liberal positions on school politics could have hurt Bradley with whites but might have helped him win Latino votes.

Conclusions

The 1969 election revealed much about the evolving nature of biracial coalition politics in Los Angeles. In some ways, Bradley's campaign was a huge success. He held the Black vote while explicitly seeking multiracial backing far more openly and extensively than any previous Black candidate in the nation. In theory, this could be a risky business (Eisinger 1983). Black support held even when the Black candidate moved out into the wider community.

Bradley came to symbolize the entire thrust of the Black movement for political recognition in Los Angeles. Willard Murray, Yorty's Black ally, conceded that "Bradley had lost the election, but in the Black community he had won" (Murray interview).

Bradley received by far the highest percentage of the white vote (37 percent) of any first-time big-city Black mayoral candidate up to that time (Hahn, Klingman, and Pachon 1976). In large cities, it remains a record to this day. He came within eight percentage points of an outright victory in the primary despite massive polarization. Finally, he had built a well-funded, citywide organization, led by loyal and tested activists.

Defeat offered sobering lessons. Maullin (1971:44) contended that Bradley's campaign had been too rigidly ideological: "[T]he Bradley campaign organization proved too inflexible in concept and too amorphous in organization to make needed adjustments in the themes of the campaign or the image of the candidate."

The road to convincing conservative and moderate white voters would be difficult indeed. Many voters observed the campaign through an ideological lens or with negative racial attitudes and in some cases, both. A less exciting election would be needed to persuade or demobilize them.

The Bradley forces may have misunderstood the viability of a Black-Latino alliance by assuming an identity of minority ideology and interests. Maullin (1971:51) asserted that Bradley's plan for a coalition with Latinos was flawed, and was based on an appeal to poorer, culturally separate Latinos: "Yorty won his support by appealing to the lower-middle-class, upward focused, status-oriented and assimilative-American trend in Mexican-American group behavior." Obviously, these Latino voters were also more likely to register and vote.

As far back as the battle over the Ninth District council seat in 1963, Los Angeles Blacks and Latinos had been competitors as well as allies. With three council seats for Blacks and none for Latinos, the argument that both were politically excluded rested on shaky ground. Liberal money and support had been flowing to Blacks, most notably Bradley, creating resentment among even liberal Latino activists. Once again, no assumptions could be made about ideology and interest; Bradley's people would have to experiment and adapt.

Furthermore, Bradley found that while Jews were his most reliable non-Black supporters, they could also feel threatened and ambivalent, and vote accordingly. Their liberalism was tempered by concerns of their own (Caditz 1976). As in his dealings with Latinos, Bradley would have to reassure Jews that their interests would be respected after his victory. When he failed to address the issue of crime, Bradley had hoped that white liberal voters would put ideology ahead of interest; but even liberals were fearful of crime. Clearly Yorty was able to turn Bradley's strengths—Black and liberal idealism—into liabilities. He did this by focusing on threatened interests and ambivalent ideologies.

Bradley's people were serious contenders for citywide power. But the Jewish liberal activists had been unable to deliver the united Jewish vote, and Latinos were unsure about joining the coalition. While race was the central issue of city politics, other concerns were inextricably tied to it— such as police accountability, schools, and taxes. The minority candidacy was embedded within a wider struggle between progressive social change and conservative resistance.

The biracial activists had learned the dangers of crusades. The tremendous energy Bradley's candidacy unleashed had created an organizational nightmare; reliance on old-time allies could not prevent—and, indeed, enhanced—an atmosphere of amateurism. The organization may have been sufficient to win the primary, but its weaknesses emerged in the harsh glare of the city finals. In order to win, the biracial forces would have to make changes.

Most of all, Los Angeles progressives had to hope for a change in the climate of chaos and fear. In a smoother environment, Bradley would be on safer ground. But with the rise of the school busing issue, much trouble could be expected.

A key lesson of 1969 was that the search for minority incorporation in Los Angeles rested on minority mobilization, biracial coalition, and liberal racial ideology, as described by Browning, Marshall, and Tabb (1984). From the Watts riot on, the city's divisions formed around race and ideology. The ideological struggle ultimately involved symbols of social order versus ideals of social justice.

Viewed historically, the 1969 election was a major step on the road to biracial coalition power in Los Angeles. The 1965 election had been the first in which the citywide alliance of Blacks and white liberals had taken shape. Bradley's 1969 campaign built on James Roosevelt's 1965 mayoral base, and expanded it. His African-American base was much deeper than Roosevelt's, and he was making inroads into the white community. The process of winning over Latinos was under way. The greatest weakness of the liberal forces was an overoptimistic and limited view of the dynamics of biracial coalition formation. Four years later, they would have another chance.

SEVEN

BIRACIAL VICTORY: THE 1973 MAYORAL

ELECTION

I N 1973 the Los Angeles biracial coalition won a historic victory—the election of Tom Bradley as mayor. In historical perspective, Bradley's victory seems even more remarkable. At the time, Bradley's election was seen as the first in a wave of crossover Black candidacies; but no such wave emerged. In fact, it was not until the 1989 election of David Dinkins in New York City that another major city without a near-majority Black population elected a Black mayor.

The atmosphere of Los Angeles politics had changed since Bradley's devastating 1969 defeat, for the better and for the worse. The last racial disorders had occurred in 1968, and the final student uprising in May 1970. As the violence subsided, racial and ideological divisions lost some of their force. The Watergate scandal seriously threatened the Nixon presidency. Researching the 1973 election through the microfilmed pages of the *Los Angeles Times* is also a short course on Watergate: the scandal was a hotter story than the mayoral race.

Watergate made the issue of government integrity highly salient. In 1969 Bradley had insistently talked reform, but without listeners. The combination of reform and Democratic loyalty would look much better in 1973 than it had in 1969.

Bradley's own standing had grown. When he first announced his candidacy in 1968, only 7 percent of the voters knew who he was; in 1973, the figure had risen to 95 percent (Robinson 1976). As Weiner noted: "It would have taken a much more powerful racist attack to undermine Tom Bradley in 1973 than in 1969 because there was much more substance to Tom Bradley than was perceived in 1969" (Weiner interview).

The Bradley strategy, then, would be to highlight Bradley's personal image and aggressively question Yorty's leadership, while preventing the mobilization of hostile whites and maintaining the enthusiasm of Blacks and white liberals. The Latino vote would be a battleground. When Yorty's inevitable attacks occurred, the argument would be brought back to issues of government and to questions about Yorty's leadership. The campaign would aim at local issues and civic pride, rather than bringing in well-known outsiders to give it a national dimension. The plan would be to avoid an emotional, gut-wrenching campaign that would lead to high turnout among conservative whites.

But Bradley had new problems to overcome. After the November 1972 general election, the California secretary of state had dropped thousands of nonvoters from the rolls. The impact on the Los Angeles Black community was devastating. An internal campaign document estimated that in precincts that were over 45 percent Black, as many as eighty thousand voters had been purged ("Voter Registration in So. Central L.A.," in handwritten, undated memo, Farrell papers). A massive mobilization effort would be needed just to bring the African-American community back to where it had been in 1969.

The volatile issue of school busing was back on the agenda. In 1970, Los Angeles Superior Court Judge Alfred Gitelson ruled in *Crawford v. Board of Education of the City of Los Angeles* that the city's schools were illegally segregated on the basis of race. A year later, he was defeated for reelection by antibusing candidate William Kennedy (Caditz 1976:3).

In the 1971 school board elections, conservatives won two of three races. Once again, the conservative constituency showed the highest degree of mobilization (see Table 7.1). At the same time, there was promising evidence of continuing biracial coalition in spite of the opposition to busing among many white liberals. The Black and Jewish districts voted in close alliance, and both were far from the preferences of the conservative Twelfth.

The three liberal candidates, Bernstein, Hardy, and Hartsfield received their strongest votes in the white liberal and Black communities. They were solidly opposed in the white conservative district, which also cast the most votes. Again, Black voters were much less likely than either white liberals or white conservatives to look down the ballot and vote for school board candidates.

The busing issue continued to show its force in 1972. Proposition 21, a

TABLE 7.1
School Board Races in Three Key Council Districts, 1971 (percent of vote)

	5th	8th	12th
Bernstein (liberal)	63.9	60.4	35.0
Chambers (conservative)	30.7	25.7	60.9
Hardy (liberal)	65.3	73.4	38.5
Swift (conservative)	28.1	9.0	57.7
Hartsfield (liberal)	54.7	73.7	31.7
Bardos (conservative)	36.4	14.0	62.4
Total	91.1	84.7	94.1
	(N = 36,116)	(N = 28,276)	(N = 38,581)

Source: City Archives.

statewide initiative to restrict the use of busing, passed with 63.1 percent of the vote. While Los Angeles voters supported Democrat George McGovern over President Nixon by 49.7 percent to 45.0 percent, a solid 57.7 percent backed Proposition 21. One is reminded of the anomaly in 1964, when the city strongly backed Democrat Lyndon Johnson but also endorsed Proposition 14 to end open housing. An indicator of Los Angeles's racial conservatism is that in Berkeley, a liberal bastion to the north, Proposition 21 received only 28.0 percent of the vote. Clearly the school busing issue could seriously damage Bradley's chances of defeating Yorty in 1973, and it was sure to threaten biracial alliances.

The Mayoral Campaign

When it became clear that Bradley would run again, the analysis of the 1969 campaign became the basis for planning the 1973 rematch. Despite the strong ideological liberalism of the Bradley organization, some key activists felt that an excess of liberal ideology had doomed the campaign. Some argued that rigid ideology had prevented the Bradley forces from mounting a successful counterattack to Yorty's charges (Maullin 1971). The political perception of the Bradley camp was captured succinctly by Don Rothenberg, who had been at the center of the storm in 1969: "There are some, not many, who assumed that what beat Bradley was the smear of the 'Left influence.' There are others who felt that racism was the major factor. To be cold about it, one can change the leftist influence; one cannot change the fact that Tom Bradley is black" (Rothenberg interview).

Anton Calleia, who had been deputy campaign manager in 1969, said, "It's not that we were naive in 1969. I think we really were surprised by some of the attacks. You're always at a disadvantage when you have to react" (Calleia interview). Bradley's aides vowed not to be thrust onto the defensive again. The Bradley people set out to change both their ideological approach and their style of campaigning. They moved toward professionalism, a process that had begun after the 1969 primary. In 1973 they ran a campaign, not a crusade. As in all such changes, there was something lost and something gained.

While still retaining his key role in the organization, Weiner was replaced as campaign manager by local attorney Richard Bronner. Weiner and the Tenth District loyalists remained as members of a highly influential campaign strategy board, which stayed largely out of public view. No major campaign decisions could be made without input from this committee.

Bradley recruited a new superstructure of campaign leadership from outside the circle of his longtime loyalists. Nelson Rising, a wealthy land developer who had just finished leading Democrat John Tunney's successful 1972 senatorial campaign, entered the campaign as chairman. He brought with him Tunney's media advisor, David Garth, a specialist in issue-oriented campaign advertising.

Garth's fees were enormous. Bradley approached wealthy liberal industrialist Max Palevsky to serve as finance chairman. In addition to volunteering nearly full-time in that role, Palevsky provided a significant share of the Bradley campaign budget through several large loans. As in 1969, Bradley outspent the incumbent mayor (see Table 7.2), but the wily Yorty held the bulk of his funds for his patented general election finish.

The Bradley organization had in several rapid steps completed the transformation from a loyalist-run mass crusade into a modern candidate organization. While this change made the Bradley group more formidable in the electoral sphere (and brought much favorable press coverage), it created strains within the Bradley network. As Weiner recalled, "For those who were familiar with 1969 and were looking for an exact repetition of everything except the results, it was something of a letdown" (Weiner interview).

The Rising-Garth-Palevsky circle had little personal loyalty to Bradley. They knew their own worth, and felt that Bradley needed them. The loyalty of the old-time Bradley hands was extremely intense. The conflict was between locally oriented Black and white liberal activists and nationally oriented, cosmopolitan campaign specialists. It is a measure of the electoral drive of the Bradley forces that the new activists were integrated, if uneasily, into the ongoing movement.

Given the abrasive nature of Garth's personality, and Palevsky's patronizing view of the loyalists (Palevsky interview), the strategy committee became a buffer between the superstructure and the organized Bradley base. Garth dealt directly with the strategy committee, which viewed his commercials before they were aired. Palevsky had his own financial group, which was separate from the main campaign.

Despite all the conflict, the loyalists appreciated what both Garth and Palevsky brought to the campaign. As Weiner reported,

One of the things that I learned in '73 is that it is not enough to run some commercials indicating that Tom Bradley had some experience in the Police

TABLE 7.2
Campaign Spending in Mayoral Race,
1973 (dollars)

	Bradley	Yorty
Primary	708,039	375,203
General election	609,487	586,961

Source: *Los Angeles Times*, 7 July 1973.

Department. You had to flood the media, not only flooding the TV. . . . If you had radio, you had to support what was on television. If you had newspaper, you had to support what was on radio and television. . . . and maybe on the 12th or 20th or 40th contact, maybe the member of the public might say, "Hey, Tom Bradley was once a policeman." I was really very naive concerning the media until meeting David Garth. (Weiner interview)

Thus, the Bradley organization had changed internally in preparation for the 1973 campaign. It had become both more professional and less ideological. The emphasis would be on mass media, backed by a grass-roots campaign, rather than the other way around. These changes reduced the crusade atmosphere that had made the 1969 campaign so appealing at the street level. To the Tenth District loyalists, however, the change was essential; after all, they had begun in 1963 with the intent to win, not to crusade.

The program was good in theory, but the entry into the race of Jesse Unruh, the most powerful Democrat in California, threw a monkey wrench into the best-laid plans. Unruh represented a serious challenge to the biracial reform coalition, and revived the power of Black factional politics.

Unruh was the leader of the regular faction of the Democratic party, and unlike Yorty, he had a solid base within Democratic Los Angeles. Among the more traditional Black and Jewish voters (low-income Blacks in South Central Los Angeles and the lower-middle-class Jews of the Fairfax area), Unruh was a well-known leader with a solid record on Democratic issues.

In addition, Unruh could call on the Black regulars—Bradley's rivals. Mervyn Dymally and his Black allies joined the Unruh campaign, posing a real threat to Bradley in the Black community. Black Assemblyman Bill Greene sent out a mailer with the phrase, "Tom Bradley can't beat Sam Yorty" (*Los Angeles Times*, 3 April 1973). Black politicians could not safely support Yorty, but they could back Unruh. Thus, just as Bradley was poised to reach out toward moderate voters, he was threatened in his own Democratic base. Early polls showed Unruh doing surprisingly well among Jews and other white liberals.

Bradley directed his fire at both Yorty and Unruh. He used an early infusion of campaign money to run television advertisements attacking Yorty's leadership. He characterized Unruh as a machine boss attempting to impose his rule on Los Angeles (Robinson 1976).

In the April primary election (see Table 7.3), Bradley finished first with over 35 percent of the vote. Yorty was a strong second, with slightly under 29 percent. Despite his strong base, Unruh finished third, and did not make the runoff.

Not surprisingly, Unruh made a strong showing in the Black and Jewish communities. Bradley and Unruh together got 88 percent of the vote in the Black community, with 76 percent going to Bradley (Halley 1974). The

TABLE 7.3
Mayoral Primary Vote, 1973

	N	%
Bradley	234,953	35.4
Yorty	191,407	28.9
Unruh	115,193	17.4

Source: City Clerk, Election Division.

Jewish community split its votes evenly between the two liberals, Bradley and Unruh. Only among Latinos and whites did Yorty obtain a substantial base.

The 1973 election is the first in which all four key council districts can be examined. The Fifth, Eighth and Twelfth have been described previously. In 1971, the city council voted by fourteen to one to alter the Fourteenth District in order to build a Latino majority. (The one dissenting vote came from the incumbent white council member in the Fourteenth, Arthur Snyder.) The new Fourteenth was three-quarters Latino and took a large share of the Latino base in the Ninth District.

While white voters in the northern part of the district still outmobilized the more numerous Latinos in the middle and southern sections, the Fourteenth could begin to represent Latino voters for purposes of analysis. But the figures on the Fourteenth need to be taken cautiously. Private polls taken as late as 1987 found that only 38 percent of the district's voters were Latino, and 45 percent were white; in 1991, 41 percent were Latino, and 49 percent were white. Latino voters were significantly more likely than Fourteenth District whites to be Democrats and to support Bradley (Fairbank, Maullin, and Associates 1987, 1991). Election figures for the Fourteenth therefore consistently underestimate Latino liberalism.

Table 7.4 shows the 1973 primary vote in the four key districts. Unruh and Bradley dominated the Black and Jewish liberal areas, and Yorty built a reasonable showing in the white conservative and Latino districts. Bradley made a surprisingly strong showing in the white conservative district.

While Bradley's primary share was lower than in 1969, he was actually in a much better position than in the earlier election. In 1969, Yorty was able to form a majority out of the voters for the other candidates—who were moderates or conservatives. In 1973, the third candidate was a traditional Democratic liberal. A *Los Angeles Times* poll taken shortly after the primary found that Bradley was the second choice of 75 percent of Unruh's voters (*Los Angeles Times*, 5 April 1973). With Unruh out of the way, Bradley could return to his planned strategy to defeat Yorty.

Another good omen was the passage of ballot measures providing low-

TABLE 7.4
Mayoral Primary Vote in Four Key Council Districts, 1973 (percent)

		Bradley	Unruh	Yorty
5th	White liberal/Jewish	30.1	27.7	23.4
8th	Black	78.6	8.6	5.3
12th	White conservative	23.2	15.1	36.4
14th	Latino/moderate white	19.3	25.1	35.7

Source: Same as Table 7.3.

income housing for the elderly and $28 million in junior college bonds. For the first time in several years, Los Angeles voters seemed open to liberal ballot propositions.

Bradley utilized a two-track campaign, involving mass mobilization of the Black community and a citywide, media-based appeal that targeted liberal and moderate non-Black voters. Although its dimensions were different and it placed much more emphasis on the non-Black community, the runoff campaign resembled what had been the enduring Bradley program since the council battles.

The African-American community campaign was a street-level project coordinated through the central headquarters. Robert Farrell, the Black community coordinator, operated a registration and get-out-the-vote drive under the general direction of key aide Warren Hollier. Most of the money was targeted into the heart of the South Central Los Angeles Black community. An internal campaign document from the primary indicated that out of a $78,970 mobilization budget, more than $55,000 had gone to South Central Los Angeles (undated memo, Farrell papers).

Farrell also served as campaign liaison to the United Clergy for Bradley. These influential Black ministers, led by Bishop H. H. Brookins, planned fundraisers and rallies for Bradley. At one point they considered linking up with Jewish rabbis and other white clergy, but chose instead to focus directly and exclusively on the Black community (minutes of United Clergy for Bradley, 29 November 1972, Farrell papers).

This community-based effort had to fight within the campaign for the resources that had been much more available in 1969. Hundreds of thousands of dollars were going into buying time for Garth's television commercials. Garth's ads focused on Bradley as a former police officer, and on Bradley's love of the city—hitting two important symbols of stability and localism. These ads were extremely effective in countering Yorty's charge that Bradley was soft on crime and allowed Bradley to attack Yorty on the leadership issue.

Yorty tried to use the same issues that had worked so well for him in 1969. He linked Bradley with Black militants and with leftist students. He charged that police officers would quit by the hundreds if Bradley were elected. In the changed climate, these charges were unable to prevent Bradley from taking the initiative. When Yorty suggested that Bradley had been a bad policeman, Bradley released his police personnel file, which was filled with glowing reports (Robinson 1976). Bradley's press aide, Bob Kholos, arranged for Bradley to hold a 9:00 AM press briefing each morning just before Yorty's 10:00 A.M. regular press conference. Thus, Yorty's briefing was often aimed at answering charges by Bradley (Sullivan interview).

Bradley charged that Yorty was bowing to political pressure from Occidental Petroleum Corporation to allow oil drilling near the affluent Pacific Palisades. This highly effective charge came back to haunt Bradley in 1985, when he reversed his own long-standing opposition to Occidental's oil drilling proposal.

Near the end of the campaign, it was revealed that some of Yorty's supporters had bought him a life insurance policy with campaign funds. Yorty defended the gift, but was hounded by criticism led by liberal council member Joel Wachs.

Some evidence arose during the campaign that Yorty's stridency was not bearing fruit in the crucial lower-middle-class white precincts of the San Fernando Valley. The *Los Angeles Times* (28 May 1973) dispatched a team of reporters to interview voters in key Yorty precincts and found them critical of Yorty's campaign.

On election day, Bradley easily defeated Yorty, with 54 percent of the vote. Bradley enjoyed high Black turnout, solid Jewish support, an increasing Latino base, and little countermobilization by conservative whites. The key was the reduced citywide turnout, which reflected the changed times and Bradley's campaign strategy.

In 1969, the overall turnout had been 76 percent. Four years later, only 64 percent of the registered voters came to the polls. The decline was greatest in the areas of Yorty's strength. As in 1969, Blacks turned out at the highest rate of all groups (Halley 1974). The election of Black mayors depends most of all on the relative strength of Black turnout (O'Laughlin and Berg 1977).

The four key districts showed clear differences (see Table 7.5). Ideological division among whites once again played a central role. The liberal Fifth District was fourteen points more pro-Bradley than the white conservative Twelfth, and cast many more votes. The mobilization of the liberal Fifth and the demobilization of the conservative Twelfth were crucial to Bradley's victory.

The importance of white liberal votes can be seen by looking at total votes cast in each of the four key council districts (see Table 7.5). Turnout does not fully measure mobilization since it is a percentage of those already registered to vote. In the Black community, for instance, there had been a large dropoff in registration since 1969 due to the purge of nonvoters from the

TABLE 7.5

Mayoral Vote in General Election in Four Key Council Districts, 1973

		Bradley Vote (%)	Total Votes Cast (N)	Bradley Margin (N)
5th	White liberal/Jewish	58	74,456	12,697
8th	Black	91	49,324	41,282
12th	White conservative	44	58,643	−6,396
14th	Latino/moderate white	44	30,705	−3,030

Source: Same as Table 7.3.

rolls. The building of a base for the Black candidate in the Fifth—one of the highest-turnout districts in the city—was a major coup for the biracial coalition.

The two-track strategy had worked. The quiet mobilization of the Black community, conducted without citywide media coverage, had not generated a white countermobilization. In fact, Bradley received a remarkable 46 percent of the white vote, and a bare majority of the Latino vote (Halley, Acock, and Greene 1976). Since white votes include Jews, Latinos were significantly more pro-Bradley than white Gentiles. The council district analysis surely underestimates Bradley's Latino vote.

While there was plenty of evidence that a core anti-Bradley vote had come from lower-middle-class whites in the San Fernando Valley, the behavior of the Twelfth District shows that the most potent anti-Bradley conservative base comprised affluent white conservatives. In both 1969 and 1973, the strongest and most active base for Yorty was the Twelfth.

Where had Bradley's Latino votes come from? Hahn, Klingman, and Pachon (1976:515) found that "in predominantly chicano areas, as income and education increased, the vote . . . for Bradley seemed to decline." The same pattern had emerged in 1969, as better-off Latinos had seemed less amenable to the coalition-of-minorities argument (Hahn and Almy 1971; Maullin 1971). Some evidence indicated that if a Black-Latino coalition was emerging in Los Angeles, it was a class coalition of the economically dispossessed.

Among whites, the reverse effect appeared. To a greater degree than in 1969, the white vote for Bradley was associated with increasing income and education. Hahn, Klingman, and Pachon (1976:517) concluded that in 1969 "in white areas of the city Bradley appeared to draw relatively undifferentiated support that was only marginally related to social status. In 1973, however, this association was enhanced markedly as he became an increasingly legitimate and viable challenger to the incumbent mayor."

Halley, Acock, and Greene (1976) found evidence for the same conclusion, showing that even among non-Jews, there was more support for

Bradley among high-socioeconomic-status whites than among low-socioeconomic-status whites. On the other hand, Jewish precincts at all socioeconomic levels gave more support to Bradley than did comparable white Gentile precincts (Halley, Acock, and Greene 1976).

Halley (1974:87) argued that even the white Gentile vote for Bradley was overestimated because "over one-third of his vote in these areas came from Jewish precincts, where he received overwhelming support." A study by two Bradley strategists of ten Jewish precincts and thirty-two white Gentile precincts showed Bradley's Jewish support at 62 percent, with that of white Gentiles at 44 percent (cited in Halley, Acock, and Greene 1976).

The results made clear that the Bradley coalition was not a simple—or single—phenomenon. Studies of biracial coalitions tend to search for a single unifying strand, such as class or racial solidarity. Looking for a single socioeconomic relationship misses the reality of biracial coalition building. To succeed, a coalition must be flexible enough to mean different things to different groups (Downs 1957).

For instance, the white vote for Bradley was, as expected, skewed toward Jews and liberals. Since Jews enjoy relatively high socioeconomic status in Los Angeles, their vote can account for some of the class bias. If this is a liberal vote, then it does not necessarily make the coalition less change oriented. In fact, quite the opposite could be true. In addition, much of the white opposition to Bradley was just as affluent. Indeed, ideological differences among whites are greatest at high-socioeconomic-status levels (Shingles 1989).

On the other hand, the Latino vote may be a class vote. Los Angeles may have a basis for a Black-Latino coalition that is quite different from the sort of coalition that could be made with whites. This Latino class vote gets pulled out of voting analysis as an "ethnic vote," but it may be important in class terms. In the search for a white working-class base for Black politics, observers may tend to miss it. If there is a working-class Latino base for the biracial coalition, its members probably have different priorities than those of white liberals. (Looking ahead to the later Bradley years, Latinos and white liberals differed considerably on class-based issues of the "quality of life.")

The Bradley victory was augmented by the election of Jewish liberal Burt Pines as city attorney. Running as an informal ticket, the Bradley-Pines team swept both Black and Jewish areas. Their vote totals were very similar except in the Black community (see Table 7.6). While Pines did not approach Bradley's Black support, he won a large share of the vote; Bradley did very well in Pines's areas of white strength. Hahn, Klingman, and Pachon (1976) suggested that the two candidates had brought each other votes.

TABLE 7.6

Pines Vote and Bradley Vote
in Four Key Council Districts, 1973 (percent)

		Pines	Bradley
5th	White liberal/Jewish	58.6	57.7
8th	Black	69.0	91.1
12th	White conservative	47.8	44.0
14th	Latino/moderate white	46.6	44.2

Source: Same as Table 7.3.

The euphoria over the Bradley-Pines victory was reduced by the defeat of two African-American candidates for the Board of Education: Diane Watson and Arnett Hartsfield. Both ran behind Bradley in the Black and Jewish districts and were clobbered in the white conservative and Latino/white moderate areas (see Table 7.7). The defeats indicated the persisting volatility of the busing issue, and Bradley's exceptional crossover appeal in a largely white city with a strong moderate and conservative base.

Bradley's election demonstrated that a small but solid and organized Black community linked to an effective white liberal constituency could elect a Black mayor in a major city. The evolution of the winning base could be seen in two districts: the liberal Fifth and the Black Eighth. These districts had been the bedrock of James Roosevelt's losing mayoral effort in 1965. Each subsequent election saw an increase in the liberal Democratic candidate's strength (see Table 7.8).

Thus the winning strategy was established. If they could resist the label of "radicals," Blacks, middle-class white liberals, and less well-off Latinos could sweep the city. In consolidating its power over the following years, the biracial coalition and its leaders came back again and again to this formula.

TABLE 7.7

School Board Races in Four Key Council Districts, 1973 (percent of vote)

		Newman	Watson[a]	Ferraro	Hartsfield[a]
5th	White liberal/Jewish	54.4	31.0	40.1	44.7
8th	Black	17.7	68.3	18.2	64.6
12th	White conservative	61.4	28.0	56.1	33.4
14th	Latino/moderate white	61.3	25.3	63.1	25.2

Source: City Archives.
[a]Black candidates.

TABLE 7.8
Mayoral Vote for Liberal Candidates in Two Key Council Districts,
1965, 1969, and 1973 (percent)

		Roosevelt 1965	Bradley 1969	Bradley 1973
5th	White liberal/Jewish	48.0	50.7	57.7
8th	Black	59.9	86.2	91.1

Sources: City Clerk, Election Division; City Archives.

Taking over City Hall

Bradley's victory set off euphoria among Blacks and liberals in Los Angeles and attracted national and international attention. A biracial reform administration, committed to protecting the environment and promoting job growth in the central city was symbolically bolstered by the drama of Bradley's individual achievement. With Bradley's election, the liberal takeover of city hall began in earnest.

Bradley's election was the centerpiece of a major ideological transformation at city hall. The conservative regime of Sam Yorty was about to be replaced by a durable, multiracial liberal coalition. In the new regime, a place would be found for racial minorities, women, white liberals, and eventually downtown business.

The first decisions that the new regime had to make were about who would actually work at city hall. These decisions were crucial, because mayoral staff would play a key role in other appointments. At the outset, Bradley adopted a stance that was to characterize much of his career—to reward those who had been the most loyal and effective members of his electoral organization. He chose the path of localism rather than creating a cosmopolitan regime of the "best and the brightest." This represented a significant difference from the approach taken by New York City's John Lindsay after his election as mayor in 1965. Los Angeles would not go to the cutting edge of social change; rather, it would be a careful, cautious governing regime. It also meant that the Bradley faction would have considerable power in the Bradley administration.

Shortly after the election, Bradley called a meeting of his top political advisors to discuss the key post of deputy mayor–chief of staff. Max Palevsky, one of Bradley's leading financial backers and the key campaign fundraiser, strongly urged the selection of William Norris. Palevsky later said that his "interest in Tom was that Tom could really be a rallying point for an organized Democratic party in this state that could get things done" (Palevsky interview).

Bradley turned instead to Maurice Weiner, his key political advisor and one of the best-known Democratic reform strategists in the city, to take over the key post. While this move alienated Palevsky, it signaled a commitment to a localized, politically careful operation. It also solidified Bradley's base on the Jewish liberal West Side. For the second deputy mayor, Bradley selected the first Latino to hold the post, Manuel Aragon. Key Black allies Warren Hollier and William Elkins were appointed president of the Board of Public Works and executive assistant to the mayor, respectively.

The administration looked much like the campaign organization, a mixture of Black and white liberal activists, joined by some Latinos and Asian-Americans. Liaison with ethnic communities was institutionalized into a system dividing the city into five geographic areas, each with a coordinator reporting to a political deputy.

The Bradley coalition that won a historic victory in 1973 was actually a highly localistic, personalized group with deep roots in Los Angeles liberal politics. It was in a position to take over city hall and extend its influence. In the next chapter, we will see how this coalition in turn transformed the Black factional politics of Los Angeles.

EIGHT

FACTIONAL CONFLICTS AND THE

CONSOLIDATION OF BIRACIAL POWER

BRADLEY'S victory showed the depth and strength of biracial coalition politics in Los Angeles. It also represented a challenge to the existing structure of local African-American politics. Until Bradley's election, the organization led by Mervyn Dymally and Jesse Unruh had been the leading political force in the Black community. But Bradley had won a famous victory and enjoyed access to the liberal reform movement. What had once been a one-sided factional battle between the Black regulars and the Black reformers was now an even match.

Emboldened by his political strength, Bradley expanded his base within the African-American community. He endorsed two victorious Black city council candidates and fostered the growth of a Bradley organization in Black Los Angeles. Bradley used this organization to challenge Dymally on his own turf—Democratic legislative primaries in the Black community. These races provide a rare insight into the inner nature of the Bradley coalition.

I argue that factional divisions among Blacks are important factors in the development of biracial coalitions for Black empowerment. The movement for Black empowerment was not only a shift in power between Blacks and whites; it also marked an important change in power relations within the Black community.

Black voting unity in Bradley's mayoral races led scholarly observers to argue that class division had not been a factor among Blacks. Hahn, Klingman, and Pachon (1976:515) wrote: "The data, therefore, did not corroborate the frequently expressed fear that the electoral choices of the middle- or upper-middle-class black areas might diverge from the voting patterns of working-class black areas, or that they might provide reduced support for black candidates."

Only a full historical analysis reveals the roots in Black factional politics of the Bradley coalition. The rise of Bradley and his allies was not only a movement for Black empowerment but also the political expression of the progressive, upwardly mobile portion of the Los Angeles Black community long overshadowed by the party regulars. When Bradley ran for mayor, this reality was obscured by voting returns that showed Blacks solidly in the Black candidate's coalition.

The Election of Allies

Like Yorty, Bradley used his electoral strength to help allies win other offices. Bradley intervened in council races; unlike his predecessor, he neither challenged incumbents, nor tried to punish opponents. But Bradley has been much more active and assertive within the Black community than many think.

Within one year of his mayoral election, Bradley had helped elect two African-American allies to city council seats, giving him a solid bloc of supporters. He came close to electing a white ally in the Jewish Fifth District. (He repeated the pattern in 1991, when vacancies appeared in the Eighth and Ninth Districts; both of his candidates won.)

Bradley's election as mayor created a vacancy in his own Tenth District council seat. He was confronted with several possible candidacies by allies. Warren Hollier, one of his closest Black aides, considered the race. Bradley appointed him to the prized, full-time post of president of the Board of Public Works. Then the Asian-American leader George Takei filed for the seat. Takei, who played the navigator Sulu on the popular television series "Star Trek," had been the Asian-American chairman for Bradley's 1969 and 1973 mayoral campaigns. Juanita Dudley, well known in the Black community, also joined the fray.

Bradley reached out and offered his help to his longtime friend and supporter David Cunningham, who said: "I called Tom right after the primary to congratulate him. He said, 'I want you to run for my Council seat.' He said to come see him when I got back. I went to see him and decided to run, then spoke to Maury Weiner" (Cunningham interview).

Cunningham remembered that Bradley promised that "he [Bradley] would put it all together." The Bradley endorsement was "a big gift," said Leslie Song-Winner, an organizer of Cunningham's winning campaign, adding that "it was totally a Tom Bradley campaign" (Song-Winner interview). Cunningham said that his support was basically from Bradley's constituency and that he himself was relatively unknown. The Cunningham campaign used Bradley's photograph to highlight the endorsement. Cunningham was backed by Bishop Brookins, and received some campaign money from the liberal West Side (Song-Winner interview).

Yvonne Brathwaite Burke, a Black Bradley ally from the Leimert Park Democratic Club, spoke out in Cunningham's favor: "What is most important is that we have just elected a new Mayor and we have to elect someone to the City Council who has a history of loyalty to Tom Bradley, someone who is not an enemy. There are some people running for that office who fought hard to defeat Tom Bradley" (*Los Angeles Times*, 4 August 1973).

While Bradley endorsed Cunningham, the mayor's highest ranking Asian-American aide, Masamori Kojima, endorsed Takei on Mayor's Office stationery. Takei told the *Los Angeles Times*: "I regret that [Bradley] had to make a formal endorsement but I am pleased that he allowed Mr. Kojima, who is in the Bradley 'family,' to endorse me. This indicates in a benign way [Bradley's] warmth and cordiality toward my campaign" (14 August 1973). And the mayor's wife signed the nominating petition of another Black candidate, Juanita Dudley.

Cunningham narrowly defeated Takei in late September. Takei put on a late surge, sparked by a get-out-the-vote operation led by young Asian-American activists (Song-Winner interview). In November, Bradley appointed Takei to the Board of the Southern California Rapid Transit District. Cunningham's strongest base was in the Black community. In his eight best census tracts, the Black population ranged from 60 to 88 percent. In each of his six weakest, the Black population was less than 9 percent.

Takei's defeat meant that the movement for Asian-American representation was unlikely to surmount the numbers and unity of the Black community. When Asian-Americans eventually won representation on the council, with Michael Woo in 1985, it would be in Hollywood's Thirteenth District, a liberal community with a small Black population.

In factional terms, the Tenth District race had presented a real challenge to Bradley. Three friendly Black candidates and one friendly Asian-American candidate had sought his support. Bradley had managed to stay on warm terms with all four candidates. Cunningham's manager later recalled that "all the candidates had a Tom Bradley picture. He was real nice to everyone" (Song-Winner interview). And he had helped a grateful ally win a seat (one that Cunningham would hold until 1987).

In early 1974, Councilman Billy Mills, a Black rival to Bradley in the early days, resigned his Eighth District seat to become a judge. A wide-open race ensued to succeed him in this Black, working-class district. Bradley's stature was such that even though he had limited organizational links in this Dymally stronghold, his endorsement would still be critical.

Robert Farrell, Black community coordinator in Bradley's 1969 and 1973 campaigns and a member of the new mayor's staff, decided to run for the seat. Farrell recalled the process of "applying" for Bradley's endorsement:

> I had made sure the Mayor would be aware of my wishes, should Billy Mills become a judge, to run for office. . . . I picked up the phone and talked to everybody several times. I asked him for his support. There were others that made their pitch, too. . . . There was a marketplace; you put your thing together. I tended to have a lot of support from the Mayor's people, and the Mayor himself. It didn't just happen by itself. (Farrell interview)

In Farrell's view, the Bradley endorsement was the key to victory: "The strongest support I had was the Mayor's endorsement, and that provided access to key sources of money. The initial loans came from friends of

Bradley" (ibid.). According to Rick Taylor, Farrell's 1974 campaign precinct organizer, Bradley called Max Palevsky, the major donor to Bradley in 1973, and obtained a $10,000 loan for Farrell's campaign (Taylor interview). For campaign staff, Farrell said that he "drew from the collective Bradley and Bradley-associate network" (Farrell interview).

Farrell won election easily, with 44 percent of the vote. According to Taylor, his base was in the older, more established parts of the district, with particular strength among city hall employees and homeowners. By the time he ran for reelection he had built a much stronger base in South Central Los Angeles (Taylor interview).

In 1975 the Bradley faction moved aggressively into Dymally territory— Democratic primaries for legislative offices in Black districts. State legislative primaries were the heart of the Dymally operation, and his people were incensed. As Willard Murray recalled, "I don't know why Tom got involved in that. What does he care who's up in Sacramento? He doesn't give a damn what they do" (Murray interview). Murray further argued that since Dymally had not interfered when Bradley influenced city council races, Bradley should have reciprocated and left the legislative races alone (ibid).

Bradley endorsed Kenneth S. Washington to run against Dymally's ally, Assemblyman Bill Greene, for the Twenty-Ninth District's state senate seat, vacated when Dymally was elected lieutenant-governor in 1974. A year later, Bradley ally Maxine Waters opposed Dymally protégé Johnny Collins for the Forty-Eighth District's vacant assembly seat. In 1978, two Bradley allies, Marguerite Archie and Willis Edwards, opposed Dymally candidate Gwen Moore in the open Forty-Ninth Assembly District.

The three districts (see Maps 8.1–8.3) covered the diversity of the Los Angeles Black community, from working-class to middle-class areas. The Twenty-Ninth State Senate District ranged from poor to middle class; the Forty-Eighth Assembly District was an East Side working-class district, and the Forty-Ninth Assembly District included affluent areas on the West Side. The two Black council districts in which Bradley allies were elected overlapped the Twenty-Ninth Senate District and the Forty-Eighth Assembly District. In other words, these elections took place in well-worn areas of Black political life.

The results were mixed. Greene beat Washington by ninety-eight votes out of more than thirty-six thousand cast; Waters solidly beat Collins; and the two Bradley candidates in 1978 split a plurality, allowing Moore to win. With a slight shift in luck and greater unity, the Bradley forces might have won all three seats. Thus a small Black community was able to sustain two powerful, evenly matched Black political factions.

The three elections placed the two Black factions in head-to-head conflict—and therefore provide a rare opportunity to observe Black factions

Map 8.1 Twenty-Ninth State Senate District Boundaries

Rendition of Maps 8.1–8.4: Phil Harris, Cris Forsyth, and Michael Burghart

Map 8.2 Forty-Eighth State Assembly District Boundaries

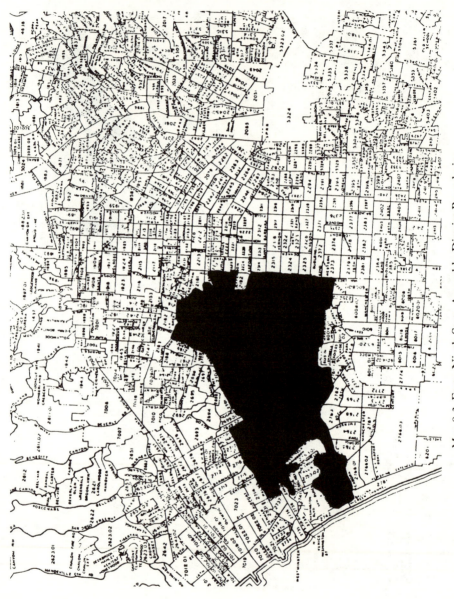

Map 8.3 Forty-Ninth State Assembly District Boundaries

at both the elite and mass levels. A number of such intraracial struggles are occurring in Black majority cities, and are beginning to provide new data on African-American factional lines (Parent and Stekler 1985).

These illuminating campaigns have never been studied. When they were covered in the Los Angeles media, they were generally seen as a "power struggle" between the two leading Black politicians. These events are much more interesting, however, when seen as reflections of social and political division within an otherwise united Black community.

In this chapter, I will tell the story of each election and analyze the vote. What was the social basis for the struggle between Bradley and Dymally? What did it mean for biracial coalition politics? I have relied on interviews of participants, state voting records, campaign contribution reports, and material from the 1970 census. I will also offer some evidence from participant observation (having been the press secretary for Washington, Waters, and Archie).

The factional lines were abundantly clear at the elite level. Bradley's allies became a sort of factional suborganization of his citywide alliance. Dymally's candidates could count on operatives based in Sacramento and big labor and Democratic party money. The Dymally people were part of the broader regular party. The Bradley group was an alliance of personal allies, Black and white liberal activists, and wealthy contributors—a sawed-off variant of the broader citywide alliance behind Bradley.

Along with the mayor's endorsement, formal or informal, came the personal and financial resources of the Bradley faction. A small network of activists provided the main staff for each of the campaigns. The key Bradley organizer was Maxine Waters, now a Democratic member of Congress. This group coordinated most of the campaigns; most had already worked in Cunningham and Farrell's council races. Only in the case of the Edwards-Archie split did this group break off from the main Bradley forces, with Waters and her people going over to Archie, while Bradley went with Edwards.

Eventually the Waters subfaction became so formidable in its own right that a Waters candidate (Archie, then Archie-Hudson) was able easily to defeat a Bradley candidate (Farrell) in a 1990 assembly primary. But Bradley's strength in city politics endured; in 1991, Bradley council candidates narrowly defeated Waters candidates in two races.

Financing for these campaigns came from Black professionals, West Side liberals, and associated politicians. Waters received the bulk of her funds in loans from Cunningham and Farrell, in both of whose campaigns she had been an integral part. Funds in the two city and three state campaigns were highly interrelated. Table 8.1 shows the donations to factional candidates by major Bradley donors in the Jewish liberal community. Table 8.2 shows donations among Bradley candidates.

TABLE 8.1
Funds Donated to Factional Candidates
by Liberal Bradley Donors, 1973–1978 (dollars)

Max Palevsky		Joan Palevsky		Stanley Scheinbaum	
Washington	1,500	Washington	2,500	Washington	1,500
Waters	1,500	Waters	50	Waters	1,000
Edwards	500	Archie	500	Edwards	100
		Cunningham	500	Archie	1,000[a]
				Cunningham	200

Sources: County of Los Angeles, Registrar-Recorder, Campaign Finance Reports; City of Los Angeles, Election Division, Campaign Finance Reports.
[a] Loan.

In light of the current debate over Black conservatism, one of the most striking features of these campaigns was the very low level of ideological disagreement among candidates. Although the two factions represented two social blocs, they generally agreed on liberal public policies. In fact, policy questions were so uncontroversial that as press secretary (and informally, issues director), I found it frustrating to develop new issues. The campaigns turned on such issues as integrity and activism and on which candidate would be the most able to bring about the changes needed in the district. The Bradley candidates portrayed themselves as energetic progressives and the Dymally candidates as status quo, tied to special interests.

The real differences were not between liberals and conservatives (since everybody was liberal), but rather in style and approach. The Bradley-Waters forces appealed to good government and political reform issues, promised a new activist leadership, and also attempted to win votes in both Black and white communities. The Dymally people hardly used issues at all, preferring to mobilize their lower-income Black voters through such standard party documents as sample ballot mailers marked with favored candidates. Farrell summarized the differences in political style: "The Tom

TABLE 8.2
Donations among Bradley Factional Candidates, 1975–1978 (dollars)

To Washington		To Waters		To Archie	
Cunningham	1,000	Cunningham	17,500[a]	Waters	3,910[a]
Archie	225	Farrell	1,500[a]		
Edwards	1,020				

Sources: Same as Table 8.1.
[a] Loans.

Bradley style is issues locked in ideals. The east side campaign tended to be a lot of individual politics, club by club, block by block. That's your technique, as opposed to stand-up debate at the Jewish Community Center" (Farrell interview).

Elite factions might not represent a significant mass base. How consistent were the voting bases of the Bradley and Dymally candidates in these races? Did class division emerge clearly in the campaigns or in the voting returns?

In order to highlight the two factions, I have considered only the votes of the Bradley and Dymally candidates, disregarding votes for others. For the election with two Bradley-allied candidates, I have joined their votes into one measure of the vote for Bradley candidates.

The factional elections were analyzed by census tract. Precinct totals were converted to 1970 census tracts. Where precincts crossed census tracts (which, sadly, was often) I estimated what percentage of each precinct belonged in each tract.

Completion of the data has thus far been possible only for the races in the Forty-Eighth Assembly District and Forty-Ninth Assembly District. The race in the Twenty-Ninth State Senate District, the only election in which social class was openly discussed as a campaign issue, has presented an ongoing challenge because of missing data and maps. The voting material on the state senate race in the Twenty-Ninth is less complete because the county used consolidated election precincts, and to my despair, neither the state nor the county could locate the consolidation guide. Only preliminary results on that election can be presented here.

In addition to the obvious estimating involved, and the joining of possibly dissimilar precincts into census tracts, the well-known ecological fallacy must be mentioned. No firm inference about individual voting behavior can be reliably made from aggregate data.

If mass preferences reflect the factions at the elite level, the vote for Bradley candidates should have been higher among upwardly mobile Blacks and among whites. As Farrell described the factional communities, the Dymally base was more homogeneously Black, and the Bradley communities were more heterogeneous, upwardly mobile, and biracial.

The Twenty-Ninth State Senate District in 1975

The Twenty-Ninth Senate District, about to be redesigned after the 1975 election, was the most heterogeneous of the three. The western portion of the district, west of Vermont Avenue, was in the diverse and upwardly mobile Tenth Council District—the base of the Bradley faction. To the east of Vermont Avenue, the district became poorer and more Black.

Dr. Kenneth S. Washington was a high-ranking state education official, an elected member of the Community College Board of Trustees, and a close friend of Tom Bradley. If qualifications alone determined electoral success, he would have been elected by acclamation. Washington was highly educated and articulate, and had a wide range of expertise on public issues.

Social class emerged openly as a campaign issue. Washington was clearly appealing to a higher-status constituency than was Greene, who had little formal education. In a press conference during the campaign, Washington expressed the sentiment that if he had more education than Greene, that was his opponent's own fault. For the only time in any of these campaigns, class had become an open issue in the Bradley-Dymally rivalry (*Los Angeles Times*, 21 February, 26 February, 2 March 1975).

Washington's campaign aides were unable to convince him to list himself on campaign literature as "Kenny Washington"; he insisted on "Dr. Kenneth S. Washington." The Greene forces were delighted, and were able to pursue the notion that Washington was an elitist snob looking down on the people of the Twenty-Ninth District. (When Washington ran for reelection to the Community College Board of Trustees in 1991, a campaign ad in the *Sentinel* [30 May 1991] listed him as Kenneth "Ken" Washington.)

The campaign worked hard to take advantage of Washington's extraordinary credentials and ability. After numerous efforts, the *Los Angeles Times* editorial board agreed to interview him, and eventually provided an unusual special election endorsement (*Los Angeles Times*, 28 February 1975). We immediately mailed it out to all Democratic voters. Constant challenges to Greene to debate were rebuffed, often accompanied by the laughter of Greene's press secretary. Brief television coverage made it difficult to showcase Washington's greater ability to discuss issues; even the turgid and uninspired Greene could sound reasonable for ten seconds.

Washington called attention to the liquor interests that had contributed heavily to Greene, and to Greene's apparent intent to evade the spirit of the state's new campaign finance law passed in 1974 (statement of Kenneth S. Washington, 16 January 1975, author's records). Bradley's endorsement was used constantly, and on the weekend before the election, the mayor took Washington on his traditional preelection tour of Black churches.

On election night, the votes were extremely close. When 169 of the 183 precincts had reported, Washington led by more than five hundred votes. All the East Side precincts had apparently reported. But at the last minute, eight precincts came in, including six from the heart of Dymally territory, carrying majorities for Greene—just enough to beat Washington by ninety-eight votes. The victory celebration turned to shock, and when Bradley addressed the crowd he voiced suspicion, noting the sudden turn of events. The next day he commented, "Up to five minutes before the final six precincts came in, Kenny Washington was ahead. . . . I am not charging that there were any irregularities, but we do want to look at the last series of precincts to see what accounted for this dramatic shift" (*Los Angeles Times*, 6 March 1975).

Later investigation revealed that an unusually high percentage of the ballots had been invalidated because of voter error. But no tampering was ever proved. Greene had won, and Dymally had eked out a victory over Bradley.

Roderick Wright, Washington's precinct coordinator, recalled that the sociopolitical dividing line in the district was Vermont Avenue (Wright interview). The clear division was East Side versus West Side. The precinct totals bear out Wright's view. Washington's best precincts were all to the west of Vermont Avenue, while his worst precincts were all to its east. These divisions can be explained by socioeconomic status (as well as Greene's incumbency in the assembly district in the eastern portion of the state senate district.)

The evidence supports Councilman Farrell's recollection: Washington's strongest base was "on the west side with the CDC people. The Bill Greene victory was a traditional victory. The votes for that victory came out of traditional turf" (Farrell interview).

In another way, the contrasts of East Side and West Side confounded expectations. In special elections, higher-status voters tend to turn out at higher rates. But the regular forces did a better job of mobilization than did the reformers. In Washington's eleven strongest precincts, the turnout was only 39 percent; in his fifteen weakest precincts, it was 44 percent.

The Forty-Eighth Assembly District in 1976

As chief deputy to the Tenth District councilman, David Cunningham, Maxine Waters was one of the highest-ranking Black women at city hall. She had managed Farrell's council campaign and Washington's senate race. Increasingly, the Bradley organization in the Black community owed its allegiance to her.

In 1976, the Forty-Eighth District assemblyman, Leon Ralph, abruptly left office. He showed up at the California secretary of state's office at the end of the last day of the filing period with a young aide, Johnny Collins. Collins immediately filed for the post. Waters had been considering running for office should one open up, and Ralph's ploy infuriated her. She called Secretary of State March Fong Eu, who reopened the filing.

Ralph and Collins were loyal members of the Dymally organization, and the Collins candidacy had numerous advantages—the endorsement of the incumbent and the financial and organizational resources of the state machine. Waters had the Bradley faction and its access to Black reform and white liberal money. She was unable, however, to obtain Bradley's formal endorsement.

Perhaps chastened by Washington's narrow loss, Bradley held back. With Washington's loss, Bradley had the worst of both worlds; he was accused of being a "boss" and was also seen as having lost influence. Waters did receive a letter of endorsement from Bradley's wife, Ethel Bradley, and was able to gain the full support of the associated Bradley network. Maurice Weiner, Bradley's closest political advisor, later commented that "Maxine, even without the full endorsement, made the best use of the Bradley group" (Weiner interview).

Waters was heavily outfinanced by the Dymally forces, but managed to survive on loans from Cunningham and Farrell. A $17,500 loan from Cunningham comprised one-quarter of her budget of about $61,000. Her organization was intact, veterans of the Cunningham, Farrell, and Washington campaigns.

The Forty-Eighth District was in the heart of Dymally territory. Unlike the Twenty-Ninth State Senate District or the Forty-Ninth Assembly District, it contained none of the West Side. As Wright recalled, "[T]he district stopped right at Vermont. It was all east side" (Wright interview).

Census tract data reveal a stark socioeconomic contrast between the Forty-Eight and Forty-Ninth Districts (see Table 8.3). However, the overall figures for the Forty-Eighth mask its division between the overwhelmingly Black poor and working-class areas and the nearly all-white city of South Gate. (By 1992, South Gate was largely Latino.) In eight census tracts, the Black population was less than 1 percent. In thirty-eight of the remaining forty-four census tracts the Black population was 80 percent or more. Thus, the Forty-Eighth was really two districts—an all-white working-class and middle-class community (not very liberal) joined to a nearly all-Black poor and working-class area. This was not a particularly promising site for the Bradley brand of biracial coalition politics—in either Black or white neighborhoods.

TABLE 8.3
Socioeconomic Indices and Black Share of Population
in Two Assembly Districts, 1970 (means of census tracts)

	48th	49th
Mean household income (dollars)	5,659	8,364
Percentage in poverty	28.1	10.2
Homeownership percentage	40.2	43.2
Black percentage	67.3	44.0

Source: Analysis of 1970 census data and precincts based on County of Los Angeles maps.

Waters built a campaign for both sectors of the district. She was well-known in South Central Los Angeles from her years of activism in the antipoverty program and with community-based organizations. Everybody seemed to know her. She also had anything but a middle-class, snobby style. She was direct, brash, and strong-minded, and she kept her issues comprehensible and community based.

Waters's campaign was a combination of traditional methods and modern issues. Her approach in South Central Los Angeles was direct mail. One piece attacked Ralph for trying to steal the election and blasted the Dymally machine; another was the letter from Mrs. Bradley. Her literature featured her numerous connections to Mayor Bradley. She sent out potholders and vegetable seeds, which were enormously popular, widely used, and relatively cheap.

I volunteered to find a way to win South Gate. I visited every newspaper editor in the city numerous times, and placed ads in South Gate papers. Waters sent a letter to the voters of South Gate highlighting that community's issues. We got to know a South Gate resident who was a minor candidate in the race. We produced a calendar of Fourth of July events in South Gate. When we sent walkers door to door, they often saw the calendar on the wall. Throughout this time, we could find no visible South Gate effort from the Collins campaign.

On election day, Waters swamped Collins all over the district, finishing with 48.2 percent of the vote to his 37.3 percent. Waters won everywhere. Of the 201 precincts, Waters beat Collins in 160 (80 percent). In South Gate, she led Collins in 48 out of 56 precincts. In largely Black neighborhoods, she won in 82 out of 109 percincts.

The census tract data indicate that socioeconomic status and race both had some effect on Waters's margin (see Table 8.4). Her margin was highest where Black population was lower and where there was less poverty and higher income. It should be noted, however, that the middle areas of each category show no clear pattern supporting this interpretation.

When the district is divided into white and Black areas, some of the socioeconomic effect is revealed to derive from the high status of white areas in which she made a very strong showing. Consistent with the Bradley faction's style, Waters had made a strong effort both in Black communities and in white areas. In South Gate, which had all but two of the overwhelmingly white (less than 1 percent Black) census tracts in the district, Waters crushed Collins by nearly 20 points. Of her seventeen best census tracts (where she won more than 60 percent of the two-candidate vote), four were in South Gate and she averaged nearly 60 percent of the two-candidate vote in that city.

Table 8.5 examines class effects in Black areas showing the Waters vote in three types of overwhelmingly Black census tracts: low, middle, and high

TABLE 8.4
Waters versus Collins Vote by Area's Income Level
and Black Population Share, 1976 (percent of two-candidate vote)

	Waters	Collins	Waters Margin
Income level			
Mean household income			
Lowest third[a]	52	48	4
Highest third	55	45	10
Percentage of individuals in poverty			
Lowest third	57	43	14
Highest third	50	50	0
Black percentage of population			
Lowest third	57	43	14
Highest third	53	47	6

Source: Same as Table 8.3.
[a]Of census tracts, in each case.

household income. These data yield no obvious class effects, even at low and high levels of Black household income, possibly because of the generally low income of Black households in the district. One item was indicative of a Black factional base. When the very lowest vote totals for Waters were examined by census tract, they clustered together. These totals were from a contiguous group of very poor, very Black tracts at the southern end of the district, and here the Dymally candidate did extremely well. In these seven census tracts, Waters lost by an average of thirty points. These tracts had a very low mean household income ($4,800), high poverty (44 percent) and high Black population (89 percent).

Of Waters's solid victory virtually everywhere in the district, Farrell commented that "a real sense of unity came when Maxine Waters brought the west to the east" (Farrell interview). Her election showed that a progressive stance and biracial appeals could take on a grass-roots flavor in territory not at all congenial to Black reformers. Waters's ability to expand her own

TABLE 8.5
Waters Vote by Mean Household Income in Black Census Tracts, 1976

	Waters Vote (%)	Number of Census Tracts
Low household income	51.9	17
Middle household income	58.9	13
High household income	51.1	8

Source: Same as Table 8.3.
Note: Black census tracts are defined as those in which Blacks comprise over 80 percent of the population.

coalition would make her a formidable rival to Bradley within the Black community years later, and allowed her to start a third movement beyond the Dymally regulars and the Bradley reformers.

The Forth-Ninth Assembly District in 1978

In 1978, the Bradley forces divided, and that division cost them an assembly seat. Facing Gwen Moore, who was backed by the Dymally machine and the state assembly leadership, the Bradley people had two candidates. Willis Edwards, a close friend of the mayor and president of the Social Services Commission, and Marguerite Archie, a member of the Community College Board of Trustees, both sought Bradley's endorsement. Loyalty and friendship won out, as Bradley endorsed Edwards. A Bradley aide commented, "Tom owed Willis" (Sullivan interview). When Waters backed Archie, her people went with her to Archie's campaign, and Bradley had to put together another set of operatives to help Edwards.

The Forty-Ninth District should have been winnable for the Bradley forces. It was heterogeneous, stretching from the Crenshaw area on the east all the way to the ocean on the west. It included working-class Black areas, middle-class Black neighborhoods such as Baldwin Hills and Leimert Park, racially mixed Culver City, and white beach communities. About one-third of the census tracts were overwhelmingly white; another third were largely Black, and the rest were mixed. Wright remembered that in this election, Crenshaw Boulevard was the dividing line; west of Vermont Avenue, this was better Bradley territory (Wright interview). It was the mirror image of Waters's Forty-Eighth District.

The three-way campaign was confused, as the two Bradley candidates fought each other as well as Moore. There was bitterness in the Bradley camp. Edwards was angry that Wright went with the Waters people over to Archie (Edwards interview). The Archie people felt that Edwards was the weaker of the two candidates and would severely hamper Archie's chances against Moore. Election night bore out Archie's fears. The two Bradley candidates split an easy plurality, most of which was Archie's. She had 21.9 percent, and Edwards had 12.4 percent. But Moore won the election with 25.2 percent.

Wright remembered that "Marguerite finished second in Culver City, second in Ladera Heights, first in Baldwin Hills and View Park, and Moore killed us on the east side. Willis won Leimert Park, Bradley's base" (Wright interview). With Leimert Park in Archie's hands, she might have won. Generally, the Bradley candidates won everywhere when their votes were combined (see Table 8.6).

Like Waters, Archie and Edwards did better where income was higher

TABLE 8.6
Combined Bradley Candidates' Vote and Dymally Candidate's Vote
by Demographic Area, 1978

	Archie/ Edwards (%)	Moore (%)	Archie/ Edwards Margin (%)	Number of Census Tracts
Income level				
Mean household income				
Lowest third[a]	53	47	6	18
Highest third	58	42	16	19
Percentage of individuals in poverty				
Lowest third	59	41	18	18
Highest third	53	47	6	19
Black percentage of population				
Lowest third	58	42	16	18
Highest third	53	47	6	19

Source: Same as Table 8.3.
[a]Of census tracts, in each case.

and poverty and Black population were lower. The same dynamic appeared
in their best and worst tracts (see Table 8.7). Clearly the Bradley candidates
did remarkably well with white voters while holding their own in the Black
community.

When we compare the three elections, some effects of Black factions at
the mass level do appear to exist. In the Forty-Eighth District, Waters managed to do very well in a wide range of Black districts, with the exception
of a contiguous bloc of very poor tracts. At the same time, she crushed her
factional opponent in a white area. In the West Side Forty-Ninth District,
the Bradley candidates again did very well with white voters but also were

TABLE 8.7
Demographics of Worst and Best Census Tracts
for Combined Bradley Candidates' Vote, 1978

	Bradley Candidates' Vote versus Opponent (%)[a]	Margin (%)[a]	Mean Household Income ($)	Black Population Share (%)
Worst third	50-50	0	7,700	55
Best third	64-36	28	10,100	24

Source: Same as Table 8.3.
[a]Refers to the percentage representing the sum total of Archie and Edwards votes compared to the percentage of the three-candidate vote gained by Moore.

very formidable among a range of Black voters. In the Twenty-Ninth District senate race, social class may have had a more powerful effect on the Black vote.

Fifth Council District in 1975

The Bradley faction also appeared in the Jewish community. As in the Black community, Bradley drew broad appeal at the mass level. Unlike Blacks, however, Jews varied in their Bradley support, depending on their socioeconomic status—the higher the status, the greater the Bradley support. In 1975, a city council election in the liberal Fifth District (see Map 8.4) illustrated some of the factional lines.

Bordering on the racially mixed Tenth, the Fifth District is the most liberal white area and has been a pillar of the Bradley coalition. In 1975 Bradley ally Frances Savitch was upset by a young Jewish activist, Zev Yaroslavsky. As in the Black community, we can search for the Bradley faction's base in the Jewish community by looking at Savitch's vote. As in the Black community, these factional lines would be hidden by looking only at the vote for Tom Bradley.

Savitch was one of Bradley's closest city hall aides, an early ally from the Tenth District, and the wife of one of his principal financial backers. She ran without Bradley's open endorsement, but her campaign chairman was Maurice Weiner, Bradley's closest political ally. She raised substantial sums of money from West Side liberal sources. Her campaign letterhead was filled with activists and elected officials from the Bradley coalition. She raised over $150,000.

Yaroslavsky, by contrast, was young and little known. His experience was largely confined to the Jewish community, in support of Soviet Jews. His base was in the Fairfax area, and he was well known in the more traditional sectors, such as the orthodox Jewish community. He raised far less money than did Savitch, and had little elite support. Yet he beat Savitch in the runoff, and eventually became one of the city's most prominent politicians.

Analysis of the 1975 race reveals some limited socioeconomic factional effects. The vote for the Bradley candidate seems to have changed hardly at all when the district is divided demographically into high, middle, and low average household income and homeownership percentage (with Black population and poverty percentages too low to be useful). However, when the Bradley candidate's vote is divided into its high, middle, and low areas, some patterns emerge (see Table 8.8).

Another way to examine the Savitch vote is to divide the district geographically, into hillside and flatland, a distinction made within Yaro-

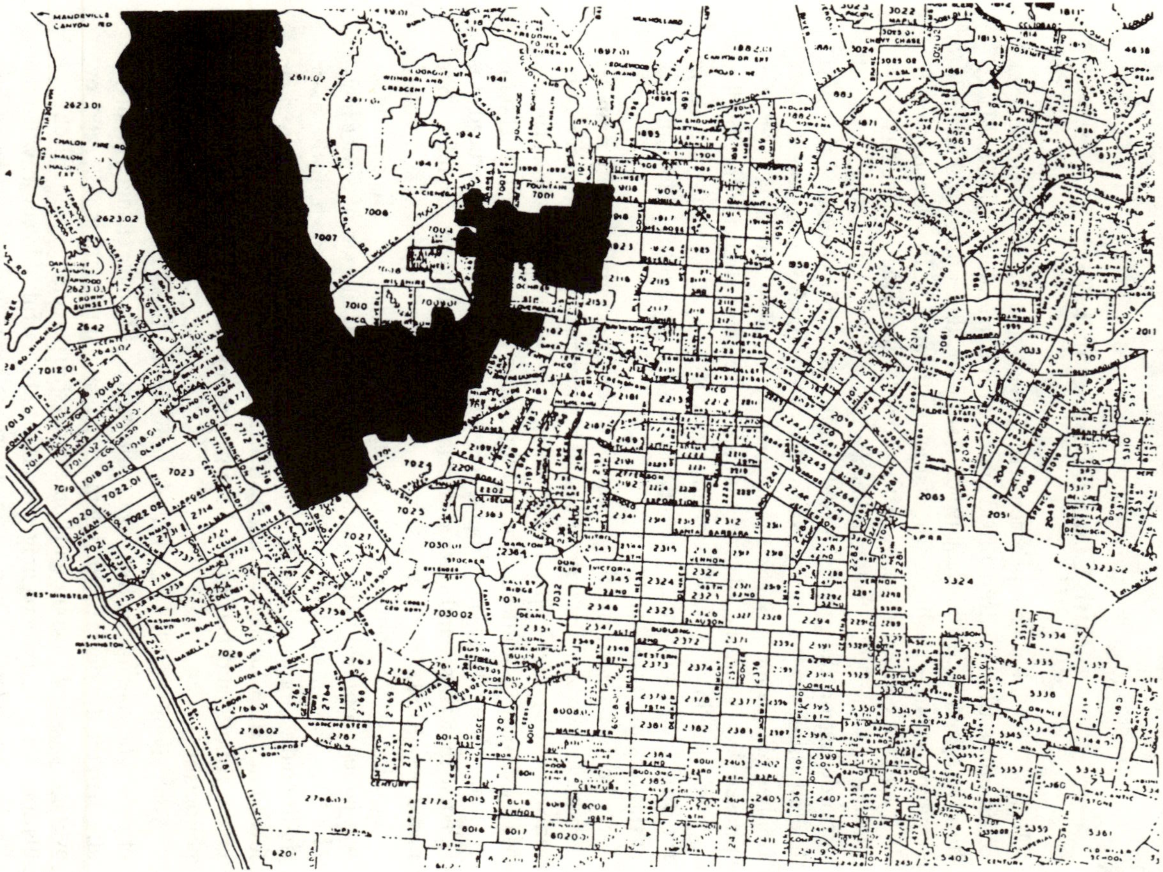

Map 8.4 Fifth Council District Boundaries

TABLE 8.8
Approximate Household Income in Savitch's Worst,
Middle, and Best Census Tracts, 1975

	Savitch versus Yaroslavsky (%)[a]	Margin (%)[a]	Approximate Household Income ($)
Worst vote	38-62	−24	10,000
Middle vote	45-55	−10	10,000
Best vote	52-48	4	16,000

Source: Same as Table 8.3.
[a]Calculated as a percentage of the two-candidate vote.

slavsky's council office (*Los Angeles Times*, 9 April 1981). Examining the census tracts north of Pico Boulevard (which include the affluent communities of Bel Air and Westwood), we find that Savitch broke even in these tracts but trailed by eight points in the tracts south of Pico. The first area had twice the mean household income of the southern area ($18,277, compared to $9,765). As in the Black community, there are some socioeconomic effects but not the clear demarcation visible at the elite level.

Private polling taken a decade later indicated that Yaroslavsky's base was still in traditional areas of the district—and like the Dymally base, this was less friendly to the Bradley faction. Yaroslavsky was strongest among older voters, especially older women, orthodox and conservative Jews, and Fairfax residents (Fairbank, Maullin, and Associates 1988). In 1969, these were the very voters who were most likely to switch to Yorty against Bradley in the runoff (Wilson and Wilde 1969).

Yaroslavsky's victory did not immediately threaten the Bradley coalition, as the young councilman generally backed Bradley in his first years on the council. When the city council divided bitterly over school busing in 1977, Yaroslavsky was one of only two white members of the council to vote against the majority resolution condemning busing (*Los Angeles Times*, 31 March 1977). But over the long haul, Yaroslavsky became one of Bradley's most formidable critics.

Thus in both the Black and Jewish communities, elite factional struggles had some echoes at the mass level. The examination of the vote also reveals that these are not communities torn apart by class division. Indeed, a careful study of interactional patterns of Los Angeles Blacks (Oliver 1986) indicated that the notion of intraracial class conflict as a replacement for interracial division is greatly overstated. Oliver examined social ties within and between the middle-class and lower-class Black areas of the city, and discovered that for both groups ties to other Blacks remain primary. Certainly, on issues crucial to the Jewish community, the Fifth District is not riven by internal conflict. And at all socioeconomic levels, Jews are more liberal and pro-Bradley than other whites. The two pillars of biracial politics in Los Angeles, Blacks and Jews, are indeed divided into core factional areas but in the context of an overall sense of internal unity for each group.

The study of the Bradley faction in the Black and Jewish communities indicates both the strengths and the weaknesses of the Bradley forces. The biracial reformers have been quite progressive, although rarely populist. They have pursued cross-racial politics and clean government. As reformers, they have opposed political machines, and have been particularly well suited to exercise power in reform-minded Los Angeles. No other progressive group or style could have won.

But these groups, amenable to interracial coalition, are likely to be vulnerable to charges of being out of touch with the grass roots. In both cases, the Bradley candidates were very formidable progressives; these were not out-of-touch elitists. But they had their weakest base in the poorest and most "ethnic" areas—South Central's poorest Black neighborhoods or the Jewish area of Fairfax. When troubles developed in the coalition, pressures from these areas on biracial leadership to be more group-centered would be likely to emerge.

Black Factions and the Origins of Biracial Coalitions

We often see the African-American community as politically monolithic. It is not. The phenomenon of Black unity is extraordinary precisely because of the important class and social divisions among Blacks. These divisions are further exacerbated by political rivalries among leading politicians. This study has not uncovered severe partisan or ideological divisions among Blacks based on social class. But it did show intensely fought political struggles that involved social bases more solid than personal rivalry by politicians.

The Black community is generally united when facing external opposition. But when one explores more deeply the styles and tactics that are accepted within the Black community, a great deal of diversity emerges. And these differences have great political implications for the development of biracial coalitions, and for how biracial coalitions assign benefits once in power. Presumably, the faction that forms the winning coalition can stamp its style on the outcome. The larger society will not see the significance of the factional inner core of the coalition.

In the presence of internal divisions, coalition building is likely to advantage some and not others among Blacks. Or, put another way, white politicians do not deal with "the Black community," but rather with sectors of the Black community that are amenable to alliance with that particular sector of the white community. For example, organized labor and traditional Democrats, such as Jesse Unruh, found it easiest to ally with Dymally and his associates. Based in the largely Black, working-class areas of the central city, the Dymally forces were amenable to the mobilization and direct mail tactics of the party regulars.

The party regulars were not attuned to the movement for citywide Black empowerment. The Bradley people were, and they took over the leadership role. The rise of upwardly mobile Black liberals meant that white reformers, stymied by traditional Black politicians, could find amenable allies of their own. As shown earlier, this alliance grew into a dominant citywide force behind Tom Bradley.

This chapter has described the extension of the biracial alliance, far from the prying eyes of a city preoccupied with Black-white citywide mayoral campaigns. In microcosm, the citywide success was repeated with a combination of Black organization and white liberal support. Only this time the opponents were not the forces of white conservatism, but, rather, the Black regulars allied with old-style Democrats. The earlier factional conflicts, subdued in the search for citywide power, thus came full circle back into the precincts of the Black community.

Biracial coalitions are a crucial factor in the attainment of African-American empowerment. This research suggests that it is not just the presence of a white liberal reform base that leads to strong biracial coalitions. There also must be a reform-oriented base among Blacks that is amenable to forging the alliance and is itself in the mainstream of the Black community. It is a two-way street, in which each community chooses and in which each must be able to cross over.

PART THREE

THE COALITION IN POWER

NINE

POLITICAL CHANGE: POWER SHIFTS

B Y 1975, biracial coalition politics had become a smashing electoral success in Los Angeles, carrying in a Black mayor, dominating citywide offices, and holding the commanding heights of the city council. Bradley's African-American faction had expanded its reach into state politics. The conservative forces led by Sam Yorty had been put to rout. The city government was in the hands of a liberal regime.

What did the regime do with its political power in the years of its political hegemony? Did the coalition implement policies substantially different from those of the previous conservative regime? How did holding power change the coalition?

How stable was the political alliance that underlay the takeover of city hall? In their study of the 1969 and 1973 Los Angeles elections, Hahn, Klingman, and Pachon (1976:520) had predicted that Bradley's coalition would be relatively unstable and suggested "the extreme flexibility and fragility of any electoral coalition between black and white electorates." How valid did this projection turn out to be?

The first two parts of this book have explored a western model of biracial coalition politics, in which African-Americans and white liberals joined together to combat a conservative political establishment. Mutual interests and shared ideology created a powerful coalition able to win citywide power.

Just as the relationship between Blacks and white liberals has been discussed in terms of eastern and midwestern models, so have Black mayors. Thus, Levine (1974) found that older views of mayoral leadership, based on pluralistic models, could not describe mayoralties in racially polarized communities. He found instead that a conflict model, rather than an entrepreneurial one, would be more apt. He noted another path, but indicated that it is highly unlikely to be followed; namely, consociational. In this model, a strong coalition is formed at the elite level, crossing polarized group boundaries. Such a regime arose in Los Angeles.

Because the western model allows greater alliance between Blacks and white liberal reformers, it makes sense that western Black mayor regimes would involve such alliances. In western racial politics, the consociational lines are more open than in eastern and midwestern cities. Los Angeles, therefore, represents something prototypically western—a community where Blacks share in governance without the population levels required in eastern and midwestern cities. But to what extent does the Los Angeles regime share the dilemmas of consociational leadership? As Levine put it,

> While consociations promise a way out of the bind of immobilism and sporadic intergroup conflict, they nevertheless still promote a certain degree of immobilism by allowing concurrent majorities to veto redistributive proposals and by narrowing policy agendas to collective-goods programs and distributive bargaining. . . . In communities governed by elite cartels, mayoral leadership is limited by the necessity to engage in continuous rounds of ad hoc bargaining. (1974:44–45)

Just as there are optimists and pessimists about biracial electoral politics, so there are two major views of the policy effects of Black mayoral regimes. Not surprisingly, the same people who are likely to believe that biracialism is electorally feasible also find significant and progressive policy change to result from African-American mayoralties. The pessimists about biracial politics tend also to be those who characterize Black mayors as unable or unwilling to challenge conservative institutions and practices, leaving the African-American community, in material terms, not much better off than before. Interestingly, each side tends to study its own set of policy issues.

Thus Cole (1976), Eisinger (1983), and Browning, Marshall, and Tabb (1984), while cognizant of the policy limits of Black mayoral power, indicated that winning municipal office or gaining incorporation into ruling coalitions does indeed bring major benefits and heightened city attention to minority concerns. They emphasized increases in minority jobs and appointments and changes in police practices. Eisinger saw in minority hiring a continuation of the pattern of patronage that helped white ethnic minorities to attain economic success.

Critics tend to see Black mayors as subservient to dominant economic interests, claiming that Black mayors "rationalize" city government for the convenience of business elites. Both Jones (1978) and Stone (1989) have argued that Black electoral success in Atlanta did not ensure Black economic equality because of the accommodations between Black political elites and local business. These critics tend to downplay such policies as city hiring and police practices, and instead look at economic policy.

Others have suggested that Black mayoral regimes have "depoliticized" the Black masses, and have reduced the likelihood of protest or working-class politics. In a comparison between Black and Irish upward mobility, Erie (1980) argued that, like the old political machines, Black mayoral regimes work closely with business and other conservative forces to reduce protest and to create a comfortable atmosphere for private investment. In this view, the jobs that are created by Black mayoral regimes tend to fit only the middle class, further sustaining class cleavages in the Black community. A direct result is the depoliticization of the Black masses.

Until recent years, the Los Angeles coalition in government received little scholarly attention, in contrast to the Yorty-Bradley mayoral battles. During its heyday (1973–1985), the coalition benefited from the mayor's popularity and the success of the 1984 Olympics. The low salience of Los Angeles politics—both to scholars and to Los Angelenos—left the era largely unstudied. The most successful years of the biracial coalition have never been chronicled. On the other hand, there was little systematic criticism of its weaknesses.

The greatest interest in Los Angeles has coincided with the most troubled period of the alliance in power. When Bradley became enmeshed in a personal financial scandal in 1989, his image suffered perhaps irretrievable losses, and his problems attracted national attention. The 1991 Rodney King case and the 1992 violence cast further shadows on Los Angeles government. Critical views of the Bradley era have dominated recent writings, largely from the political economy point of view.

Some argue that most of the political benefits of Los Angeles coalition politics accrued to the Jewish, not the Black community (Jackson and Oliver 1988). Others contend that the Bradley coalition was basically a corporate-centered alliance of economic elites interested largely in advancing the interests of the wealthy (Regalado 1991, 1992). Davis (1991) portrays the liberal coalition as an elite economic alliance between West Side and downtown, with minimal progressive value. Negative views of the Bradley era have begun to harden.

We still do not have a balanced portrait of the Bradley years in government—of the nature of the evolving coalition and the gains and limitations of minority incorporation in Los Angeles. I hope to contribute to such a view, giving credit where credit is due, and placing blame where blame is called for. The current conventional wisdom about the Los Angeles coalition may be as shortsighted as the previously uncritical approach. Only through a historical analysis can a fair assessment be made. To begin, we must examine the political context within which the biracial coalition took power.

Just as the political rise of a liberal coalition was affected by the nature of the western metropolis, so were the opportunities for social change. Los Angeles government in 1973 very much fit the model of the entrepreneurial political economy, with a boomtown ethos and an underdeveloped political system. For the Los Angeles liberal coalition to survive and thrive, it needed to fit in with the reform culture of the city. While Los Angeles's political reformism was a factor in Bradley's electoral success, it was also a formidable obstacle to any policy that would entail massive change.

The reform political culture resisted the changes that popular movements might demand. Planned as an alternative to the party machines of New York City and Chicago, modern Los Angeles government was designed to reduce the influence of elected officials over the resources of government. The civil service was deeply entrenched, and the charter severely limited the mayor's formal powers. The city council had an unusually large amount of power, and city departments were run by general managers supervised by mostly part-time mayoral appointees to city commissions.

With its underdeveloped public sector, Los Angeles lacked the long tradition of public works and the use of government to bring about equality. In Los Angeles, the mayor controlled at most several hundred jobs, but even these could be filled only with the agreement of the city council. Such structural limitations have been typical of the West, and played a role in the ten cities explored by Browning, Marshall, and Tabb (1984:201–3). In fact, Browning, Marshall, and Tabb found that structural changes increasing the power of elected officials were crucial to making minority incorporation work.

The reform of Los Angeles politics goes well beyond the structure of political institutions. Political machines and bosses are anathema to the city's voters, to the dominant *Los Angeles Times*, and to the major business interests. Activities that draw charges of "boss rule" in Los Angeles would be easily accepted in eastern and midwestern cities, and even in San Francisco. (In many ways, San Francisco is a western anomaly, with its active ethnic enclaves, pluralistic politics, and strong political organizations.) Political interference in bureaucratic decisionmaking is a risky business in Los Angeles.

The LAPD's extraordinary power and prestige illustrate the point. As shown in the Rodney King case, the removal of a Los Angeles police chief can be a cataclysmic political event—a sort of urban parricide. Few politicians dared to challenge the mighty police, fearing a public backlash or private blackmail. Yet the liberal coalition had to take on the police in order to respond to its minority and liberal base.

The liberal coalition also had to deal with business. Until the rise of Sam Yorty, the local business community dominated city politics in alliance with the conservative *Los Angeles Times*. Yorty's victory over the probusiness mayor in 1961 and changes at the *Times* allowed a more pluralistic system to flourish.

But the role of business in local politics remained formidable. As the costs of local campaigns skyrocketed, business interests (especially land developers) were the leading source of badly needed campaign funds. Business had a major stake in city policy, and had the resources to make that role effective. Even the initially hostile Yorty made his peace with business, realizing how essential it was to his governing success.

Many Black mayors have turned to business for the resources of governing, often at the cost of alliance with middle-class whites (Eisinger 1983).

Thus the Los Angeles coalition faced the complex task of linking itself to business support without losing white liberals; after some years, it became harder and harder.

Finally, the coalition needed to remain within its relatively narrow electoral mandate. Los Angeles African-Americans and white liberals expected significant progressive change to emerge from the long road to electoral power. Their constituencies expected a more responsive bureaucracy, restraints on police behavior, economic opportunities, and high levels of representation at city hall. At the same time, many white and Latino voters had supported Bradley only after he had calmed their fears of sudden alterations in the city's fabric.

Winning the 1973 election involved a long process of confidence building. Bradley won by convincing the voters that there would not be a sudden and drastic shift in the city's policies, especially toward Blacks, and that white leftists would not radicalize the city. Bradley had to convince Latinos that he would not turn the city over to the Blacks. Photographs of Bradley in a police uniform reassured elderly Jews living in the Fairfax area. While Blacks and white liberals were the core of the coalition, they could not claim all the policy benefits of victory. With its long record of racial and ideological moderation, Los Angeles was no San Francisco or Berkeley.

Having power expanded and transformed the biracial coalition. The most far-reaching change was its incorporation of business. Bradley's campaign financing had been heavily dependent on the Jewish and Black communities. His money and his votes came from similar communities. As city hall turned toward its ambitious redevelopment plans, the coalition dramatically expanded to incorporate the economic sector. This expansion included a major role for labor unions, particularly the construction trades (Regalado 1991). In turn, the incorporation of the economic sector changed the nature of the regime's financial support. Now the votes and the money were coming from overlapping, and at times different, places.

The incorporation of business had many benefits for the coalition; its liabilities only became clear as time passed. The coalition became a sort of hybrid: a progressive biracial alliance dedicated to police accountability, affirmative action, environmental planning, and antipoverty programs, joined to a moderate elite alliance devoted to growth, downtown redevelopment, and the creation of a "world-class" city. Bradley and his council allies were now committed to a balancing act—a situation made more ambiguous by the vast amounts of business money available to incumbents.

The transition from insurgents to insiders allowed the coalition to increase its power greatly and to influence policy. But it also carried the great risk of blunting the momentum for change when the financial advantages of power emerged. Campaign war chests—not just for Bradley, but for other citywide officeholders and council members—allowed incumbents to insulate themselves from public accountability. For activists, access to city contracts could become a lucrative way to connect to the regime.

With this minority-economic alliance in place, how did the Bradley coalition change Los Angeles, in light of the city's limits on progressive social change? How did the coalition handle the outsider-insider contradictions inherent in taking power in a city without party organizations and with a strong business base?

In this chapter, I will examine the regime's policies in three areas considered by Browning, Marshall, and Tabb (1984) and widely discussed in the urban literature: commission appointments, police accountability, and affirmative action. These can be considered political issues, with some economic implications.

But Browning, Marshall, and Tabb explicitly left out such economic issues as redevelopment and the role of the business community in governing coalitions. In the next chapter, I will discuss the far more murky question of economic policy. Within these two sets of issues lie most of the dreams and demands that emerged from the urban riots of the 1960s—for representation, accountability, and economic equality.

I will examine the political response that emerged from these eras in two chapters. The first dozen years of the Bradley coalition were an era of hegemony, in which political challenges were few and far between. But from 1985 on, important and growing political difficulties severely undermined the coalition's stability and power. Finally, the Rodney King case and the violence in South Central Los Angeles bring up to date the condition of the coalition in power.

Commission Appointments

Holding few political jobs with which to reward supporters, Los Angeles mayors have trouble building political machines. One area of city government where a mayor can redistribute political power is through appointments to city commissions. Each city department is under the general direction of city commissioners nominated by the mayor and confirmed by the city council.

With the exception of the Board of Public Works, commissioners serve part-time. Part-time status means that most commissions have an uphill battle supervising full-time department managers. But when backed by the mayor and city council members, city commissioners can be quite important. They are often seen as the mayor's representatives in departmental matters. In Bradley's "hidden hand" governing style, commissioners have assumed extraordinary importance.

In this section, I will compare how Mayor Yorty and Mayor Bradley approached their commission appointments. How did each indicate the nature of his coalition, and which groups and interests were rewarded and recognized? In particular, how were minorities treated by each mayor?

For Yorty's commission appointments, I used newspaper records and city archives to unearth the names of the 155 commissioners who were serving when Bradley defeated Yorty in 1973. I excluded temporary or unimportant commissions. I was able to locate the individual council files for all 155. In most cases, these files contained home address, council district, background, and occupation.

While the files were hardly jam-packed with information, it was possible to assess ethnicity, occupation, council district, and religion for the majority of commissioners. For 120 of Yorty's commissioners, occupation could be identified; for 133, council district and ethnicity could be assessed. Examining commissioners in place on Election Day 1973 highlights the difference between the old and new regimes.

Bradley made two large sets of commission appointments, first upon his election in 1973, and again in 1984. Public accounts of Bradley's appointments make it possible to assess proportions of groups, and the individual examination of names allows further details to emerge. Council resentment over Bradley's 1984 commission appointments led to a city study completed in 1988 providing further information about the geographic location of Bradley commissioners. Finally, I obtained recent data on commissioners as of November 1991.

Analysis of the records showed that the overwhelming majority of Yorty commissioners were business executives (see Table 9.1). Despite his populist image, Yorty stacked his commissions with corporate executives and owners.

Yorty appointed some minorities to city commissions (see Table 9.2). The numbers should be taken with some caution. There were eleven Blacks among Yorty commissioners, and in his early days Yorty appointed a number of Blacks to key city commissions. But his actions alienated even some of his Black appointees, and by the end of his reign, his appointees were less likely to be active in the movements for Black empowerment. Two of the eleven Black appointees were Celes King and his wife, both active Republican conservatives. Yorty's Latino and Asian-American appointees tended to come out of the labor movement or nonpolitical professions, such as acting, and included few community activists.

Women commissioners had little independent standing. Of Yorty's twenty-three women appointees, five were actors and nine were described as housewives, with most of the latter the wives of male political or business leaders. The wife of a former councilman and the widow of former police chief William Parker were among them. Only one environmental activist,

TABLE 9.1

Occupations of Yorty Commissioners,
1973

	%	N
Business executive or	50	60
owner	9	11
Attorney	8	9
"Housewife"	5	6
Union leader	5	6
Minority activist	4	5
Actor	4	5
Academic	4	5
Media	3	4
Minister	3	3
Medical doctor	1	1
Environmental activist	4	5
Other		
Total *N*		120

Source: City Archives (analysis of city council files for individual commisioners).

male or female, was appointed, and she was reappointed by Bradley in
1973.

The prototypical Yorty commissioner was a middle-aged, white, non-
Jewish male who was either a corporate executive or the owner of a business. This commissioner was likely to own a construction or real estate
company, or to be an executive in an oil corporation.

Table 9.3 shows the district breakdown of the Yorty commissioners.

TABLE 9.2

Minority Representation
among Yorty Commissioners, 1973

	%	N
Blacks	6	11
Latinos	9	12
Asian-Americans	1	5
Jews	11	15
Women	17	23
Total *N*		133

Source: Same as Table 9.1.

TABLE 9.3
Yorty Commissioners
by Council District, 1973

	N	%
1st	6	5
2d	25	19
3d	3	2
4th	13	10
5th	15	11
6th	3	2
7th	2	2
8th	6	5
9th	5	4
10th	7	5
11th	14	11
12th	9	7
13th	5	4
14th	16	12
15th	4	3
Total N	133	

Source: Same as Table 9.1.

These districts predate the 1972 city redistricting. The largest number of Yorty commissioners came from the Second District in the near Valley, where Yorty's residence was located, and from the bordering West Side Eleventh District. Nearly one-fifth of all Yorty commissioners came from the Second District. While the pre-1972 Fourteenth District was heavily represented, most of the appointees from that area were not Latinos.

Yorty's government base can be envisioned as crossing from the white sections of the East Side through downtown, and then north to the Valley. However, as with his populism, Yorty did not reward the far reaches of the Valley with political power to the degree that many believed.

Yorty's commission base resembled his electoral coalition, but with some important differences. He incorporated the Second and Fourteenth districts, where he had done exceptionally well, but did little for the Twelfth District, which was to become the hard-core conservative base of city politics. The West Side Fifth and Eleventh districts did well despite the growing support for Bradley in those areas—testimony to the active behind-the-scenes civic involvement of the West Side.

Even under Yorty, the main West Side districts, the Fifth and the Eleventh, were significantly represented on commissions. These districts have the highest level of education, and are also among the highest in political participation. Since commissionerships are generally unpaid, a premium is placed on civic participation and high status. For instance, two West Side districts, the Fifth and the Eleventh, comprised 22 percent of Yorty's positions. On the other hand, both these districts were below the levels of the north-central districts, the Fourth and the Fourteenth. And even together, they were nearly matched by the prime Yorty district, the Second, with 19 percent.

With Bradley's election, the power structure at city hall changed dramatically. The Yorty commissioners were highly resistant to the new regime. Traditionally, incumbent commissioners offer their resignations when a new mayor is elected. But a number of Yorty commissioners simply refused to resign their posts.

The council files indicate that some Yorty commissioners sent gracious resignation letters to Bradley, which made clear their desire to continue. Many others resigned. But the entire Metropolitan Water District Board refused to go, arguing that they were engaged in crucial negotiations that should not be interrupted. Phill Silver, a postelection Yorty appointee to the Housing Authority, demanded the right to remain in his position.

Bradley eventually received all the resignations, but the road had not been easy. The Bradley organization took great care with the appointment process. City hall received over a thousand applications for commissionerships. Clearly a significant change was expected. Bradley appointed a blue-ribbon commission headed by former governor Pat Brown to assess the applications. But behind the scenes, Bradley's key political advisors were scrutinizing the same list (Weiner, Moore, and Farrell interviews). The final appointments included a large number of people who had been part of his electoral victory.

Of the new mayor's first 140 appointments, 17 were holdovers from Yorty. These appointments were not, however, to the top commissions. The Bradley commissioners as a whole were far more likely than the Yorty people to be minority, Jewish, female, and liberal.

In ethnic terms, the Bradley commissioners included twenty-one Blacks, thirteen Latinos, and ten Asian-Americans (see Table 9.4). Of the 140 commissioners, 45 were women. The role of the Asian-American community in the Bradley coalition, less visible than the Black-Jewish alliance, is indicated by the inclusion of Asian-Americans on numerous city commissions.

The Bradley appointments also reflected a major geographic shift, from the north-central area of the city to the West Side–South Side axis that underlay Bradley's victory. Of the two key components of Bradley's base, the West Side played the more prominent role in commission appointments, although the South Side grew significantly over Yorty's years.

Throughout the Bradley era, West Side representation on city commis-

TABLE 9.4

Minority Representation among Bradley Commissioners,
1973, 1984, and 1991

	1973		1984		1991	
	N	%	N	%	N	%
Blacks	21	15	23	19	42	20
Latinos	13	9	19	16	34	16
Asian-Americans	10	7	11	9	28	13
Women	45	32	40	33	99	47
Total appointments	140		120		213	

Sources: 1973—*Los Angeles Times*, 8 August 1973. 1984—ibid., 2 August, 3 August 1984. 1991—Office of the Mayor.

sions has been extraordinarily high, and minority representation has been substantial. Minority incorporation also benefited white liberals; the rise of the Bradley coalition reflected in part the ascendancy of West Side power centers (Davis 1991). The area least advantaged by Bradley's victory was the northern/central portion of the San Fernando Valley. Not surprisingly, this redistribution reflected the large ideological gap between the West Side and Valley whites.

The Fifth District, the core of Bradley's Jewish support, accounted for 22 percent of Bradley's appointments, compared to 11 percent of Yorty's. Outraged Valley council members noted that nearly half of Bradley's initial appointees came from the West Side or from affluent hillside areas of the near Valley (*Los Angeles Times*, 9 August 1973).

At the same time, minority representation increased rapidly both in quantity and in political involvement. Yorty had appointed conservative and moderate Blacks to less important commissions. The Human Relations Commission, for example, was a place where minorities could be safely stuck. Bradley appointed Blacks and Latinos (and in many cases Asian-Americans), along with white liberals, to virtually every important city commission. Minorities were placed on commissions that had previously had no minority members. For example, Robert Collins became the first African-American to serve on the Airport Commission. Warren Hollier became president of the Board of Public Works; Sam Williams eventually led the Police Commission; and Arnett Hartsfield soon headed the Civil Service Commission.

On most key policymaking commissions, a liberal–minority majority existed. The Civil Service Commission could pursue affirmative action in city hiring, while the Police Commission could seek to obtain civilian control of the LAPD. By being part of a majority on each commission, Blacks had obtained incorporation in major policy areas. Thus the 1973 election brought to power a multiracial liberal coalition substantially different from that of Sam Yorty.

Geographically, the Bradley regime could be seen in its appointments. The heart of Yorty's regime lay in the old Second Council District, the near Valley, and the city's northeast. His people tended to be white male businessmen; the women tended to be "housewives."

Bradley shifted the balance of power to the upwardly mobile minority communities and to the liberal West Side. The center of the Bradley coalition's inner power structure lay in a swath from the Tenth District westward through the Sixth, Fifth and Eleventh, a narrower base than his broader electoral constituency. The power base of the coalition at city hall was solidly liberal, minority, and middle class.

After eleven years in power, Bradley made a clean sweep of commissionerships in 1984, creating another opportunity to assess the appointment process. The new Bradley commissioners were somewhat more conservative than the original group, but ethnic diversity had continued to grow. In percentage terms, each minority had increased. The largest increases came among Latinos, who nearly doubled their share of commission spots. A larger number of positions were allocated to the Valley, forty-six in all. But the controversy over these appointments increased. Some of the new Valley members came from the West Side districts that reached into the Valley (the Fifth and the Eleventh). Twelfth District councilman Hal Bernson called on the mayor to provide more Valley and less West Side representation. The council called for a study of the issue, and in 1988 issued a report showing the extraordinarily large base of the West Side.

According to city figures, 36.2 percent of the city's commissioners were from the Fifth and Eleventh districts. Another 17.2 percent were from the Sixth and the Tenth, West Side and central Black districts of upward mobility. Oddly, none at all were from the heavily Black Eighth District, and few were from the Ninth. During the 1991 council election in the Ninth District, candidate Bob Gay noted, "[A]t present, no citizen of the 9th district south of the Santa Monica Freeway serves on any city commission" (*Los Angeles Times*, 19 May 1991).

The issue so agitated the council that a debate ensued over whether to restructure the commission selection process. One plan called for the city to be divided into regions with equal appointments. Third District councilwoman Joy Picus feared that her Valley district would be joined to the West Side districts, and thereby lose influence (Council Minutes, 1 July 1988). Nobody wanted to be in the same pot with the West Siders.

As of 1991, the Bradley appointments continued to be diverse. Women and Asian-Americans continued to rise in political prominence.

The bulk of 1991 commissioners continued to come from Bradley's political base—upwardly mobile minority communities and the white liberal districts on the West Side. The racially mixed and upwardly mobile Sixth and Tenth districts provided 22 percent of commissioners; another 30 percent came from the liberal Fifth and Eleventh. With Hollywood's liberal Thirteenth added in at 10 percent, these districts, only one-third of the city's fifteen districts, provided two-thirds of the commissioners.

The commission appointments of Yorty and Bradley differed in many ways. At the most obvious level, Bradley brought African-Americans, Latinos, Asian-Americans, Jews and other white liberals, and women into the high places of city hall through appointments to major commissions. By creating liberal majorities on most major commissions, Bradley established the means to create liberal policies.

Both the white liberal West Side and minority communities increased their political power through appointment to city commissions. The Bradley regime substantially increased minority representation on city commissions. In addition, the new commissioners were incorporated into the dominant city coalition.

The Los Angeles case fits in well with the findings of Browning, Marshall, and Tabb (1984:156–61). Incorporation led to minority representation on city commissions. And the higher the level of incorporation, the more often these appointments were to important, policymaking commissions.

Affirmative Action in City Hiring

Affirmative action programs generally take a long time to accomplish, and Black mayors make a significant difference (Eisinger 1982). Like most Black mayoral regimes, the Bradley coalition had a strong commitment to affirmative action.

The issue arose at city hall just before Bradley's 1973 election and pitted Mayor Yorty against the city council. In a "tumultuous 2 hour session," (*Los Angeles Times*, 9 August 1972) on August 8, the council created a twelve-member affirmative action panel to advise the general manager of the Personnel Department. The committee was to include four Blacks, four Latinos, two Asian-Americans, and one American Indian and would also be empowered to appeal decisions by the Personnel Department to the Civil Service Commission. The council coalition was typical: a ten-three majority, with Valley members Bernardi, Lorenzen, and Wilkinson in opposition (ibid.). The majority was veto-proof.

But much of the movement on affirmative action came from outside city hall: pressure from the federal government and lawsuits filed by the Western Center on Law and Poverty. A major lawsuit filed against the LAPD in 1972 and a Department of Labor report issued in 1974 castigated the police and fire departments. Later, a lawsuit was settled with the Department of Water and Power.

Terry Hatter of the Western Center on Law and Poverty was one of Bradley's first appointees at city hall, and the new administration was obviously far more serious about affirmative action than Yorty had been. The appointment of African-American activist Arnett Hartsfield to the Civil Service Commission further cemented the affirmative action program.

The Bradley administration undertook several steps to support city hiring of minorities. A mayoral executive order called for individual departments to increase minority hiring. One of the mayor's top deputies, Bill Elkins, was placed in charge of a committee to evaluate the progress of departments. The group met regularly and reviewed departmental reports.

The earliest year for which statistics are available is 1973—a convenience in measuring the transition from Yorty to Bradley. Beginning in that year, cities have had to compile affirmative action statistics for the federal government. In this section, I will compare the minority share of the city government workforce and of top-level city government jobs in June 1973 to that in June 1991; the percentages are derived from data supplied by the city.

Between 1973 and 1991, the city's overall employment changed to reflect demographic groups in the city (see Table 9.5). The white share of the city workforce dropped from nearly two-thirds to less than one-half. Blacks increased slightly in percentage; women gained substantially. The Black increase is interesting because it coincided with a steady decline in the Black share of the city's population, from 17 percent to 13 percent. Latinos and Asian-Americans, who had greatly increased their population shares, registered the largest percentage gains, each group doubling its share of city jobs.

TABLE 9.5
Composition of City Government Workforce,
1973 and 1991

	1973		1991	
	N	%	N	%
Whites	26,681	64.1	21,088	46.0
Blacks	9,135	21.9	10,286	22.4
Latinos	3,879	9.3	9,112	19.9
Asian-Americans	1,659	4.0	3,452	7.5
Women	6,660	16.0	11,705	25.5

Source: Comparative analysis of data from City of Los Angeles, Numerical Progress, 1973–1991.

This success is probably attributable in part to earlier lack of access, a factor cited by Browning, Marshall, and Tabb (1984).

Within specific job classifications, a more complex picture emerges. Between 1973 and 1991, all groups gained substantially in the most desirable jobs (see Table 9.6). The biggest change for Blacks over the Bradley years was the shift from low-status jobs to higher-status ones, rather than increased overall representation in the city ranks. It would appear superficially that even in 1973, Blacks were overrepresented relative to their share of the population. But at the end of Yorty's term, the vast majority of Blacks were in the lowest classifications. More than half of service or maintenance workers in 1973 were Black, and 40 percent of all Black city workers held such jobs. By 1991, Blacks had gained increased representation in higher-level positions, and were less concentrated in the service/maintenance area (see Table 9.7).

For Latinos, the changes were both in overall numbers and in quality of jobs. Latinos, Asian-Americans, and women all experienced a pronounced shift toward more professional jobs between 1973 and 1991 (see Table 9.8). Latinos continued to be concentrated in blue-collar positions (40.5 percent of all Latino city workers in 1991) but had greater numbers of workers in "protective services" (police and fire departments) and in the professional ranks. Asian-Americans had the best profile, with one-third of Asian-American city employees in professional positions and another third holding clerical spots. Three-quarters of women employed by the city in 1973 had clerical jobs; by 1991, only one-half held clerical positions, and nearly one-fifth held professional positions.

In short, all minorities fared well under Bradley. Blacks gained both numbers and status despite their loss in population share. Latinos gained both numbers and position, although not in proportion to their share of the

TABLE 9.6
Minority Representation in Top-Level City Jobs,
1973 and 1991 (percent of jobs)

	Officials and Administrators		Professionals	
	1973	1991	1973	1991
Whites	94.7	70.9	81.4	54.9
Blacks	1.3	10.5	5.0	12.0
Latinos	2.6	7.5	4.6	11.1
Asian-Americans	1.3	8.0	8.0	15.4
Women	3.0	14.9	11.9	29.9

Source: Same as Table 9.5.

TABLE 9.7
Blacks in Low-Level City Jobs, 1973 and 1991 (percent)

	1973	1991
Share of service and maintenance jobs held by Blacks	57.6	42.6
Share of jobs held by Blacks that were service and maintenance jobs	40.0	23.5

Source: Same as Table 9.5.

population. Asian-Americans did exceptionally well, developing a solid niche in "good" city jobs. Women began to move out of the "pink ghetto" into more varied and important jobs.

But there is still a long way to go. In class terms, the city workforce is divided along racial lines. While Blacks comprise a smaller share of the service/maintenance force, Latinos have picked up the difference. Blacks and Latinos comprised 72.3 percent of these workers in 1973, with Blacks providing 57.6 percent. In 1991, Blacks and Latinos still comprised 72.3 percent of service/maintenance workers, but Latinos accounted for 29.7 percent and Blacks for 42.6 percent. In both years, whites provided most of the remaining quarter.

The top-bottom racial division is particularly acute within the police department. Gains for Latinos depended heavily on "protective services" (see Table 9.8), and this was also the case for Blacks. Under court pressure both the police and fire departments have made progress in hiring minorities. However, the LAPD in particular has been slow to promote minorities. On several occasions, the LAPD agreed to court rulings requiring that

TABLE 9.8
Job Classifications of Latino, Asian-American, and Women City Employees, 1973 and 1991 (percent of group)

	Latinos		Asian-Americans		Women	
	1973	1991	1973	1991	1973	1991
Officials	0.2	0.5	0.2	1.5	0.1	0.8
Professionals	6.8	10.1	27.8	37.3	10.3	21.2
Technical	8.2	8.3	17.5	13.9	7.0	4.9
Protective services	15.4	24.2	2.0	7.6	3.0	13.0
Paraprofessionals	0.8	1.2	0.4	1.4	1.0	2.0
Service	23.2	18.4	6.6	3.4	2.2	4.0
Skilled	23.3	18.8	14.3	14.3	0.1	1.0
Clerical	22.1	18.5	31.2	20.7	76.3	52.8

Source: Same as Table 9.5.

TABLE 9.9
White Representation in LAPD
Employment, 1980 and 1988
(percent white)

	1980	1988
Chief	100	77.8
Commander	90.0	82.4
Captain III	92.6	83.3
Captain II	95.2	93.8
Captain I	87.1	90.0
Lieutenant II	85.1	83.1
Lieutenant I	89.8	85.9
Detective III	87.4	86.7
Detective II	85.1	80.9
Detective I	88.6	78.3
Sergeant II	88.8	82.1
Sergeant I	88.5	85.4
Patrol III	79.3	67.8
Patrol II	76.3	61.9
Patrol I	60.9	42.8
Overall	80.2	68.2

Source: LAPD statistics.

a set share of new hirings be minorities. But promotions have been a much harder battle. While minorities provide an increasing share of patrol officers, they continue to be nearly completely shut out at the officer levels. The overall figures indicate a substantial increase in the minority share of the force. Yet three-quarters or more of each rank of sergeant and above remained white as late as 1988 (see Table 9.9).

To sum up, the gains of affirmative action have been significant, but must be sustained over a very long period of time to make a real dent in the top-bottom division of the workforce. Even so, the coalition's affirmative action record supports Eisinger's (1982:391) view that "affirmative action in city employment is redistributive of existing resources, and to some modest degree those redistributive processes appear to be subject to the pressures of local black political influence."

Police Accountability

The coalition's most contentious and divisive conflicts have been with the police department. These battles have represented the continuation by nonelectoral means of the city's ongoing ideological and racial struggle. The

LAPD came to represent a sort of government-in-exile for conservative Los Angeles in the face of the electoral success of the biracial regime. The LAPD was well-prepared to play such a role—better prepared in fact than the city's conservative political leaders.

The traditional pattern was for mayors and council members to defer to the chief of police. Even when mayors appointed Black police commissioners, they were toothless. Jesse Brewer recalled: "We've always had a black police commissioner. That was going on when I came on. His name was [Dr. J. Alexander] Somerville. And I asked someone, 'Gee, does he know what's happening to us? Is he someone I could appeal to?' And I was told, 'No, forget it'" (Brewer interview). Brewer added, "We didn't have a lot of faith in those commissioners who were appointed by Yorty. Whatever Parker asked for, he got. There were no bad shootings" (ibid.).

Woods (1973:6) summarized the situation: "Formal and informal police organizations campaign for conservative office seekers. Threats have been issued that the election of certain candidates will result in mass resignations from the police force. The department utilizes its huge union treasury to obtain benefits that threaten the city's financial structure. . . ."

Bradley and his allies were unwilling to play the passive role the LAPD expected of them. The top brass actively helped Yorty against Bradley. In all subsequent elections, the chief has either considered running or helped Bradley's opponents. Even ex-chiefs nurse a grudge: Ed Davis endorsed Councilman Nate Holden against Bradley in 1989.

The reason for this ill will is that the coalition has pursued a persistent, if only moderately successful, program to bring some civilian accountability to the police department. The key vehicle has been the Police Commission. With Bradley's election, the atmosphere of the department changed. The biracial regime represented the first serious challenge to the LAPD's hegemony in city politics since the rise of Chief Parker. Comprised of racial minorities and liberal reformers, the coalition was led by the groups against which the LAPD had historically aimed its political efforts. It was the department's worst nightmare come true.

Even more threatening to the LAPD, the coalition's leader was an African-American former police officer with intimate knowledge of the department's actual workings—a man who would not be as easily manipulated as previous mayors. The department had already been concerned by Bradley's work in the council, where he was the leading liberal spokesperson for police accountability.

Bradley's first appointments to the Police Commission indicated that the pattern of "kept commissions" was unlikely to continue. Within the first year, he selected some of his closest allies, all of whom were strong liberals with a commitment to holding the department accountable. These included Sam Williams, a Black lawyer who had served as a staff member on the

McCone Commission on the Watts riot, and Stephen Reinhardt, a Jewish liberal lawyer. Over the years, commissioners maintained a pattern of a Bradley majority with a critical attitude toward the department, although the criticism was much toned down during the 1980s.

The appointment of former deputy police chief James Fisk to the commission was a major challenge to the department. Fisk had been an outsider for years, calling for more liberal policies. Brewer said:

> Jim Fisk was one of those who was in the forefront of trying to sensitize this department to minority relations. And because of that he became persona non grata to the rest of the staff and was kind of isolated, ostracized as a deputy chief. Jim, like Tom, knew the inner workings of the department and knew what kinds of questions to ask. Fisk knew where the bodies were buried. (Brewer interview)

Conflicts between the chief and the mayor, the chief and the city council, and the chief and the Police Commission became routine at city hall. On several occasions, the commission reprimanded Chief Gates for intemperate comments. The commission explored police shootings, which had always been "rubber-stamped" by Poulson and Yorty commissioners. It was unable, however, to stem the tide of police shootings.

The inner workings of the department, including the cost-effectiveness of its operations, had to be repeatedly justified to the commission. Over time, the relationship moved into the normal interaction of strong adversaries, but it never became the sort of cooperative, or co-opted, relationship of before.

On the political front, the biracial regime dealt with the department on roughly equal terms. It did not destroy the department, nor was it in the chief's pocket. On the economic front, the regime was able over time to reduce the share of the city budget accruing to the police. The LAPD had carved out a growing share of the city budget. Along with the fire department, it had also won an extraordinary pension system, which was on the verge of bankrupting the city. Table 9.10 shows the share of the city budget going to the LAPD, from Yorty's first to his last budget.

Thus in Yorty's last term, the LAPD moved beyond a stable budget share to a significantly higher proportion of the city budget. It is interesting that the biggest jump occurred after the police helped Yorty beat Bradley in 1969. That tells only half the story of the economic benefits won for the uniformed services by alliance with city hall.

In 1971, the council placed before the voters a proposition to tie police and fire pensions to the cost-of-living index. Passed overwhelmingly, the measure led to explosive pension increases as inflation rose through the 1970s. Pensions were becoming a major burden on the budget. In Yorty's first year in office, the police budget and the fire and police pensions had

TABLE 9.10
Yorty's Police Budgets, 1962–1974

	LAPD Budget		Police/Fire Pension Plan	
	Total (millions of dollars)	Share of City Budget (%)	Total (millions of dollars)	Share of City Budget (%)
1962–1963	50.8	19.9	14.5	5.6
1963–1964	53.9	19.3	21.3	7.6
1964–1965	55.5	18.4	23.9	7.9
1965–1966	61.4	19.3	27.7	8.7
1966–1967	63.7	18.8	31.1	9.2
1967–1968	71.8	19.5	36.8	10.0
1968–1969	85.7	19.2	49.6	11.1
1969–1970	97.2	20.8	50.0	10.7
1970–1971	110.2	21.0	56.5	10.8
1971–1972	131.1	22.1	68.9	11.5
1972–1973	143.5	23.0	73.0	11.7
1973–1974	161.4	22.1	86.6	12.5

Source: City of Los Angeles annual budgets.

consumed 25.5 percent of the city budget; in Yorty's last year, these items comprised 34.6 percent of the city budget.

The pension burden outlasted Yorty. In the Bradley era, mandated changes in the pension plan brought its share of the city budget as high as 15.0 percent in the recession year 1981–1982, and represented an astounding annual city contribution of $211,545,649. The Yorty regime continued and expanded a long-standing city hall policy of political and economic deference to the LAPD. Yorty was rewarded with strong political support, covert and overt, and a reputation for supporting law and order in an era of great social unrest.

The police budget itself was only slowly brought under control. Public pressure to hire more officers was relentless. The mayor and council supported propositions to increases taxes or fees to pay for police, but were persistently rebuffed by the city voters. Key electoral opposition to these measures, ironically, came from the Valley conservative districts most vocal in supporting the department. With the passage of Proposition 13 in 1978, city funds were strained to the limit, and the share of budget going to the police fell as well.

Budget times were contentious. Bradley repeatedly cut from the police budget items that he considered useless, incurring the anger of the LAPD leadership. As Bradley said, the chief "asked for everything from a tank to a submarine to an airplane and I took those out of the budget" (Bradley interview).

At the same time, Bradley and his council allies pursued ways to reduce the explosive fire and police pensions. In 1980, they placed a measure on the ballot to exempt new police and fire hires from the cost-of-living pension. Despite the strong opposition of the uniformed unions the measure passed, with 57 percent of the vote. In early 1982, the council placed on the June ballot a more powerful measure to end the cost-of-living allowance for all, with the exception of those already receiving pensions. In fiscal year 1981–1982, the pension plan reached its all-time high: 15.0 percent of the city budget.

The political struggle was furious. Bradley was on the same ballot as a candidate for the Democratic gubernatorial nomination, and the police and fire unions, backed by high departmental brass, said they would ruin his statewide bid. Mass resignations were threatened—as they had been to prevent Bradley's election as mayor—and other dire predictions were made.

In fact, the unions made good on part of their threat. They were extremely useful to Republican George Deukmejian in the November general election, helping him make the case that Bradley was "antipolice" and soft on crime in his own city. These were key issues in Bradley's narrow defeat.

But the liberal coalition prevailed at the polls, as the voters easily approved the proposition on pensions. Black voters, who had previously backed pension increases, led the charge for the limits in 1982 (*Los Angeles Times*, 17 June 1982). As a result, the costs of police services and pensions were finally gotten under control (see Table 9.11), allowing the city to pass through the rigors of Proposition 13 without going into severe crisis.

In the hotly contested issue of police shootings, the Bradley regime made uneven progress. The old days in which there were no bad shootings had ended. But the ability of the Police Commission to investigate and oversee police shootings was always limited. The famous 1979 case of Eulia Love, a Black woman whom police officers shot numerous times in a confrontation involving an unpaid bill, and the controversy over chokeholds at least raised enough public pressure to counterbalance the department's power. But the absolute number of fatal shootings by LAPD officers barely changed between 1978 and 1987 (LAPD statistics).

During the height of the coalition's power, Bradley had the help of council liberals in confronting the police. For example, Zev Yaroslavsky, later one of Bradley's chief rivals, established a strong record in the 1970s as a critic of the LAPD. He helped Bradley end the use of the police chokehold and was instrumental in limiting the LAPD's intelligence program. He was heartily disliked by Chief Gates, who once referred to "Zev and his Marxist friends" (Krikorian 1983:417).

Among the many contentious issues involving the police, one stands out for its redistributive element: police deployment. The 1984 Olympics were

TABLE 9.11
Bradley's Police Budgets, 1974–1988

	LAPD Budget		Police/Fire Pension Plan	
	Total (millions of dollars)	Share of City Budget (%)	Total (millions of dollars)	Share of City Budget (%)
1974–1975	162.7	21.7	89.5	12.0
1975–1976	197.0	22.3	103.3	11.7
1976–1977	210.4	21.5	110.7	11.3
1977–1978	226.2	22.0	116.0	11.3
1978–1979	208.6	19.8	131.0	12.5
1979–1980	241.1	21.1	160.3	14.0
1980–1981	271.9	20.5	177.0	13.4
1981–1982	292.0	20.6	211.5	15.0
1982–1983	315.6	21.0	192.2	12.8
1983–1984	344.0	19.9	213.4	12.4
1984–1985	386.5	19.9	219.8	11.3
1985–1986	378.3	17.8	226.5	10.7
1986–1987	404.9	17.1	269.4	11.4
1987–1988	436.1	17.6	279.7	11.3

Source: Same as Table 9.10.

marked by excellent police deployments in minority communities, leading to a remarkable drop in crime. Grass-roots organizations tried eagerly to maintain this momentum by reexamining the police deployment formula. Under the existing formula, dollar value of stolen property was a key factor. Crimes against property were valued relatively highly compared to crimes against persons. As a result, the formula increased deployments in white areas of the Valley and West Side but underserved South Central Los Angeles. Bradley's police commission eventually revised the formula, actually moving officers from white areas to minority areas.

The police issue was most salient in the African-American community, and the ruling coalition was generally responsive. Indeed the transfer of officers hurt the white liberal West Side. While commission appointments may have been more helpful to white liberals than to minorities (although both were helped), policies on police accountability were probably most skewed toward the interests of the Black community.

The scandalous beating of a Black motorist by a claque of police officers in 1991 set off an epochal battle between the Bradley coalition and the LAPD. But by the time of the Rodney King beating, the liberal coalition had begun to divide, and Bradley could not count on the city council to back his efforts.

Chapter Thirteen delves fully into this controversy, but a crucial outcome deserves mention in this section. The passage by the voters of a ballot measure to restructure the LAPD (Proposition F) in June 1992 represented a victory for the biracial coalition that would have been inconceivable in any other circumstances. The new law limited the terms of police chiefs and removed their civil service protection. It also expanded the power and resources of the Police Commission. Chief Gates left office, and a new African-American chief, Willie Williams, took his place, pledging to implement community-based policing. Even with a divided mayor and council, the hard-earned victory was won.

By comparison to other cities, in which liberal regimes succeeded in creating civilian police review boards, these might seem like modest changes. But the extraordinary power of the Los Angeles police must be taken into account. Few civilian regimes have encountered anything quite like it. The Bradley coalition made a real difference in accountability in the face of tremendous political pressure exercised by the department. For the first time in modern Los Angeles, a civilian regime could stand on equal terms with the department and on occasion rein it in. The regime's efforts support Saltzstein's (1989) conclusion that African-American mayors make a real difference in police accountability.

In the liberal regime, the police did not meet their master, but they did meet their match. The department never created the sort of relationship it had had with previous regimes, in which initial conflict was replaced by police hegemony. In fact, the Yorty era continued to represent an ideal to the department that would be unattainable in the Bradley era. As one former chief recalled:

> "Yorty and his commission were essentially people who said, 'We want to have a crime-free city; what can we do to help you?'" said [Ed] Davis, who served under both mayors. "[Bradley] appointed high-quality commissioners, they came in every week with something new to pick on. . . . We never seemed to do anything right; we never got any credit or help. We were always dissected, turned over and looked at.
>
> The difference between Yorty and Bradley [is] day and night and it's still night." (*Los Angeles Times*, 14 October 1986)

Conclusions

In the area of political power, the Bradley coalition represented a major, durable shift from conservative, white control of city hall to a multiracial power base with a generally liberal ideology. This shift involved the incorporation into major city policies of a wide range of previously excluded groups, and also represented a fundamental power shift from conservative to liberal whites.

These political changes were significant. Political issues change, but the capacity to make decisions for the city allowed the coalition and its members to shape future policies as they emerged. The hostility of city hall to minority assertion shifted to a working alliance of minorities and white liberals making policy. Hegemony and unity were essential to the political victories of the coalition.

The most pronounced and clear policy outcomes of the political movement led by Bradley were, not surprisingly, political—the redistribution of power and the increased accountability of bureaucratic agencies. These areas of social change had one thing in common: they did not depend on major financial resources. While they may have been politically risky, they did not require alterations in the city's economic fabric. The administration could change the composition of the city workforce, hold the police accountable, and change the structure of appointments without raising taxes or dealing with business interests. Progress could continue with relatively little regard for changing fiscal conditions. In the next chapter, the troubling questions of economic change in an era of fiscal limits are explored.

TEN

ECONOMIC CHANGE: A MIXED RECORD

THE WATTS rebellion of 1965 generated a major debate in Los Angeles about poverty and government. Liberals called for an active effort to help the inner city, including the search for federal funds. Conservatives considered such efforts wasteful, and argued that local government could do little to reduce poverty. One of the defining goals of the liberal coalition was to win this political battle, and gain the responsibility for new policies.

Two and a half decades later, after years of liberal hegemony at city hall, inner city despair remained—an explosive mixture of poverty, crime, and drugs. And on April 29, 1992, South Central Los Angeles exploded once again. For the second time in three decades, violence in Los Angeles raised profound questions about the fate of minority communities in big cities. What happened to the original optimism and hope of the liberal agenda? We must go back to the original liberal plan and see what worked, and what failed.

By the time the liberal coalition took power in 1973, it had a clear agenda for economic policies in the city. It could not be called redistributive in city terms, but it meant to bring additional resources into the inner city without shaking the existing pot of city resources.

This agenda had four great pillars: (1) federal and state aid for expanded social services; (2) downtown redevelopment, based on "tax increment" financing, with the hope of generating funds for affordable housing; (3) maintenance of local taxes within moderate levels unless the voters provided explicit approval for tax hikes; and (4) affirmative action in city hiring.

Such a program, if successful, could achieve substantial improvements for minorities without major political risk. As "free money," grants would expand city resources while taxes stayed down. Business investment would generate funds to create low-income housing. With unapproved taxes generally left off the agenda, a countermobilization of angry taxpayers would be unlikely. Social service programs would therefore be less likely to arouse significant opposition. In Los Angeles, city hiring was a much less salient issue than in the patronage-rich cities with political machines; affirmative action might therefore have a low profile.

The success of the coalition depended on all four elements' working in tandem. In a nutshell, while all were in place, the coalition's policies had the greatest positive impact. But in later years, the pillars weakened, and the regime did not have a sustainable strategy for generating local resources for economic equality. Conflicts over economic policy in these years severely weakened the coalition. It was only after several years of floundering that the Bradley administration began to find some tentative answers. Indeed, it was only the breakdown of political hegemony and unity that allowed new approaches to arise.

In economic terms, the Bradley record can be divided into three eras: (1) the progressive, antipoverty period, 1973–1980; (2) the pro-business growth period, 1980–1987; and (3) the postgrowth period that began in 1988. What makes the economic issue so hard to evaluate is that all three elements have been present all along. One can find evidence of almost any characterization of the biracial coalition on the economic front over its twenty years of power. The trick is to evaluate which element dominates each period.

The Progressive Period

Bradley's 1973 election set off a period of progressive economic change in close alliance with the federal government. Buoyed by Bradley's popularity and national reputation, Los Angeles became the site for numerous state and federal grants and innovative programs. Two major efforts dominated the era: the search for federal aid for social and economic programs and the downtown redevelopment program. To a young person working in the administration, as I did in those years, the Bradley government provided a framework for new ideas and programs.

Maurice Weiner, a progressive activist, was the deputy mayor, and former insurgents were walking around city hall working for the government. In one office, former VISTA and Peace Corps volunteers were designing innovative projects, and the mayor was holding monthly open houses at which anybody could ask him questions.

Federal aid was at the heart of the coalition's progressive policies. As "free money" (a characterization much disputed by local conservatives), federal aid allowed the coalition to pursue a wide range of social programs. Yorty and council conservatives had been extremely suspicious of federal grants, and missed the full wave of federal funds that emerged in the 1960s. John S. Gibson, Jr., who represented Watts (the Fifteenth District) on the council in those days, recalled the difficulty of mobilizing the city to pursue federal money: "Yorty would only help a councilman [on a grant] if there was something in return. He would stir up a fuss with Congress, and he had higher ambitions" (Gibson interview). Gibson helped Bradley and other council liberals create the Board of Grants Administration over Mayor Yorty's veto. A former federal official noted that in those days, "the feds wanted more city leadership. While Bradley was in the council, leadership was coming from the council. They dealt directly with federal officials" (McFarlin interview).

C. Erwin Piper, Yorty's city administrative officer (CAO), was highly suspicious of grants. He felt that much of the money went "down the drain" for "welfare type projects rather than economy projects" and remembered being besieged by minority group activists (Piper interview). An official with the Department of Housing and Urban Development recalled that Yorty wanted the federal money but did not want to use it in neighborhoods, or to deal with community-based organizations (Roberts interview).

Bradley's approach could not have been more different. He hired former federal officials as mayoral staff, actively pursued grant funds, and was accordingly rewarded. Federal officials who worked with Los Angeles under Yorty and Bradley thought it was like night and day. They practically had to beg the city to take money under Yorty, while Bradley was prepared and enthusiastic (Roberts and McFarlin interviews).

Within the first month of Bradley's election, the U.S. Department of Health, Education and Welfare found a leftover half-million dollars in its San Francisco regional office. They sent it to Los Angeles to coordinate social service programs (Ostrow interview). The mayor multiplied these funds as seed money for other grants, including the development of an innovative City Volunteer Corps with funds from the federal ACTION agency. Additional funds came from the Department of Labor for job-training programs.

The mayor's office scored its greatest grant-obtaining coups in economic development. After Jimmy Carter's election in 1976, the U.S. Economic Development Administration (EDA) made funds available to save or produce jobs. The Bradley administration obtained a remarkable share of funds under Title IX, for economic adjustment and dislocation. Bradley was also highly successful in the competitive Urban Development Action Grant (UDAG) program sponsored by the U.S. Department of Housing and Urban Development.

Directed by an innovative staff person, W. Bradford Crowe, the mayor's economic development office obtained multimillion-dollar grants to save and restore the tuna cannery in the harbor and the flower and produce markets downtown. Thousands of blue-collar jobs were saved. After the demise of the EDA, Bradley hired the agency's regional director, Wilfred Marshall, to head his Office of Small Business Assistance.

Bradley's closest council ally, David Cunningham of the Tenth District, was himself an experienced grant seeker and became the first council member to hire a full-time grant specialist when he hired me for that position. Cunningham's office soon obtained a $495,000 EDA Title X grant to renovate two obsolete fire stations as community facilities. One became a senior citizen center; the other, a multiethnic arts center. Cunningham used CETA Title VI funds to set up a community service center to help individuals and organizations utilize federal programs.

Inner city members of the council were strong supporters of grant seeking and active grant seekers for their districts. Even conservative members of the council began to show keen interest in obtaining the maximum available federal funds for their districts. Although quite conservative, Arthur Snyder, the council member from the largely Latino Fourteenth District, was among the most aggressive and successful. When Ronald Reagan was elected president in 1980, council president Joel Wachs appointed Twelfth District councilman Hal Bernson, a Republican, as head of the Council Grants Committee (Smith interview). In time, a "grants consensus" grew within the city government. When Piper retired as city administrative officer, his potential replacement, Keith Comrie, was asked by Bradley about his attitude toward grants in his job interview (Comrie interview).

The council distributed money throughout the city, building grants ties to all members. Originally federal funds could only go to inner city neighborhoods, but the council succeeded in amending the formula so that other districts could benefit. One federal official commented, "The city is masterful at maneuvering money among council people; HUD can't do anything about it" (Roberts interview). Bradley's clout with federal officials was bipartisan. His ties to downtown business gave him credibility with the Republicans, and his political base gave him huge support from the Carter administration.

Federal funds so expanded the size of the mayor's office that in 1975 the mayor and council created the Community Development Department (CDD) to handle most federal programs. The mayor kept the citywide economic programs in his office, and moved the social service programs into the CDD. Through the 1970s the CDD grew significantly and provided a wide range of services to low-income communities.

State and federal grants to the city jumped from $99.1 million in fiscal year 1972 to $412.7 million in fiscal year 1978; in fiscal year 1978, Los Angeles received $275 million in operating revenue from the federal government, 400 percent more than in fiscal year 1972 (Ross 1980). Much of the increase was determined by formula, and reflected a greater emphasis on western cities, but the Bradley administration made every effort to maximize its federal and state support.

Federal aid increased the power of elected officials over the government. Those council members allied with Bradley were able to share Bradley's power over new programs; federal officials strongly preferred to deal with elected officials. In the long run, the coalition's use of federal aid helped reverse some of the city's inherent tendencies to limit the power of politicians (Saltzstein, Sonenshein, and Ostrow 1986; see Ross [1980] for a view that the change was only temporary). But it also increased the power of community-based organizations sophisticated enough to enter the grants process (Ross 1980). Grass-roots community organizations became skilled grants agencies providing services to low-income communities; they developed elaborate ties to the mayor and the city council (Saltzstein, Sonenshein, and Ostrow 1986).

Ross (1980:46,50) found that the federal money helped the city meet social needs. She estimated that of the major operating grants, 66 percent benefited low- and moderate-income groups. The community development block grants could have done more, in her view, had the council not been able to spread the money into areas of less need. On the other hand, the block grants helped open up city hiring and assisted affirmative action.

The incorporation of community-based organizations into the city grants process was both a blessing and a problem. Deputy Mayor Grace Davis described the blend of city agencies and community-based organizations as "one big family" (Davis interview). But the danger arose that these groups would become too adept at working the system, and lose touch with their obligation to serve the community. Moreover, their skills in manipulating the grant system would be less useful if external funds were removed— which, of course, is what happened. When it did, the low-income communities found that they had lost political organizing skills in order to develop the sort of "patron-client" dynamic that Hamilton (1979) found in New York City's antipoverty politics. Indeed, after the loss of federal funding, it was several years before a new model of community politics again developed in Los Angeles—the Alinsky-style pressure group from the grass roots.

The second pillar of economic policy was downtown redevelopment. In the 1960s, Los Angeles urban renewal had been a liberal issue. Opposition to downtown renewal came from Yorty's allies—conservative council members and representatives from the San Fernando Valley. Conservatives, generally uninterested in downtown, feared federal involvement and potential costs to the city. Liberals argued vehemently for a greater city role in renewal efforts, although perhaps downtown and the inner city became mixed together in many people's minds.

Even when renewal became redevelopment in the early 1970s, the coalition lines remained the same. The difference was the much stronger interest and involvement by the downtown business community. In the early 1970s the Central City Association jointly funded with the city council a feasibility study of a downtown redevelopment program using tax increment financing and the city's Community Redevelopment Agency (CRA).

Under this program, an area of downtown would be declared blighted, and its tax rates would be frozen. The CRA would condemn and purchase property for eventual development. As the tax assessments rose, the "increment" between frozen and real tax rates would be diverted from county coffers into CRA redevelopment projects. Thus downtown renewal would be self-financing, although at a substantial cost to the county treasury.

With Bradley's election in 1973, the renewal coalition became far stronger at city hall. The council president, John S. Gibson, Jr., reshuffled committee assignments to put liberal Bradley ally Pat Russell (Sixth District) in charge of redevelopment instead of Valley council member and chief opponent Ernani Bernardi (Seventh District). Business again financed a study, and the new proposal called for a massive redevelopment program covering 255 downtown blocks.

The new plan generated great controversy, and significant negative media attention (with the exception of the *Los Angeles Times*). The liberal coalition was firmly behind redevelopment. During hearings in the city council, some opposition was voiced. But a parade of witnesses from liberal and minority communities praised the plan, and argued that it was essential (*Los Angeles Times*, 4 July, 12 July 1975). Even then, however, there was some West Side opposition, voiced by Eleventh District councilman Marvin Braude (*Los Angeles Times*, 20 November 1975).

A committee organized by the mayor's office and headed by Terry Hatter mobilized public support. The chief opponents were county conservatives (especially Peter Schabarum), Bernardi, and Valley assemblyman Alan Robbins, who ran against Bradley in 1977. Bernardi's lawsuit succeeded in placing a $750 million cap on CRA spending downtown; by the time the city was approaching the cap, in the late 1980s, the consensus behind the CRA had fallen significantly.

The city's redevelopment program eventually brought a great deal of business support to the liberal coalition, but later became the symbol of liberal disenchantment with the Bradley regime. When Los Angeles seemed to be stagnating, the notion of creating growth was a progressive concept. Redevelopment also tied downtown business to the mayor and his council allies. Major campaign contributions flowed to these incumbents, powerfully reinforcing their political positions.

The Bradley coalition in those days managed to mix its economic goals comfortably. With federal funds, it was possible to redevelop downtown but also to save jobs in outlying areas. Social services could be expanded in innovative ways without breaking the city budget. Among major cities receiving grants funds, Los Angeles was one of the most astute at not becoming "dependent" on federal funds (Ross 1980). With redevelopment concentrated on downtown, no conflict arose with environmentalists on the West Side and coastline. There were, however, areas of weakness.

Even in that progressive period, the coalition government did a poor job in the area of low-income housing, foreshadowing later disillusionment with the redevelopment program. Both the Los Angeles City Housing

Authority and federally funded housing programs came under fire from community activists and the federal government. The federal government charged the city with mismanaging federal housing funds. A federal audit charged that despite a growing shortfall of affordable housing, the city had failed to spend $51.7 million in federal grant money in due time (*Los Angeles Times*, 25 January 1980). Longtime Bradley friend Homer Smith mismanaged the Housing Authority and despite considerable pressure held his job (*Los Angeles Times*, 28 November 1982). When federal housing cutbacks hit in the early 1980s, the city's lack of an affordable housing program exacerbated the crisis.

The end of the progressive era was foreshadowed by the passage of Proposition 13 in 1978. The tax-cutting initiative reduced the property tax rate in Los Angeles by 80 percent, and collections fell 50 percent between 1978 and 1979 (Ross 1980:viii). A warning shot from the tax revolt, the measure was reinforced by Ronald Reagan's election in 1980. Suddenly, federal and state support dried up, and the city was left to its own devices. In economic policy, the crushing fiscal blows of the new decade left the city without a coherent plan for economic equality.

The Progrowth Era

The decline in federal aid after Reagan's election had profound implications for the coalition's plan for economic equality. Without outside resources, the only choices were higher local taxes, redistribution of needed services, or new ways to tap the city's economic growth. These choices were politically painful, and pushed the coalition to expand the downtown redevelopment angle as the solution for equality. The same trend was visible in many cities (Browning, Marshall, and Tabb 1990). It turned out to be an imperfect answer.

In this era, Bradley's leadership centered around making Los Angeles a "world class" city. Expanding his already close ties to the downtown business community, Bradley was able to make Los Angeles the site of the 1984 Summer Olympics. In accordance with his low-taxes program, Bradley helped pass an initiative to prohibit the taxpayers from picking up the Olympics tab. He traveled widely to foreign countries to solicit business for the harbor and other Los Angeles industries. He increasingly described Los Angeles as a Pacific Rim city.

Bradley's growth program became the basis for his centrist campaign for governor in 1982. He highlighted his record of producing jobs and his quiet leadership; liberal political changes in the city were muted in his campaign. He raised an extraordinary amount of campaign money, with significant contributions from business (Kindel interview). His nearly successful campaign reflected the second-stage Bradley rather than the earlier progressive program. But there was a limited market for a probusiness Black mayor in a partisan race against an even more probusiness Republican (Sonenshein 1990).

During the 1980s the city's economic program increasingly centered around redevelopment and the CRA. As the city boomed, business investment moved well beyond the downtown area, pushing into the West Side. This shift was to have major political implications for the ruling coalition. It forced into the open the conflict between West Side and downtown power bases noted by Davis (1991).

Bradley was completely committed to a controversial downtown strategy. Critics often pointed out that Los Angeles might be more suited to a multicenter approach, and that downtown might become a ghost town at night. Defenders noted that the CRA rebuilt neighborhoods outside downtown, and that without downtown growth the city would fall far behind. With strong business support, Bradley stuck to his strategy, and downtown boomed—with mixed consequences for the city.

In the next ten years, the CRA fundamentally rebuilt downtown Los Angeles, but did little to solve the city's problem of affordable housing. Other cities were doing much more to fill the housing shortage. By 1984, for instance, Boston had imposed a "linkage fee" on new development that was sustaining large blocks of new housing (*New York Times*, 5 August 1990). Suddenly conservatives were joined by liberals and minority activists in questioning the CRA.

Bradley remained involved in the inner city through persistent efforts to build shopping centers and other facilities in South Central Los Angeles. Bradley pushed hard to find "anchor" stores that would locate in the area. The negotiations were painful. The mayor was bucking the trend among businesses to leave cities for suburban growth areas. Many years of lobbying by Bradley and Sixth District councilwoman Pat Russell finally led to the construction of the Baldwin Hills Shopping Center.

The end of the second era happened slowly. As Bradley's progrowth approach continued, he found that elements of his original coalition were losing their enthusiasm. For different reasons, African-Americans and white liberals were feeling uncomfortable. Several events may be seen as warnings: the 1984 Jesse Jackson campaign, and the oil-drilling decision of 1985.

Jackson's campaign restored the challenge of minority-liberal progressivism in an era of political and economic retrenchment. By comparison, Bradley seemed more and more a figure of the establishment, and the Jackson campaigns pushed him in his own minority base. In later years, the Jackson-style pressure on Bradley was increased by Maxine Waters.

In the first days of 1985 the city council sent Bradley a plan to allow oil drilling at the Pacific Palisades. Bradley's opposition to the plan had been one of the central features of his 1973 election and one of his clearest contrasts to Yorty. But to the dismay of his closest friends and advisors, Bradley agreed to the ordinance (*Los Angeles Times*, 13 January 1985). The uproar among environmentalists was extremely intense.

As the CRA and redevelopment coalition split asunder, the liberal economic agenda floundered. There appeared to be no plan by which the interests of minorities and liberals could be joined for economic equality without outside aid.

The Postgrowth Era

The third phase of the coalition's economic program began in the mid-1980s. Under great pressure from homeowner groups and the public, Bradley began to seek out a middle ground. Calling himself an advocate of "balanced growth," Bradley began to rebuild his frayed ties to environmentalists. With his gubernatorial ambitions shattered by a second defeat in 1986, Bradley inaugurated a new era. He named environmentalist Michael Gage as deputy mayor, and began to appoint environmental activists—who had been among his severest critics—to city commissions. A key turning point came in January 1988, when Rob Glushon, a Bradley appointee to the Environmental Quality Board, resigned in protest against Bradley's policies (*Los Angeles Times*, 5 January 1988). Bradley replaced Glushon with Felicia Marcus, a strong environmental critic of the Bradley administration (*Los Angeles Times*, 6 January 1988). Two days later, Bradley proposed to spend $2 billion of CRA money over twenty years for housing (*Los Angeles Times*, 8 January 1988). On April 18, he gave a State of the City speech in which he proposed to utilize $700 million of CRA money to fund an innovative after-school program for the city schools (*Los Angeles Times*, 19 April 1988).

Bradley soon undertook policies that moderated his previously probusiness stance. For example, he pushed a ban on downtown truck traffic during certain hours. The controversial and widely praised proposal set off huge protests from business interests—groups Bradley would never have tackled earlier.

In the area of housing—perhaps the key weakness of the administration—Bradley created a Commission on Affordable Housing, hired a new city housing director, and brought more critics of his policies into the government. He appointed Legal Aid activist Michael Bodakin to a key position in the housing department. In a revealing comment in a housing policy report, the city's commission on affordable housing noted: "The City must solve its own housing problem, state and federal assistance is insufficient. . . . Local solutions will require locally generated subsidies" (City of Los Angeles,

1991:4). In 1991, Bradley pushed for the "linkage fee" in Los Angeles (*Los Angeles Times*, 15 August 1991). The proposal was strongly opposed by business, but won conditional acceptance from the city council. Articles and reports began to appear labeling Los Angeles and California an "anti-business" environment (*Los Angeles Times*, 18 December 1991; Los Angeles Headquarters City Association 1992).

Bradley began to alter his policies on the CRA. While he worked to increase the CRA cap to $5 billion, he allocated a larger share than required to building affordable housing. He announced his innovative program to provide after-school child care in the elementary schools using tax increment money. In 1992, he agreed to a council proposal to tap CRA funds to maintain city services.

Finally, Bradley began to put greater pressure on local banks to invest in South Central Los Angeles. This policy was likely to be much stronger than the "anchor store" approach alone. Small businesses could not easily receive bank loans in the inner city, yet were known to be the most reliable source of new jobs. In association with Eighth District councilman Mark Ridley-Thomas, Bradley pushed a city ordinance to consider bank lending practices in the placement of city deposits (*Los Angeles Times*, 9 November 1991).

Bradley's neoprogressive approach was received much more skeptically than his earlier progressive period had been. His long period of progrowth leadership—particularly the oil-drilling decision—had made him the symbol of unsettling economic change. His "balanced growth" position left him with suspicious homeowner associations and nervous business allies. But it did allow Los Angeles to become, for the first time, a site for creative urban ideas in the post-federal aid period.

Oddly, then, after a long period of becoming disconnected with progressive economic policies, Bradley had come to a potentially creative position on the eve of the 1992 Los Angeles violence. A city with linkage fees to build low-income housing, a serious plan to compel local banks to invest fairly in the inner city, and a regime willing occasionally to confront downtown business would be in a good position to make some progress—largely with local resources—in helping South Central Los Angeles. But the policies had not been fully implemented by April 1992, and in the edgy, postviolence atmosphere, there was little trust in the plans of political leaders. One African-American columnist wrote that Bradley "rebuilt downtown, the westside, the valley, the whole city while his own beginnings turned to blight and despair . . . certainly after almost 20 years [Bradley has] set aside enough chits to spend a few rebuilding South Central" (*Herald Dispatch–Watts Star Review*, 21 May 1992).

South Central Los Angeles had itself changed dramatically in the Bradley years. A largely Black community in the 1960s, it had become an ethnic mix of Blacks and Latinos. The Latino community had a large number of recent immigrants, many from Central America, whose interests were not adequately represented by either the traditional Latino politicians on the East Side or the Black politicians in South Central. In 1980, 67.8 percent of the area was Black, and only 23.8 percent was Latino. The 1990 census showed that in the South Central planning area, 47.6 percent of the population were Black, and 44.7 percent were Latino (Los Angeles City Planning Reports).

Socioeconomic census data yield a bleak picture of South Central (1990 U.S. Census, Selected Social Characteristics, Summary Tapes 1A and 3A). In 1990, only 6.1 percent of its residents had a college degree, and fewer than 50 percent were high school graduates. The official unemployment rate stood at 15.2 percent, but many were not in the labor force. Strikingly, 97,427 residents (nearly one-fifth) had entered the United States after 1980. Of 149,440 households, 38,073 were without a car; of 158,941 housing units, 11,111 were without a telephone. The poverty rate stood at 32.9 percent.

Evidence of the biracial coalition's impact must be sought indirectly. For one thing, it could be seen in the mobility of those who had left. The political and economic power of the coalition did allow for the continuance of upward mobility—on the Bradley model—for many African-Americans. In addition, local government provided some base, even for those left behind. Of the 175,284 workers in the area, 31,869 worked for the government; 19,747 worked for *local* government. Government jobs mean families fed and clothed (Eisinger 1982). But South Central remains a poor community in which many are trapped without hope or prospects.

Davis (1991:304), himself a critic of the Bradley coalition's economic policies, has noted that "critics who accuse the Bradley administration of 'killing Southcentral L.A.' usually ignore its achievements in integrating the public workforce." He captured the paradox of these policies: "[I]t may be equally true that Black political leadership in Los Angeles County has sponsored significant economic advance and contributed to the community's benign neglect at the same time."

The biracial coalition and Bradley cannot be held solely responsible for the crisis in South Central Los Angeles. They could not halt the political and economic forces that have greatly increased economic inequality in the nation. They could not restore the massive cuts in crucial social programs under the Reagan administration. They could not force city taxpayers to agree to a redistribution of city tax resources to aid the inner city. They can point to some very solid achievements that would not have been done by the city's previous regime. But they could have done more. In the period of retrenchment of the early 1980s, it was all too easy to become comfortable with a booming city backed by substantial business support. There were few voices in city government for those excluded. Only after a period of turmoil in city politics—upsetting the comfortable applecart—did creative policies that might really make a difference move to the top of the city agenda.

Conclusions

The Bradley coalition in government is clearer to see in the previous chapter than in this one. Fairly consistently, the Bradley coalition promoted affirmative action, police accountability, and minority representation on commissions. But what is it in the economic arena? The coalition striving to place shopping centers in minority communities and preserve the coastline from oil drilling? Or the one energetically developing downtown while affordable housing languishes? Or the one proposing new policies to tax downtown business to pay for affordable housing and demanding that banks invest in minority communities? Or all of them?

When backed by federal resources, Bradley's coalition was economically progressive. When left without federal aid and with little public pressure, its leaders were supportive of the status quo, probusiness, and not very innovative. When pushed hard in the post–federal aid era, the regime was able to generate new internal creativity to solve problems.

Hegemony had bred serious economic problems. It had been too easy for the mayor and the council to build their campaign war chests and downtown buildings while problems festered. Political division, which weakened the regime's ability to reach such political goals as police accountability, played an essential and useful role in reconnecting the coalition to its original purpose of economic equality.

Numerous constraints limited the ability of the biracial regime to bring about fundamental economic change in Los Angeles. However, in political and social areas, the regime significantly increased the benefits available to racial minorities. These benefits were shared with white liberals, particularly in the area of political representation and decisionmaking. Latinos and Asian-Americans, despite representing secondary coalition partners, received significant benefits, especially through commissions and affirmative action. Business and labor received large economic benefits through the ambitious redevelopment program.

The biracial regime provided these benefits in a manner very different from that of the Yorty regime and much like that of Black mayoral regimes in cities with larger Black populations. In some highly visible areas, such as the police, the regime had greater difficulty imposing change than did Black mayors in such cities. In less visible areas, such as affirmative action, it made significant progress. In affordable housing, the regime was ineffective—although it showed considerable promise in its later years— while it was enormously successful in promoting downtown development.

A biracial regime with heavy white involvement had much the same goals and techniques as did coalitions more heavily dominated by large Black populations. In most areas, white liberals shared the goals of minority politics and acted as allies in seeking social change. In other areas, serious disagreements—particularly over the nature of growth and development— highlighted the class differences within the coalition.

At the public and symbolic level, much greater care had to be exercised by regime leaders than would have been necessary in a city with a larger Black population. Bradley was much less a "race mayor" than Black mayors in cities with larger Black populations, and therefore offered much less symbolic satisfaction to Los Angeles Blacks, while being very positively viewed by whites. But in policy terms, often behind the scenes, Bradley and his allies operated in a manner remarkably similar to that of most Black mayoral regimes.

The coalition in power expanded the power of elected officials over government. But this was a double-edged sword. It could help make the police accountable to minority communities, but it could also place redevelopment beyond the reach of democratic accountability. By the early 1990s, both progressives and conservatives feared a loss of public control over economic decisions made by elected officials.

ELEVEN

POLITICAL HEGEMONY: 1973–1985

THE REGIME demonstrated a high degree of stability during its first dozen years of power, through both its "progressive liberal" period and its "progrowth" period. Indeed, these years can be called the era of hegemony. The regime's political power rarely faced sustained challenge.

During the years of hegemony, a stable pattern developed in city, state, and federal elections. Indeed, the pattern had begun in 1964 and continues to this day. African-American voters were the most consistently liberal, and white, homeowning, non-Jewish areas in the northwestern San Fernando Valley were the most conservative. High-turnout, white liberal districts on the West Side, with their large Jewish and educated populations, differed substantially from white conservative areas. Latino areas offered increasing levels of racial liberalism but persistently low mobilization. The solid combination of minority (especially Black) and white liberal voting was the leading edge of the Bradley coalition's power base.

The patterns also appeared in statewide partisan politics. For instance, in Bradley's two gubernatorial races and in the 1984 and 1988 presidential elections, the Twelfth was the bedrock conservative district. The Fifth was on the other side.

In 1982, Bradley beat Deukmejian by more than twenty-eight thousand votes in the Fifth, winning 66.9 percent of the vote. Bradley's poorest showing, by far, was in the Twelfth, where he received only 39.9 percent of the vote. In 1986, Bradley won 56.5 percent of the vote in the Fifth, with a 12,689-vote edge, while he won only 31.5 percent in the Twelfth. The difference was twenty-nine percentage points in 1982, and twenty-seven points in 1986.

The Twelfth was fertile territory for Reagan's presidential campaigns. He won only 36.7 percent and 36.8 percent of the Fifth District's votes in 1980 and 1984, respectively, while the corresponding figures in the Twelfth were 60.8 percent and 65.4 percent. In both elections, the Twelfth was Reagan's best district in the city.

Soon after taking power, the regime made room for business and labor through a major downtown redevelopment program. Despite its liberalism, the Bradley regime operated much as did other Black mayoral regimes, focusing heavily on economic growth through business. The support of the business sector played a major role in protecting the regime's hegemony, because of its crucial role in campaign finance. It became next to impossible to defeat the minority-liberal-business coalition.

A network of liberal elected officials moved from insurgency to incumbency. With their high name recognition and campaign treasuries, they were close to unbeatable. Bradley, other citywide elected officials, and liberal council members rarely fought in public and enjoyed the insulation of successful insiders.

I will closely examine the four key council districts that have been discussed throughout this book: the white liberal Fifth, the Black Eighth, the white conservative Twelfth, and the Latino/moderate white Fourteenth. By 1973, they were relatively stable in district lines and provide excellent continuity. Once again, the reader is cautioned to remember that although the Fourteenth is 75 percent Latino, Latinos actually represent a smaller share of the electorate than of the population; Fourteenth District whites include many Republicans and conservatives. I have supplemented this council district material with information from the *Los Angeles Times* poll and private surveys conducted by Fairbank, Maullin, and Associates.

Mayoral Elections

During the dozen years after Bradley's first election, his position at city hall was virtually unassailable. He won three consecutive reelections with great ease, each time gaining a majority in the nonpartisan primary. In his 1985 reelection, Bradley set a city record by winning nearly 68 percent of the vote and all fifteen council districts (see Table 11.1).

But the Bradley vote varied widely throughout the city (see Table 11.2). His strongest base of support was in the Black community and among white liberals; his weakest base was among white conservatives. Latinos were substantially more pro-Bradley than white conservatives. Later polls found Latinos to be heavily Democratic and strongly pro-Bradley, probably closer to Jews than to non-Jewish whites (Fairbank, Maullin, and Associates,

TABLE 11.1
Bradley Vote and Opponent Vote,
1977, 1981, and 1985 (percent)

	Bradley Vote	*Opponent*	*Opponent Vote*
1977	59.4	Alan Robbins	28.1
1981	63.8	Sam Yorty	32.3
1985	67.6	John Ferraro	30.5

Source: City Clerk, Election Division.

TABLE 11.2

Bradley Vote in Four Key Council Districts, 1977, 1981, and 1985 (percent)

		1977	1981	1985
5th	White liberal/Jewish	61.7	68.7	71.6
8th	Black	90.2	91.5	92.4
12th	White conservative	40.3	44.3	49.4
14th	Latino/moderate white	54.8	52.8	58.3

Source: Same as Table 11.1.

various years). Even with a heavy white vote, the Latino Fourteenth kept its distance from the vote in the white conservative Twelfth.

Clearly, the Eighth and the Fifth have been the strongest pro-Bradley districts among the four, with the Twelfth the least so. No district has been more anti-Bradley than the conservative Twelfth. In both 1977 and 1981, it was the only district Bradley lost. Electoral stability can also be seen in the relative ranking of the Bradley vote in each district (see Table 11.3).

Meanwhile, the Fifth's support for Bradley continued to grow, as did its gap from the Twelfth. The white liberal base for Bradley, while not as high in percentage terms as the Black vote, had great importance because of its extremely high mobilization (see Table 11.4). The Bradley margin of votes in the Fifth District was an important contribution to Bradley's overall margin. This, of course, is a function of the high education and income in the Fifth. But it again suggests the great importance for Black Los Angeles of having formed an alliance with a highly mobilized, politically alert white liberal community. Otherwise, the votes of the Black community would have been wiped out by highly mobilized white conservatives.

How was Bradley so easily reelected? First, Bradley was able to deter the strongest possible opposition. Bradley's toughest opponents would have been either white liberals or conservative police chiefs. Testimony to Bradley's strength in the liberal community was the refusal of strong liberal candidates to run against him. The same was true of strong conservatives.

TABLE 11.3

Relative Ranking of Bradley Vote in Four Key Council Districts,
1977, 1981, and 1985

		1977	1981	1985
5th	White liberal/Jewish	4	4	5
8th	Black	1	1	1
12th	White conservative	15	15	15
14th	Latino/moderate white	11	11	12

Source: Same as Table 11.1.

TABLE 11.4

Bradley Margin in a White Liberal District
and a Black District, 1969–1985 (number of votes)

	5th–White Liberal	8th–Black	Difference
1969	1,866	47,901	46,035
1973	12,697	41,282	28,585
1977	16,930	29,565	12,635
1981	18,684	29,617	10,933
1985	19,379	35,932	16,553

Source: Analysis of data from City Clerk, Election Division.

In each campaign year, major candidates considered challenging Bradley. In each case, the police chief would consider a race, and one or more white liberal politicians would do the same. In 1980 Chief Daryl Gates began to explore a mayoral bid. Also mentioned were two liberal Jewish politicians, council member Zev Yaroslavsky and city controller Ira Reiner.

Gates was still thinking over his options when Reiner stunned city hall by announcing his decision to run instead for city attorney. He cited Bradley's large lead in the polls and said that fundraising to run against Bradley would be very difficult (*Los Angeles Times*, 18 November 1980). A *Los Angeles Times* reporter commented, "Bradley is, within the liberal community, unassailable" (ibid., 19 November 1980), and quoted a political professional as saying:

> Bradley is fantastically popular, there aren't enough conservatives in the city and with the possible exception of the Chicanos, he won't be able to crack any of the elements of the vast liberal coalition. And that's not to mention money. Where is he going to get the money, the big bucks? You need at least $1 million and the businessmen are solidly behind the mayor. (cited ibid.)

All these problems failed to deter Gates, and he asked the Police Commission for a three-month leave of absence to campaign. Gates even said that he wanted to avoid retiring so that if elected he could appoint a new Police Commission and thereby influence the choice of his successor (*Los Angeles Times*, 30 November 1980). Not surprisingly, the Bradley Police Commission refused to help Gates run against the mayor, and refused his request for a leave. Shortly thereafter, Gates decided not to run, and Bradley had a clear field.

The districts have displayed comparable behavior in other citywide races, although the differences between the Eighth and the other districts have been reduced because of the absence of a Black candidate. In that setting, the similarities between the Eighth and the Fifth become even clearer.

The most striking fact is that since 1973 every citywide candidate backed in the Black community has won election. To a varying degree, these victories have been aided by white liberal support. When the two communities vote in tandem, they cannot lose. When they have been only moderately in alliance, the greater unity of the Black community has prevailed. In two cases, candidates backed by the African-American community defeated candidates backed by the liberal, Jewish Waxman-Berman machine.

Table 11.5 displays the vote in four contested citywide races in 1981 and 1985. In 1981, James Kenneth Hahn was elected city controller, and Ira Reiner was chosen city attorney. In 1985, Hahn was elected city attorney and Rick Tuttle was elected controller.

The Black community clearly picked the winner in each election, and voted as a bloc, making African-Americans a crucial part of any citywide coalition. In Hahn's two races, he had a strong base in the Black community due to the name recognition of his father, Supervisor Kenneth Hahn, and Bradley's endorsement. In 1981, he also had a strong base on the West Side and with Latinos; but in 1985, facing West Side candidate Lisa Specht, he actually was weakest among white liberals. Yet he still won.

Tuttle's 1985 race had the standard lineup of Blacks and moderate support from white liberals and Latinos. Reiner's 1981 victory illustrated his strong appeal to minorities, white liberals, and even white conservatives. Reiner is rarely mentioned as a mayoral force today, but—at least until the fiasco in the Rodney King trial—he continued to be the one city politician other than Bradley with such a broad appeal. All the winning candidates were white liberals, indicating the citywide strength of the liberal coalition.

During the period of hegemony, Bradley enjoyed close support from a majority of the city council. Key Bradley allies Pat Russell and David Cunningham rose to high positions, with Russell becoming council president. Zev Yaroslavsky, a future opponent of the mayor, remained a firm Bradley supporter and Russell ally during this era.

TABLE 11.5

City Attorney and Controller Races in Four Key Council Districts, 1981 and 1985
(percent of vote)

		Hahn, 1981 City Controller	Reiner, 1981 City Attorney	Hahn, 1985 City Attorney	Tuttle, 1985 City Controller
5th	White liberal/Jewish	51.7	70.8	38.5	48.3
8th	Black	89.0	73.5	64.4	82.4
12th	White conservative	34.5	53.8	48.4	39.6
14th	Latino/moderate white	51.1	57.0	52.4	50.5

Source: Same as Table 11.1.

At the same time, newer members joined the council in place of older, conservative council members. Joy Picus won the Third District seat in 1977 in a major upset of council member Donald Lorenzen. Conservative stalwart Arthur Snyder of the Fourteenth left the council in 1985, to be replaced by Latino Richard Alatorre. By the mid-1980s, the council was younger, more diverse, and more liberal than it had been in the 1970s. Until the mid-1980s, Bradley's support on the council was so solid that there were few cases of a council member publicly speaking against the mayor, let alone opposing his policies.

Fiscal Measures — the Conservative Riposte

The Achilles' heel of this liberal hegemony was fiscal. While conservatives were clearly out of power, the ballot provided great scope for influence over the government. (The other conservative influence came through the political power of the police department.)

Public votes on revenue measures have been important aspects of Los Angeles government. In times of fiscal austerity local taxing authority is crucial to achieving social goals. Beginning with Proposition 13 in 1978, conservative voters took advantage of the fiscal ambivalence and low mobilization of minorities and white liberals on tax issues to limit the city government's ability to raise revenue. While they were unable to defeat the liberal coalition's candidates, they were more than able to tie the hands of the liberal government. On fiscal matters, they knew what they wanted, and generally won. The requirement of a two-thirds vote to increase taxes greatly aided the conservative cause.

Table 11.6 shows the vote on the famous tax-cutting measure Proposition 13 in 1978 and on two city measures to increase taxes to pay for policing, Proposition A in 1981 and Proposition 1 in 1985. While the pattern of

TABLE 11.6
Prospending Votes in Four Key Council Districts,
1978, 1981, and 1985 (percent)

		No on Proposition 13, 1978	Yes on Proposition A, 1981	Yes on Proposition 1, 1985
5th	White liberal/Jewish	45.7	49.5	49.0
8th	Black	77.9	50.5	59.2
12th	White conservative	20.0	29.9	25.2
14th	Latino/moderate white	48.8	36.9	37.2

Sources: County of Los Angeles, Registrar-Recorder; City Clerk, Election Division.

voting on these measures resembles that for candidates, there are important differences. The tax/revenue question made all the groups less liberal. With the exception of Proposition 13, however, there was a clear revenue alliance between Blacks and white liberals. The revenue aspect brought the two groups closer together, because it made Blacks less liberal in supporting expenditures.

The overwhelming opposition to taxes among white conservatives, even to support their well-loved LAPD, is striking. With its high turnout, and with fiscal ambivalence in the liberal Fifth District, the Twelfth District had its way on the main revenue measures of the era, thereby limiting the gains of minority incorporation at city hall. The prospending side lost all three times.

These results strongly indicate that while analysts often focus on how business at the elite level prevents the attainment of the economic goals of minority incorporation, an overlooked problem at the mass level may be the resistance of local voters to taxes. They also show that there is no unity on revenue among whites or minorities. If there is no effective constituency for local taxation, then there is not likely to be an easy political route to the redistributive programs that critics expect a progressive local regime to undertake.

Thus, with only a few exceptions, the basic liberal coalition in Los Angeles joined solid Black voting, the overwhelming share of the highly mobilized West Side, and a less mobilized share of the East Side against the conservative Valley. The pattern was repeated again and again, and in Bradley's case became stronger with each election. There is no denying the central importance to Los Angeles biracial politics of minority mobilization and unity combined with ideological division among whites.

Clearly, the coalition that brought the biracial regime to power in 1973 was not shaky. It became stronger as time went on, as Black and liberal votes (and Black and liberal money) became linked to business money. This coalition crossed class lines, and was not reduced in effectiveness by the obvious class contradictions. Class and minority affinities between Blacks and Latinos grew. Between 1973 and 1985, this liberal biracial coalition reigned supreme in city politics. As long as Blacks and white liberals stuck together, the coalition was unbeatable.

Pillars of Hegemony

During this hegemonic period, several elements held the coalition together and made its position unassailable. Put briefly, Bradley's coalition was a popular alliance at the mass level, managed by a tightly knit biracial organization at the elite level, and fueled by a powerful fundraising machine. In addition to shared ideology at the mass level, the three main pillars of hegemony were Bradley's style, campaign money, and the inner leadership of the Bradley faction.

Making the coalition operate in government depended partly on Bradley's personal style—a combination of "hidden hand" government and personal popularity. Tom Bradley avoids conflict. Levine (1974) has noted that conflict can be a means of generating policy in cities that elect Black mayors, but such an approach would be completely foreign to Bradley's coalition. This is not to say that conflict has not been useful to other Los Angeles mayors; the combative Sam Yorty served three straight terms. But both from personal preference and because of the political context, Bradley has taken the stance of consensus.

Robinson's (1976) psychological biography of Bradley assessed him as "active negative," highly devoted to work but not comfortable in personal interactions. Robinson suggested a virtual horror of personal conflict, dating back to early childhood. The same feature has been often noted by journalists making rare forays into the inner world of the Bradley administration.

While he avoids conflict, Bradley also values personal loyalty. In the service of personal loyalty, he will even risk conflict. Bradley's unwillingness to fire 1969 campaign aide Don Rothenberg after his earlier Communist Party membership had been revealed probably cost him many votes (Maullin 1971). His friend Frank Terry said, "I think Tom had one weakness; he has what I consider almost a blind loyalty to people. If he was convinced you were loyal to him, then he was loyal to you to the bitter end, regardless of what you did" (Terry interview).

Bradley's loyalty was tested in crises involving two of his closest political allies. When his long-time deputy Maurice Weiner was arrested on a morals charge in 1976, Bradley testified on his behalf in open court; Weiner subsequently resigned (Los Angeles Times, 12 February 1976). A few years later, Bradley's appointment of Warren Hollier as president of the Board of Public Works became an albatross when Hollier was investigated by the Los Angeles Times for abuse of power and financial irregularities, charges that eventually led to his resignation (Los Angeles Times, 26 November 1980).

Avoidance of conflict and placing a high value on personal loyalty combine with a workaholic pace to create the sort of environment that is highly stable, if often unimaginative. In political terms, this style helped prevent coalition erosion because the constant emphasis on consensus made disruption difficult to undertake. The emphasis on hard work is consistent with Bradley's own values, but had the further advantage of making potentially conflictual issues into technical ones, and draining the hot blood out of them. This is hardly an atmosphere for rhetoric and emotional issues.

Bradley works seven days a week, fifteen or sixteen hours a day. He is protected by rotating bodyguard-drivers, who have a hard time keeping up with his pace. He keeps a full schedule of community visits. His wife rarely sees him: he leaves the house very early and comes home very late at night.

At the same time, he operates at the private level to be a "helper" to a wide range of people. (The revelation of Bradley's private style of assistance became a major factor in the personal scandal that engulfed his mayoralty in 1989.) This comes as no surprise to those who have known Bradley all along. His friend Terry said:

> When he was at the police department, people would call him in the middle of the night and he helped people on a one-to-one basis. He has that kind of ability to give you a resource or check into it. When he says he'll check for something he'll do it and the next thing you know it's somehow done. And you haven't exchanged twenty words with him, but somehow he has responded. . . . And I think that's the key to his success. (Terry interview)

Bradley is not much of a public speaker, rarely coins a dynamic phrase, and often sits quietly in meetings. He does not inspire familiarity, but does generate a great deal of respect and deference from those who are close to him.

I spent a morning with Bradley and his staff on a visit to the African-American community. While the mayor sat in the front seat with his driver and quietly read the morning paper, I sat in the crowded back seat with his aides. Nobody interrupted the mayor's reading. When we went to a local grade school, he was greeted very warmly by students and faculty. We met with a group of Black reporters from newspapers and radio stations in a sort of informal press conference. While we ate breakfast, no one came up to chat with the mayor. All left him alone to eat in peace, quite unlike the usual position of a major politician. The questions were friendly and quite respectful; when asked about programs for South Central Los Angeles, Bradley mentioned his efforts to bring commerce and investment into the area. Throughout the day, I felt that Bradley was an important, respected figure but not someone to slap on the back; this distance has been both his strength and a weakness.

But he is a very active executive, with a style similar to Greenstein's (1982) analysis of President Dwight D. Eisenhower's "hidden hand" leadership. Until recent years, this covert style worked very well in a city where politics had low salience. Bradley's pattern has been to work behind the scenes through a network of people, allowing an issue to take shape and exerting his influence indirectly. When he debated councilman John Ferraro in 1985, for instance, Bradley claimed that he had nothing to do with the shift of police from the Valley to the inner city. Key staff people became his link to evolving issues, and somewhat mysteriously let the mayor's wishes be known. Of course, in the long tradition of Los Angeles reform politics, everybody then denied at length that any influence at all was being exerted.

When this strategy worked poorly, Bradley got caught between irreconcilable forces not amenable to his mediating influence. As council deference to Bradley declined, his "hidden hand" approach was harder to sustain. For example, several council members angrily disputed Bradley's statement in 1991 that he had had no involvement in the Police Commission's decision to place Police Chief Gates on leave. Bradley's style in dealing with the CRA behind the scenes left community groups suspicious and resentful.

Bradley's conciliatory style and behind-the-scenes approach has had its most beneficial effect in defusing intergroup conflict. The survival of coalitions depends as much on what leaders do not say as on what they do say. Mayor Ed Koch of New York City often felt that he had been given insufficient credit for progressive policies, but his publicly spoken words could turn difficult situations into disasters. It would be hard to find many cases during Bradley's tenure when his public statements made intergroup relations worse. Bradley's approach in times of conflict has been to call leaders and activists to private meetings to discuss their differences. Black community leaders and Korean-American storeowners found Bradley taking the same role when their difficulties reached serious levels in the last several years.

Bradley has always publicly denounced racism and anti-Semitism, even when this stance has caused him political problems. His record on fighting Black anti-Semitism has been very consistent, going back to his early years in politics, and was a substantial reason for his strong elite and mass ties to the Jewish community. For example he spoke out publicly in 1975 against the UN resolution condemning Zionism: "To decry Zionism as racist is an act of international hypocrisy. I firmly condemn the U.N. resolution" (*Los Angeles Times*, 8 November 1975).

In the broadest sense, a major resource of the coalition has been Bradley's popularity. This public appeal is the product of his style, and of the meaning attached to having a successful Black mayor. Bradley was well-placed to symbolize the dream of interracial harmony and to tie together the aspirations of minorities and liberal whites. He was able to act as a "bridge," and to help people feel good. Especially in his early years, Bradley's achievements inspired those who faced long odds, especially in the face of racism. The symbolism of Bradley's campaigns obviously appealed to many whites. In addition to the ideological reasons for supporting a minority candidate, Don Rothenberg described a more subtle dimension:

> Most whites in our society have very little contact with black people. Tom
> Bradley, welcomed into the heart, the home, the mind of a white person

becomes a meaningful experience for that individual. Indeed, a reason for supporting him is that he is black and this makes a white person feel good that he or she was able to overcome that obstacle and can feel clean. (Rothenberg interview)

Bradley's style helped hold his coalition together for many years and helped it survive, albeit in much diminished form, into the 1990s. It was a resource of great importance. But it was supplemented by a very practical advantage—campaign money.

Throughout his years at city hall, and even in his mayoral challenges in 1969 and 1973, Bradley has held the financial edge. To a remarkable degree for a minority candidate, he has managed to make money one of his key advantages. His Tenth District recall campaign raised more than $10,000 from the Black community, especially from doctors and lawyers. In his mayoral races, he raised a huge sum from the West Side Jewish community. In preserving his incumbency, Bradley became a major fundraiser among the business and Asian-American communities. The diversified portfolio of Black, Jewish, Asian-American, and business money has been a pillar of hegemony.

After 1973, Bradley made a transition from his Black and Jewish financial base to an alliance with business. Bradley's enthusiastic support for the reconstruction of downtown was obviously the key policy move in this shift. Maureen Kindel, a key Bradley fundraiser said: "I recall that [Bradley aide] Fran Savitch was designated to take me to lunch and to ask me if I would become finance director of the mayor's re-election effort [in 1977]. They knew that they had really raised their money from a rather narrowly-based coalition of liberal west side Jews and homeowner associations" (Kindel interview).

Kindel undertook "a sixteen-week fundraising effort which raised over a million dollars" (ibid.). She arranged for Bradley "to have breakfast with the downtown business community and luncheons with Republicans. In 1977 what we saw is a lot of support from the downtown business community which is mostly white and Republican" (ibid.). Kindel became a member of the Bradley inner circle and was eventually named to the top commission post in the city, president of the Board of Public Works.

Bradley was not the only one with a money advantage. His council allies became major fundraisers, increasing the already established power of developers and other big donors. Council war chests in the hundreds of thousands of dollars were not uncommon. As long as the mayor and council majority were on the same side, money operated as a means of maintaining coalition hegemony. Money also helped reduce accountability, however, by reducing competition. Hegemony bred neglect. Of course, when togetherness ceased, competing fundraising bases multiplied the conflicts that undermined the coalition.

While the shared ideology of the white liberal and minority communities helped lay the groundwork for the coalition, leadership has been of great importance. Leadership has been particularly crucial in maintaining links between African-Americans and Jews. Indeed, Black-Jewish conflict between 1977 and 1979 came close to disrupting the hegemony of the Los Angeles coalition—and was likely prevented from doing so largely by a leadership network associated with Bradley.

Bradley's 1973 election had surmounted the rise of the busing issue in 1970 and 1971, but the court battles continued until the late 1970s. A dramatic series of events then cast a pall over Black-Jewish relations. A Jewish assemblyman and foe of school busing, Alan Robbins, opposed Bradley for mayor in 1977. A Jewish member of the Board of Education, Howard Miller, was recalled in 1978 by a resurgent antibusing movement; its leader and eventual replacement for Miller on the school board was Roberta Weintraub. Weintraub joined with fellow Jewish antibusing activist Bobbie Fiedler on a divided board. Conflict arose immediately between the antibusing members and Black member Rita Walters; the perception grew among Blacks that the Jewish community was turning heavily to the right. Indeed, Jews in the San Fernando Valley were much more antibusing than the Jewish leadership; one liberal Jewish activist remembered: "[W]e had 100 percent of the Jewish leaders; they had the Jewish grass roots" (Plotkin interview).

During this divisive period, the well-known firing of UN Ambasssador Andrew Young took place. President Carter removed Young after the ambassador had met with a representative of the Palestine Liberation Organization (PLO) in violation of U.S. policy. Black-Jewish conflict arose nationwide, as many Blacks blamed Jews for Young's removal.

The Bradley forces managed to overcome these extraordinary and deeply threatening crises through an extension of Bradley's "hidden hand" style of leadership. The vehicle was a network of Black and Jewish community leaders, who met in private and reached a modus vivendi.

In 1977 Bradley had detailed two of his top aides, Bill Elkins and Ethel Narvid, Black and Jewish, respectively, to establish a dialogue among Black and Jewish leaders. The initial impetus was the busing controversy. A small group of leaders outside government began to meet. The Black leaders represented churches, labor organizations, and professionals. The Jewish leaders came from Jewish communal organizations, synagogues, and other community activities. The members on both sides were sophisticated in dealing with other communities, while also representing important interests of their own group.

The Jewish leaders were generally opposed to the Weintraub-Fiedler team on the Board of Education. The Black leaders had worked with the Jewish community in the past. Virtually all had been active in Bradley's campaigns and most knew one another.

By 1979, the group had become formalized into the Black-Jewish Leadership Coalition and had undertaken an array of joint projects. Members donated $2,500 each into a $50,000 seed fund for low-income housing in South Central Los Angeles, initiated a program to encourage Jewish employers to hire Black youths, and created a program bringing Black and Jewish youth together. In the spring of 1979, members of the group took a tour of Israel, spending two weeks together.

The group's activities extended the small-group trust that had been present in the biracial campaign to elect Bradley to the city council in 1963. Reading the files of one key group member, I noticed a high degree of interaction across racial lines on important issues (Giesberg papers). When Rita Walters, a Black member of the group, was elected to the Board of Education in 1979, the group celebrated. Her involvement with the coalition's Jewish members also meant that when she faced severe conflict with Weintraub and Fiedler, she could remember her more positive interaction with other Jewish leaders. When the Young firing occurred, the group had therefore not only been meeting for several years but had also traveled abroad together. The coalition therefore provided an excellent vehicle for dealing with the local fallout from the Young controversy.

Over a period of weeks, the members of the group met privately four times. The meetings were often extremely angry, particularly on the part of the Black members. It was generally understood that proceedings of the meetings were not to be leaked to the media. Bradley was not present, but Elkins and Narvid played key roles and the mayor's interest was clear (Giesberg interview).

In November the group held a press conference with Bradley to release a joint statement both on the Young incident and on Black-Jewish relations (*Los Angeles Times*, 30 November 1979). The statement attracted a great deal of public attention and favorable news coverage in the *Los Angeles Times* as well as in several Jewish and Black newspapers. The *Sentinel* was very positive in its coverage. There was some criticism from traditional parts of the Jewish community that the statement indicated that the Black members favored negotiations between Israel and the PLO, and there was substantial letter writing back and forth on the subject (Giesberg papers).

The public announcement and the model of closed-door discussion made Los Angeles unusual among cities during the Young controversy. There were bitter recriminations between Blacks and Jews in cities where there were few existing biracial groups backed by a popular Black mayor in a position to mediate.

As it turned out, both before and after the Young incident, the supposed Jewish turn to the right was evanescent. For example, in the 1977 mayoral race, Jewish antibusing candidate Robbins was clobbered in the Fifth District. In school board elections, the West Side-South Central coalition generally remained in place. But leadership ties were crucial in preventing a more severe shakeup in the coalition relationship.

Conclusions

The biracial regime between 1973 and 1985 achieved a high level of political stability. The key to this stability was the maintenance of a political alliance between Blacks and white liberals, slowly expanded to include Latinos, Asian-Americans, and the business sector. The strength of the regime on the Black South Side and the liberal West Side preempted some of the strongest political challengers to Bradley, and the availability of other citywide offices and congressional seats gave room for liberal electoral ambitions.

The alliance was built on shared political incorporation, giving leaders of both African-American and liberal communities a large stake in the maintenance of the regime. When business became a full partner, the leaders of the regime found that their incumbency was advanced by business campaign contributions. One of the most important pillars of the coalition was the ideological symbolism with which Bradley has been invested, both for Blacks and for white liberals.

Between 1973 and 1985, the coalition surmounted potential problems and continued to maintain its political stability. It even enlarged itself, gaining greater control in the council, and the Bradley faction within the Black community became a formidable force.

The original expectation of those who had studied Bradley's 1973 election—that the interracial coalition would be extremely unstable and unlikely to survive—was obviously not met in reality. But a broader look at historical trends indicates that while the Black-liberal relationship was stronger than many expected, it was also subject to strains.

Hegemony had its costs. What helped maintain social peace and advance a progressive agenda also fostered secretive economic decisions. Those who were most friendly to the coalition in its first decade became much more suspicious of the closed circle of economic hegemony.

From 1985 on, the biracial coalition entered a more challenging and problematic phase. The pillars of hegemony began to shake. A split grew between the white liberal and Black communities. The new phase can help explain some of the factors likely to threaten biracial coalitions. While the

Black-liberal alliance was stronger than most had presumed, it was hardly unshakeable.

When conflicts of interest and ideology began to separate white liberals from racial minorities in the mid-1980s, the political strength of the coalition was reduced. The 1989 mayoral election was the first serious challenge to Bradley, and Blacks and Latinos began to draw closer together. The politics of class reduced the strength of a cross-class biracial coalition. Thus, over the long sweep of time, the contradictions within the regime began to tell—but only after a remarkable period of political hegemony.

TWELVE

THE BREAKDOWN OF CONSENSUS: 1985–1990

I N APRIL 1985, Tom Bradley earned his most overpowering political victory, winning reelection to a fourth term with a record 68 percent of the city vote. He swept all fifteen council districts. The lone holdout in 1977 and 1981—the northwestern Valley Twelfth District—reported a Bradley victory for the first time. The electoral fortunes of the Bradley coalition appeared assured, with no clouds on the horizon.

And yet, as often happens with landslide victories, the high point of electoral success was also a crest. Beyond it lay the seeds of downturn and perhaps downfall. The signs had begun to accumulate before the 1985 election and long before a serious Bradley financial scandal threatened the regime. As economic alignments shifted, ideological alliances became frayed.

There had always been the potential for conflict between minority and white liberal constituencies in Los Angeles. While ideology provided an important common bond, differences of class interest and personal ambition started to crystallize after 1985. The threads of the coalition's balancing act—an ideological interracial alliance and an economic coalition between minority leaders and downtown business—began to unravel.

Black-Liberal Conflict

One of the major pillars of the regime's hegemony had been its ability to hold the white liberal and business sectors in the same house. Eisinger (1983) has argued that keeping business and the white middle class together has been very difficult for most Black mayors. Like Bradley, white liberal and minority politicians consistently tapped business for campaign contributions. But their constituents were becoming increasingly wary of the power of developers to affect their daily lives.

While many cities were losing population, Los Angeles was booming. The growth strategy had paid off. The city entered 1980 with a little under three million people, and added another four hundred thousand residents by the 1990 census. The continuing effects of Proposition 13 and federal aid cutbacks meant that the city had fewer resources to provide amenities for a growing city. City hall became a major focus of public distress.

Until the early 1980s, the West Side liberal communities were largely untouched by the boom in commercial construction set off by the regime's downtown redevelopment program. It was more than possible for Bradley and his allies to be for both a clean coastline and a growing downtown in such a physically expansive city. But as growth moved out from downtown into other parts of the city, commercial development became first an irritant, and then a crisis. The lack of affordable housing, skyrocketing rents, and tightening traffic all were blamed on unrestrained commercial growth. West Side areas were highly sensitive to the change, particularly the neighborhoods of Westchester and Westwood.

The basis for a severe conflict between the liberal middle class and the business sector had begun to form. The regime's strong ties to both sectors meant political trouble. This conflict in turn had an influence on conflicts between liberal middle-class and minority communities. It undermined the comfortable progrowth positions held by liberal and minority city council members.

Bradley's progrowth position was not unpopular in the Black and Latino communities, if it meant bringing shopping centers and new jobs into these underdeveloped areas. Such commercial developments as the Baldwin Hills Shopping Center were among the few real economic benefits (other than city jobs) that Bradley could offer his minority constituency as long as cutbacks in state and federal funds continued. But in minority areas there was also increasing resentment at feeling abandoned by downtown in the face of drugs and crime. Many wondered if the benefits of redevelopment were trickling down.

The potential conflict at the core of the coalition also involved a shift in the structure of group ambitions. The Bradley coalition had brought white liberals to the head table at city hall. But liberal power had not yet crested. Voter registration and campaign donations continued to be very high on the liberal West Side. National Democratic candidates came to West Los Angeles to raise funds. Liberal candidates were literally lined up to run for various offices. Guerra (1987) found that while the 1960s and 1970s were the era of the Black candidate, the 1980s were the period of Jewish assertion (see also Willens 1980).

The roots of the conflict of ambitions went back to Bradley's narrow loss in the gubernatorial race of 1982. Had Bradley won, white liberal politicians would have had the opportunity to move up, stengthening the coalition's morale. Fifth District councilman Zev Yaroslavsky, for example, intended to run for mayor if Bradley had been elected governor.

At the elite level, an important element in this assertion was the liberal machine run by congressmen Henry Waxman and Howard Berman. They slated other Jewish liberal candidates for legislative and congressional offices, relying heavily on the technological skills of Berman's brother, Michael, and his partner, Carl D'Agostino. In time, they came to dominate state legislative and congressional offices with West Side constituencies.

The Waxman-Berman group generally stayed in the background of Los Angeles city politics. West Side Jews were so deeply tied to the Bradley coalition that there would have been no credible base for attacking the Bradley regime. As reformers themselves, Waxman and Berman had been on the same side as the Bradley people during the bitter intraparty fight against the party "regulars" headed by Jesse Unruh and Mervyn Dymally. They had helped Bradley in his mayoral races as far back as 1969. In 1975, they had joined the Bradley forces in unsuccessfully backing Frances Savitch for the Fifth District council seat won by insurgent Zev Yaroslavsky.

In 1985 Bradley made two decisions that built a bridge between Yaroslavsky's grass-roots base and the more affluent West Side communities. The mayor ended his long-standing opposition to Occidental Petroleum Corporation's plan to drill for oil in the Pacific Palisades. The oil-drilling decision helped make Bradley and his allies the focus of resentment over the city's declining "quality of life." Many West Siders, especially on the coast, felt deeply betrayed by Bradley. It was no longer possible for Bradley to be prodevelopment downtown and proenvironment on the coastline; his two worlds collided.

Also in 1985, Bradley found himself caught between his Jewish and Black allies when Nation of Islam leader Louis Farrakhan came to Los Angeles. Ordinarily Bradley would have immediately denounced Farrakhan's well-known anti-Semitic views. A group of Black leaders asked Bradley to avoid such an early condemnation, promising that they would get Farrakhan to tone himself down. The delay devastated and angered many Los Angeles Jews, even when Bradley condemned Farrakhan after his public address attacked Jews (*Los Angeles Times*, 13 September, 16 September 1985).

The Farrakhan controversy indicated that the Black community itself had a growing presence of elite forces ready to loosen the alliance and go it alone. With the oil-drilling decision and the Farrakhan confrontation, a similar sense of cutting loose was developing on the West Side. When Black and Jewish leaders came together during the Farrakhan incident, there was little common ground and much animosity (Giesberg interview).

By 1985 the Waxman-Berman group had begun to show great interest in becoming an independent force in city politics. The oil-drilling and Farrakhan decisions provided a wedge, and Bradley's problems provided a political opportunity. Just as a machine needs new patronage jobs, a slating combine needs new offices. Los Angeles's city hall fit the bill. Citing Bradley's oil-drilling decision, Waxman and Berman withheld their endorsement of Bradley's mayoral reelection until the last minute. They unsuccessfully backed Lisa Specht for city attorney against Bradley's choice, James K. Hahn.

Waxman and Berman were acting in their pattern of "hostile takeovers," last seen in their bitter, failed 1979 assembly speakership battle against Leo McCarthy. Their approach had been to be the first to take on a vulnerable incumbent on the theory that if troubles persist, other challengers will emerge (Littwin 1976; Weiss 1985). Their chief local ally became Zev Yaroslavsky.

Yaroslavsky and the Waxman-Berman group strongly endorsed Gary Hart in the 1984 Democratic presidential primary. Bradley endorsed Walter Mondale. In 1985, Waxman and Berman backed Lisa Specht for city attorney against James Hahn, the candidate endorsed by Bradley. The Hart and Specht candidacies indicated some of the emerging dynamics in Black-white liberal politics.

In the 1984 Democratic presidential primary, Los Angeles Democrats (who would be central to any white liberal mayoral challenge) divided among Walter Mondale, Gary Hart, and Jesse Jackson. At the time, the Mondale-Hart split was taken as emblematic of the emerging generational conflict in the Los Angeles coalition (*Los Angeles Times*, 11 March 1984). In the final vote, it became clear that, while appealing, Hart—and by implication Yaroslavsky—had some citywide limitations.

An analysis of the 1984 primary returns reveals that Mondale won a solid citywide victory, with 133,633 votes (32.8 percent); Hart was second with 99,969 votes (24.5 percent), followed by Jackson with 94,865 votes (23.3 percent). These returns present some problems for research. The 1984 California Democratic primary in California was conducted by congressional district. Each candidate ran a slate of delegates. In order to assess votes, I took the county's report of delegate votes by council district. For each congressional district falling within the council district, I took the average vote for delegates on each candidate's slate to be the representation of the candidate's vote.

The Bradley-style candidate (Mondale) running against a Yaroslavsky-style candidate with strong appeal on the West Side (Hart) held his own both there and in the Black community against Jackson (see Table 12.1). Because this was a Democratic primary, the Latino influence on the Fourteenth District outcome was probably higher than it would have been in a nonpartisan election.

TABLE 12.1
Democratic Presidential Primary Vote in Three Key Council Districts, 1984 (percent)

		Mondale	*Hart*	*Jackson*
5th	White liberal/Jewish	37.5	33.7	12.5
8th	Black	18.7	2.3	51.6
14th	Latino/moderate white	37.2	22.6	11.6

Source: Analysis of data from County of Los Angeles, Registrar-Recorder.

Mondale beat Hart in all three areas, and beat both Jackson and Hart in the liberal Jewish and Latino communities. Hart had absolutely no appeal in the Black community; in fact, Jesse Jackson did better in the liberal Jewish Fifth than Hart did in the Black Eighth! If the analogy held, Yaroslavsky would be in a weak position among Democrats against Bradley, who would monopolize the Black community and surely do better in Yaroslavsky's own area than Jesse Jackson had. Yaroslavsky would also have been vulnerable to a Mondale-type white candidate with some appeal on the West Side and a strong (or by comparison, any) minority base.

Looked at by congressional districts, a similar pattern emerges. Of Jackson's votes, 62 percent came from two Black districts, the Twenty-Eighth and Twenty-Ninth, and 66 percent of Hart's votes came from West Side districts represented by Waxman, Berman, and liberal Anthony Beilenson. On the other hand, Mondale was more diversified. Half of his votes came from the West Side districts and another 19.5 percent from the Black districts.

The results show the great difficulty of a "West Side only" political movement. Los Angeles white liberals are more powerful as part of a progressive alliance than on their own. Of course, Jesse Jackson's totals reveal the equally poor prospects for a "Blacks only" campaign that alienates the West Side. Mondale's campaign indicates the strength of a crossover candidacy that joins both white liberals and minorities.

In 1985 Yaroslavsky and the Waxman-Berman forces backed Lisa Specht against James K. Hahn for city attorney. The Black-backed candidate, Hahn, gained a huge edge in South Central Los Angeles, and did well on the West Side. Specht, confined largely to a West Side base, was boxed in.

Hahn won the election in the primary, with 50.2 percent to Specht's 39.6 percent. (With his majority, he avoided a runoff.) The results once again revealed the isolation of the liberal West Side when separated from its minority allies. Even the conservative Twelfth District in the northwestern Valley voted for the Bradley candidate over the West Side liberal candidate (see Table 12.2)—certainly a sobering portent for a Yaroslavsky mayoral bid. There was no evidence of a cross-ideology white solidarity movement linking the Valley and the West Side.

The united power of the Black community had been demonstrated once again. Of Hahn's 50,621 vote margin over Specht, nearly 40,000 came from the five districts with the largest Black populations. Of the fifteen council districts, Hahn won ten handily and broke even in three. The only two districts that Specht solidly won were the West Side Fifth and Eleventh.

By the mid-1980s the meaning of Los Angeles liberalism had become seriously muddled. In the period of challenge to Los Angeles conservatism, Blacks and white liberals had both felt the sting of political exclusion. In the period of hegemony, they both enjoyed the fruits of power. But economic

TABLE 12.2
City Attorney Primary Vote in Four Key Council Districts, 1985

		Hahn (%)	Specht (%)	Hahn Margin (N)
5th	White liberal/Jewish	38.5	53.5	−5,625
8th	Black	64.4	27.0	13,728
12th	White conservative	48.4	42.5	1,963
14th	Latino/moderate white	52.4	36.6	2,594

Source: City Clerk, Election Division.

issues crosscut the simple ideological confrontation between Left and Right. Both the Bradley coalition and its critics were damaged by the loss of ideological clarity.

The antibusiness position that comprised a main line of criticism against the regime could be interpreted either as a progressive assault on private privilege or as resistance by middle-class people to economic growth benefiting the poor and minority neighborhoods. Under pressure, Bradley began to attack the slow-growth position as elitist (Boyarsky 1988). For the first time, Bradley was acting to undermine a cross-racial, cross-class coalition on a key issue.

Oddly, a new coalition linking slow-growth West Siders and minority neighborhoods, upset for different reasons by the progrowth policies of the regime, could have been a severe threat to Bradley. In that sense, conflict between the two groups for a time served the survival interests of a regime constructed on cooperation between the two.

The increasing demands of Asian-Americans and Latinos for political power further complicated the picture. Even as Blacks and white liberals had their conflicts with each other, the very strength of that core relationship tended to raise ambivalence among Latinos and Asian-Americans. They wondered if their own roles in the regime were sufficient. This was especially true of Latinos, who, unlike Asian-Americans, did not have the resources to participate behind the scenes as campaign donors to the regime. There appeared to be some room to work things out; private polling showed that Asian-Americans and Latinos remained among the most consistent of pro-Bradley groups (Fairbank, Maullin, and Associates, various years).

During 1985 and 1986, Bradley and his council allies faced the issue of council reapportionment under the threat of lawsuits by Latinos. The need to maintain existing coalition strength led one way; accommodating Latinos, another, and accommodating Asian-Americans, yet another. Finally Bradley intervened to veto a council plan that would have eliminated the only Asian-American council member. Only the sudden death of a sitting council member, Howard Finn, allowed the problem to be resolved to the satisfaction of all (Regalado 1988b). By 1986, the fifteen-member council had two Latino members and one Asian-American.

In 1986, Bradley was badly defeated in a second try for governor. Some saw in the returns further evidence of the fracturing of his local coalition (*Los Angeles Times*, 21 December 1986), noting that his vote totals had declined in Black and Jewish neighborhoods. The greater problem was that, unlike his narrow 1982 defeat, his landslide loss made him seem politically vulnerable to city hall politicians. In 1986 city voters overwhelmingly passed Proposition U, an initiative to limit the city's growth championed by West Side council members Zev Yaroslavsky and Marvin Braude. The widely popular measure passed in minority communities as well as on the West Side.

In 1987, Bradley suffered two crushing council election defeats. Ruth Galanter upset Bradley's ally Pat Russell in a Sixth District election that pitted slow-growth white West Siders against midcity Black residents. In a contest between Black candidates, Nate Holden badly beat Bradley's friend and endorsed candidate Homer Broome in Bradley's own Tenth District by highlighting the city's neglect of services. Most important, Yaroslavsky pursued a serious mayoral challenge, backed by the Waxman-Berman machine. Unlike previous contenders (including himself), Yaroslavsky showed little inclination to pull out.

Before each mayoral election, strong opponents scouted out the chances of beating Bradley. At various times since 1973, district attorney Ira Reiner, Yaroslavsky, police chief Daryl Gates, and others have conducted exploratory searches. Each backed down in the face of Bradley's popularity and fundraising power. Therefore, what was most remarkable about the 1989 preelection was how close a strong candidate came to running against Bradley.

These electoral and organizational trends cast in sharp relief the challenges faced by the Bradley regime in the late 1980s. For the first time since Jesse Unruh ran against Bradley in the 1973 primary, a mayoral challenge was sustained by a white liberal politician, the council member from the Fifth District. This candidacy had the potential to shear middle-class liberals (especially Jews) from racial minorities. There seemed to be a genuine crisis at the heart of the biracial coalition. The stage was set for the 1989 mayoral election.

The Mayoral Campaign

The preelection competition lasted nearly two years between Bradley and his most vocal opponent, Yaroslavsky—from the 1987 council elections until Yaroslavsky's decision not to run against Bradley in January 1989. In the formal election, Bradley faced two less well known opponents, Black city councilman Nate Holden and former county supervisor Baxter Ward. In April 1989 Bradley narrowly won the nonpartisan primary, with 52 percent of the vote.

By 1987 Yaroslavsky had emerged as Bradley's chief critic. As chairman of key council committees, Yaroslavsky criticized the mayor's budget and allocation of police positions. He was available to the increasingly active local media to provide critical comments about Bradley. Local reporters were delighted to finally have a "horse race" at city hall, and sought out Yaroslavsky after each Bradley statement or decision.

Yaroslavsky's challenge seemed credible because he was able to keep up with Bradley's fundraising. No one had ever outspent Bradley in a mayoral race, not even Sam Yorty, the incumbent. But Bradley was struggling to keep up with Yaroslavsky. By the end of 1987, Yaroslavsky had more cash on hand than did Bradley, who was still retiring his debt from the gubernatorial race; the councilman had $801,726 to Bradley's $552,314 (*Los Angeles Times*, 3 February 1988). Eight months later, each candidate had more than $1.1 million (*Los Angeles Times*, 8 September 1988). For the next several months, the candidates' campaign finance reports were closely watched to see who was ahead.

In August 1988, the Yaroslavsky campaign suffered a major blow with the leak to the press of a devastating memo written for Yaroslavsky by consultant Michael Berman, disparaging Blacks, Jews, and many other groups and individuals (*Los Angeles Times*, 9 August 1988). The privately expressed fears of Jewish leaders that a Bradley-Yaroslavsky contest would damage Black-Jewish relations developed greater strength.

The Bradley administration struggled for quite a while in the face of an unaccustomed level of criticism from a liberal West Side councilman. In time, however, Bradley and deputy mayor Michael Gage responded by reinvigorating the mayor's office, and incorporating environmental groups into city policy. In one key turning point, the mayor intervened in a Westwood development on the side of environmental groups, leaving Yaroslavsky in the progrowth position in his own council district (*Los Angeles Times*, 23 December 1988).

After a year of pushing Bradley, Yaroslavsky's own polls showed that he had barely made a dent against the mayor. On January 5, 1989, he announced that he would instead run for reelection to his own council seat. Yaroslavsky indicated that he could not surmount Bradley's popularity.

A private poll (Fairbank, Maullin, and Associates 1989) found Bradley well ahead of Yaroslavsky (57 percent to 23 percent). Yaroslavsky's only bases of support were in the Jewish community, where he trailed Bradley 33 percent to 39 percent, and among Republicans, where he trailed 30 percent to 47 percent. Like Lisa Specht, Yaroslavsky had his core support in coastal and West Side areas, while Bradley was strong all over. Indeed, by council district, Bradley was beating Yaroslavsky with a majority everywhere except in the white liberal areas—the Fifth, Eleventh, and Thirteenth districts.

Over the long haul, the difficulty of Yaroslavsky's position became clear. His own record of support for the development of Westwood would have placed him in a difficult spot. Like a number of liberal politicians, he had been strongly progrowth for years, while taking massive contributions from developers. It was hard for Yaroslavsky to run as an antigrowth populist while facing a neighborhood revolt against him in Westwood. In fact, when he decided not to face Bradley, he encountered his first serious challenge for his own seat since his first election from a slow-growth advocate.

Coming out of the white constituency most supportive of Bradley, Yaroslavsky was extremely weak in minority areas. He would have had to destroy Bradley on the West Side by painting him as unprogressive, and then win over the conservative whites in the Valley. Yaroslavsky, not known or trusted in minority neighborhoods, could not tie together the slow-growth white West Side and the minority groups for whom growth meant jobs.

Bradley could have run to Yaroslavsky's right in the Valley, as Hahn did against Specht in 1985. A larger concern for progressives might be that a Black-liberal mayoral contest would cede an unusually large role to conservatives as the possible balance of power. The *Los Angeles Times* found a similar structural impediment to a West Side–led coalition in their examination of the November 1988 election returns: on oil drilling and cigarette taxes, white liberal and minority districts diverged, indicating difficulties for Yaroslavsky's approach (*Los Angeles Times*, 20 November 1988).

The broader problem for Yaroslavsky was that Bradley, like Mondale and Hahn, had access to the key formula for progressive power in Los Angeles—interracial politics. With a solid base in the African-American community and a strong share on the West Side and among Latinos, such candidates start out way ahead of everybody else. And it is difficult for a West Side white liberal to make the case to Valley conservatives (already angry that political power has shifted from them to the West Side) that a West Side–led change at city hall would be desirable.

One way for Yaroslavsky to win would have been to be unpredictable—to embody maverick populism and to attack the regime as the establishment. Yaroslavsky had won his council seat in 1975 with just such a campaign. Had the Bradley scandal arisen earlier, he might have been able to pull it off. But by now Yaroslavsky was himself part of the establishment and a member of a West Side political machine in nonpartisan Los Angeles.

Had Yaroslavsky actually entered the race, it would have created major complications for the biracial coalition even if Bradley won. Yaroslavsky would be asking his constituency in the Fifth District to repudiate the politician they had consistently and enthusiastically backed for many years. It would have been essential to his strategy to drive a stake into the heart of the biracial coalition, since Bradley's interracial symbolism was one of his greatest assets on the West Side. Yaroslavsky's candidacy would have threatened the existence of coalition politics (especially between Blacks and Jews). Activists in both the Black and Jewish communities were concerned. As early as August, an "Alliance of Black and Jewish Clergy" condemned the Berman memo, and other community leaders were undoubtedly ready to get involved. Indeed, Yaroslavsky's decision not to run was itself a crucial elite decision with important coalition implications.

With the withdrawal of Yaroslavsky, it seemed that all the drama had been drained out of the 1989 election. Bradley had survived his toughest challenge, and declarations of the end of his regime seemed to have been premature. His two best-known opponents in the primary were cash-poor mavericks Nate Holden and Baxter Ward. It looked like a cakewalk. By March, Bradley had over $1 million on hand; Holden had $67,252, and Ward had followed his longtime practice of accepting no campaign contributions (*Los Angeles Times*, 6 April 1989). By the time the campaign was over, Bradley had spent over $2.6 million, while Holden had spent only $226,723 (*Los Angeles Times*, 3 August 1989).

Bradley campaigned very little, and expended most of his funds at the end. Meanwhile, Holden and Ward vigorously attacked him. Holden showed particular ability to use the media to highlight the street-level shortcomings of the regime. Near the end of the campaign, a Bradley financial scandal emerged, tarnishing Bradley's personal image for the first time. With Yaroslavsky out of the race, voters could send Bradley a message without removing him from office. The combination of barely visible storm signals and Bradley's quiet campaign created the conditions for an upset.

In the final week, Bradley's forces sensed trouble with the arrival of a poll showing him with only a bare majority. To fall below that level would force him into a runoff, where anything could happen. But the normal strategy of Black mobilization was complicated by Holden's presence. For the first time since Unruh ran in the 1973 primary, the Bradley forces could not consider every Black vote a Bradley vote.

Private polling (Fairbank, Maullin, and Associates, 1989) showed Bradley with only 54 percent of the vote. The slowly emerging scandal was hurting him with two groups: Jews and white Republicans. His minority support was still quite strong, although sentiment that it was "time for a change" was surprisingly widespread. One-quarter of Blacks, more than one-third of Latinos, and nearly one-half of Jews felt that way. There were definite signs of softness in Bradley's base as election day neared.

When the returns came in, Bradley had narrowly won reelection, with the lowest turnout in the city's history. Fewer than 20 percent of the voters had come to the polls. Holden had indeed cut into Bradley's base in the Black community, and Ward and Holden together had hurt him in white and Latino areas. The overall results are displayed in Table 12.3. The three main candidates won over 95 percent of the votes cast for mayor. Both Holden and Ward obtained significant shares of the vote. Together, they made a formidable combination, winning over 43 percent of the votes cast.

Table 12.4 shows the vote by key council district. Both Ward and Holden did reasonably well throughout the city, although Ward showed absolutely no strength in the Black community, receiving only 308 and 333 votes, respectively, in the Eighth and Ninth council districts. The strongest area for both opposition candidates was the same: the conservative San Fernando Valley. Both Holden and Ward received their highest totals in the Second, Third, and Twelfth districts—the white Valley districts. Holden benefited from strong police backing; both the police union and former chief Ed Davis supported him.

Because neither Ward nor Holden enjoyed the general recognition of Bradley and other city leaders, it seems wise to combine their votes into an "anti-Bradley vote." This has been done in Table 12.4, next-to-the-last column. In the last column, I have indicated Bradley's vote margin over the sum total of Ward and Holden. With 95 percent of the votes coming from these three candidates, the margin over *both* opponents was the key to getting Bradley over 50 percent.

Seen in this way, the election seems quite close, and important differences among districts emerge. Bradley won seven districts by substantial margins, lost three by substantial margins, and broke even (less than one thousand votes either way) in five districts. Given the private polling results before the election, it seems unlikely that a bigger turnout would have made much difference.

Of the seven districts Bradley won, five were the districts with the largest African-American populations. The other two had white liberal

TABLE 12.3
Mayoral Primary Vote, 1989

	N	%
Bradley	165,599	51.9
Holden	89,184	27.9
Ward	48,923	15.3
Holden + Ward	138,108	43.2
Total	303,706	95.1
Total vote	319,088	

Source: Same as Table 12.2.

TABLE 12.4
Mayoral Election Vote in Four Key Council Districts, 1989

		Total Votes (N)	Bradley (%)	Holden (%)	Ward (%)	Holden + Ward (%)	Margin (N)
5th	White liberal/Jewish	39,739	51.8	25.4	13.9	39.3	4,949
8th	Black	19,064	73.2	17.0	1.6	18.6	10,407
12th	White conservative	29,466	39.1	32.9	19.6	52.5	−3,930
14th	Latino/moderate white	13,219	45.5	24.9	17.7	42.6	372

Source: Same as Table 12.2.

majorities—the West Side Fifth District and the Hollywood Thirteenth. Only in the Fifth did Bradley exceed 50 percent of the vote among districts with white majorities. The three districts Bradley lost were in the Valley and were overwhelmingly white. The break-even districts included the two Latino districts, the First and the Fourteenth; one Latino-white Valley district, the Seventh; the West Side Eleventh, and the midcity Fourth.

Thus the core of Bradley's narrow victory seemed to rest on the original base of his coalition—Blacks and white liberals—in opposition to the Valley conservatives. Latinos were somewhere in the middle, and had low mobilization. Private polling showed that Latinos represented only 6 percent of registered voters (Fairbank, Maullin, and Associates 1989). In terms of the coalition's history, nothing could be more familiar.

The 1989 results take on added meaning when they are viewed in historical perspective. Bradley won four straight primary reelections for mayor. In 1977, 1981, and 1985 he defeated one main challenger each time, whereas in 1989 he faced two. I will compare the 1989 results to these three previous elections with reference to the four key council districts. Table 12.5 displays the vote for Bradley in mayoral primaries in the four districts. Obviously, Bradley's 1989 showing was weaker in all four areas, after a long period of steady increases in his vote. The decline appeared to be across the board.

TABLE 12.5
Bradley Primary Vote in Four Key Council Districts, 1977–1989 (percent)

		1977	1981	1985	1989
5th	White liberal/Jewish	61.7	68.7	73.7	51.8
8th	Black	90.2	91.5	96.6	73.2
12th	White conservative	40.3	44.3	50.3	39.1
14th	Latino/moderate white	54.8	52.8	60.2	45.5

Source: Same as Table 12.2.

Table 12.5 indicates percentage support, but does not address the level of effective backing Bradley received from each district. Margin is a useful index here because it combines percentage support and votes cast. Table 12.6 indicates Bradley's vote margin in each election. Table 12.6 reveals the consistency of Black political unity behind Bradley over four elections, as well as the solidly mobilized base in the liberal Jewish area. Given the low turnout in 1989, white conservatives had considerable clout against Bradley, and Latino support for the mayor was muted by low mobilization. But the table also indicates that in 1989 the strength of Bradley's base fell short of that in previous elections, and that the effective conservative surge was relatively stronger.

The next two tables explore the structure of Bradley's base. How do the various elements of the coalition compare to one another over time? Have their positions changed relative to one another? Tables 12.7 and 12.8 rank the four council districts on Bradley vote and Bradley margins in the four primary elections. The results indicate strong stability, even as the coalition was being shaken.

In all four elections, the liberal 5th district was the most important Bradley base among districts with white majorities. With its high turnout, the value of the margin Bradley gained in the 5th district placed it behind only the main Black districts (8, 9, and 10) in three of the four elections. And this included the 1989 race, in which Black-liberal conflicts had emerged as threats to the coalition.

One of the great ironies of the 1989 mayoral election is that Bradley may have won his majority because Yaroslavsky faced an unusually strong challenge for his own council seat. Against Laura Lake, a slow-growth candidate with appeal in Westwood, Yaroslavsky won only 62.7% of the vote. With his enormous district popularity, this was quite a surprise. Private polling showed him vulnerable in the area of developer campaign contributions (Fairbank, Maullin, and Associates 1988).

TABLE 12.6

Bradley Margin in Mayoral Primary in Four Key Council Districts, 1977–1989 (number of votes)

		1977[a]	1981[a]	1985[a]	1989[b]
5th	White liberal/Jewish	16,930	18,684	19,379	4,949
8th	Black	29,565	29,617	35,932	10,407
12th	White conservative	−1,183	−1,755	721	−3,930
14th	Latino/moderate white	4,549	2,391	3,933	372

Source: Analysis of data from City Clerk, Election Division.

[a]Margin against main challenger.

[b]Margin against two main challengers combined.

TABLE 12.7

Ranking of Bradley Percentage in Four Key Council Districts, 1977–1989

		1977	1981	1985	1989
5th	White liberal/Jewish	5	5	5	5
8th	Black	1	1	1	1
12th	White conservative	15	15	15	15
14th	Latino/moderate white	8	10	9	9

Source: City Clerk, Election Division.

The Lake-Yaroslavsky race increased the already high turnout characteristic of the Fifth District (see Table 12.9). Just under forty thousand voters came to the polls, ten thousand more than in the conservative Twelfth District, more than twice as many as voted in the Black Eighth District, and three times the total in the Latino Fourteenth District.

Despite all the strains in the coalition, Bradley's enduring strength in the Fifth District combined with strong Black support to save him from an unpredictable runoff. The 1989 Los Angeles mayoral primary revealed a sharp decline in the strength of the Bradley coalition, but also indicated remarkable stability in the structure of the coalition. The engine was not running as well as before, but it was pushing the same car.

The Bradley regime had lived to fight another day. This was a dicey time, in which an upset was in the air. Had the financial scandal hit with full force in early 1989, Bradley might have been forced into a runoff if he had been running against both a strong liberal and a strong conservative. The *Los Angeles Times* poll concluded that had Yaroslavsky run, he could have forced Bradley into a runoff (*Los Angeles Times*, 16 April 1989).

The Yaroslavsky challenge, even though unconsummated, opened up the Bradley administration to new directions in city policy by breaking up the long era of noncompetitive political hegemony enjoyed by the regime. Hegemony had bred neglect, and had stifled creativity. The regime had made the transition from its growth program to policies that offered improvement in the basic quality of life. It had been led to accommodate new

TABLE 12.8

Ranking of Bradley Margin in Four Key Council Districts, 1977–1989

		1977	1981	1985	1989
5th	White liberal/Jewish	4	4	5	4
8th	Black	1	1	1	1
12th	White conservative	15	15	15	15
14th	Latino/moderate white	11	11	12	9

Source: Analysis of data from City Clerk, Election Division.

TABLE 12.9
Primary Votes Cast in Four Key Council Districts, 1989

		Total Votes Cast
5th	White liberal/Jewish	39,739
8th	Black	19,064
12th	White conservative	29,466
14th	Latino/moderate white	13,219

Source: City Clerk, Election Division.

social conditions and incorporate new groups and approaches. New positions emerged on affordable housing, one of the central failures of the regime.

The 1989 Los Angeles mayoral election testified both to the surprising resilience of the Los Angeles biracial coalition and to its potential vulnerabilities over time. In the 1980s some Los Angeles Blacks and white liberals found that while they had much in common, their interests and beliefs also conflicted. Elite activists seeking political power sought to forge new types of politics outside the existing biracial coalition. Other elites worked to hold the coalition together. The coalition survived, as the long-standing ideological alliance between white liberalism and minority politics retained its vitality. But it had been severely wounded, and its future was uncertain. The events surrounding the 1989 mayoral election illustrate the shifts that can occur in a biracial relationship over time.

In fact, the relationship between Blacks and white liberals in Los Angeles has not always been smooth. Things can go the other way as well, as today's Los Angeles so clearly shows. The movements began separately, enjoyed a long stretch of joint effort, and have recently become clouded by conflicts of interests and values. These shifts represent an important reminder of the importance of independent power politics in any discussion of biracial coalitions.

In both Chicago and New York City, comparable shifting can be seen in recent years. Harold Washington's 1983 and 1987 mayoral victories in Chicago depended mostly on Black mobilization, but his final margins of victory required the support of Latinos and a small bloc of white liberals (Kleppner 1985). When Washington died, tensions arose among the Black, Jewish, and Latino communities, which enabled a white candidate to gain enough white liberal and Latino support to win the mayoralty (Starks and Preston 1990). In New York City, Blacks and liberals were isolated from each other after the end of the liberal Lindsay administration in 1973. But in 1989, minorities joined with a share of white liberals to take the mayoralty behind David Dinkins.

The conditions through which a Black-liberal alliance could dominate

Los Angeles have faded. The success of the biracial coalition helped change these conditions. It was the very size of the white liberal community that made an extraordinary biracial coalition possible. But such a powerful white liberal community would inevitably have its own political interests, which would in time lead to competition with a Black community itself anxious to retain its autonomy.

The Financial Scandal

Even as Bradley was narrowly winning a fifth term, he was becoming engulfed in a devastating financial scandal. For most of 1989, Bradley faced charges that potentially threatened his political career.

In the last days of March, just before the primary, reports began to circulate about Bradley's ties to local banks and savings and loan associations. In a very unusual arrangement for a big-city mayor, Bradley received an annual stipend from two financial institutions. Far East National Bank, one of Bradley's employers, was involved with the city government through its efforts to obtain lucrative deposits of city funds. While Bradley had publicly reported the stipends all along, the potential for impropriety was obvious.

On March 31, the city attorney, James K. Hahn, announced that he was beginning an investigation into Bradley's financial arrangements. The story, which was reported first in the *Los Angeles Herald-Examiner* and then in the *Los Angeles Times*, arose too late to affect the mayoral primary. But it snowballed throughout the next several months.

By April and May, the media were exploring the whole range of Bradley's personal finances. Federal authorities began looking at Bradley's stock investments with the ill-fated firm of Drexel Burnham Lambert. The ability of Bradley's friends, associates, and campaign contributors to obtain access to city hall was carefully studied, and the stories were damaging.

The focus of the city investigation turned ultimately on the charge that Bradley had intervened to maintain city deposits in the Far East National Bank. Bradley had called the city treasurer after allegedly receiving a request from the bank's president inquiring about city deposits. The city had restored the bank's $1 million deposit and added another $1 million. A notation on the treasurer's record "per the mayor" had been whited out. In May, Bradley dramatically appeared in the council chamber to acknowledge that he had made mistakes (*Los Angeles Times*, 11 May 1989).

The city attorney issued a report on September 13 that accused Bradley of serious ethical misjudgments, but stopped short of a criminal indictment. In testimony before the city council committee on ethics, Hahn's deputies indicated that it was hard to nail down the connection between Bradley and the city treasurer's action. Had the records been better, they said, criminal charges might have been filed; such charges could well have ended Bradley's political career. The next day, Bradley defended himself in a forty-minute speech on local television.

The financial scandal profoundly damaged Bradley. It struck at the image of personal integrity and honesty that Bradley had possessed for decades. It eroded the reform edge that had been essential to the coalition's rise to power. It led people both inside and outside government to consider his resignation, and many believed that he would be a lame duck in his fifth term.

As the scandal hit the papers, any remaining reserve among city politicians against attacking Bradley disappeared. Latina council member Gloria Molina chastised the city attorney for not filing criminal charges. As polling over the next several months indicated, the scandal also seriously damaged Bradley's stature among the voters.

We begin with two polls conducted by the *Los Angeles Times*, the first on May 12 and 13, 1989, and the second on September 14, 1989. The first poll came after substantial media coverage of the scandal and Bradley's dramatic speech to the city council, in which he admitted serious errors. The second was conducted after the release of the Hahn report.

Bradley's overall approval rating in the first poll was 53 percent, well below his previous ratings (see Table 12.10). Among whites, only 46 percent approved, and 39 percent disapproved. Among Blacks, Latinos, and Jews, Bradley was approved by over 60 percent. It is noteworthy that his strongest base (as it would be several years later) was among Latinos.

The scandal was having a serious effect on Bradley's base in the Jewish community, which was already upset by the oil-drilling decision in 1985 and the Farrakhan case in the same year. While Latinos were most likely to

TABLE 12.10
Bradley Job Performance Ratings during Financial Scandal, 1989 (percent)

	Early Stages of Scandal		After City Attorney Filed Lawsuit against Bradley	
	Approve	Disapprove	Approve	Disapprove
Total	53	30	41	37
Whites	46	39	—	—
Blacks	60	24	—	—
Latinos	65	15	—	—
Jews	62	29	—	—

Sources: *Los Angeles Times* Poll, reports 182 (May 12–13, 1989) and 192 (September 14, 1989).

be unaware of the scandal (51 percent, compared to 24 percent for whites and 25 percent for Blacks), Jews were least likely to be unaware (8 percent). And Jews disapproved the most (52 percent, compared to 44 percent for whites and 21 percent each for Blacks and Latinos).

But Jews were no more likely than Blacks or Latinos to want Bradley to step down even if he was not completely cleared of the charges; whites were much more likely to say that he should. Jews were the least likely of all groups to favor a recall election. Finally, Jews retained their very favorable view of Bradley (see Table 12.10).

When given alternative mayoral candidates, more Jews picked Yaroslavsky than picked Bradley (36 percent to 23 percent). Blacks picked Bradley first, but a surprisingly large minority chose Maxine Waters (43 percent to 31 percent). Whites chose "don't know," followed by Zev, and then Bradley (24 percent to 17 percent to 14 percent). Latinos chose Gloria Molina, followed by Bradley, and then Alatorre (39 percent to 25 percent to 25 percent). In other words, Bradley had serious competition, but he was the only one picked consistently by groups other than his own.

Finally, only 41 percent of all voters said they would have chosen Bradley if the April election had been held that day; 34 percent of whites chose Bradley, as did 45 percent of Jews, 49 percent of Latinos, and only 58 percent of Blacks. Clearly, Bradley was very fortunate that the scandal did not arise months before the campaign, and that he did not face a viable mainstream challenger who could have forced him into a runoff.

Months later, Hahn issued his report offering criticism and partial exoneration for Bradley. The second *Los Angeles Times* poll was not divided by group. It did show, however, a clear erosion of Bradley's support, to 41 percent approval, and 37 percent disapproval. Nearly half of the respondents (45 percent) said Bradley was guilty of a conflict of interest; only 27 percent said he was not. A bare majority (54 percent) said he should not resign, but 31 percent thought he should. Another slim majority (51 percent) thought Bradley had lied about his financial affairs. Bradley's overall favorability rating declined to 45 percent, with 46 percent holding an unfavorable view. Hahn, on the other hand, was seen favorably by 44 percent and unfavorably by only 17 percent. If the election had been held that day, Bradley would have received only 34 percent of the votes, with 28 percent of the voters unsure.

The enormous public attention to the financial scandal completed a process that Bradley's regime had itself begun—the development of Los Angeles into an important, noticeable city. Elected officials were much more powerful than they had been before the coalition took power. The media had become increasingly sophisticated about city politics, and acted in a more "national" manner—skeptical about politicians. No longer could

Bradley operate comfortably behind the scenes, with little public, elite, or media notice.

But after the city attorney's report, the story slowly disappeared, and with the lack of attention by the media, the council lost interest. Over time, Bradley steadily regained his popularity, but not the full trust of the public. The Rodney King case was the first test of how strong Bradley's recovery had been.

THIRTEEN

THE RODNEY KING CASE AND LOS ANGELES

COALITION POLITICS

W HEN THE WATTS uprising blasted Los Angeles in 1965,
people were quick to draw national conclusions, to show how
the violence explained much about American society. The local
political context of the riot was overshadowed. Yet it was the local political
fallout that eventually created the major national lessons of Watts—how
racial polarization could emerge out of civil disorder and, paradoxically,
how a biracial coalition could form and take power in a polarized city with a
small African-American population.

On Wednesday, April 29, 1992, anger exploded in Los Angeles once
again. The storm of the last days of April was indeed profound—lives lost,
trust shattered, property destroyed, neighborhoods turned to rubble. The
city will never again be the same. But politics remain. Just as with Watts, we
may not know the real lessons of 1992 until we explore the political fault
lines of the city and how they may have changed.

In the shocked aftermath of the cataclysm, how will the various threads of
the city's political life form and re-form? Can politics respond to the overwhelming in the interests of the overwhelmed? What are the implications of
the violence for the city's biracial and multiracial coalitions?

A historical perspective on local racial politics makes one humble when
making postriot predictions for Los Angeles in 1992. Many of the most
important developments in 1965 emerged very slowly. But we can at least
place the rebellion into its political context—before and after—in a way
that can increase our understanding of what might come next. And by
comparing the political contexts of 1965 and 1992, we may learn even more.

Before the Violence

In the summer of 1965, a conservative ruling coalition headed by Mayor
Yorty was at the height of its power and could ignore Black Los Angeles
with impunity. Triumphantly reelected in April over liberal Democrat
James Roosevelt, Yorty could see good news everywhere. His only weak
spots were in African-American neighborhoods and in the largely liberal

Jewish Fifth District. He dominated the Valley and was relatively popular among Latinos.

With his mayoral reelection, Yorty took control of the city's antipoverty program (*Los Angeles Newsletter*, 17 July 1965). Among big-city mayors, Yorty was clearly the most hostile to federal social programs (Greenstone and Peterson 1973). His alliance with the police chief, William Parker, was a political shield that allowed him to attack minority and white liberalism. He ignored warnings from council members Tom Bradley and Rosalind Wyman of the liberal Jewish Fifth District that minority discontent with the police was explosive. With Bradley as the connecting force, a Black and liberal insurgency was growing into a powerful challenging coalition, but was largely invisible within citywide politics. The biracial coalition was not to take power until Bradley's mayoral victory in 1973.

The 1992 violence took place in a very different time—long after the biracial challengers to Los Angeles conservatism had assumed power. Now the biracial coalition was itself part of the establishment and had generated substantial dissent from within its core constituencies.

When an amateur cameraman captured on videotape the beating of a Black motorist by Los Angeles police officers, the repercussions were felt nationwide and throughout the world. Within Los Angeles, remarkable events unfolded. The seemingly unassailable police department faced mounting calls to reform its practices. More dramatically, pressure arose to remove the police chief, Daryl Gates. Chief Gates agreed to retire by April 1992, and the city began the process of choosing a successor. Then Gates announced that he would stay until June. Finally on June 26, 1992, Gates retired, and a new police chief, Willie Williams, took office.

The politics of the Rodney King case provide an extraordinary window into the evolving coalition politics of Los Angeles. The drama includes many of the actors so far introduced—minority communities, white liberals and conservatives, the police, and the downtown business community. We can utilize the Rodney King case to draw a snapshot of the state of coalition politics nearly two decades after the first Bradley victory.

The police have been at the heart of the struggle for minority incorporation in Los Angeles, and controversies over police accountability have sustained durable coalition patterns. Even before the riot, the King case breathed new life into conflicts and alliances among the city's major groups.

The Rodney King case had a lot to do with restoring the coalition lines that had been fraying as the city grappled with the growth issue (Sonenshein 1992). Growth issues divided minority and white middle-class communities. While minority communities were desperate for growth, middle-class white neighborhoods felt choked by buildings, traffic, and people. By contrast, the search for police accountability brought liberal whites and minority groups closer together. Reforming the LAPD had been one of the central goals of the liberal biracial coalition. While Bradley has often been characterized as terminally cautious, he challenged the police even at severe cost in moderate and conservative white support. His long struggle with the LAPD certainly hurt him in his unsuccessful 1982 gubernatorial race against Republican George Deukmejian.

When the King beating took place, Los Angeles coalition politics were already in a state of flux. Bradley had few allies and many challengers within the city council. The media were often critical. The financial scandal had devastated Bradley, leaving him "just another politician" to many voters and to many in the city's elite. While his standing among the voters had risen to higher levels, his image of probity had not recovered. There was no longer a united progressive coalition leading the city, combining the separated governmental powers. Many politicians were looking ahead to the 1993 mayoral election and anticipating Bradley's retirement.

One wonders what might have happened had camcorders been in wide use during the period of coalition hegemony, when the mayor and the council majority constituted a strong alliance. But what is truly remarkable is that the King case haltingly and inconsistently rebuilt some of the coalition lines that had eroded, and ultimately led to an astonishing coalition victory—a popularly supported reassertion of civilian control over the police.

The tape of the March 3 King beating first aired on the evening of March 5. The emotional impact of the video was unprecedented. Civil liberties organizations noted that the beating itself was hardly uncommon, but the visual images made all the difference. A *Los Angeles Times* poll (Report #245, 7–8 March 1991) found that a huge percentage of the city had seen it. Soon pressure began to build on Gates to accept responsibility, and, indeed, to resign.

The dramatic events that comprised the King controversy piled one atop the other. They began with the airing of the tape, continued through Bradley's call in late March for Gates to resign, the Police Commission's decision to place Gates on leave (a decision immediately overturned by the city council), city council elections in April and May, and the release of the Christopher Commission report in July.

The initial period of the controversy seemed to support the notion that liberal coalition politics had died in Los Angeles. Bradley's council base was virtually nonexistent. Two of the three council seats representing Black districts were in effect vacant: Gilbert Lindsay of the Ninth District had died, and the retiring Robert Farrell of the Eighth District was a lame duck. The third seat was held by Nate Holden, a bitter enemy of the mayor and a Gates supporter. Liberal politicians were reluctant to take on the chief.

Many felt that the case would mark the long-predicted end of the Black-liberal coalition (Meyerson 1991).

Table 13.1 shows white, Black, and Latino support for Bradley and Gates in several successive polls. In a poll taken shortly after the controversy began, the *Los Angeles Times* found that, as after the Watts riot, Blacks differed from whites and Latinos in evaluating the chief of police. For example, Blacks were far less likely than either whites or Latinos to approve of Gates. But the difference was far smaller than in 1965, when Black approval of then-Chief Parker was virtually a mirror image of his white and Latino ratings.

A key difference between Blacks and Latinos concerned the LAPD as a whole. Latinos had more confidence than did Blacks or whites in the ability of the police to fight crime in their neighborhoods, approved of the LAPD more, and were more likely to think the LAPD was honest. The silence or vacillation of such Latino elected officials as Gloria Molina and Richard Alatorre may make more sense in this context. At the same time, Latinos were solidly pro-Bradley at the time of the first poll (see Table 13.1).

The most dramatic elite development in the first period was the public statement by the council's only Asian-American member, Michael Woo, that he favored Gates's resignation. While Bradley and his staff worked

TABLE 13.1

Approval and Disapproval of Bradley's and Gates's Job Performance,
1991–1992 (percent)

	After Rodney King Beating	Before Bradley Called on Gates to Resign	After Bradley Called on Gates to Resign	After Release of Christopher Commission Report	After the Riots
Bradley					
Total	61–28	57–30	53–39	48–41	38–55
Whites	56–34	49–41	41–48	—	27–70
Blacks	66–27	54–34	64–31	—	47–41
Latinos	66–22	66–18	63–32	—	49–42
Gates					
Total	33–55	31–61	35–57	28–64	16–81
Whites	36–55	42–52	45–46	—	18–79
Blacks	23–75	12–81	13–82	—	5–93
Latinos	32–49	20–70	29–62	—	16–79

Sources: Los Angeles Times Poll, reports 245 (March 7–8, 1991), 247 (March 20–21, 1991), 249 (April 3–4, 1991), 254 (July 11–14, 1991), and 281 (May 9–12, 1992).

Note: The first value in each cell is the percentage of respondents approving; the second value is the percentage disapproving.

behind the scenes to remove Gates, Woo's public stance placed him alone out front. Woo had taken an extraordinary gamble.

For those who favor the "coalition of color" theory, Woo's move could be seen as reflecting rainbow politics. But Woo cannot be understood only as an Asian-American. He is also the representative of a white liberal district, the Thirteenth. His position on Gates, along with Congressman Howard Berman's similar position (Meyerson 1991) provided the first signs of liberal support for the Black position.

Bradley was being pressed within the African-American community to take a stronger stand; at the same time, his "hidden hand" program to remove Gates was sparking criticism from the city council and resentment from the public. In the Black community, the atmosphere grew more and more intense. When county supervisor Kenneth Hahn backed Gates, he faced significant opposition. To the *Sentinel*, Hahn "may have uttered words that could forever taint his longstanding popularity with L.A.'s Black community" (4–10 April 1991). Bradley faced strong pressure to call for Gates's resignation. Black voters reported strong interest in Sixth District council member Ruth Galanter's position as a factor in their vote for council (*Los Angeles Times*, 10 April 1991).

The pages of the *Sentinel* bear witness to the high voltage of the King case in the Black community. It was the headline story virtually every week that it was in the news. Each week, there were a half-dozen or more stories, editorials, and columns. On several front pages, the *Sentinel* showed extremely graphic, color photos of victims of police beatings.

When Black councilman Nate Holden, a strong Gates supporter, attended a public meeting on the issue, the *Sentinel* reported: "Then in walked Holden, to an onslaught of jeers and profane verbal fireballs. . . . Just why Holden attended the rally . . . is a mystery. . . . All he did was walk into a boiling cauldron of malcontent—malcontent for him" (17 April 1991).

A *Los Angeles Times* poll two weeks later revealed that Bradley was being hurt among whites and Blacks but not at all with Latinos (see Table 13.1). Gates himself was losing minority backing and gaining white support as the controversy continued. The police issue was reconfiguring public opinion.

The controversy took a dramatic turn on April 2 when Bradley publicly called on Chief Gates to resign. Bradley's police commission placed Gates on indefinite suspension for the period of the investigation. An outraged city council overruled the commission on April 5. It reached an agreement with Gates to preempt his threatened lawsuit against the city by restoring him to office.

The vote to override the police commission was ten to three. Even liberal council members were nervous about confronting Gates, and their conflicts with Bradley led them to feel no obligation to support him. Joining Woo in opposition were only Black council member Farrell and Ruth Galanter, who was facing reelection under tremendous pressure to oppose Gates in her biracial Sixth District. At the same meeting, another, less publicized vote was held to appropriate $150,000 for a Police Commission investigation of the LAPD. The voting lines were much closer on that vote to "normal" coalitions. The motion by Yaroslavsky and Ferraro passed nine to four, with all four Valley council members opposed.

These days were the climax of the controversy, and seemed to show a city government in chaos. The *Los Angeles Times* editorialized, business leaders called on the mayor and council to get together, and the public was confused. The establishment pressure on Bradley took its toll; soon he was meeting with Gates and council president John Ferraro to make a tentative peace (*Los Angeles Times*, 10 April 1991).

Like Woo, the cautious Bradley had taken an extraordinary gamble. A *Los Angeles Times* poll taken during and shortly after these events showed that his public support had again shifted dramatically (see Table 13.1). Clearly, the Gates issue was an electoral loser for Bradley among whites, whether he vacillated or acted. But Bradley had salvaged a deteriorating situation among Blacks, and neither position seemed to affect his standing among Latinos. In a hypothetical mayoral race between Bradley and Gates, Bradley now won easily among minorities but only narrowly among whites (see Table 13.2).

The three-day climactic controversy in early April placed Bradley in a highly risky position. He took on the Los Angeles city council and Gates, and the council stuck with the chief. At the same time, he reoriented his base of support. While his overall popularity fell, his minority base solidified. This was well within the pattern of coalition politics, despite the image of Bradley as a nonracial mayor. The biracial coalition was first built in the Black community before it expanded into a citywide coalition, and without its Black base, it is lost.

On the Tuesday after the three days in April, the city held a primary election. There were contested races in the Sixth, Eighth, Ninth and Twelfth districts. The Eighth and Ninth were Black districts; the Sixth was

TABLE 13.2
Bradley versus Gates in Hypothetical Mayoral Race,
1991 (percent)

	Would Vote for Bradley	*Would Vote for Gates*	*Would Vote for Neither*
Whites	37	28	26
Blacks	62	2	21
Latinos	64	14	12

Source: Los Angeles Times Poll, report 249 (April 3–4, 1991).

a biracial liberal district, and the Twelfth was the white conservative district.

The Gates issue was a part of each race. In the biracial Sixth, Galanter had to justify her balancing act on the issue. In the Twelfth, Bernson used strong support from Gates to combat liberal slow-growth challenger Julie Korenstein. In the Eighth and Ninth, Black candidates competed to stand out against Gates. The Black community was about to shift its representation, with the retirement of Robert Farrell of the Eighth District and the death of Gilbert Lindsay of the Ninth District. With Holden's election in the Tenth in 1987, a new generation of Black representation would sit in the council. As the primary returns came in, highly competitive runoff elections were set for May.

For some time, a new factional division had been growing in the Black community, which was considerably different from the earlier Bradley-Dymally split. That division, the basis for the early biracial coalition, was along class lines and placed the Bradley forces on the progressive left of the moderate Dymally regulars tied to Jesse Unruh. Bradley's organizational base was in upwardly mobile Black communities, while Dymally's home ground was poorer and working class. The Bradley forces were the reformers.

In the 1980s and beyond, Bradley's new Black competitors came from the left. He himself had long ago moved to the moderate center. Jesse Jackson's 1984 and 1988 presidential campaigns challenged Bradley to reconnect himself to the Black community, as Jackson explicitly pushed Black and progressive themes. Jackson's ally Maxine Waters emerged as a rival of Bradley in the African-American community.

Waters had been Bradley's close ally in the 1970s and was the key organizer of Bradley's factional challenge to Dymally. A dynamic activist, Waters soon carved out her own base. She established a strong low-income and working-class constituency in her Forty-Eighth Assembly District. Her political strength was such that she was soon independent of Bradley. The mayor failed to formally endorse Waters in her 1976 assembly campaign, but she won anyway. In Sacramento, Waters became a close ally of Speaker Willie Brown, and soon amassed considerable legislative power, all independent of Bradley. In 1978, a split in the Bradley camp led to the election of a Dymally ally in the Forty-Ninth Assembly District. Waters endorsed Marguerite Archie, and Bradley backed Willis Edwards. Waters's candidate did far better than did Bradley's (see Chapter Eight).

By 1984, Waters was becoming well known as a progressive leader, and she had formed a close alliance with Jesse Jackson. In 1988, she was one of Jackson's national chairpersons and a member of his inner circle. In 1990, Waters left her Forty-Eighth assembly seat to run for Congress and endorsed Archie (then Archie-Hudson) for her seat. Bradley endorsed Robert Farrell. Again Waters's candidate easily defeated Bradley's.

The Waters-Bradley rivalry had its roots not in class conflict, but rather in ideology and style. Waters, like Jackson, is issue-oriented and a passionate advocate for minority and low-income communities. She is much more Black-oriented than Bradley and is also a national feminist leader. When she selected candidates in the city council races, her endorsement carried major clout.

Bradley had never been an issue leader, and had always been more a problem solver. As a big-city, coalition-oriented mayor, he had become a symbol of the status quo and a figure of the establishment. Waters's issue-based approach and her own experience as a local problem solver challenged Bradley's style in his home base in a way that Jesse Jackson could not. Her constituency—working-class, minority, and Democratic—allowed her to take progressive stands that Bradley could not take as mayor of the city.

The Rodney King case highlighted their differences. Waters was the dominant figure in the Black protest against Gates, leading rallies and demanding Gates's resignation. When Supervisor Hahn backed Gates, Waters led a protest by Black leaders. She maintained steady pressure on Bradley to call for Gates's resignation. In the May runoffs, Waters and Bradley backed opposing candidates. Waters backed Robert Gay in the Ninth to succeed Lindsay, while Bradley supported Rita Walters. Waters endorsed Roderick Wright in the Eighth against Bradley's choice, Mark Ridley-Thomas.

Another runoff election far to the northwest would also be influenced by the Rodney King story. Councilman Hal Bernson was facing a strong challenge from liberal Julie Korenstein in the city's most conservative district. The issue was development—in particular, Bernson's support for a large Porter Ranch project. To widespread surprise, Korenstein was making serious inroads into Bernson's base. While the council races in the Black districts would test Bradley's strength in the Black community, the Twelfth District race tested Gates's electoral power. Gates strongly backed Bernson, who made massive use of this endorsement in the conservative Twelfth.

Bradley's power base in the African-American community was narrowly confirmed in May. Bradley headed off Maxine Waters's group as both his candidates won. Walters defeated Gay by fewer than one hundred votes, and Ridley-Thomas narrowly defeated Wright. These victories enhanced Bradley's power reputation among elites, aided by Gay's tearful, televised concession: "The mayor is an extraordinarily influential individual in this city" (*Los Angeles Times*, 6 June 1991). Now Bradley had two Black allies on the council, both assertive opponents of Gates.

In the Twelfth, Bernson barely beat Korenstein, and his victory confirmed Gates's conservative drawing power. As Gates's political reach demonstrated, the city still had a strong conservative constituency. The message would not be lost on vulnerable city council incumbents.

Bradley suffered a major citywide defeat with the passage of Charter

Amendment 5. The measure was placed on the ballot after Bradley inadvertently signed it, and increased the council's power over the government. The measure became an indirect test of citywide support for Bradley's executive power during the Rodney King controversy. The measure passed with over 59 percent of the vote.

The city divided along racial lines on Charter Amendment 5. The only districts in which Amendment 5 did not receive a majority were four Black or biracial areas: the Sixth, Eighth, Ninth, and Tenth districts. As the data in Table 13.3 show, a considerable gap existed between the Black Eighth and the three other key districts. In the latter, the vote was close to identical in percentage. The biggest gap in margin was between the Black Eighth and the white conservative Twelfth.

The vote on Charter Amendment 5 indicated that in the precarious, posthegemony world, Bradley's coalition had become much narrower. Indeed, the city council was making important inroads into his governmental power. With Charter Amendment 5 in place, the new council was likely to challenge Bradley further. But the Bradley forces' success in the council races in the Black districts and the Twelfth District victory of Gates's candidate, Bernson, meant a revival of ideological and racial politics. On the police issue, where would the city's other constituencies and leaders jump?

Now that minority support had realigned on the Gates issue, and was set in the city council, Bradley's only strategy for a citywide victory on the police controversy was to reframe the issue. With his reputation injured by the financial scandal and the rise of conflict with the council, Bradley would have failed if he had made the issue a referendum on himself. Ironically, the progressive position was able to win only because its chief historical symbol stayed in the background. The vehicle was the blue-ribbon commission headed by Warren Christopher.

In July the Christopher Commission made its report—and it was a shocker. Unexpectedly, the commission issued a stinging report, which highlighted the failure of the LAPD and other city officials to rein in police brutality. Most dramatically, the commission released transcripts of police

TABLE 13.3
Vote on Charter Amendment 5 in Four Key Council Districts, 1991

		Yes (%)	No (%)	Margin (N)
5th	White liberal/Jewish	61.2	38.8	3,458
8th	Black	50.1	49.9	185
12th	White conservative	62.4	37.6	7,966
14th	Latino/moderate white	61.0	39.0	1,708

Source: City Clerk, Election Division.

conversations on car computers. The transcripts contained numerous examples of racist and sexist phrases, including the infamous reference to "gorillas in the mist" (Independent Commission 1991:71–74).

Almost immediately, the Christopher Commission report overrode the conflicts between the mayor and the city council. It drew strong elite support, including that of the *Los Angeles Times*, which, however, gave little credit to Bradley. Minority spokespeople expressed surprise and satisfaction that the report was so hard-hitting. Most remarkably, the lineup in the city council shifted rapidly. For a short time, city leadership looked as it had during the era of coalition hegemony. As long as city leaders were discussing not Tom Bradley but only the commission Bradley had appointed, they were lavish in their praise.

The commission report ended the Black isolation on the issue and built a majority constituency in the face of Bradley's citywide political liabilities. A *Los Angeles Times* poll (Report 254, July 11–14, 1991) showed very strong support for the commission's recommendations; private polls showed that backing for the report crossed racial and many ideological lines (Fairbank, Maullin, and Associates, various dates).

With the release of the Christopher Commission report, the elite breakdown in the coalition began temporarily to mend itself, as coalition members rallied behind the recommendations. The antireform group, predictably, comprised white Valley council members, and liberal council members joined the anti-Gates majority. By now, Bradley had two new allies on the council; Gates's strongest base was in the Twelfth. In September, the council's ad hoc committee recommended a series of twenty-one provisions, most of them in line with the Christopher Commission recommendations. The council placed a measure on the June 1992 ballot to implement the report.

We can examine coalition lines through a private citywide poll conducted by Fairbank, Maullin, and Associates in September 1991. On the question of Daryl Gates, the city divided right along familiar racial and ideological lines. Overall, 41 percent of the voters approved of Gates. But when the ratings are broken down by party, religion, and race (pillars of coalition politics in Los Angeles), the lines are clear (see Table 13.4). Democrats were twice as likely as Republicans to view Gates unfavorably. Blacks and Latinos were close together, with under a third of each group viewing Gates favorably. Of all groups, Jews had the least favorable view of Gates, and they were only one-fourth as likely as white Protestants to view him very favorably.

In this book I have argued that evolutionary perspectives are necessary to understand coalitions. Each stage of coalition development in Los Angeles began with an initial period of polarization of key groups, followed by vacillation and re-formation of others. Generally, Blacks started out on the

TABLE 13.4
Evaluations of Gates Citywide, 1991 (percent)

	Democrats	Republicans	Whites	Blacks	Latinos	Asian-Americans	Jews	White Protestants
Very favorable	16	36	29	8	10	18	9	37
Somewhat favorable	17	23	20	18	7	30	27	25
Somewhat unfavorable	24	17	15	39	34	36	18	12
Very unfavorable	31	16	28	29	24	0	36	16

Source: Survey by Fairbank, Maullin, and Associates, September 1991.

left, and white conservatives on the right, with white liberals and Latinos in the middle. This process, at both the elite and mass levels, operated once again in the Rodney King case. As the Rodney King issue evolved well before the riots of 1992, fragmented coalition lines shifted and re-formed into a pattern closely resembling the long-term coalition patterns of the city's politics.

The Black community represented the firmest base for the progressive position. At the start, this was more at the mass level than at the elite level because of Bradley's cautious response and the turnover of Black council members. After the events of April and May, the Black community was strongly unified around opposition to Gates, with the exception of maverick Nate Holden. (Holden had been endorsed by the police union and former police chief Ed Davis in his 1989 campaign against Bradley.)

The Latino community did not provide strong support for the Black position in the early phases of the controversy. Such officeholders as Alatorre and Molina were close to invisible. On the surface, this looked like 1965, when Latinos were just like whites. But there were important differences. By 1991 Latinos were registering very strong support for Bradley in the *Los Angeles Times* polls and in private polls. During the period of Bradley's toughening stance, this support hardly changed. By contrast, Blacks started out positive, and then became less favorable as Bradley seemed to vacillate; when he toughened on Gates, their support grew.

As the issue evolved, the Latino position shifted at the mass level, and then, with Mike Hernandez's election to succeed Molina in the First District, at the elite level as well. Latino anger at Los Angeles County sheriffs for violence against Latinos began to shape a common effort, and the polls showed a steady shift toward the Black position among Latinos.

The Rodney King case restored and strengthened the long-term coalition conflict in Los Angeles by turning the city's attention from economic policy toward the racial and ideological issues that had divided and energized city politics since 1964. With the publication of the Christopher Commission report, a dithering city council, which in April had scuttled a Police Commission proposal to place Gates on leave, pulled together and placed on the June 1992 ballot a charter amendment to implement the commission's recommendations. This amendment, Proposition F, changed the city charter to set term limits for Police Commission members and the police chief (two consecutive five-year terms for the latter); create an independent staff for the Police Commission; change the method of choosing and removing the chief; and revise the process of disciplining police officers, including adding a civilian member to officer misconduct panels.

As the Ventura County jury went into its deliberations in Simi Valley in late March 1992, Bradley's coalition had come to a position of strength— although surely not the hegemony of earlier years. Liberal opponents, such as Yaroslavsky, were drawn into the confrontation with Gates, and Asian-American councilman Michael Woo directly called for Gates's resignation.

There was every reason to believe that the June measure, backed by Bradley's elite allies in the business community, the *Los Angeles Times*, African-Americans, Latinos, and white liberals, would pass in a low-turnout election. That prediction assumed what nearly everybody assumed —that the jury would bring in a guilty verdict on some or all of the charges against the LAPD officers.

The political context of the 1992 violence, then, was the survival of a wounded, aging political coalition dominated by African-Americans, white liberals, and downtown business. Latinos, though restive with the shape of city politics, were still supportive of Bradley. Conservatives were on the defensive because of the Rodney King videotape. There was no vital insurgency from either the left or the right to challenge the regime, but there was also little enthusiasm behind it. Against all odds and predictions, the coalition still held power.

After the Violence

The 1965 and 1992 uprisings were profoundly different events. The Watts riot began with the arrest by the California Highway Patrol of Black motorist Marquette Frye, on suspicion of drunk driving. When a crowd gathered and formed the impression that a pregnant African-American woman was being brutalized, rock throwing began. The violence spread, and soon there was burning and looting (Conot 1967). The violence lasted for several days, and the toll was staggering. Thirty-four people were killed (thirty-one Blacks and three whites). There were 1,032 injuries, and 3,438 adult and 514 juvenile arrests. Property damage was estimated at $40 million (Governor's Commission 1965:23–24).

The Watts riot was clearly a struggle between Black and white. The causes were obscure to those outside the African-American community, since the violence had been precipitated by an event the public had never seen. The violence had a powerful political content, as indicated by interviews with those arrested (Sears and McConahay 1973). Surveys at the time showed little public sympathy among whites or Latinos for the Black protest. Vast majorities of both groups rejected the tactics of violent protest, and strongly supported then-Chief Parker. By contrast, African-Americans overwhelmingly opposed the police chief, and strongly backed virtually all Black and some white liberal public officials (Sears and McConahay 1973).

The Watts riot greatly strengthened the positions of Mayor Yorty and Chief Parker. They were seen as the guardians of public order and were able to characterize the rioters in the most negative possible terms. For example, Parker called the rioters "monkeys in a zoo" (Sears and McConahay 1973:151).

In 1965, liberal government was firmly in control in Washington, and federal money was available for Los Angeles. Although much federal funding eventually flowed to the city, the amount could have been greater. Mayor Yorty and conservative city council members resisted the federal role, even when chided by federal officials for their lack of interest. Many years later, former federal officials recalled their frustration; they had money to give to Los Angeles, but city hall was reluctant to take it (Saltzstein, Sonenshein, and Ostrow 1986).

The mismatch between federal resources and local political greatly strengthened the liberal biracial coalition. It gave Bradley and his allies a platform. If they took power, they would obtain maximum federal resources to rebuild the inner city without raising local taxes.

The violence in 1992 was more complex and varied. Some have called it a "class riot"; others have called it the first "multiracial riot." While some have found major political content in the violence, others disagree. There will be a tendency to attach a single definition to the 1992 violence, but that search for simplicity may be misplaced. Perhaps the most accurate assessment would be that it was several different, overlapping riots.

Black anger against the innocent verdict in the Rodney King case was obviously at the heart of the uprising. The verdict came after the Latasha Harlins case, in which a Korean-American grocer had received a light sentence for killing a young African-American woman during an argument in the former's store. While most people were shocked by the jury's decision, the rage in the African-American community went much deeper—and was about much more than the individual verdict. To African-Americans, more than to any other group, the verdict was the straw that broke the camel's back, rather than an exception to the rule of justice. A long stream of police misconduct toward Blacks of all social classes had built a wave of resentment; the Simi Valley decision seemed to endorse all the times that police officers stopped, insulted, or injured African-Americans.

The scope of the violence in 1992 was much greater than in 1965. The death toll reached 58; there were 2,383 injuries, over 17,000 arrests, and an estimated $785 million in property damage (*Los Angeles Times*, 11 May 1992, special issue). The South Central Los Angeles riot was both more frightening and more widely understandable than the Watts conflagration. It spread outside the Black community to threaten Hollywood, the Korean-American community, and even Beverly Hills. There was no sense of safety anywhere—and that universal dread may have important political consequences. But unlike 1965, the precipitating moment of the violence was clearly visible outside the African-American community. Millions of Americans had seen the Rodney King beating on videotape, and the great majority of those who heard the verdict found it unjust. But who had seen the arrest of Marquette Frye in 1965?

Potentially, the 1992 violence could have played the same role for the conservative leader, Chief Gates, that the Watts riot had played for Yorty and Chief Parker in 1965. A strong and effective response to the violence might have strengthened Gates's hand and doomed the June police reform measure. Of course, this did not occur. Gates's dereliction of leadership—symbolized by his attendance at a fundraiser against the June measure while the city burned—brought a storm of criticism. While the rioters were villified in 1992, that negative perception shared space with public perceptions of Gates as the instigator of a monumental government fiasco. Thus the inference that the riot would be politically advantageous for local conservatives was muddied by the massive decline in Gates's professional reputation. Weeks after the violence, Gates's disapproval rating reached an astonishing 81 percent (*Los Angeles Times*, 15 May 1992; see Table 13.1). By contrast, in the wake of the Watts violence, 79 percent of whites and 74 percent of Mexican-Americans had viewed Chief Parker favorably, and Blacks, with a 10 percent approval rating of Parker, had been far from the other groups (Sears and McConahay 1973:59, 165).

But the violence hurt Bradley as well. His reputation as a peacemaker had been one of his greatest political assets. Yorty could treat civil disorder as a vindication of his hard-line policies; Bradley had no such way out. The riot made it more difficult to bridge the racial gap—a difficulty already apparent in the struggle with Gates. Bradley's conflict with Gates may have helped him with minority communities, but it hurt him citywide. Even though Gates seemed to be the real loser in the riot, continuing evidence of Bradley's conflict with the police chief reduced the mayor's support. Post-riot polls confirmed that decline, as Bradley's overall support fell to 38 percent (*Los Angeles Times*, 15 May 1992; see Table 13.1).

Within the Black community, the violence may have shifted the ground under the earlier Bradley-Waters rivalry. After the riot, Bradley could not easily speak for the African-American community, and, of course, he had only rarely been a racial spokesperson before. There he was preempted by Congresswoman Waters, whose eloquent and militant statements of the Black position captured great public attention. Where there is no middle ground, the center is a tough place to occupy. Bradley's centrist governing style now seemed too mild for South Central Los Angeles.

While the 1965 violence generated much federal aid, few expected massive federal help to flow to Los Angeles in 1992. Then it was Los Angeles that was reluctant to participate; today it is Washington. Federal money and the redirecting of city resources allowed progressive leaders in the 1970s to initiate new programs without unduly raising city taxes. Los Angeles will be forced to come up with local solutions—and local money to pay for them. While this crisis gave Bradley an opportunity to make his business links work for South Central Los Angeles and to influence local banks to invest more heavily in the inner city, it also left the local coalition vulnerable to blame if positive change did not occur.

Proposition F

Almost unnoticed in the cascade of violence and public debate was the ballot measure to reform the Los Angeles Police Department, scheduled for the June 2 election. The campaign for police reform had brought much of the old liberal biracial coalition together one more time. It received substantial support from minority and white liberal organizations (although a number of white liberal elected officials delayed supporting the measure until later in the campaign). Max Palevsky, one of Bradley's earliest Jewish financial backers, provided $25,000 toward the reform campaign fund (*Los Angeles Times*, 24 March 1992). Downtown business, drawn in part by its association with attorney Warren Christopher, provided major funding for the Proposition F campaign (ibid.).

Reporter Frank Clifford noted: "[T]he campaign has a familiar ring, combining downtown financial muscle with an ethnically diverse campaign committee made up of civil rights and religious leaders from all over the city. It is much the same mix of corporate money and ethnic variety that has provided Mayor Tom Bradley with a winning edge over the past two decades" (ibid.). The conservative opposition, led by Gates and former Mayor Yorty, was just as familiar.

Disorder in the city seemed likely to jeopardize Proposition F, perhaps galvanizing conservatives in opposition. But public and private polling indicated that police reform had developed a solid base of support (see Table 13.5). A strong majority favored the proposition's passage before and after the Simi Valley verdict. Blacks, Latinos, and Jews—the pillars of police

TABLE 13.5

Public Support for Proposition F, before and after the Riots, 1992 (percent)

| | Before the Riots February 1992 | | After the Riots | | | |
| | | | May 1992 | | May 9–12, 1992 | |
	Favor	Oppose	Favor	Oppose	Favor	Oppose
Total	57	20	57	19	61	17
Whites	52	27	56	21	55	23
Blacks	76	8	59	6	82	3
Latinos	66	12	62	17	66	11
Jews	60	15	—	—	—	—

Sources: February 1992 and May 1992—surveys by Fairbank, Maullin, and Associates. May 9–12, 1992—*Los Angeles Times* Poll, report 281.

reform—were the backbone of Proposition F, but whites were also generally in support.

On June 2, 1992, the city's voters passed Proposition F by a two to one margin. This extraordinary event marked the first time since the rise of Chief William Parker in 1950 that the city government had restored civilian control of the police. The coalition lines in the vote showed the durability of the patterns underlying the biracial coalition. The base for Proposition F was in the African-American community (see Table 13.6). In the three council districts with the largest Black populations, 92 percent, 90 percent, and 86 percent voted yes. The opposition lay in the Valley. Nevertheless, even in the three white Valley districts, 52 percent, 54 percent, and 46 percent voted yes. Only in the conservative Twelfth did more vote no than yes (54 percent to 46 percent).

In white liberal districts, Proposition F won easily. Michael Woo's Thirteenth District cast 74.3 percent of its ballots in favor of the proposition. The Fifth District offered 71 percent approval, once again 25 percentage

TABLE 13.6

Proposition F Vote and Margin in Four Key Council Districts, 1992

		Yes (%)[a]	No (%)[a]	Margin (N)
5th	White liberal/Jewish	71.1	28.9	22,645
8th	Black	92.0	8.0	24,024
12th	White conservative	46.3	53.7	−3,420
14th	Latino/moderate white	65.4	34.6	6,408

Source: Analysis of data from County of Los Angeles, Registrar-Recorder.
[a]Percentage of all votes cast on Proposition F.

points more liberal than the white conservative Twelfth District. And the Fifth District cast the most ballots in the city, maximizing its impact. The measure passed easily in the two Latino districts (70 percent and 65 percent), but with a smaller number of ballots cast.

The crucial importance of biracial alliance on police reform is shown by the margin of victory in the Black Eighth District and the white liberal/Jewish Fifth District. They were very close together, and both provided key contributions to Proposition F's passage.

The dramatic events of 1991 and 1992 took the Bradley regime and the people of Los Angeles to peaks and valleys of discord, confrontation, and change. In the end, Bradley managed to obtain an extraordinarily valuable and costly victory—the beginning of reform of the LAPD. But his own support suffered serious erosion, and the city passed through a massive civil trauma.

The winning campaign to implement police reform must be considered one of the greatest victories of the biracial coalition that took power in 1973. Few had the inclination to stop and applaud, however, in a city still digging itself out from the shells of hundreds of burned buildings, and the raw taste of injustice and violence. The future remained unsettled and uncertain for the Los Angeles community; only later might people look back and see what had been accomplished.

Mayor Tom Bradley and Police Chief Daryl Gates air their differences over the police and fire pension system, July 14, 1981. (Herald Examiner Collection, Los Angeles Public Library.)

City councilman Michael Woo, the city's first Asian-American elected official, winning in 1985 the Thirteenth Council District. (Photo by Ellen Kelsey, courtesy of the office of Councilman Michael Woo.)

Mayor Bradley with two often feuding leaders in the Latino community, Councilman Richard Alatorre and then Councilwoman Gloria Molina at a press conference on toxics found in the home, February 19, 1988. (Herald Examiner Collection, Los Angeles Public Library.)

The police assault on demonstrators supporting the Justice for Janitors movement in Century City, June 1990. (Photo by Tom Ramsay, courtesy of the Service Employees International Union.)

Rivals Tom Bradley and council member Zev Yaroslavsky prepare to speak in support of the Justice for Janitors movement at a rally in Century City, June 1990. (Photo by Tom Ramsay, courtesy of the Service Employees International Union.)

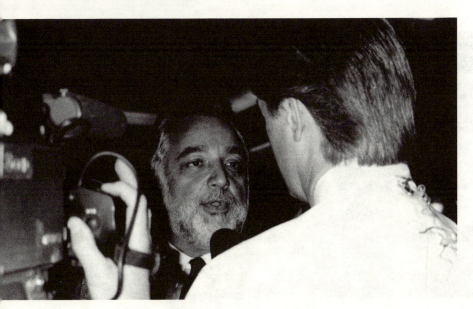

Danny Bakewell, an African-American community activist involved in the controversy over minority hiring in the wake of the 1992 violence. (Photo by Corecia Davis.)

Congresswoman Maxine Waters. (Photo by Narishimah Osei, courtesy of the office of Congresswoman Maxine Waters.)

Mark Ridley-Thomas, council member from the Eighth District, and a rising leader in the African-American community. (Photo by Corecia Davis.)

Scenes from the 1992 violence. (Photos by Frankie J. Quintero and Mathew Lyle Warnock.)

Aftermath of the violence. (Photo by Corecia Davis.)

Mayor Tom Bradley and his wife Ethel greet guests at the press conference at which Bradley announced that he would not seek a sixth term as mayor. (Photo by Corecia Davis.)

PART FOUR

ENDINGS AND BEGINNINGS

FOURTEEN

BIRACIAL COALITION POLITICS IN LOS
ANGELES AND NEW YORK CITY

THE EXPERIENCE of the Los Angeles biracial coalition suggests
an important puzzle. If Blacks and white liberals have an affinity
for alliance, why do they not always coalesce? More specifically,
why has biracial politics developed so differently in New York City than in
Los Angeles? Why did the city with fewer Blacks and white liberals develop
the far stronger biracial coalition?

Between 1973 and 1985, Los Angeles politics was dominated by a biracial
coalition linking Blacks and white liberals, particularly Jews, behind a
popular Black mayor. This coalition exercised leadership in the city council
and underlay the other two holders of citywide offices.

The contrast with New York City is stark. Until 1989, New York City
was an example of minority exclusion from the ruling coalition, with
Blacks, Latinos, and white liberals mutually isolated and unable to form a
challenging coalition (Mollenkopf 1990a). In 1989, Black candidate David
Dinkins narrowly won election as mayor. And still the cloud over interracial
politics in New York has failed to dissipate.

Until Dinkins's election, observers of New York City politics were deeply
concerned about the inability of African-Americans to win political incorporation (*New York Times*, 31 March, 26 May 1987). Mollenkopf (1990a) saw
New York City as "the great anomaly" in the theory of minority incorporation advanced by Browning, Marshall, and Tabb (1984). Before Dinkins,
there had been no serious Black mayoral contender in modern New York
City, and those Black candidates who had sought important offices had not
even received full Black voting support (Hamilton 1979).

At the same time, relations between African-Americans and Jews (generally the most liberal whites) have been severely strained. The 1988 Democratic presidential primary in New York State, in which Jesse Jackson and
then-Mayor Edward Koch argued bitterly, was only the latest of a string of
incidents dividing Blacks and Jews—the crucial building blocks of biracial
coalitions. New York City has often been used to support the pessimistic
view of biracial coalitions, showing the limits of Black-liberal and Black-
Jewish relations.

In the first part of this book, I introduced the idea that there are three major factors in the formation of biracial coalitions: ideology, interest, and leadership. In this chapter, I will explore these three factors in New York City and Los Angeles.

The two cities are particularly useful because they represent alternative urban models. New York City is, of course, an older city with traditional party structures. In that sense, it shares many qualities with a large number of eastern and midwestern cities.

Los Angeles is a model of the newer, western cities developed in the late nineteenth and early twentieth centuries, shaped by midwestern Protestant migrants who hoped to devise an urban alternative to the "old, corrupt" cities of the East and Midwest (Singleton 1979). The antiparty norms of the Progressive movement found their greatest expression in the West (Shefter 1983), and were central to the development of the Los Angeles political community. Party organizations have been virtually nonexistent in Los Angeles (Adrian 1959; Carney 1964).

Both New York City and Los Angeles fall in the middle range of Black population—large enough to compete for power but too small to depend on Black mobilization alone. New York City has a large population of European Catholic immigrant groups and is also by far the larger center of Jewish population. Together, the New York City and Los Angeles metropolitan areas hold 60 percent of America's Jews (Fisher 1979).

Los Angeles has the larger Latino and Asian-American population of the two cities and a significant Jewish population; it lacks the large working-class white Catholic group so prominent in New York City. Its Black population is significantly smaller (see Table 14.1 for 1980). The combined minority populations of the two cities are quite comparable.

Both cities have significant white Protestant populations, but their political orientations are vastly different. Harris and Swanson (1970) found that New York City's white Protestants were relatively liberal on racial matters. Los Angeles is different. The analysis of private polls in Los Angeles (Fairbank, Maullin, and Associates 1989, 1991) reveals that the bookends

TABLE 14.1
Minority Population Shares in New York City
and Los Angeles, 1980 (percent)

	New York City	*Los Angeles*
Black	25.2	16.7
Latino	19.9	27.5
Jewish (est.)	20.0	7.0

Source: Census data and estimates.

of white ideology are Jews on the left and white Protestants on the right.

Ideology

Where liberalism is strongest, both in numbers and in prestige, African-American political success ought to be greatest. Where Blacks are in a position to compete for power, white liberals will be essential to victory. By this standard, New York City ought to be the home of biracial politics.

New York City is the spiritual center of American liberalism. When conservatives wish to satirize liberalism, they generally cite two cities: New York City and San Francisco. New York City has been in the forefront of welfare services and an innovator in social policy. The public sector in New York City is immense, reflecting the government's commitment to providing social services. (After the fiscal crisis of 1975, a number of these services were cut back.) For many years, the city offered a public university free of charge, financed public hospitals and major public works, and operated the largest school system in the country.

A high level of party strength has been counterbalanced by an effective, Manhattan-based reform movement, which has competed successfully for citywide power. Since the 1930s, liberal reform has been a major force in city politics, sustaining the LaGuardia and Lindsay "fusion" regimes in the 1930s and the 1960s, respectively. The ideologies and interests of the "amateur Democrats" have made them the natural allies of racial minorities in modern city politics. In fact, liberal mayoral candidate John Lindsay won office in 1965 with minority support, long before the citywide success of the Bradley coalition in Los Angeles.

The presence in New York City of an immense Jewish population further suggests the potential power of biracial politics, since Jews have historically been the white group most amenable to alliance with Blacks. The Jewish population of New York City is around 20 percent, compared to 7 percent in Los Angeles. The Jewish influence in the city is extraordinary—culturally, intellectually, and politically.

There are certainly enough Blacks and white liberals to make biracial liberalism work in New York City. Something must have gone wrong in the dynamic of biracial politics. The linkage between minority and liberal reform politics has failed to arise, and each has been weaker as a result.

Why has Los Angeles found itself with strong biracial politics, even after civil violence, while in New York City, the liberal center, biracial politics is a mess? To more fully explain the situation it is necessary to explore the realm of interest, and the concepts originally presented by Carmichael and Hamilton (1967).

Interest

Carmichael and Hamilton (1967:76) suggested that the ideological support given to Blacks by white liberals is contingent on self-interest: "[W]e do not seek to condemn these groups for being what they are so much as we seek to emphasize a fact of life: they are unreliable allies when a conflict of interest arises. Morality and sentiment cannot weather such conflicts, and black people must realize this."

Interest conflicts grow out of the nature of the city struggle for power, and the extent to which the elected city government controls material stakes. When the minority struggle for political representation directly threatens the interests of white liberals, the odds of biracial politics ought to decline. Conflicts between African-Americans and white liberals should arise when white liberals hold public jobs, or have already achieved political incorporation when Blacks challenge incumbent regimes or public institutions. Even the strongest ideology is unlikely to become a formula for a persistent reduction in self-interest.

The material stakes in city politics are far higher in New York City than in Los Angeles. In New York City, these stakes are the most likely to include the interests of white liberals. In contrast to Los Angeles, white liberals in New York City have been concentrated in public jobs, and were heavily incorporated into ruling regimes. Thus the Black movement was a much more direct threat to liberal interests.

Table 14.2 compares public jobs in the two cities in 1982. Clearly, on a per capita basis, New York City (5.32) dwarfed Los Angeles (1.36) in its level of city-controlled public employment. New York City's workforce included education and hospitals; these categories account for about one-third of city jobs.

Even the smaller number of public jobs in Los Angeles overstates the

TABLE 14.2
City Government Employment in New York City and Los Angeles, 1982

	New York City	Los Angeles
Population	7,071,639	2,968,579
Number of city jobs	376,512	40,560
City employees as share of population	5.32%	1.36%

Source: U.S. Bureau of the Census, *Government Employment* (Washington, DC: GPO, 1984), vol. 3, no. 1, tab. 2.

level of political stakes. Political control of public hiring is limited in Los Angeles by both severe formal strictures and powerful local norms. The mayor controls no more than several hundred public jobs, and the city council controls even fewer. The civil service system covers virtually everybody else, and there is a local premium on bringing people up through the merit system. There are just not as many material stakes to fuel interest conflicts in Los Angeles or to sustain party machines.

New York City lacks a central machine, but has a large number of public jobs at stake because of its huge public investment. As the 1987 municipal scandals illustrated, vast discretion could be exercised through city hall, the Democratic party, the borough presidents, the former Board of Estimate, and the city council. Education and hospitals are strongly influenced by the city government in New York City, leading to gut-wrenching decisions by the mayor and other political leaders. The schools, for instance, are very much at stake in New York municipal elections and offer a basis for struggle between Blacks and white liberals.

The city's very progressivism created a vast network of programs employing many white liberals. As poor and minority people sought to improve their power position in the city, they inevitably came up against white liberals in positions of power over them. (In recent years, these public service programs have increasingly been staffed by minorities, perhaps leading to greater intraminority conflict.)

Thus, the very success of old-fashioned liberalism in New York City, in that it predated the rise of Black consciousness, set up interest conflicts that would ultimately complicate biracial politics. In particular, the large Jewish community, among the city's most liberal whites, had been at least partially incorporated into ruling regimes and city employment for decades. Despite the absence of a Jewish mayor until the election of Abraham Beame in 1973, Jews had numerous avenues for political power. Jews participated in the La Guardia regime, the Democratic party, the Liberal party, and in the Reform Democratic movement.

The rise of an Italian-Jewish coalition behind reform mayor Fiorello LaGuardia in 1933 brought Jews into the high points of city hall at the expense of the Irish (Bayor 1978). Previously, Jews had been "outsiders." As a result, Jews moved into all levels of public service, including teaching. In 1970, the Jewish percentage of the city's teachers was estimated at more than 50 percent, and an even higher share of school principals were Jewish (Glazer and Moynihan 1970a). This differed from the role of Jews in other cities:

> In New York, as contrasted with cities where the Jewish population is smaller, there is a huge lower-middle class. . . . One-seventh of the government employees in New York are Jewish. This is smaller than the Jewish proportion in

the city, but much greater than the proportion of Jewish government employees in other cities. (ibid.:146)

The Jews of New York City were far more incorporated politically than the Jews of Los Angeles before the rise of the Bradley coalition. Inevitably, New York City's Jews were ambivalent about joining an insurgent coalition against an establishment in which many played a role. While Jews represented the most liberal group in the city, they also had a stake in the establishment—a stake that was severely challenged in the 1968 school strikes.

The same ambivalence was experienced by many Blacks. A highly elaborate system of pluralistic bargaining left wide scope for fragmented incorporation of Blacks through the party organizations and the trade unions. In addition, the five-borough system further fragmented the Black community (Mollenkopf 1990a). By contrast, the Los Angeles regime largely excluded Blacks, and there was no party ladder to provide an alternative path to the top.

The larger working-class population of Jews in New York City had fewer opportunities for residential mobility, and longer ties to neighborhoods than the Jews of Los Angeles. Thus, a larger proportion were likely to be "trapped" in declining neighborhoods, surrounded and threatened by minorities. Political liberalism would thereby be counterbalanced by an urban conservatism born of fear and discomfort.

By contrast, the Jews of Los Angeles, more affluent than in New York, moved steadily westward out of the central city in the face of the minority advance (Vorspan 1969). Less than in Brooklyn, for instance, did the Jews of Los Angeles rub raw against minority neighborhoods.

Fisher and Tanaka (1986:216) have reported that California Jews as a group are younger and more affluent than the Jews of New York. Both their youth and the higher educational levels that accompany their affluence may make them more likely to be amenable to the ideology of racial liberalism.

The 1968 school strikes profoundly injured relations between Blacks and Jews in New York City (Harris and Swanson 1970). Both communities felt wronged. The strikes began after a Black-led experimental school board in Ocean Hill-Brownsville transferred nineteen teachers out of the district, setting off three bitter strikes by teachers.

The strikes pitted activist Blacks as "outs" against a school bureaucracy led and staffed disproportionately by liberal and moderate whites (including many Jews). Liberals were cast as "ins" in traditionally liberal New York City; it was a strike against institutional liberalism. The high degree of Black-Jewish conflict produced by the strikes helped shift much of the city's liberal base into a moderate, conservative alliance with white Catholics; this link became the base for the Koch regime (Mollenkopf 1990a; Harris and

Swanson 1970). The result left African-Americans without political incorporation.

Such an event would have been far less likely to occur in Los Angeles. The reform structures of the city worked to insulate city hall from school issues. Los Angeles city leaders have little impact over the schools. The schools are run by a separately elected school board, which has wrestled with such divisive issues as busing. There was, indeed, intense Black-white and to some extent Black-Jewish conflict over busing in Los Angeles. But when Bradley's opponent sought to inject school busing into the 1977 mayoral election, he failed.

In addition to characteristics of the Black and white liberal communities, the nature of the ruling regime in each city had an impact. The rise of minority political coalitions described by Browning, Marshall, and Tabb (1984) typically occurred in opposition to incumbent conservative regimes. In this setting, minorities and liberal reformers joined together to oust unsympathetic regimes and thereby gained political incorporation.

The Los Angeles case fits this model very closely. In the 1950s the city was still ruled by a conservative, business-oriented regime with a small-town point of view. The upset victory of Sam Yorty in 1961 ultimately changed little. Yorty continued the conservative thrust by fighting against federal aid, alienating minorities and liberal reformers, and allying himself closely with the police and conservative white homeowners. While Yorty tried mightily to co-opt Black leaders, his unpopularity among Black voters made success unlikely. The reform system of Los Angeles government would have made it difficult for Yorty to offer material inducements for Black support even if he had desired to do so.

The Yorty regime provided a unifying target for a challenging biracial coalition. As the Black and reform movements rose in strength, their efforts were joined; the result was both an insurgent victory and the shared memory of exclusion under Yorty.

New York City's establishment was both more liberal and more sophisticated than Yorty's artlessly reactionary government. When New York City's vibrant liberalism is examined more closely, it has two streams: the upper-middle-class reform liberalism of "amateur Democrats," and the more traditional working-class and middle-class liberalism of the political parties and trade unions. Both have exercised substantial political clout in local politics, and both have made strong appeals to racial minorities and Jews.

Because of the existence of two appealing sorts of liberalism, it was more difficult for the reform Democrats, whose interests and ideologies were most closely allied with Black political empowerment, to win full control of the liberal spectrum. A substantial percentage of Jews and Blacks were in working-class and middle-class occupations, and were amenable to the appeals of party organizations and trade unions.

New York City's establishment was itself liberal—hardly surprising in a city with such a strong liberal tradition. The doctrine that emerged from this political culture was interest-group liberalism, a pluralistic struggle for public benefits, which inevitably expanded the public sector to meet new demands (Greenstone and Peterson 1973). New York City's leaders practiced a highly elaborate system of pluralistic bargaining, perhaps best represented by Mayor Robert Wagner. Potential insurgencies could be co-opted with the huge public resources available in the city's politics.

The simple conservative establishment in Los Angeles, with its disdain for expansion and openness, sustained the common interests of African-Americans and white liberals. Exclusion from traditional party politics or from conservative regimes created a common interest in political incorporation. Black mayoral candidates often run as liberal, antiparty reformers (Tryman 1974). In most cities, the greater likelihood of white liberals' holding professional positions in noncity employment may reduce potential interest conflicts in the allocation of city jobs. In fact, a Black reform regime may multiply the access of white reformers to higher-level, policymaking positions in the new government.

In Los Angeles, white liberals and Blacks shared major political interests. The Los Angeles biracial coalition originated as an alliance of the "outs"— who happened to be Blacks and white liberals. They built a coalition together as outsiders on the basis of shared ideology and a mutual desire for political incorporation. Bradley's victory brought Black and white liberal leaders the top political jobs in the city (Sonenshein 1984).

Thus, interest conflicts between African-Americans and white liberals in New York City help explain the failure of the predicted model of Black political incorporation through Black mobilization and white liberal support. In Los Angeles, ideology and interest flowed together, at least until recently, to make possible a strong coalition. It has been argued that the incentives for reform politics are "purposive" (ideological) rather than material (Wilson and Clark 1961). But even to reformers, nonideological political benefits provide powerful incentives for political action.

Los Angeles politics was far simpler than New York's, and offered fewer reasons for ambivalence about the establishment. It excluded Blacks and liberal reformers and was therefore a shared target. In New York City, the establishment was both more responsive and more flexible, and absorbed much of the energy that could have gone into an insurgency.

Leadership

In Los Angeles, biracial political success depended fundamentally on African-American leadership and political organization. In New York City, the absence of outstanding leadership helped ensure the early failure of biracial politics. When leadership arose in New York City, it came both too early and too late. A crucial difference between the two cities was the far more sophisticated and unified Black political community in Los Angeles and its more fortuitous timing.

The evolution of the Los Angeles biracial coalition was marked by sophisticated and unified Black political work, from the 1962 nomination of Tom Bradley for a council seat by a community convention to the highly effective mobilization of the Black vote in Bradley's mayoral elections. The African-American rise to citywide power was preceded by strategic bloc voting by Blacks. In 1961, Los Angeles Blacks provided Sam Yorty's margin of victory over an incumbent mayor, in direct opposition to the position of white liberal reformers. Two years later, Blacks won three seats on the fifteen-member city council.

In sum, to successfully achieve political incorporation, Blacks in Los Angeles have in actual practice tended to follow some of the advice of Carmichael and Hamilton. The basis for long-term coalition is best laid in the home base of the Black community. While pursuing this path, they have also succeeded in maintaining links to liberal whites, as suggested by the advocates of ideological coalition, and as ruled impractical or unwise by the Black Power theorists.

In New York City, Blacks were less successful in mobilizing as an independent political force until the late 1980s. Blacks in New York City were comparatively reluctant to back Black candidates for borough or citywide offices. Unlike Black communities in other cities, which provided overwhelming support for Black candidates, New York City's Blacks voted in the 50–60 percent range for Black candidates (Hamilton 1979). The same complaint is heard in Boston (Travis 1990). Mollenkopf (1990a) has noted that New York City's Black political leaders are in many cases incorporated into the regular party and do not seek to lead a reform coalition.

The chances for developing a corps of biracial leadership may have been diverted by the premature success of a liberal electoral coalition behind John V. Lindsay in 1965. Lindsay's election was a beacon to those who favored liberal coalitions, while Los Angeles progressives languished under a strengthened Yorty regime. True to its image as a liberal center, New York City had elected a liberal reformer with major appeal to racial minorities—two years before the election of the first Black mayors in Cleveland and Gary, and in the same year that Sam Yorty crushed the liberal challenge in Los Angeles's mayoral election.

This early success, paradoxically, may have retarded the development of an independent minority movement for citywide incorporation and a body of experience and knowledge about the political tactics necessary to build a biracial coalition. The premature victory of reform liberalism in New York

City was made possible by an electoral system that allowed mayors to be elected without a majority of the vote. In Los Angeles, by contrast, citywide defeat in 1965 and 1969 helped move along both minority mobilization and the art of coalition building by providing crucial feedback from the electorate.

Running on the Republican and Liberal lines, Lindsay won 43.3 percent of the vote, but a majority of no major group. He was able to piece together significant minorities of Jews, Blacks, and Latinos (*New York Times*, 3 November 1965). The Democratic and Conservative candidates split over 55 percent of the vote between them. Democrats won all the other citywide offices, and the Democratic candidate for council president, Frank O'Connor, outpolled Lindsay by over two hundred thousand votes.

Such a result could not have occurred in Los Angeles, where a nonpartisan primary leads to a runoff between the top two finishers. A mayor could not be elected with less than a majority of the vote. Oddly, liberal James Roosevelt's crushing defeat by Yorty in 1965 was not much different from Lindsay's victory. In basically a two-man race, Roosevelt won 36 percent of the vote. In Bradley's 1969 mayoral defeat, he received a higher share of the vote (46 percent) than Lindsay did in victory in either 1965 or 1969. Thus, the difference between victory and defeat in the two cities was more one of electoral structure than of general support. Appearances to the contrary notwithstanding, biracial liberalism in 1965 was no closer to a majority in New York City than in Los Angeles; its political strength was overestimated in New York and underestimated in Los Angeles. When Lindsay won reelection in 1969 as an independent after losing the Republican primary, he collected only 41.8 percent of the vote (*New York Times*, 6 November 1969).

Despite the narrowness of the victory, the election of the glamorous Lindsay transformed New York City government. It seemed that a liberal reform coalition would not have to undertake the slow process of tempering its idealism with the hard discipline of practical coalition building. Victory had already arrived, and it was time to change the city's policies. No longer would the slow cultivation of minority candidacies be required. The mayor himself would be so sympathetic to minority concerns that independent minority politics would be extraneous, and, indeed, threatening.

The Lindsay victory made it appear that a new coalition would be able to dominate the city. Moynihan and Glazer (1970b) proposed that in alliance with Blacks and Puerto Ricans, a new alliance led by upper-status Protestant and Jewish reformers had taken the city away from the Catholics. Later events were to show this conclusion to be highly premature.

During his first term in office, Lindsay backed the community control forces in the antipoverty program; developed a scatter-site housing program to place low-income housing in middle-class areas; supported a ballot measure to create a civilian police review board; and provided early support for the Black challenge to the teachers' union that led to the 1968 teachers' strike (Bellush and David 1971).

Lindsay's program represented a major challenge to the middle-class institutions of the city without a durable majority coalition to back it up—much like the dream of progressives in Los Angeles today. Its reach may have exceeded its grasp. By contrast, the Bradley group assiduously cultivated its coalition garden (at times missing opportunities to undertake creative efforts in public policy). It had taken them a long time to build their majority, and they had no intention of giving it up.

The Lindsay coalition emerged from the amateur reform movement, with all its disdain for practical politics. Lindsay had little real experience with minority politics, and his people tended to view minority needs through an ideological lens. This tendency had been seen among liberal reformers in several cities (Greenstone and Peterson 1973). What happened was that Lindsay won while still quite naive about minority politics.

Thus, it followed that Lindsay chose minority allies from outside existing political organizations with an electoral base. As a reformer, Lindsay shared the perception of minority electoral politics as incompatible with reform philosophy. Wilson (1962) found this view among reformers in New York City, Los Angeles, and Chicago.

Lindsay was able to join forces with community insurgents against the leadership of the federal antipoverty program (Greenstone and Peterson 1973). By directing their efforts at "soft money" federally funded programs, however, these activists may have lost their focus on the "hard money" controlled by city hall. A decade later, Hamilton (1979) found the city's minority politics still pointlessly preoccupied with such efforts.

These developments contrasted sharply with what was happening at the same time in Los Angeles. By 1963, the Los Angeles liberal insurgency had joined forces with an independent Black movement that had secured three council seats. Unlike the New York City amateurs, Los Angeles CDC members were centrally involved in the election of a Black candidate, Tom Bradley, in one of these districts.

Thus, the connection between African-American political empowerment and liberal reform was made early in Los Angeles. In Los Angeles, it would have been inconceivable for political reformers to ignore Bradley and look for unconventional, nonelectoral Black allies. Furthermore, the Los Angeles reformers and Blacks had already been using the political tactics necessary for biracial coalitions in the 1963 council race. The concept of reaching Blacks and whites with separate, if overlapping, appeals had already been successfully tested in Bradley's 1963 council election.

The Los Angeles progressives had no choice other than to seek citywide power after Yorty took complete control of the antipoverty program in 1965. "Soft money" battles were hopeless in the face of Yorty's opposition and the city's disdain for federal money.

There were Black reformers in Los Angeles with independent legitimacy and political ambitions who were taken seriously by white reformers. In Los Angeles, the biracial coalition began in the Black community, and then radiated outward to meet an ascendant liberal reform movement. In New York City, the Lindsay coalition was directed by white reformers, who had reached out to minorities but not to the heart of the minority political community.

In fact, the white liberal mayor in a time of racial polarization also faces great challenge from minority political empowerment. Lindsay had to be concerned about the rise of a serious minority candidate, such as Herman Badillo or Percy Sutton. In fact, Badillo nearly won the 1969 Democratic mayoral primary; had he done so, Lindsay might have failed to be reelected.

Lindsay's approach had the effect of separating minority elected officials from minority street activists, leaving no class of activist-politician-reformers analogous to those in Los Angeles. His early victory headed off the development of such a class, partly because such a group would have threatened his incumbency. The result was bold and creative policy but self-destructive politics. The legacy of the split between progressive politics and the city's middle class remains today (Sleeper 1990).

The election of Lindsay was a source of great excitement and creativity in New York's government. But in some ways, both the co-optative powers of the liberal regime and the surprise election of Lindsay delayed the growth of the sort of minority political incorporation described by Browning, Marshall, and Tabb (1984). And the combination of material appeals from pluralistic bargaining and reform liberalism eventually led to fiscal crisis.

By contrast, the Bradley regime followed the well-trod path most widely used by Black mayors: affirmative action in city hiring, aggressive pursuit of federal funds for social programs, steady pushing for police accountability, and support for downtown redevelopment. Following these policies, Bradley continued to expand his support in the white middle class while retaining a minority base. While the coalition weakened in the 1980s and was severely threatened by racial violence in 1992, it had a remarkably long run at the top.

In one other way, the prospects for a biracial coalition to govern successfully in Los Angeles were far greater than in New York City. The liberal regime that preceded the Lindsay era was already financially overextended. In fact, the city's emerging fiscal crisis was a theme of Lindsay's 1965 campaign. Interest group liberalism had accommodated numerous groups, but at a huge cost. Mayor Wagner had reached expensive agreements with municipal unions. In short, the previous regime had already mortgaged much of the city's fiscal slack. To help racial minorities—and as a white mayor, Lindsay would have to provide a lot—would require cutting back union settlements, thereby risking strikes.

By contrast, Los Angeles' conservative leaders had left a huge gap in their use of city and federal resources to solve social problems. There were limits to union power, no party organizations to mobilize patronage, and a conservative distaste for federal funds. Redevelopment was starved. Thus the incoming liberal regime had a great deal of fiscal slack with which to carry out its objectives. Federal aid alone increased enormously with Bradley's election. Therefore, reaching Bradley's more modest goals required far less confrontation.

The question of leadership goes beyond mayors, to the people at the activist level who sustain coalitions. A key to the Los Angeles biracial coalition was a personal link at the leadership level between middle-class Black activists and white reformers. Carmichael and Hamilton rightly argued that white reformers often ignore Blacks or impose their own interests on them (1967:64–65). This was true generally of the CDC movement in California (Wilson 1962; Jones 1962). In fact, the priorities of Blacks and liberal reformers in Los Angeles often differed on such issues as the importance of Black political representation (Wilson 1962). Bradley's leadership in the liberal CDC movement was therefore a major factor in building cross-racial links.

A Los Angeles Black religious leader, H. H. Brookins, has since 1963 been a major force in connecting Black electoral interests to the ideological support of white liberals. In Bradley's 1963 council campaign, Brookins developed a strategy to reach white liberals (Patterson 1969). In later years, he counseled Bradley to form an alliance with liberal councilwoman Rosalind Wyman (Littwin 1981). Brookins's close alliance with Bradley has been a major factor in maintaining Los Angeles' biracial liberalism.

A loyal network of white liberal CDC activists have also worked closely with Bradley since 1963. They have helped protect his interests in the liberal community and have provided a direct, personal link with the Bradley network in the Black community. The biracial leadership of the Los Angeles coalition was highly active in reducing Black-liberal tensions whenever they arose in the city, often meeting behind closed doors to air differences.

The experience of New York City shows that in the presence of interest conflicts, leaders may tend to protect their own group first, and avoid the search for creative, overarching solutions. Leaders in the Black and Jewish communities did little to prevent intergroup hostility from arising during the 1968 school strikes. Black anti-Semitism emerged and was not repudiated by Black leaders. The teachers' union publicized Black anti-Semitic remarks in order to mobilize support for the union's position (Gittell

1971:153). The school strikes left deep scars. No real network has linked Blacks and white liberals in recent years.

Thus leaders influenced the historical difficulties of biracial politics in New York City and its success in Los Angeles. And the prospects for leaders differed in the two cities. While interest and ideology matter greatly, the outcome is not fixed. The presence of a Black mayoral candidate and the active creation of biracial networks may make the difference.

On November 7, 1989, David Dinkins was narrowly elected as New York City's first African-American mayor. The long drought for minority incorporation in New York City appeared to be over. The election of Dinkins seemed a major, though precarious, milestone in the revival of biracial coalition politics in the nation's largest city.

If Lindsay was elected too early, Dinkins may have been elected too late. Dinkins's style and approach have been comparable to Bradley's, but the conditions of contemporary New York City politics have conspired to make his road much harder.

The Dinkins election, following the pattern of other cities, grew out of a mobilized Black political community energized by the 1988 Jesse Jackson campaign (Thompson 1990; Mollenkopf 1990b). For the first time, a viable African-American candidate in New York City could draw on a mobilized, unified Black vote. Like Dinkins, Tom Bradley won the mayoralty despite a relatively small Black population. Minority mobilization combined with liberal and Jewish votes were the keys in the two largest Jewish communities in America. And the Black candidates were ideal crossover politicians, moderate and reassuring.

But there are important differences. Clearly, Los Angeles has had a stronger and more durable coalition between Blacks and Jews. A Black-Jewish coalition, particularly at the leadership level, has been at the heart of Tom Bradley's success. Dinkins built his victory with stronger Latino support than Bradley received in the early days and a lesser degree of Jewish support.

Dinkins was confronted with a fiscal crisis of major proportions, the criticism of the powerful *New York Times*, and the persistence of well-publicized racial conflicts in the city. He arrived as a mediator in a city that seemed to have given up on mediation. If Tom Bradley were beginning in 1989 instead of 1973, even he might have found a far less hospitable environment for a new Black mayor.

Many New Yorkers believe that Dinkins will be unable to expand his white base if this requires improving relations between Blacks and Jews. Tensions have, indeed, been high between the two communities since at least 1968. But New Yorkers tend to be unduly pessimistic on the subject of Black-Jewish relations—an attitude that can be self-fulfilling. Every incident, every comment by even the most marginal person, becomes magnified.

Expecting Jews to be as big a part of the Dinkins coalition as they are in the Bradley one is unrealistic. The political and social conditions for Black-Jewish alliance were more promising in Los Angeles than in New York City. But the Los Angeles case indicates at the least that Black-Jewish conflict is not inevitable. Coalition expansion is still a possibility.

Conclusions

This book has argued that the success of a biracial electoral coalition between Blacks and white liberals depends primarily on ideology, but with crucial roles for interest and leadership. Two explanations for the difficulties of biracial politics in New York City compared to Los Angeles emerge—conflict of interest and inadequate leadership. The settings in which Blacks and white liberals interacted were much more likely to foster conflict in New York City. The very strength of New York City's liberalism and the high stakes of its politics reduced the viability of the sort of coalition that dominated Los Angeles. Potential coalition partners faced a significant conflict of interest, which would have required adept leadership to overcome. By contrast, the Blacks and white liberals of Los Angeles shared a strong alliance of political interest.

A corps of white liberal and Black leaders, sharing common experiences and a desire for political power through the electoral process, arose in Los Angeles long before the racial conflicts of the mid-1960s. In New York City, by contrast, the premature winning of citywide power by a liberal coalition in 1965 short-circuited the process of realistic coalition formation. This victory also had the paradoxical effect of weakening the impetus for an independent minority movement. By the time an African-American mayor was elected, much of the damage to biracial politics had been done. By contrast, in Los Angeles, the uphill battle faced by liberalism and minority movements against a common enemy made unity more likely. And, the long path to coalition victory forced leaders to patiently forge a winning and stable majority.

It was Los Angeles's relative conservatism that made the long-term victory of a biracial coalition possible, and it was New York City's dynamic and multifaceted liberalism that helped delay and dilute minority political incorporation through biracial coalition. But even in New York City, minority mobilization eventually joined with racial liberalism to achieve an uneasy and precarious minority incorporation.

Not surprisingly, the other metropolis heavily influenced by liberal political culture, San Francisco, was one of the cities studied by Browning, Marshall, and Tabb (1984) where racial minorities were unable for quite some time to obtain independent political incorporation. In many ways, San Francisco is an eastern city that happens to look out on the Pacific Ocean.

Thus, too much liberalism, as well as not enough, may be a deterrent to Black political incorporation. An established liberalism can have the paradoxical effect of stifling the development of an independent Black political movement, while promoting policies on ideological grounds that could bring some material benefits into minority communities (see, e.g., Mollenkopf 1990a; Browning, Marshall, and Tabb 1984:162). In such a city, even moderate regimes would have to adopt policies to preempt the formation of a potentially popular minority-liberal coalition.

The analysis of this chapter indicates lessons for activists in both cities. Los Angeles activists take their biracial coalition for granted. As a new generation of liberal and Black leaders arise, they are generally unaware of the self-discipline that created and sustained the Bradley coalition. They do not remember the days of joint exclusion under the Yorty regime, seeing only that under the present coalition they do not get all they want. The 1992 rebellion will also make Los Angeles activists cautious in building coalition lines.

New York City's biracial activists have the opposite problem. They have lived with interracial tension for so long that they have forgotten what it is like to be part of a durable biracial coalition. However, the long period of joint exclusion may impel these activists to do it right this time—to undertake the slow, patient development of cross-racial links between ideological allies who recognize that a coalition involves distinct, independent groups.

In the broader sense, the experiences of New York City and Los Angeles indicate that the ideological affinity between the minority search for equality and white liberalism represents only a potential base for biracial coalition politics. While drawn together, Blacks and white liberals do not have identical interests. Each group has its own interests, and its own sensitivities. In order to succeed, biracial coalitions must first transcend interest conflicts between Blacks and white liberals. Then the coalition must develop an agenda that allows expansion beyond those two groups—or at least one that does not so threaten other groups that the coalition's survival is jeopardized.

The lesson of New York City is that ideology is not enough. Building biracial coalitions requires a mixture of political pragmatism and strong idealism. Thus it is essential for the strong ideologies of African-American political empowerment and liberal reform to be tempered by shrewd political strategy. A pragmatic sense of politics advanced by effective leaders is essential to make biracial coalitions work.

The search for real political power in the African-American community leads inevitably into biracial coalition and to the search for allies in the white liberal community. Over the last twenty years, New York City's biracial politics would have been greatly advanced by a substantial dose of real Black political power.

In Los Angeles, Black power and biracial coalition politics were complementary; in New York City, they are still seen as contradictory. This has slowed the creation of a true biracial coalition, based on two pillars: white respect for independent Black political activity and Black renunciation of anti-Semitism. Neither Blacks nor liberals can rule a great city without the other. They can enjoy the shared goal of political incorporation only with a due respect for each other.

FIFTEEN

MULTIRACIAL COALITIONS IN THE FUTURE

OF LOS ANGELES: POLITICS BEYOND BLACK

AND WHITE

THE FUTURE of Los Angeles coalition politics has been dramatically and irrevocably altered by the demographic changes recorded in the 1990 census. Both Black and white population shares have declined. The growth of non-Black minority communities portends major shifts in the city's political context. One writer called Los Angeles "the capital of the Third World" (Rieff 1991). What is the role of biracial and multiracial coalitions in this new Los Angeles?

Between 1980 and 1990, the city's overall population increased by more than 10 percent. Four hundred thousand more people lived in the city. The composition of Los Angeles reflected the growth of Latino and Asian-American communities, especially growth due to immigration (see Table 15.1).

In the context of this new city, what comes next for minority politics? The great surge of political mobilization that began in the 1960s has led to a substantial degree of minority political power. We are now moving rather unsteadily into the postincorporation era, an uncharted territory in which new minority and progressive strategies must be devised.

This book's primary focus has been the relationship between African-Americans and liberal whites. New coalitions must move beyond Black and white to include Latinos and Asian-Americans. But building new coalitions is not simply a matter of adding up the population numbers of the various groups. Any multiracial strategy will have to consider that Blacks and whites in Los Angeles have been far more likely to participate in electoral politics and have the most experience in coalition politics, that Asian-Americans have been most active in campaign donations, and that Latinos have been relatively inactive in both elite and mass political mobilization in the city.

DeLeon and Powell (1989) have explored the potential for a new urban populism, a neighborhood-based social agenda based on limiting development while increasing community services. They propose that such coalitions could link antigrowth whites with minorities, and found such an alliance to have formed in a recent slow-growth ballot measure in San

TABLE 15.1
Population of Los Angeles
by Race/Ethnicity, 1990

	%	N
White	37.3	1,299,604
Black	14.0	487,674
Latino	39.9	1,391,411
Asian-American	9.8	341,807
Total		3,485,398

Source: Census data.
Note: Percentages total more than 100 because of rounding.

Francisco. How likely is such an urban populism to form in a sustained manner in Los Angeles? If such an urban populism were to form, which groups would be the most likely participants in a multiracial coalition, and what would be its prospects for success? Is there a chance for a sort of urban populism crossing racial and ethnic lines and maintaining the potential momentum of progressive change, or is balkanization the most likely outcome?

I have argued in this book that the prospects for biracial coalitions between Blacks and white liberals depend on three main factors: ideology, interest, and leadership. Of these, ideological compatibility has been the most important, but both interest and leadership have played crucial roles. In the previous chapter, the model helped explain why Black-liberal alliances were much deeper and stronger in Los Angeles than in New York City.

In this chapter, I will apply that model, originally aimed at a two-part coalition for incorporation, to the more complex puzzle of coalitions among Blacks, white liberals, Latinos, and Asian-Americans in a postincorporation setting. Thus the model will have been used to analyze the development of the Los Angeles coalition, to compare interracial politics in Los Angeles and New York City, and finally to explore multiracial coalitions in the Los Angeles of today.

Ideology

To what extent do minorities and liberal whites still share an ideological agenda? Are there significant ideological divisions between white liberals and white conservatives? Have these ideological patterns shifted significantly in recent years?

The four council districts used in this long-term study can contribute to some answers. In particular, I will look at several types of elections, searching for patterns of alliance and conflict. Because there is no council district with an Asian-American majority, I will rely on other published research to estimate ideologies of the Asian-American community. Public opinion polls will supplement voting analysis.

I examined: (1) party registration and party voting; (2) city nonpartisan voting for mayor and for other citywide offices; (3) measures and referenda on revenue, development, and social issues. The elections I studied mostly took place in the 1980s; the most recent was in 1992. My goal is to move beyond the early coalition era, and observe group behavior leading to the future.

Table 15.2 indicates the proportion of registered voters in each district who were Democrats in 1984, 1988, and 1990. While all four areas had a smaller percentage of Democrats in 1990 than in 1984, the basic pattern shows Blacks as by far the most Democratic, Latinos and white liberals as strongly Democratic, and a significant gap between the three groups and white conservatives. The values in the table underestimate the Democratic registration of Jews and Latinos. A private poll of the Fourteenth Council District in 1987 found that 87 percent of its Latinos were Democrats, compared to 55 percent of whites; four years later the ratio was 79 percent to 54 percent. The same organization conducted citywide polls in 1989 and 1991. In 1989, 82 percent of Jews were Democrats, compared to only 46 percent of white non-Jews (including Catholics); in 1991, 75 percent of Jews were Democrats compared to 38 percent of white Protestants (Fairbank, Maullin, and Associates, 1987, 1989, 1991). An academic survey of Los Angeles Jews found that 5 percent were radical, 41 percent were liberal, 35 percent were moderate, and only 16 percent conservative (Sandberg 1986:165).

Table 15.3 shows how the districts voted in four partisan elections—

TABLE 15.2
Party Registration in Four Key Council Districts, 1984, 1988, and 1990 (percent Democratic)

		1984	1988	1990
5th	White liberal/Jewish	66.8	62.2	62.1
8th	Black	89.0	87.5	87.1
12th	White conservative	47.5	43.9	43.3
14th	Latino/moderate white	70.1	66.1	65.1

Source: County of Los Angeles, Registrar-Recorder.

TABLE 15.3

Vote for the Democratic Nominee in Four Key Council Districts,
1982–1988 (percent)

		1982 Bradley	1984 Mondale	1986 Bradley	1988 Dukakis
5th	White liberal/Jewish	66.9	59.2	56.5	64.6
8th	Black	93.1	85.2	90.1	84.9
12th	White conservative	39.9	31.1	31.5	40.5
14th	Latino/moderate white	60.5	55.6	56.5	62.5

Source: County of Los Angeles, Registrar-Recorder.

when Tom Bradley ran for governor in 1982 and 1986, when Walter Mondale ran for president in 1984, and when Michael Dukakis ran for president in 1988. Once again, Blacks were the most Democratic in these elections, with the white liberal and Latino districts quite close to each other. White conservatives were far to the right of all three groups. Again, the figures for the Fourteenth understate Latino Democratic voting. Erie, Brackman, and Ingram (1992:11) found that 73 percent of Los Angeles Latinos voted for Bradley in 1986.

Asian-Americans in Los Angeles present a more complicated picture. Erie, Brackman, and Ingram (1992:54) found "a small but discernable tendency for the region's Asian Pacifics to vote Democratic." Nakanishi's (1986:34) study of the Los Angeles "Asian Corridor" found that 54.4 percent of Asian-Americans were Democrats, compared to 28.1 percent who were Republicans (1990:34). In addition, Asian-Americans are the least likely of Los Angeles' minority groups to vote. Nakanishi (1990) found that fewer than half of the most active group, Japanese-Americans, were registered to vote. Uhlaner, Cain, and Kiewiet (1989) have found low voting participation among Asian-Americans across all socioeconomic levels.

If we explore the nonpartisan mayoral races in Bradley's four reelection campaigns, a somewhat different pattern emerges. At the height of Bradley's popularity in 1985, the Jewish liberal and Black districts provided support well in excess of their votes for Democratic gubernatorial and presidential candidates (see Table 11.2).

In all four elections, the Latino district provided less support for Bradley than it had for Democratic state and national nominees. Again, the council district numbers probably understate Latino support for Bradley. Interestingly, the vote of the white conservative district, still far from that of the three other groups, was generally higher for Bradley than it was for Democratic nominees. In Bradley's narrow 1989 reelection, his vote declined in all four areas; the Fifth was the only white district to give him a majority.

On two occasions, city voters have voted on propositions that became virtual referenda on business development in the city. In 1986, Proposition U limited heights of city buildings. Widely viewed as a slow-growth measure, it passed overwhelmingly. In 1988, Proposition O was designed to prevent oil drilling in the Pacific Palisades. On the same ballot, Occidental Petroleum proposed measure P to allow the drilling plan to proceed and to use revenue for social programs. A slow-growth position would be yes on U, yes on O, and no on P. Table 15.4 displays the votes on these measures.

The votes on these economic measures revealed the first major divergence in coalition patterns. In all three elections, the white liberal base was the core of the antibusiness sentiment, and the other three groups were rather close to one another. While the city does not have a probusiness electorate (on all three measures the business position lost citywide), growth issues do, indeed, change the nature of coalition politics. This divergence also provides a way in which business can continue to wield power in city politics through dividing progressive forces. The oil-drilling campaign involved aggressive campaigning in minority communities, in which the West Side was cast as the villain.

The *Los Angeles Times* (20 November 1988) also found a gap on economic issues between white liberals and minorities, noting that this could present severe problems for a white liberal, slow-growth candidate for mayor. The history of the Bradley coalition indicates that when he was able to join minorities and white environmentalists on the West Side in 1973, he had built his winning coalition (Sonenshein 1986). Indeed, the crucial consideration in building a postincorporation urban populism in San Francisco would be the resolution of the gap on growth issues (DeLeon and Powell 1989).

The last set of issues represents divisive social questions. These are generally assumed to be cross-cutting issues that fracture coalitions. Los Angeles voters have had the opportunity in recent years to express themselves on two social issues: the death penalty and gun control.

On the 1982 statewide ballot, voters overwhelmingly rejected Proposi-

TABLE 15.4
Slow-Growth Position in Four Key Council Districts, 1986 (percent)

		Yes on Proposition U	Yes on Proposition O	No on Proposition P
5th	White liberal/Jewish	75.9	64.4	72.9
8th	Black	68.5	43.9	60.1
12th	White conservative	62.0	45.2	59.7
14th	Latino/moderate white	66.1	49.5	67.5

Source: City Clerk, Election Division.

tion 15, a handgun control measure. Four years later, the voters turned out
Chief Justice Rose Bird, largely as a referendum on the death penalty. The
results are presented in Table 15.5. A yes vote in each case, to approve
Proposition 15 and to retain Bird, would be seen as a liberal social vote.

The results were mixed. On gun control, as on growth, the cutting edge
was the white liberal community. As in the voting on the business initiatives, the minority and white conservative communities strongly resisted
the liberal position, undoubtedly for different reasons. On the Rose Bird
(death penalty) issue, the picture was different. Blacks were the leading edge
in opposition, although white liberals were once again on the same side as
Blacks. Latinos were mixed, and white conservatives were overwhelmingly
pro–death penalty. The difference between white liberals and white conservatives on the death penalty was as large as that on partisan and city
elections.

Private polling on a number of recent issues underscores the ideological
division among whites. For example, police issues strongly divided Jews
and white Protestants. Latinos differed considerably from white non-Jews,
and most closely resembled Jews despite major differences in socioeconomic status (Fairbank, Maullin, and Associates, various years).

These results challenge the prevailing view. The two high-turnout, high-
status white districts revealed large ideological differences among whites,
with significant electoral consequences. Polling confirms the evidence from
the council district analysis. In light of the high political participation of the
city's whites, these differences will continue to have profound political
consequences.

The vision of a "minority-majority city" run by whites implies a level of
unity among whites that is profoundly discouraging, but is factually incor-
rect. Efforts to increase minority incorporation may continue to draw support from mobilized whites. Liberal whites are far closer to the minority
position than whites as a whole (and, indeed, conservative whites are further away).

TABLE 15.5
Liberal Vote on Social Issues in Four Key Council Districts,
1982 and 1986 (percent)

		1982 *Proposition 15*	*1988* *Rose Bird*
5th	White liberal/Jewish	55.5	52.4
8th	Black	39.7	68.1
12th	White conservative	38.3	25.8
14th	Latino/moderate white	44.2	42.7

Source: County of Los Angeles, Registrar-Recorder.

Latinos are consistently more liberal than conservative whites; they are comparable to white liberals, but much less mobilized. We see renewed evidence that Blacks are by far the most liberal group in the city. Asian-Americans in Los Angeles display a moderate degree of Democratic liberalism, but to a lesser degree than do either Latinos or Jews.

Rather than whites on one side, Blacks on the other, and Latinos in the middle (Jackson 1988), my picture shows Blacks on one end and white conservatives on the other. These are still the poles of Los Angeles city politics. White liberals and Latinos are in the middle, and Asian-Americans are between these two groups and white conservatives. Latinos and Asian-Americans mobilize at low levels, but Latino participation seems likely to increase as the community's socioeconomic status rises. There has been no real erosion at the mass level of the electoral base for multiracial politics in Los Angeles. General liberal ideology, support for minority incorporation, and Democratic loyalty and voting seem to remain extremely solid.

Petrocik and Patterson (1986:11) found much the same thing in their analysis of party coalitions in Los Angeles: "The pro-Democratic bias of Hispanics, Jews and Blacks is virtually unaffected by income." The data also show, however, that there are important areas of electoral conflict among potential progressive allies. The most important are attitudes toward economic growth, social issues, and raising of taxes to provide public services. These divisive issues are crucial in the formation of a big-city coalition and in the ability of a winning coalition to provide important benefits.

Ideological agreement provides only the beginning of a multiracial coalition. Coalitions are more complex than electoral affinity; they also involve group competition (interests) and long-term elite transactions (leadership). How are these dynamics likely to affect future coalitions in Los Angeles politics? How have the 1992 riots affected the potential for building intergroup alliances?

Interest

In the postincorporation city, the framework of minority and coalition politics has changed. Minorities once joined with white liberals to unseat the conservative regime, win political incorporation, and implement progressive policies. In the postincorporation era, the liberal coalition has become divided over economic issues and political power. The consensus on downtown redevelopment as a means of revitalizing the local economy has collapsed as the city has choked on high-intensity growth while basic services have been starved. Class conflict has emerged within the biracial alliance, with many middle-class whites opposing growth and minorities calling for economic development.

The flow of federal funds for social programs has been halted, perhaps permanently. Federal aid had once helped solve the local political problem of the minority-liberal coalition: how to promise change without unduly raising local taxes. Now leaders must balance the political demand for low taxes with the call for greater city services. Poverty, once targeted for major reduction through a combination of federal aid and redevelopment, has worsened.

Minority incorporation has advantaged some minorities over others. Generally, the greater mobilization and unity of African-Americans has brought them much more incorporation than Latinos and Asian-Americans have enjoyed. These newer groups are growing by leaps and bounds and are themselves seeking a greater political role. Can a new urban politics incorporate Blacks and white liberals, themselves divided over issues of growth, and the newly emerging minorities?

Most of all, the idealism that animated the creation of minority incorporation and that allowed minority and liberal leaders substantial latitude is fast eroding. New coalitions must offer new benefits—particularly in the areas of economic equality and the quality of life—in order to establish a stable base of support. Moreover, all these trends had been in place long before the jury reached its verdict in Simi Valley.

The formation of a biracial coalition in Los Angeles was promoted by the mobility of the Black and Jewish communities. They were not economic competitors, and the Jewish community was moving westward even as Blacks were moving into the neighborhoods its members had vacated. Conditions are different in Los Angeles today. At the street level, where groups interact, there are many more opportunities for conflict and competition.

Blacks and Jews are increasingly likely to experience economic and political competition—a reflection of the increasing social and economic success of the Black community. An example is conflict over the role of Blacks in the film industry of Hollywood; resentment at the small number of Black artists in the executive levels of the studios took on a Black-Jewish tinge.

A broader area of conflict between African-Americans and liberal whites is the political issue of economic growth. The slow-growth movement has been led by West Side liberals, and many inner city activists resent the implication that the city has grown too much. In the central city, economic growth is still eagerly sought—as long as there are limits and people are not displaced.

On the other hand, there are still ways in which Los Angeles tends to be relatively free of Black-white liberal interest conflicts. The vast spread of the city and the continuing mobility of the population prevent some of the zero-sum living situations characteristic of eastern and midwestern cities. For example, Jews and other white liberals are still less likely to be inner city store owners than in New York City.

Blacks and white liberals are now in the paradoxical position of both sharing an interest in a status quo in which they are highly represented and being competitors for power in the city. This creates an ambivalent relationship through which assertive Latino and Asian-American political forces can increase their own power.

While the most successful Blacks may find themselves in competition with liberal whites, less successful Blacks are facing pressure from Latinos and Asian-Americans in their neighborhoods. There has been a very significant movement of Latinos into the South Side Black areas. Indeed, the central areas of the city are beginning to become outposts of interethnic rivalry among minority groups (Johnson and Oliver 1989).

More than the numbers has changed. South Central Los Angeles is in the midst of a crisis of ethnic succession. The movement of Latino communities in two directions will change Los Angeles. Upwardly mobile Latinos have been moving into the southern end of the San Fernando Valley, the location of the Seventh Council District. Latinos there are entering traditionally white, homeowning areas of the Valley. Working-class and poor Latinos have been heading in the other direction, into South Central Los Angeles and into traditionally Black neighborhoods. Many are immigrants, and a large number are Central American.

There has been conflict between Blacks and Latinos in the schools, in the public hospitals, and in political decisionmaking. The Black community has found itself outnumbered within its own historical area. For example, in the aftermath of the 1992 violence, Black activist Danny Bakewell has been pressuring contractors to hire only Blacks from South Central Los Angeles for rebuilding work. Latinos have been removed from jobs as a result of Black protests, and are reacting angrily.

The African-American community continues to hold the political power in South Central Los Angeles and to control the public institutions serving the community. In one of the supreme ironies of emerging Los Angeles, inner city Black leaders are increasingly in the position once held by the Jewish community of New York City—holding political and social sway with declining numbers over new minorities. The resultant tensions may lead to conflicts not dissimilar from those in New York.

Important bases for alliance between Blacks and Latinos still exist, including the desire for economic growth and the call for year-round schools, both of which are opposed on the liberal West Side. All the evidence indicates that as class issues grow in importance, Black-Latino alliances will strengthen. But leadership will have to borrow some of the techniques that worked successfully in building Black-Jewish coalitions—somehow expressing each community's real interest while building bridges across group lines.

The role of Korean-American store owners in Black communities adds another dimension to the difficulties of building coalitions. A series of violent confrontations in 1991 between Korean-American shopkeepers and local Blacks greatly increased tensions. One of the underlying causes of the 1992 riot was outrage at a lenient sentence given to a Korean-American grocer who had killed a young Black woman in her store. The 1992 violence involved great destruction of Korean-American stores, and in the aftermath, city hall has been buffeted by the competing demands of Blacks and Asian-Americans.

A city ordinance to limit the rebuilding of liquor stores in South Central Los Angeles has highlighted the direct conflict of interest between the two groups. The controversy over the rebuilding of liquor stores in South Central Los Angeles pitted grass-roots organizations, primarily in the African-American community, against merchants, many of whom were Korean-American. The Community Coalition for Substance Abuse Prevention and Treatment put pressure on city hall to exempt liquor stores from "fast track" rebuilding authority. Eighth District council member Mark Ridley-Thomas took the lead in the council to restrict the liquor store rebuilding.

When the city council and the mayor agreed to the exemption of liquor stores, there was a strong political reaction from the Korean-American community. A group of Korean-American merchants stood outside city hall for nearly two weeks, beating on drums and demanding a meeting with Mayor Bradley. Bradley finally did meet with them.

The liquor store controversy, which was not resolved by the interim council measure, indicated the complex political impact of the rebellion. Groups that had hitherto remained silent, or had been overshadowed by others, were emerging. Asian-Americans, feeling exposed and vulnerable after the violence, were becoming more politically active and undertaking actions that would have been unthinkable before April. They were unlikely to continue the pattern of political support for politicians without policy responsiveness in return, which introduced an important new dimension into minority coalition building. At the same time, African-Americans and Latinos in South Central Los Angeles were establishing new criteria for rebuilding the community.

The social and economic life of the city is in great transition. The likelihood of conflict among potential allies is greater today than when the original biracial coalition was formed. The city is much more heavily populated, and there are substantial areas of social and economic competition.

One of the great pillars of the biracial coalition was the shared outsider status of Blacks and white liberal reformers. Each group could assert itself, while expanding the power of the coalition. Those conditions have changed in the postincorporation city. The Black community is relatively certain to lose some of its direct political representation, even if its considerable voting clout remains a key force in city politics. Its leaders have been insiders at city hall since 1973, with a Black mayor, three city council members, and numerous city hall officials.

When Tom Bradley leaves office, it is unlikely that he will be succeeded by another Black politician. In the increasingly Latino Ninth Council District, Black council member Gilbert Lindsay died and was replaced by a Black politician. But Latinos, who have been half "in" and half "out" during the hegemony of the biracial coalition, may have a chance someday to win the seat in the Ninth District. In 1992 Latinos pressured the city council to redistrict both council and school board seats to increase Latino representation. The spread of Latino population in the city means that within a few years as many as five council districts could have Latino representatives. The trends in the working-class cities, such as Bell Gardens, that surround Los Angeles and have been long dominated by white officeholders, indicate that Latino numbers may soon be followed by major mobilization. Latino takeovers of these small cities have begun.

The combination of African-American decline and Latino assertion is likely to create tensions in the political system, and is certain to reduce incentives for coalition building. Black and Latino political development can be mutually reinforcing up to a point, but Latinos have done less well as Blacks have won substantial incorporation (McClain and Karnig 1989). What if Blacks lose substantial incorporation as Latinos gain theirs?

There is substantial evidence that interest conflicts may be growing among Blacks, Latinos, Asian-Americans, and white liberals. In comparison, the preincorporation period was characterized by strong grounds for interest alliance. Certainly, in comparison to the preincorporation period, the stakes of city political and social/economic life are higher and more conflictual. The simple, underdeveloped city of the 1960s has evolved into a sophisticated metropolis with alert groups seeking advantage. There are still areas of alliance; the margin of safety for interest conflicts has, however, clearly narrowed.

Leadership

It will not be easy for leaders in the postincorporation era to build multiracial coalitions among ideological allies in the face of important interest conflicts. Those who would build new coalitions in Los Angeles face a system in which African-Americans and white liberals are already incorporated at high levels, and fear reduction in power. The "common enemy" argument of first incorporators is not available. And Latinos and Asian-Americans certainly expect to be at the head table in any new coalition that is formed.

There is even a substantial question as to whether political incorporation can bring lasting benefits. The persistence of minority poverty, even in a highly incorporated city, has changed the perspectives of many activists. In the first flush of minority incorporation, there was much more optimism that politics would lead toward equality. Leaders will have a harder time earning leeway from their constituents for coalition bargains.

Can you teach a new dog old tricks? In essence, that is the problem facing multiracial leadership in Los Angeles. In a city where biracial politics are taken for granted, and in which few are aware of the leadership moves necessary to preserve it, there is little accumulated knowledge of coalition formation and maintenance. Little is known about how the biracial coalition preserved itself because to talk about it openly would have weakened its ability to maintain the peace.

The example of Chicago certainly indicates that there is nothing inevitable about the preservation of minority incorporation. After the death of Harold Washington, the progressive coalition was unable to escape the resurgence of the political machine behind the son of the late Mayor Richard Daley (Starks and Preston 1990). Mollenkopf (1990a) has indicated that rollback of minority gains must be a consideration in the analysis of minority politics. Even liberal San Francisco turned away from the urban populism of Mayor Art Agnos after one term, and elected a former police chief in 1991. Surely the chances for rollback in Los Angeles, and a conservative victory, are not to be discounted. In light of the massive urban violence, the potential for a long-term backlash against progressive politics cannot be ruled out.

The 1993 Mayoral Election

As of early September 1992, the 1993 Los Angeles municipal election promised to be a major milestone in the city's political history. In the aftermath of the riots of 1992, the long-standing political structure dominated by Mayor Bradley's biracial coalition of African-Americans, white liberals, and business was finally only one of several claimants for power. The rebellion had brought new issues, which had been simmering just beneath the surface, into the center of city life—divisions not only of race but of class, and the rise of open competition among the bewildering array of groups who call Los Angeles home. Whether or not Bradley ran for a sixth term, the 1993 spring election was certain to be the most competitive and important since Bradley's first victory in 1973.

The biracial coalition would not disappear. Rather, it would continue in a subsidiary role, as a part of city politics. But something new was clearly in the air: what would it be? Some saw a rainbow coalition of minorities united against a white minority; others saw a class war of the poor against the rich; yet others feared a balkanized war of each against each. Clearly, newly assertive minorities, such as Asian-Americans and Latinos, would play a considerable role in the election.

There might well, however, have been some points of continuity with previous coalition patterns. Observers might have once again prematurely ruled out a role for alliances between whites and minority groups. For instance, my examination of the vote on the police reform measure (Proposition F) passed in June 1992 revealed a clear alliance between long-standing partners—the South Central Los Angeles Black community and white liberal voters on the West Side and in Hollywood. Research on 1993 ought therefore to be open to the possibility that ideological differences between white liberals and white conservatives might have continued to play a role in the search for power.

The main mayoral candidates would struggle hard to create a coalition in what might well have been a transitional period in city politics. The coalition with which a candidate won might later shift, as had Yorty's 1961 coalition; he came in as a progressive, and soon built a powerful conservative coalition.

On September 24, 1992, Bradley held a press conference to declare his intentions. He announced that he would not seek a sixth term as mayor. The race for mayor was now wide open, and many politicians sought to win the seat. Bradley's base in the African-American community became the subject of competition, and candidates sought to create their own coalitions. For the first time in decades, Los Angeles was in search of a new governing majority.

The candidate whose coalition style was closest to Bradley's was Michael Woo, a council member from the Thirteenth District. An Asian-American elected to the council in 1985, Woo represented a white majority district in Hollywood with a significant Asian-American population. His district was one of the city's most liberal. Woo had been outspoken in his opposition to Chief Gates, calling for his resignation at a time when only African-American leaders were taking that position. Woo was likely to mobilize the Asian-American community, which was already a major, if less than visible, force in city campaign fundraising. With his liberal constituency, he was popular on the West Side and could claim credentials as both a reformer and a coalition builder. As Woo had discovered in his losing 1981 council race, however, bias against Asian-Americans could be a liability in city politics. His opponent in that race, council member Peggy Stevenson, had raised the specter of shadowy Chinese financial backers to successfully sow doubts among the voters.

County supervisor Gloria Molina, formerly a city council member from the First District, was the major prospect in the Latino community. A formidable campaigner, Molina could make the strongest claim to the reform tradition. As county supervisor, she had been a major force in changing the board's secretive and autocratic practices. Her public reputation as a gadfly would be a major asset in a mayoral race. She had also demonstrated an ability to mobilize the Latino vote and had supported voter registration efforts to expand the Latino base. Her candidacy could be a galvanizing force for a long-dormant Latino community. Her liabilities included her long-running feud with Latino council member Richard Alatorre and her strained relations with other elected officials. Her candidacy could both mobilize Latinos and divide Latino politicians.

Experience running citywide would be an important advantage for any mayoral candidate, and neither Woo nor Molina had run such a race. City attorney James K. Hahn had the potential to build a citywide coalition. In his previous citywide races, Hahn had demonstrated a strong base in the African-American community, with the support of both Bradley and his own father, long-time county supervisor Kenneth Hahn. In addition, he had drawn votes in the Valley and other areas of the city. The problems experienced by a potential rival, county district attorney Ira Reiner—beginning with the Rodney King case and continuing in the trial of those accused of beating a white truck driver during the violence—increased Hahn's chances. Hahn's law and order image and his minority alliances, however, were counterbalanced by his liabilities as a long-time insider in city politics in a year likely to favor advocates of change.

There were a number of potential Jewish candidates for mayor, drawing from both the West Side and the San Fernando Valley. Zev Yaroslavsky, a Jewish council member from the Fifth District, had pulled out of a potential 1989 race against Bradley, and might have faced trouble mobilizing support for 1993. While he remained a formidable figure on the West Side, he had built few links to minority communities. Jewish assemblyman Richard Katz and Jewish council member Joel Wachs (Second District) represented Valley districts and were political moderates. They could be successful if they drew support from the liberal West Side, built links to minority groups, or mobilized the Valley to a new level of prominence.

The African-American community was unlikely soon to launch a successor to Bradley. Council member Nate Holden (Tenth District) was a long-time Bradley enemy, and his early support for Chief Gates was unlikely to endear him to African-American voters. Council members Mark Ridley-Thomas (Eighth District) and Rita Walters (Ninth District) had been elected in 1991, and were unlikely to take on mayoral races so soon. Congresswoman Maxine Waters, Bradley's most powerful rival in the African-American community, was unlikely to seek citywide office. Her strong advocacy of progressive and minority interests had made her a leading force, but would limit her potential as a citywide coalition builder.

Strikingly absent was a major established conservative in the 1993 race. Only maverick Richard Riordan could hope to mobilize the conservative base. The political damage that had crushed Daryl Gates's career as police chief had also ended his long-standing mayoral aspirations. The reformed LAPD was in no position to help a conservative challenger—a significant change from previous elections. The business community was likely to divide among a number of contenders. Conservative voters, however, would be an important constituency in a close and diverse campaign. Thus, all the candidates were likely to address issues important to conservatives, such as keeping taxes low.

The main leaders in the city today have been limited in forming new coalitions by ties to particular policies or groups. The West Siders, represented by Yaroslavsky, have been slow to build cross-racial alliances around the slow-growth issue. Clearly, they must offer other groups more than the preservation of an affluent lifestyle on the West Side. Until recently, Mayor Bradley had been so closely tied to a downtown redevelopment strategy that he had cut himself off from the environmental movement on the West Side. Latino leaders, such as council member Richard Alatorre and county supervisor Gloria Molina, have been caught up in their struggles with one another, limiting their ability to build citywide coalitions. In the African-American community, dynamic leaders, such as Maxine Waters, are emerging as racial partisans, able to speak with credibility to their own community, but looking for new bridges to other groups.

When the Bradley administration began to move away from its sole focus on business development, it promoted some new linkages between minorities and the liberal West Side. Facing Yaroslavsky's challenge, Bradley brought in an environmentally oriented deputy mayor, Michael Gage, and began appointing environmentalists to key city commissions. After Gage left the mayor's office, Bradley appointed him and a number of other environmentalists to the board of the Department of Water and Power, and Gage was soon elected president of the board. Bradley initiated a program to charge developers' fees to build low-cost housing, a policy used in some other cities but long shunned by his administration. He appointed vigorous new staff to save an affordable-housing program that had been long mismanaged and neglected. After he was battered in a conflict-of-interest scandal, Bradley proposed wide-ranging reforms of city political practices.

With Bradley moving in this direction, it became safer for other politicians to question the development focus without alienating minorities. While Bradley's policies are often questioned in the African-American community, any attack on him or his policies from the outside is greatly resented. A continuing problem, however, is that a new generation of

African-Americans may be less inclined to support coalition politics than the current generation of activists. If, for example, anti-Semitism develops a strong cultural acceptability among younger Blacks, biracial ties will suffer.

Councilman Michael Woo, the city's only Asian-American elected official, has been in the best position to develop a citywide constituency. Unlike other minorities, Asian-American officeholders tend not to be ethnic representatives (Cain, Kiewiet, and Uhlaner 1986). For that reason, Woo is able to participate in minority politics without being too closely accountable to his own group. Indeed, with their focus on campaign fundraising, Asian-Americans may play a pivotal role not only as a mass constituency but as an organized semielite.

What appears to be missing today in Los Angeles is a set of elite ties between potential allies. Elite trust earned over time is a crucial factor in the formation of coalitions (Hinckley 1981). Such trust could be found over a twenty-year period among the Black and white liberal activists who built and sustained the biracial coalition. The common effort in electing Bradley to the city council from the multiracial Tenth District in 1963 and then to the mayoralty a decade later helped cement that trust.

One place where such ties may begin to develop is in the activities of grass-roots organizations, rather than in those of elected officials. (The origin of the Bradley coalition was in informal Democratic organizations, not among incumbent elected officials.) With the decline of federal funding, community-based organizations have arisen to advocate rather than provide services. Examples include the South Central Organizing Committee in the Black community and the United Neighborhood Organizations in Latino communities. Alliances with neighborhood and issue-oriented organizations on the West Side could begin to foster elite ties that might later be highly productive.

Because these groups focus so heavily on specific, concrete issues, they may suffer less from the racial and ethnic "identity politics" that is increasingly arising in Los Angeles. They may be able to avoid such inflammatory actions as Black activist Danny Bakewell's campaign to remove Latinos from jobs rebuilding South Central Los Angeles in favor of Blacks. Instead of protesting against companies or institutions—a common enemy—Bakewell faced off against Latino workers. Inevitably, Bakewell's approach will force a similar response from Latinos, and another bridge will have been broken. Further, such conflict strengthens Latino conservatives, just as Black-Jewish conflict bolsters white conservatives.

The broader challenge for new Los Angeles leaders, beyond who wins in 1993, is to reframe issues in a cross-racial, cross-class manner. For example, organizations focused on white middle-class issues tend to ignore the concerns of minorities. Feminist organizations, environmental groups, and AIDS organizations have tended to draw from middle-class white communities without expanding to minority communities. An encouraging development is a small environmental group that has been promoting its issues in South Central Los Angeles, one of the principal areas of environmental impact (*Los Angeles Times*, 5 December 1991).

An additional area of possible coalition activity is labor organizing, particularly among low-wage Latino workers. It is difficult to see how the movement for Latino empowerment can strictly limit itself to electoral tactics in light of the high percentage of noncitizen Latinos who are working in nonunionized industries at very low wages. One study contends that 46 percent of the Spanish-origin population of Los Angeles are not citizens (Pachon 1990:84). Labor efforts in this area can have important coalition-building consequences, even if the original effort is not electoral.

In June 1990, such cross-organizing took place during a strike by janitors in a Century City office building. A major cleaning firm had refused to sign a labor agreement with the mostly Latino immigrant janitors, while having such contracts with workers at other locations. The Justice for Janitors strike was supported by the Service Employees International Union, which led a march on the location.

The LAPD intervened when the marchers reached Olympic Boulevard, attacking viciously, and injuring a number of marchers. The violence drew widespread attention, and brought a call from Mayor Bradley for an investigation of the police action. The company soon settled, in an extraordinary victory for the low-wage workers. Bradley and liberal Jewish councilman Zev Yaroslavsky, in whose district Century City is located, held a joint press conference to announce the agreement.

Los Angeles coalitions in the postincorporation city must cross the line from electoral politics to a sort of hybrid electoral-labor politics. The electoral experience of the biracial coalition needs to be expanded to incorporate workplace concerns.

Conversely, those who are seeking to focus political efforts on low-wage workers need to learn and understand the connections to electoral politics. The literature on transformations of the city workforce into low-wage labor contains precious little analysis of politics and coalitions. A new focus on both politics and economics may provide the basis for constituting a new progressive regime.

Future Los Angeles Coalitions

Long before the violence and even before the beating of Rodney King, much rethinking had been under way about the Los Angeles biracial coalition. On the left, Bradley's liberal coalition politics—especially the coalition's ties to business—had never been particularly appealing. Among progressive African-Americans, Bradley's style of coalition leadership has always fallen short of strong advocacy for that community's own interests. Latinos and Asian-Americans, noting their increased numbers, have chafed at the city's focus on Black and white politics.

Much of the new thinking has involved rainbow coalitions of color and class. The rainbow ideal derives from Jesse Jackson's 1984 and 1988 presidential campaigns, but can be traced back even earlier to Stokely Carmichael and Charles V. Hamilton's *Black Power* (1967). In Carmichael and Hamilton's theory, interracial coalitions based on ideology (ties with white liberals) will fail to advance the Black community. The best coalitions form on the grounds of self-interest. Color and class are elements of self-interest and, in this view, provide a solid base for coalition politics.

Rainbow politics have obvious appeal for Los Angeles progressives. With Latinos and Asian-Americans increasing in numbers, an alliance of Blacks, Latinos, and Asian-Americans would represent a clear majority of the city. As class issues increase in Los Angeles politics, economics could provide a common way to overcome racial animosities. Superficially, the rainbow coalition should be a perfect fit for the new era of multiracial politics.

The problem is that on closer examination Los Angeles rainbow coalitions look less promising than advertised. As Erie, Brackman and Ingram (1992:89) have noted, "The rainbow model . . . is an ideological gloss that obscures as much as it illuminates the realities of ethnic power in Los Angeles." Ethnic conflict and economic competition significantly undermine the potential of such alliances. Further, ideological differences will not be easy to overcome. In a survey of California Blacks, Latinos, Asian-Americans, and whites, Cain, Kiewiet, and Uhlaner (1986:29) found: "Whether there will be a political coalition of minorities depends on which issues prove to be most salient in the future. On many issues that separate lower and higher income groups, Latinos and Blacks will coalesce in opposition to most Whites and Asian-Americans." Uhlaner (1991) argued that while there are no insurmountable obstacles to Black–Latino–Asian-American alliances, the participation of Asian-Americans would likely be limited to immigrant generations. Her data also showed strong affinities between Blacks and Latinos, as compared to whites. These studies provide an invaluable taste of reality for those who hypothesize the easy formation of coalitions of minorities. Well before the riot, numerous interminority street conflicts had been increasing in the city (Oliver and Johnson 1984; Johnson and Oliver 1989). These conflicts are unlikely to be assuaged by the violence, and in some cases will be severely exacerbated.

The most likely rainbow coalition is between Blacks and Latinos. Ideological compatibility seems to be much higher between these two groups than it is with either Asian-Americans or whites. While alliance with Asian-Americans is not ruled out in any of these studies, their higher economic status and relatively conservative partisan and ideological positions mean that alliance will require substantial cultivation.

In his study of Los Angeles, Jackson (1988:26) found that "the voting data presented here clearly demonstrate the prospect for a coalition forming between the Black and Hispanic communities of Los Angeles." In general, Jackson found "extreme polarization between the Black and white communities of Los Angeles," reporting that "we would find Blacks at the liberal end of the spectrum and Anglos at the conservative end. Hispanic voters would fall in between."

The 1992 riots revealed just how difficult rainbow politics could be. The Los Angeles East Side, a strongly Mexican-American community, remained largely uninvolved in the rioting. To the extent that there was Latino participation, it came primarily from communities of recent immigrants, many of them from Central America, in South Central Los Angeles (*Los Angeles Times*, 8 May 1992). The political leadership in the Latino community had displayed considerable ambivalence about the police throughout the King controversy, and the "rainbow riot" picture is therefore too simplistic.

Most powerfully, the assault on businesses owned by Korean-Americans was one of the most violent interminority confrontations in memory. The images of a shooting war in the streets will remain vivid long after the unrest settles. The closest analogy is the role of Jewish shopkeepers in Black New York City neighborhoods decades ago, but even those brittle relations never escalated to heavily armed and violent confrontation. The bond of "common color" is likely to be a thin reed indeed.

An underlying and unspoken assumption of the rainbow model has been the exclusion of white liberals. That, indeed, has been part of its appeal to those unhappy with liberal biracial coalitions. This rainbow approach is based on "rational choice" coalition theories, in which coalition members maximize their advantages and can create coalitions anew from common interest (Riker 1961).

Mike Davis (*Los Angeles Times*, 1 June 1991) dramatically expressed this picture of a city divided, in which the only choices are between a minority coalition and white dominance, and a city in which there are no longer relevant differences between white liberals and white conservatives:

> In the first case . . . minority white rule in the city is re-established by the continuing collusion of neo-liberal and conservative council members. The Hollywood Hills cease to be an important ideological divide. . . . In the second scenario . . . a new generation of activists . . . start to lay the foundation for a durable rainbow coalition whose fulcrum is a black-Latino alliance.

The vision of a city divided between resentful minorities and comfortable, conservative whites (the "*Bladerunner*" scenario) is dramatic, but both misleading and self-fulfilling. The reality is that color is likely to be a shaky ground for minority alliances, and that whites are much more politically diverse than expected. Urban violence generally leads people to presume the extinction of cross-racial alliances. This belief was widespread after the Watts riot. Yet well after Watts, ideological differences among whites were crucial aspects of the minority struggle for political power (Browning, Marshall, and Tabb 1984).

The *"Bladerunner"* assumption even influences research: testing this rainbow model does not require scholars to search for ideological differences among whites. Whites instead become a politically monolithic comparison group. Where white divisions are considered relevant, they are often examined by social class (Hahn and Almy 1971; Jackson 1988). But not all ideological division among whites will emerge from a class analysis; indeed, some of the strongest ideological divisions among whites are among whites of comparably high social status (Shingles 1989).

Experience suggests that coalitions *for* minority equality may not only be coalitions *of* minorities. Coalitions *for* economic equality may not only be coalitions *of* the dispossessed. The missing piece, and a critical key to the puzzle of Los Angeles's future, is the potential role of liberal whites in minority coalitions.

The critique of coalition theory advanced by Hinckley (1981) may provide a more realistic way to explore future coalitions in Los Angeles. Hinckley drew attention to the role of historical memory and elite trust in coalitions. While acknowledging the importance of rational self-interest, Hinckley argued that new coalitions do not arise out of thin air; they incorporate the previous experiences of potential coalition partners. In short, the most likely coalition to form may be the coalition that already exists.

If Black-liberal-Latino alliances, in various permutations, were the most common features of the incorporation period, these three groups should be the starting points for discussions of subsequent coalitions. While the question of coalitions of color or class is highly appealing to explore, it may have limitations as the sole basis for exploring potential coalitions for minority empowerment.

While much has stayed the same, much has irrevocably changed in Los Angeles. The dramatic struggle over the police department revived the historical coalition lines of the city. But that development obscures the great need for new politics and new policies in the city. The model of downtown redevelopment trickling down to the inner city is no longer viable as Los Angeles's sole economic policy. New ways must be found to generate resources and apply them directly to the areas that need help. Without federal aid, local leaders will have to take on the awesome task of enlisting private financial centers and taxpayers in the reconstruction.

The biracial government led by African-Americans and their white liberal allies must deal with the rise of Latinos and Asian-Americans. The reapportionment of city council seats in 1992 is likely to set off important conflicts between ascendant Latinos and council incumbents. The Latino presence highlights the growing gap between voters and residents of the city. Business as usual will be to represent voters. But Latinos will have to contest that approach; otherwise, the long lag in turning residents into voters will set the community back even more. For a time, Latinos (and, on occasion, Asian-Americans) may find that they need to challenge existing coalitions in order to carve out a senior role in coalitions yet to form.

The biracial coalition will likely continue in some form after Bradley leaves office. The relationship between Blacks and white liberals has been long-standing, not just in Los Angeles but in less polished forms in other cities and in national politics. It has a deep base, as well as deep conflicts. Blacks and white liberals have shared a loyalty to the Democratic party and to racial liberalism. They have collaborated in the election of African-American mayors.

One possibility is that the future of Los Angeles coalition politics will be a kind of overlay, in which the biracial coalition will continue to exist, but in a more fragile state. The coalition will share power with ascendant minorities and will have to negotiate with community-based organizations. The city will develop far more pluralistic politics, but the new politics will not be like the party politics of the East and Midwest. Rather, it will be a Los Angeles version. Politics change as groups low in voter registration, or even in citizenship, mobilize in the workplace and begin to change the rules themselves.

When the biracial coalition took power in 1973, it defeated a long-dominant conservative coalition. The conservative base did not disappear; it only became weaker. It lodged in the chief of police and in such areas as the northwestern Valley's Twelfth District. It fought rearguard actions, and sometimes won; it exercised a substantial veto over city policy through bloc votes against city tax increases. It still exists today, although further weakened by the fall of Daryl Gates.

Conclusions

The sad history of New York City stands as a sobering lesson for activists seeking to shape the future of Los Angeles. Faced with a changing New York City in the early 1960s, progressives in Black and white communities chose to pursue a path that eventually severed the ties between the minority struggle for equality and the city's middle class. The result was tragic—and continues to reverberate in the city today (Sleeper 1990). The rebellion in

South Central Los Angeles has placed Los Angeles at a similar turning point; making the best possible choice is urgently important.

But Los Angeles has the benefits of two histories that New Yorkers did not have in 1965. First, the experience of New York City shows what can go wrong if the best path is not chosen. Second, the history of Los Angeles's biracial coalition shows a path to moderate, progressive social change, the threads of which can be tied into the future. But the violence of 1992 casts things in a new light. Can groups learn to trust each other in the aftermath of civil violence?

Minorities and white liberals still remain the most viable partners for a multiracial coalition in Los Angeles. Theoretically, a basis exists for a coalition for minority equality that crosses racial and class lines. Ideological affinity in most areas remains strong, although there is disagreement in others. But ideological agreement is only the beginning, and the groups have significant and growing interest conflicts.

A multiracial coalition would have to redefine the economic goals of the city government, expand the issues addressed by predominantly liberal middle-class organizations, and open up the realm of minority politics to include the interests of low-wage minority workers. Strict campaign finance laws are needed to create a level playing field for Latino mobilization, or else Latinos will fall farther behind Jews, Asian-Americans, and Blacks, who supplement voting with campaign donations.

A new generation of leaders able to bridge these differences and construct new coalitions has yet to take center stage. If New York City's activists have too little experience in constructive coalition politics, Los Angeles' future leaders are unaware of the struggles to create and sustain their own. But grass-roots efforts are taking place on an issue-by-issue basis. The prospects for multiracial coalitions in postincorporation Los Angeles therefore are cloudy but can be viewed with a glimmer of cautious optimism.

Minority activists will have to confront the continued political power of the white middle-class in Los Angeles. If the liberal Fifth District and the conservative Twelfth District end up on the same side, they can dominate the city's politics. But the evidence in this book shows that whites are not united on many important issues. Conversely, white liberals who hope to have influence in the Los Angeles to come must step back into the conversation with minority activists—and must come with an open mind and a fresh outlook. Minority and white liberal politicians have started to learn that they cannot go it alone—either without one another or in opposition to other minority aspirations.

Any minority or white liberal candidacy in Los Angeles must respond to two basic imperatives of the city's politics and culture. Los Angeles politics is by necessity coalition politics. No candidate or group can pursue its own objectives citywide without at least one partner in another community. This has great implications for the type of leaders who can rule Los Angeles.

Any group seeking citywide power must respond to the powerful symbols of political reform that still dominate Los Angeles in the postincorporation era. The biracial coalition took the city's values as its own, and then turned them into progressive values. As the city grows and changes, the same understanding of the city and its history will be essential to new steps for social change.

The city is becoming more complex, more international, more politically attuned. New groups coming in will now have to deal with not only the earlier conservative stratum but also the remaining power of the Black and white liberal alliance. Out of that mixture of old groups and new, old ideas and new, will arise the halting and hopefully creative political responses that will shape Los Angeles in the years to come.

SIXTEEN

CONCLUSIONS AND IMPLICATIONS: TOWARD A

NEW CONTRACT FOR BIRACIAL POLITICS

LOS ANGELES—where political life has been rarely studied—provides a remarkably useful case study of minority incorporation. Despite a relatively small population, Los Angeles' African-Americans were surprisingly successful in obtaining an important share of municipal power. Until the early 1960s, Blacks had held very little political clout in Los Angeles. They had elected no officeholder in city government, and were excluded from citywide coalitions.

Between 1961 and 1963, Blacks succeeded in eroding some of the barriers to their participation. In 1963, three Black candidates rode a wave of Black mobilization into council seats. In the three decades since, African-Americans have held these three seats, a higher share of the fifteen-member council than the Black share of the population (by the 1990 census, Los Angeles was only 13 percent African-American).

In 1973, the city elected a Black mayor, Tom Bradley, who was reelected in 1977, 1981, 1985, and 1989. With Bradley's election, Los Angeles Blacks obtained a core role in the dominant citywide coalition. Shifts in the city council expanded the base of that coalition over time. Black-supported candidates won all citywide offices.

The initial victories in city council races were largely conducted under African-American leadership appealing to a Black mass base. Bradley's citywide victory was part of a wider coalition with white liberals, principally Jews. This coalition was highly stable. Joint membership in this citywide liberal coalition has meant that Blacks have had more than representation; they have had incorporation.

Significant policy changes occurred in city government as a result of Black incorporation. The first real limits were placed on police conduct in the minority community after years of city hall subservience to the department. Substantial amounts of federal aid were obtained for social service programs, in contrast to Los Angeles's lackluster previous record.

Higher proportions of minorities were appointed to city commissions, including the most important posts. Substantial increases occurred in the city's minority hiring. While these changes often fell short of the expectations of the coalition's supporters, they represented a great improvement over the previous conservative practices. Opportunities for upward mobility increased for previously excluded groups.

The goal of economic equality for minority and poor neighborhoods, however, was not achieved through the economic revitalization of the downtown. As a result of restrictive federal policies, changing demographics, and the limited equalizing benefits of downtown redevelopment, the city's economic life is not more equal today than when the regime came to power. The shocking violence that hit South Central Los Angeles in 1992 underscored the inequality that remains.

The political alliance that underlay Black incorporation combined Black mobilization and white liberal support. Secondary assistance came from the Latino and Asian-American communities. Downtown business and labor became pillars of the incumbent coalition, as redevelopment policies favored their interests.

At the mass level, the persistence of ideological division among whites was remarkable. The pattern can be seen as far back as the 1964 vote on Proposition 14, which sought to preserve housing discrimination, and as recently as the 1992 vote to reform the LAPD. Over a wide range of elections, high-turnout white liberal areas differed significantly from high-turnout white conservative areas. When combined with the heavily mobilized and unified Black vote and less-mobilized Latinos, the multiracial liberal community in Los Angeles attained extraordinary electoral strength.

When these communities divided, particularly over growth issues, the coalition substantially weakened. The rise of Latino and Asian-American aspirations has profoundly challenged the biracial coalition, as have the decline in federal aid and tensions from within.

At the elite level, the coalition was effectively created, managed, and preserved by an alliance of Black and white liberal activists who had known each other for many years. Their ties dated back to Bradley's election to the city council in 1963 in the biracial Tenth District. From within the Black community, leadership came from a progressive faction based in the upwardly mobile areas of the community. Elite trust provided an essential bridge over troubled waters that might have sunk another coalition. These cross-racial leadership ties were important reasons why Black-Jewish conflict rarely threatened coalition survival.

Elite alliance in the political sphere was strengthened by sharing a common goal—winning elections and changing public policies. Relatively equal status enhanced the ability of people from different sides of the racial divide to work together.

In short, the Los Angeles case casts doubt on the widely accepted notion that elite and mass coalitions between Blacks and white liberals are dead. They have shown, in Los Angeles, substantial signs of life.

A small Black population in a big city wins substantial political power, and then shares in the development of new city policies benefiting minorities. Is this a unique phenomenon, or indicative of some broader pattern? Bradley's electoral victories are often presented in the urban literature as inexplicable exceptions to the rule of racial polarization. In reality, the Los Angeles story differs in degree but not in kind from the evidence gathered in other American cities. It is part of the history of the movement for Black empowerment. It is a key signpost in a broader model of biracial coalition politics than has yet been brought into the literature.

Among western cities, the Los Angeles case study offers strong confirmation of the patterns Browning, Marshall, and Tabb (1984) found in ten northern California cities. In each of their cities, conservative coalitions had been dominant until 1960, and minority representation had been extremely limited. In the 1960s and 1970s, Blacks and Latinos obtained power and policy change at a very different level in the ten cities. The key factors were the extent of Black mobilization and unity, and the level of white liberal support. Latinos joined Black-liberal coalitions as secondary partners.

The city in which African-Americans attained the highest level of incorporation, Berkeley, followed a path surprisingly similar to that of Los Angeles. In Berkeley, Blacks organized in the late 1950s and early 1960s to win initial incorporation; then, in alliance with white liberal reformers, they formed a citywide progressive coalition able to win full incorporation. As in Los Angeles, the coalition elected a Black mayor. Substantial policy change (much more than in moderate Los Angeles) followed the development of a winning coalition.

In sum, Los Angeles stands as the first big-city confirmation of a model peculiarly suited to western, reform-dominated cities. It also shows that the model works in conservative southern California as well as in more liberal northern California.

This research suggests that a western model of biracial politics deserves much more attention than it has received. In settings where reform structures are strong, where the African-American population is of moderate size, where conservative regimes frustrate liberal aspirations, and where racial antipathy is relatively low, the path to liberal biracial coalition seems relatively auspicious. In such settings, the likelihood of biracial politics seems greater than in the eastern and midwestern cities that generally frame the discussion.

In western communities, the opportunities for white liberals and Black activists to meet in political situations where they are peers—a crucial precondition for biracial elite linkages—may be greater as well. Yet these conditions are more fragile in the 1990s, and much exploration needs to be done about the prospects for coalitions in the postincorporation era.

How does the Los Angeles case fit with those of other large cities in the East and Midwest, which have been the basis of the polarization model?

Applicability does not have to be limited to western states where parties are weak and African-American populations are relatively small. In other words, there may be elements that unify both the crossover and polarization models into a more general model of biracial coalitions.

A unified model accepts that Black mobilization and white liberal support are core factors in the success of Black incorporation. In many polarized cities, the slice of white support for Black incorporation is much smaller than in Los Angeles, and the Black population much larger. But the pattern is much the same. Pettigrew (1971) found that Black mayoral candidates in Gary, Newark, and Cleveland received white support from similar populations as in Los Angeles. The difference was in the degree of white support. The same result was found in Ransom's (1987) Philadelphia and Kleppner's (1985) Chicago.

The intensity of racial conflict is so great in cities such as Chicago that it tends to overshadow ideological conflict among whites. But that ideological division can be a significant—even a determining—factor in outcomes. Harold Washington's 1983 victory in Chicago was made possible by overwhelming Black (and Latino) support and a slice of white liberal voting. The 1989 mayoral election between an incumbent Black mayor and challenger Richard M. Daley depended heavily on the votes of white liberals. This group had provided the key swing voters for Harold Washington's victories in 1983 and 1987. With Black and white voters so evenly divided, the small slice of ideologically liberal whites became extremely important, and eventually handed the mayoralty to Daley.

In short, the difference between Los Angeles's crossover politics and the polarization model of eastern and midwestern cities is in part a difference of degree and emphasis. If the two models share a common framework—Black mobilization and unity combined with white liberal support—they differ significantly in the emphasis on each element. Los Angeles represents one "bookend," in which white liberal support is a truly major share of the equation. Chicago represents another, opposite "bookend," in which the overwhelming need is for Black unity, with some small increment of white support.

These differences in degree matter, because they affect the tone and direction of city politics. In Los Angeles, coalition politics is always in the air and is the beginning of all citywide strategy; in Chicago, it may be the last consideration. Even Harold Washington did not get around to cultivating a white liberal base until after he had won the 1983 Democratic primary.

In both models, African-American mobilization and biracial coalition are needed in order to achieve minority incorporation. The situation is particularly complex in New York City, where the Black population percentage is higher than in Los Angeles but lower than in Chicago. Minority strategists have often seemed caught in the middle between mobilization and coalition, sometimes achieving neither. With the election of David Dinkins as mayor of New York City in 1989, the largest U.S. city now constitutes a sort of bridge between the polarization and crossover wings of a broader model of interracial politics. The racial experience of New York City has strong elements in common with both Chicago and Los Angeles.

New York City has been more polarized than Los Angeles, but it has a much deeper white liberal base than Chicago. The biracial coalition behind Dinkins is broader (if more precarious) than the late Harold Washington's but quite a bit weaker than Tom Bradley's. Perhaps the New York City experience, which has until now been one of the main arguments against the viability of biracial coalitions, will someday help in the process of devising a new, expanded view of biracial politics that incorporates both the polarization and crossover experiences.

In national perspective, Los Angeles represents (along with other western cities) one end of a broad continuum of Black mobilization and white liberal support. For too long, the other end of the continuum (polarization) has been treated as the whole continuum. Placing the second-largest U.S. city in its correct place therefore helps shift the weight of the analysis of minority incorporation and biracial coalitions.

New Thinking on Biracial Coalitions

If biracial coalitions between Blacks and white liberals are not dead, then the widely held belief that the civil rights movement died in 1965 must be reexamined. Clearly the ideological alliance that provided the basis for the civil rights movement did not disappear with the completion of its legislative agenda. But that alliance did undergo a profound shift that has been unrecognized by either Blacks or white liberals.

After 1965, the racial coalition became much narrower, at least in terms of white participation, and the role of Black mobilization became much greater. This shift is of considerable importance because it has been overemphasized by African-Americans and underemphasized by whites. In short, the role of whites in the modern movement for Black political incorporation is qualitatively different than it was in the civil rights movement. But it still exists, and is crucial.

The civil rights movement was a broad coalition around a series of agreed-upon issues of great moral force. It was oriented toward changing government policy through external pressure and protest. The whole nature of the modern enterprise is different. While moral force and persuasion are parts of the new movement, they share the stage with an overt plan to obtain minority political empowerment. The new movement is aimed not only at changing policies but at gaining the political power to make policies. It also involves much straightforward politics, seeking to win and hold public office. More than the civil rights movement, the new era is about both morality and politics.

This presents both an opportunity and a problem. It is an opportunity because politics is an activity with enough specific goals to make common goals possible. The problem is that if the civil rights movement model does not evolve, it cannot easily survive when politics are involved.

If the broad model explaining minority incorporation in the 1960s and 1970s is a combination of Black mobilization and white liberal support, then many things need to be rethought. The whole accepted basis of biracial coalitions needs to be reexamined. Previous efforts have failed to take into account the paradoxical nature of a phenomenon with two distinctive elements.

The most widely discussed liberal views of biracial coalitions tend to emphasize what amounts to a philanthropic model, derived from the civil rights movement. In this view, racial progress emerges from the goodwill of liberal whites, who choose to offer assistance to Blacks. This model suggests that ideology is the basis of biracial politics. The failings of this model lie in two areas.

White liberals often fail to acknowledge the leading role of the African-American community in the search for racial equality. It is all too easy to redraw history to portray Blacks as victims and whites as saviors. Studies of Black mayors may highlight their relationships with the white community, rather than the African-American community base that has been essential to their self-reliance and political success.

The liberal model is also at a loss to explain conflict between Blacks and white liberals. If biracial politics is about ideology, what happens when there is a conflict of interest between the two groups? Sometimes the conflict is denied, or explained away. Liberals may withdraw from the struggle for equality, unable to confront the apparent contradiction. It is equally hard to acknowledge evidence that white benefits derive from minority political efforts. Ideological politics can break down when interest conflicts cause groups, and their leaders, to defend their threatened interests.

White liberals ought to understand that many minority activists are justifiably cautious about committing themselves to biracial coalitions that may founder when hard, divisive issues arise. Where liberalism is too strong, as perhaps has been the case in New York City and San Francisco, it may even inhibit the development of independent minority politics. Thus, the health of a Black-liberal coalition—indeed, of any minority-liberal alliance—may depend on a balance of strength.

The best biracial politics is not a form of philanthropy; when liberal support seems like charity, baffled liberals may find their hands bitten by the "ungrateful" recipient. As Hamilton (1979) has pointed out, votes provide reciprocity; mutual need can add a reliable and dignified glue to good intentions. While the Black Power argument too quickly dismisses the consistent support of white liberals, liberals tend to understate the importance of realistic group conflict and pragmatic cooperation.

In 1967, Carmichael and Hamilton sought to create a new model of biracial coalitions that would overcome the inadequacies of the liberal model. They intended to move beyond the sentimentality of the civil rights movement into a more pragmatic focus on African-American interests. For the first time they presented biracial coalition as a conscious political choice made by Blacks, thereby fundamentally altering the terms of the discussion. They constructed a listing of preconditions for biracial coalitions that emphasized Black self-determination.

Carmichael and Hamilton argued that whites played too dominant a role in the civil rights movement, and that when their own interests were threatened, such whites would desert the Black cause. The only answer was to abandon alliances of ideology in favor of interest-based coalitions.

The Black Power movement fractured the confidence of advocates of biracial coalitions. Instead of being seen as philanthropic, white liberals were characterized as patronizing and domineering. The removal of white liberals from the leadership of civil rights organizations became a painful issue. Now African-Americans saw themselves as picking and choosing coalition partners, rather than asking for the benevolent assistance of whites.

Since the publication of *Black Power* in 1967, many have emphasized the role of Black unity as the cause of Black empowerment. Full credit for African-American empowerment is given to the Black community, with other supporters banished to the fine print, unless the allies are nonwhite. Evidence of racial polarization is reemphasized in order to downplay any role for whites in the sharing of credit for success.

The pain engendered on both sides by the fracturing of the old coalition has meant that the opening presented by Carmichael and Hamilton has been inadequately extended and tested. Generally, the subject gets addressed in the course of Black-Jewish conflict, often with reference to alliance efforts several decades old. Such battles do not encourage people to devote full attention to a new understanding of the relationship.

Carmichael and Hamilton had hit on a crucial point. Their argument could be read as saying that there had been an implicit contract in the early coalition, in which white liberals felt noble and Blacks got needed political support. In *Black Power*, Carmichael and Hamilton sought to devise a new, more explicit contract that would end the "patron-client" relationship.

The problem is that their hard-eyed view is, in its own way, just as myopic about the nature of biracial coalitions as the more romantic liberal view. Goodwill alone is not enough, but neither is cold self-interest. But the debate largely ended with the publication of *Black Power* in 1967. It is long past time to reopen that discussion, with a new perspective beyond the sentimental and the cynical.

Black Power argued that Blacks had been overshadowed in the civil rights movement, and that liberal alliances were generally useless. It argued instead for alliances based on economic issues and links to the Third World. It should be obvious that there is a direct line from *Black Power* to the Jesse Jackson presidential campaigns. Jackson's campaigns presented an important alternative to liberal coalitions, and his approach came right off the pages of Carmichael and Hamilton's book. Such a coalition would begin with racial consciousness among Blacks, and the candidate would openly act as the Black candidate. Allies would then be sought in areas of common economic interest—white workers, Latinos, and others.

Only the most progressive whites—those able to support the candidate's agenda in full—would be incorporated. No effort would be made to accommodate those whites, such as Jews, who had reservations about some aspects of the program. Finally, strong linkages would be forged with Third World peoples. Combined in a single package, these elements of the rainbow coalition fit all the preconditions for successful coalitions offered in *Black Power*.

But virtually every case of Black political incorporation since the publication of *Black Power* has followed a model substantially different from Jackson's model. These victories were built on Black mobilization and the careful cultivation of white liberal support.

The main problem with *Black Power* is not its theory of Blacks, but rather its theory of whites. The book performed a tremendous service by highlighting the necessity for African-American independent action and political self-reliance. (In its argument against white domination of the civil rights movement, however, the book made the same mistake that many whites have made: underestimating the actual Black leadership role. In Los Angeles and other cities, Blacks were creating an independent political base long before 1967.) The theory set out a highly dignified role for Blacks, based on the pursuit of their group interest, but then confined whites to a role that is highly unrealistic and close to demeaning.

Carmichael and Hamilton (1967:77, emphasis in original) indicated that a coalition must be based on the following premise: "All parties to the coalition must perceive a *mutually* beneficial goal based on the conception of *each* party of his *own* self-interest." However, in the sections that followed, they did not apply this notion to liberal whites. Liberal whites who defended their own interests were defined as betrayers. In fact, Carmichael and Hamilton specifically defined an appropriate role for white progressives, without regard for whether such a role would be acceptable to them: "There is a definite, much-needed role whites can play . . . educative, organizational, supportive" (81).

Whites were then urged to rid themselves of racist values and bring other whites to the correct view: "[T]hey might also educate other white people to the need for Black Power" (82). Culturally, whites must seek to overthrow their own way of living because it is dead and jaded. Those whites who are devoted to racial justice are actually escapees from sick environments: "They have sought refuge among blacks from a sterile, meaningless, irrelevant life in middle-class America. They have been unable to deal with the stifling, racist, parochial, split-level mentality of their parents, teachers, preachers and friends. . . . Anglo-conformity is a dead weight on their necks, too" (83).

When biracial coalitions are to be formed, they must be wholly directed by African-Americans:

> It is our position that black organizations should be black-led and essentially black-staffed, with policy being made by black people. White people can and do play very important supportive roles in those organizations. . . .
>
> There are white lawyers who defend black civil rights workers in court, and white activists who support indigenous black movements across the country. Their function is not to lead or to set policy or to attempt to define black people to black people. Their role is supportive. (83–84)

Even with due allowance for the period in which this was written, the role defined in such coalitions for white liberals is constricting. They are invited to open for inspection their cultural values, renounce their families and communities, act in a supporting role without input into policy, and, in effect, ask permission to be part of a progressive movement. How could such a process produce healthy politics? How could such whites ever be expected to deliver a bloc of white support?

In this light, the conflicts between Jesse Jackson and the Jewish community can be seen in a new light. With their strong sense of community and family, Jews are unlikely to accept as terms of participation in progressive politics the agenda laid out in *Black Power*. To do so would be to violate the very conditions for strong coalition laid out in that book. As Carmichael and Hamilton stated, no coalition can survive that is not based on the survival and protection of the groups involved. Both must be able to prosper through coalition.

Thus, *Black Power* made a major contribution by laying to rest a naive view that goodwill will solve everything. But it left the job of constructing a realistic biracial coalition unfinished. It is to that task that I now turn.

We now know that African-American political incorporation (a political expression of the doctrine of Black Power) came about over the last several decades through a combination of Black mobilization and white liberal support. Blacks and liberals often saw these events differently. Blacks tended to see the great effort put toward Black unity. White liberals often noticed how at the crucial junctures, the support of whites like themselves put the Black movement over the top.

Coalitions can certainly survive the different interpretations of their members. Such differing perspectives may be crucial to coalition survival (Downs 1957). But when the views pull too far apart, how people understand their contributions to coalitions can actually affect the chances for coalition success.

For example, if African-Americans feel that white liberals are generally hypocrites, they will fail to cultivate ideological support. If white liberals fail to appreciate the Black political base and its importance, they may place pressures on a Black leader that he or she can ill afford.

It is therefore time to try to draw up a new contract for biracial politics—one in which both sides can thrive. The philanthropic model underestimates the role of Blacks, and the Black Power model underestimates the role of whites. Is there a new model that can serve the interests of all parties, and can allow coalitions to be built on a solid foundation? Can such an approach be helpful in forming new coalitions among Blacks, Latinos, Asian-Americans and liberal whites in the postincorporation era? Such a foundation will, of course, be built among leaders. But leaders affect the masses through their statements and actions.

The first element of a fair contract is to give credit where credit is due. Thus it is fair to indicate that the political successes of the past decades are due to both Black political mobilization and white liberal support. Liberals need to recognize that the African-American movement precedes their involvement; and Blacks need to recognize that without white liberals, many of their greatest victories would not have taken place.

Objectively, white liberals are, indeed, very different from white conservatives. The differences are obvious, in polls and in elections. Denial of the evidence is useless. Without a split among whites on ideological grounds, Black political mobilization would be unable to succeed. That split can be cultivated. It is crucial for white liberals, however, not to take more than their fair share of credit. Revising history to accentuate the white role is highly damaging, as is ignorance of the leading Black role in the development of minority incorporation.

Biracial politics should be understood on both sides as a mixed-motive game. The sentimental liberal view holds that ideology is everything; Black Power theorists see hypocrisy in liberalism whenever there is a conflict of interest. But most coalitions between groups are based on both conflict and cooperation.

Even when ideology draws groups together, there are numerous opportunities for conflict of interest. One would not realistically conclude that therefore the ideological affinity is meaningless. Rather, one would seek to manage or isolate the conflict of interest if the coalition were on balance successful. Caditz (1976) wisely suggested that white liberals should be realistic about their own racial ambivalence. She considered this an antidote to liberal "rigidification." They should avoid the tendency to ascribe only the loftiest of motives to their own political actions. On the other hand, others should also be realistic about liberalism.

Given the cynicism with which Black Power theorists view liberals, it is striking how disappointed they are when liberals define their own interests. If ideology does not matter, why would a progressive be expected to sacrifice his or her own interests and take full direction from others? The realism about coalitions shown in *Black Power* should be extended: white liberals are much more inclined than white conservatives to support the African-American movement, except when their own interests are threatened. These interests are not always threatened, and sometimes are advanced by the Black movement. In this view, a biracial coalition need not collapse because of a conflict of interest—unless both sides have developed, without knowing it, an overly sentimental view of coalitions.

There is no weakness in cultivating a coalition partner. White liberals may believe that they have a claim on the Black community, but this is not realistic. Coalition is a choice, not an end in itself, and there are times not to coalesce. For instance, in 1961 Blacks went for Sam Yorty while liberals hated him. Latinos have fought both Blacks and white liberals—their ideological allies—to win changes in the Los Angeles council reapportionment.

Conversely, it is only good politics to cultivate liberals to participate in the minority movement. It is surely not strength, for instance, to purposely alienate Jews from a coalition on racial equality. All ethnic groups who have used politics have also allied with other groups; that is a sign of strength.

Is there in fact a contradiction between Black Power and biracial coalition? On the rhetorical level, there may be a severe conflict. The public stances that define each position may often be in opposition. But in real politics, not only is there not a contradiction—there is a mutuality of philosophy and interest.

Generally speaking, biracial coalition building is likely to be undertaken as a result of successful minority mobilization. It is the outcome of an internal process of, as Carmichael and Hamilton (1967:vii) put it, how "black people in America must get themselves together." The early stages of Black political incorporation are spent forging unity. This means nominating conventions, the development of Black media themes, and the building of street-level precinct organizations.

In Berkeley and Los Angeles, citywide biracial coalitions were built on top of existing African-American political movements of great strength and duration. In Los Angeles, the Black community became even stronger politically as a result of the citywide coalition. After several elections, it was clear that the Black community was the single most important factor in citywide elections. Black power was at the heart of all the mobilization efforts behind African-American mayoral candidates. Yet as a part of the electoral effort, these candidates built biracial coalitions. This was not out of weakness, but due to the proximity of victory.

Where Black power is weak, there tends to be a corresponding atrophy of biracial coalition. For example, in New York City the Black and Jewish communities together comprise nearly half the city's population. Yet until Dinkins's election in 1989, there had never been a serious Black mayoral candidate. One crucial reason for the failure of Black incorporation in New York City has been the stultification of an independent Black movement. For many reasons, New York City did not become a site for such activism. Hamilton (1979) complained that New York City Blacks had failed to go after electoral power, settling instead for a patron-client relationship with federally funded agencies.

Not surprisingly, the city also failed to develop the sort of biracial coalition that Los Angeles did. In fact, conflicts of interest between Blacks and Jews escalated rapidly without the moderating influence of citywide politicians. Thus, New York City's biracial coalition politics would have been greatly advanced by a substantial dose of Black power.

It is necessary to accept the distance that separates Blacks and white liberals. One of the problems of the civil rights movement was that the attempt to bridge the distance through human relations alone was insufficient. When whites were involved in the definition and leadership of the African-American movement, it was inevitable that there would be severe strains. Human relations will be most effective as a supplement to activities that recognize the distinct interests and identities of groups.

In the same manner, the view that there is only one progressive movement, led by Blacks, omits the ability of white liberals to define their own progressivism. The recognition that Blacks and white liberals have distinct, overlapping movements can be liberating. The same will undoubtedly be true in the long effort to build alliances between Blacks and Latinos.

The bridge building does not need to be conducted at the mass level, where such bridges are notoriously open to misinterpretation. Coalitions are more likely to succeed when leaders, operating as peers in a competitive political environment, form relationships of mutual trust and respect. These leadership groups can be highly successful in muting the sort of conflicts that can be devastating to a biracial coalition.

In the best of all possible worlds, African-American unity is forged and leaders arise who can translate this unity into alliance. White liberals are themselves in need of political power after being excluded. An alliance is forged that is both ideological and pragmatic—an alliance of both shared beliefs and shared ambitions. One can imagine no better conditions for biracial coalition. These were the conditions in Los Angeles. But even where racial polarization has burned its way into the heart of a city, the possibilities for biracial alliance remain.

It is time to lay to rest the notion that the development of the African-American political community stands in opposition to a broad progressive movement among white liberals. As long as white liberals do not try to define the minority movement, and as long as Blacks do not seek to narrowly circumscribe the political expression of white liberals, the outlines of a powerful coalition for change can be seen. It will be stymied by conflicts of interest, but will be pushed ahead by shared ideology. When interests are shared under certain political circumstances, major victories with lasting value will be won.

AFTERWORD

THE 1993 LOS ANGELES MAYORAL ELECTION AND THE CRISIS OF URBAN PROGRESSIVE POLITICS

BY 1993, the long era that began with the election of the first African-American mayors in 1967 had crested and had begun to recede. In city after city, Black mayors had been replaced by whites. Moderates and conservatives, including some Republicans, displaced liberals. Most dramatically, white mayors succeeded African-Americans in each of the four largest American cities—New York City, Los Angeles, Chicago, and Philadelphia. In Los Angeles, the remarkable twenty-year coalition dominated by Mayor Tom Bradley was followed by a conservative alliance led by millionaire Republican Richard Riordan. Los Angeles, no longer the model of biracial politics, became the more problematic center of multiethnic politics, severe social conflict, and the rollback of minority gains.

The prospects for urban interracial coalitions seemed uncertain. In Los Angeles and elsewhere, the coalitions that had sustained progressive urban politics seemed to have lost their force, and those who sought greater equality were forced to consider new directions. The issue of the rollback of minority political gains moved from the theoretical to the urgently practical, as the feared long-term reaction to progressive urban politics (see Chapter 15) seemed to be becoming a reality.

These developments set off a frenzy of interpretation and speculation. The *New Republic*'s November 1, 1993, cover story, "The End of the Rainbow?" suggested that conservatives had created a new urban coalition led by whites, but drawing significant support from non-Black minorities (Sleeper 1993). Harold Meyerson (1993b) asked in the *L.A. Weekly* if this was "the end of urban liberalism?" He noted that defeated Los Angeles mayoral candidate Michael Woo "was simply the candidate of the city's multiculti future."

Writing in the *New York Times*, Nicholas Lemann (1993) suggested that

> What generated the feeling that cities like New York and L.A. would ordinarily have black mayors was an idea that all urban "people of color" would stick together politically and look to African-Americans as their natural leaders. This was the premise behind Jesse Jackson's Rainbow Coalition— but it hasn't proved true.

A general consensus seemed to be emerging that the breakdown of progressive politics at the big-city level marked the defeat of rainbow-coalition politics by conservative coalitions.

But are progressive urban politics only about the rainbow coalition? Those who have analyzed the dramatic electoral shifts in America's cities have often used the terms rainbow and biracial interchangeably. The differences are subtle, but they are nonetheless very important. The distinction is a crucial one that goes to the heart of an implicit debate over political strategy in the movement for racial equality.

The rainbow approach, popularized by Jesse Jackson's two presidential campaigns, seeks to activate demographic blocs of people of color and low-income and working-class people of all colors in service of dramatic social change. As exemplified by Jackson's campaigns, the coalition appeals to the left, and may often offer a leading role to African-Americans.

While the rainbow coalition theoretically invites white support, that appeal comes with some conditions. A potential for common economic interests suggests that working-class whites would be suitable partners in the rainbow. Strongly progressive ideology may make the most liberal whites seem to be good members. Most middle-class liberal or moderate whites, including many Jews, are neither poor enough nor progressive enough to be actively recruited. They may tend to be suspicious of rainbow coalitions, feeling that their own interests and beliefs will not be represented. Jewish voters in particular will be acutely sensitive to the rainbow coalition's attitude toward anti-Semitism.

By contrast, the biracial or interracial model—exemplified by Tom Bradley's Los Angeles coalition—is built on race, liberal ideology, religion, and Democratic party loyalty. The biracial coalition seeks to build majority coalitions, which call for less dramatic social change than that promised by the rainbow coalition. In clear contrast to the rainbow model, the interracial coalition features active, explicit appeals to middle-class whites, both liberal and moderate. Jews are openly encouraged to join the coalition, with assurances that their interests and beliefs will be respected. The support of people of color is not assumed on the basis of a common non-white status, but is sought competitively in a manner tailored for each group. It is a center-left coalition.

Shared liberal ideology allows members of biracial coalitions to build temporary bridges across racial lines. Such coalitions have provided the basis for the rise of minority political power in a wide variety of settings (Browning, Marshall, and Tabb 1984), and for the Bradley coalition in Los Angeles.

Both models are housed largely in the Democratic party; both are broadly progressive; both draw huge support from African-American voters. Not surprisingly, the rainbow model draws less white support than the biracial model and has greater difficulty developing majority coalitions. It does, however, maintain a higher degree of ideological purity than the biracial coalition, which must make significant adjustments to policy goals to hold its support.

In the heat of a political campaign, progressive candidates knowingly or unknowingly transmit signals to the voters that indicate whether they are taking a rainbow or a biracial approach. White, Latino, and Asian-American voters will be acutely aware of the difference, and will closely observe the tone of the campaign toward their interests and beliefs. Conservative competitors will offer a comfortable home to them, but they may not go in that direction if they feel well-wooed by the progressive side.

Biracial coalitions tend to be rainbow coalitions plus a significant share of whites; rainbow coalitions are more limited because of their smaller appeal to white voters. Rainbow coalitions are formidable contenders, but even before the recent decline of urban progressive coalitions, rainbow alliances had never been sufficient to win and hold power. Indeed, the belief that cities that had elected Black mayors would always do so was not based on a presumption of a rainbow alliance alone, but rather on the presumed unity of African-Americans and the willingness of a significant number of whites to cross over.

The debate between rainbow and biracial models has been largely conducted within the progressive camp. In the midst of this lively interchange, it is all too easy to forget that a third model waits in the wings—the conservative coalition. Unlike either the rainbow or the biracial models, the conservative coalition begins not in the African-American community but among whites. It seeks to win power by holding a huge majority of whites and picking off pieces of various minority constituencies. It is the reverse of the progressive coalition. In 1993, such conservative coalitions triumphed in both Los Angeles and New York City.

What does the 1993 Los Angeles mayoral election have to say about the prospects for biracial or multiracial coalitions in a multiethnic city? What did the Los Angeles election indicate about the future of an urban progressive politics? The crisis of progressive politics in Los Angeles is not simply a defeat in a major election; there is now a great uncertainty about the progressive direction and vision. Throughout the country urban progressive politics seem increasingly isolated from the leadership of urban majorities.

Oddly, at the same time that progressive coalitions were in retreat in city politics, Democrat Bill Clinton won the 1992 presidential election. How might that dramatic development at the national level affect the struggle for equality?

The material for this Afterword was based on an analysis of the vote by city council district, interviews with campaign polltakers for the two leading mayoral candidates; examination of the detailed poll reports of the *Los Angeles Times*; and personal observation at various campaign events.

Background

The context for the 1993 Los Angeles mayoral election was the inexorable decline of the Bradley coalition that had ruled Los Angeles since 1973. While the coalition had been in failing health since 1985, events moved more swiftly after the 1991 videotaped beating of Rodney King. Bradley's support fell steadily, especially among whites, as he sought to remove Police Chief Daryl Gates and to institute police reforms. Table A.1 shows the decline in Bradley's popularity over the two-year period between the beating of Rodney King and the runoff election in May 1993.

In the second May 1993 poll Bradley was supported by only 26 percent of whites, 43 percent of African-Americans, and 39 percent of Latinos. By the election, Bradley's political capital was virtually exhausted.

To the surprise of very few people, Bradley announced in September 1992 that he would not run for reelection to a sixth term. For the first time in over fifty years there would not be an incumbent in the mayoral race. For the first time since 1957, Los Angeles would have a mayor who was neither Sam Yorty nor Tom Bradley.

Under the nonpartisan rules of California city elections, an open primary for all candidates was scheduled for April 20, 1993. If no candidate received a majority, a runoff would be held between the two leading candidates on June 8. There had been no mayoral runoff in Los Angeles since Bradley's 1973 defeat of Yorty.

A huge field of mayoral candidates appeared, but a number of very strong candidates stayed out: Latina county supervisor Gloria Molina, Jewish city council member Zev Yaroslavsky, and city attorney James K. Hahn. The leading contenders among those who did enter were three members of the city council, Michael Woo, Joel Wachs, and Nate Holden,

TABLE A.1
Bradley Approval, 1991–1993

Date	Approval
March 1991 (a)	61
March 1991 (b)	57
April 1991	53
July 1991	48
May 1992 (a)	44
May 1992 (b)	38
February 1993	39
May 1993 (a)	33
May 1993 (b)	38

Source: Los Angeles Times poll.

state assembly member Richard Katz, deputy mayor Linda Griego, attorney J. Stanley Sanders, and millionaire businessman Richard Riordan.

Woo was the early favorite. A Chinese-American elected in 1985 to represent Hollywood's 13th district, Woo was the natural successor to Bradley. He was young and liberal, a crossover minority candidate, and had built bridges to the African-American community through his public calls for Gates's resignation. Woo also had substantial financial resources, drawn in major part from the growing Asian-American community. As an Asian-American, he seemed the perfect candidate to take the biracial coalition into the multiracial era. To all appearances, it was his race to lose.

Wachs and Katz were centrists cut from similar cloth, Jewish moderates with bases in the San Fernando Valley. Holden and Sanders, both African-American, were only moderately well known, although Holden had run for mayor in 1989. Griego was the best-known person from the Latino community in the race, but she was still barely recognized.

The great unknown factor was Riordan. A venture capitalist with an estimated $100 million fortune, Riordan had long been a familiar figure at city hall. He had given campaign funds to a wide range of politicians, with the largest amount going to Bradley. Bradley had appointed him to the Recreation and Parks Commission. Known as a pro-business conservative, Riordan was not particularly ideological. With his ability to place virtually unlimited funds into his campaign, he could not be discounted even with his extremely low name recognition.

The 1993 election seemed likely to introduce Los Angeles to a new rainbow age. The population was now two-thirds nonwhite, leading some to argue that interracial politics were no longer necessary. But when it came to actual voters, the image of a rainbow Los Angeles evaporated. While demographics had changed rapidly, eligible voter proportions had

TABLE A.2
Population vs. Registration (percent)

	Population	Registration	1993 Vote Share in	
			Primary	Runoff
Whites	37.3	65	68	72
Jews*	7.0 (est.)	15	16	19
Blacks	14.0	15	18	12
Latinos	39.9	11	8	10
Asian-Americans	9.2	4	4	4

Sources: Population, U.S. Census; registration, summary of various estimates; vote in 1993 from *Los Angeles Times* exit polls.

*Jews, not included as a category in the U.S. Census, are treated as a subset of white voters in this table.

TABLE A.3

The Mobilization Gap in Two Council Districts, 1992–1993

	Population	18+ Population	Citizens 18+	Registered Voters	Primary Ballots Cast, 1993
1st	228,695	160,576	58,547	36,804	10,118
5th	236,423	203,451	174,199	151,020	53,018

Source: Pactech Consultants, report to the Los Angeles City Council 1992; votes cast, from city clerk election division.

stayed stable. The electorate constituted virtually a different city from the population (see Table A.2). Two thirds of the city's residents were minorities; two thirds of the voters were white. One third of the city's adults were not citizens (Pactech 1992).

Table A.3 displays the city council districts with the lowest and highest rates of participation: the First, a Latino district on the east side; and the Fifth, the westside liberal Jewish district.

Table A.3 clearly shows the hole in the electorate. Age opens up one important gap; the Latino community is much younger. But the huge drop is citizenship, reducing the potential voting bloc in the First district to only one-third of the Fifth. Then registration and voting bring the First down to only one-fifth of the Fifth district's vote per population. Standard turnout figures obscure this difference. While about one-third of the registered voters turned out in each district in the April primary, there were more than five times as many voters in the Fifth.

Indeed, despite the enormous demographic changes in Los Angeles, the political community in 1993 looked remarkably similar to what it was when Bradley fought Yorty in 1969 and 1973: a white majority, a stable one-sixth Black base, and a significant but surprisingly small Latino bloc (see Chapters 6 and 7).

When Riordan, a white Republican, won the election, many observers were stunned that he could be elected mayor in a "minority-majority" city. But whoever had won the mayoral election—whether the sixty-two-year-old white businessman or the forty-one-year-old Asian-American council member—would have been elected by a majority of a minority in the new Los Angeles.

In the primary campaign, the large field of varied candidates toured the city, met in group debates, or, when funds were available, produced campaign commercials. At campaign forums, the main target was Woo, who appeared to be the front-runner. Katz and Wachs attacked each other, as each fought to become the established white moderate candidate. The local media, particularly television reporters, largely ignored the primary (*Los Angeles Times*, 22 March 1993). It was therefore extremely difficult for those candidates who were not well funded to make an impression on voters. When the primary votes were counted, the two candidates with the most campaign money emerged victorious.

Riordan did exceptionally well in the primary, finishing first with 32.0 percent of the vote. Woo finished second with 24.5 percent, and the two Jewish centrists, Wachs and Katz, finished third and fourth, splitting another 20.2 percent of the vote. Woo and Riordan were set to face each other in the runoff election.

There was significant damage to the Bradley coalition even in the primary. Woo failed to hold key areas of coalition strength. The results showed some interesting changes from previous patterns, as well as some continuity. Throughout this book, I have examined four key council districts in elections covering several decades. They are white liberal and Jewish (the 5th); African-American (the 8th); white conservative (the 12th) and Latino and moderate white (the 14th). Over the past thirty years a pattern developed. The Black district was the most liberal and the white conservative district represented its polar opposite. The liberal Jewish district and the Latino area provided crucial support to the African-American position, building a powerful multiracial electoral coalition.

The primary vote in the four key council districts is shown in Table A.4. I joined the Wachs and Katz vote as "centrist". The *Los Angeles Times* exit poll for the primary presented another view of the vote (Table A.5).

Woo apparently fought his way into the runoff with a very solid showing among African-Americans, a respectable bloc of Latinos, but with relatively few Jewish backers. Most Jews were drawn either to Wachs or Katz. Woo did well with white liberals, but shared that bloc with the centrist candidates. The implication was clear: a rainbow alliance would not be nearly enough to win a majority without substantial support from whites drawn to centrist politics. Woo's coalition would have to be more than a rainbow; it would have to be biracial. It was also disturbing news for Woo that the turnout was so low in the minority neighborhoods, but

TABLE A.4
Primary Vote by Key Council District (percent)

	Riordan	Wachs + Katz	Woo	Votes (#)	Turnout
5th White liberal	29.8	33.9	18.5	53,018	35.1
8th Black	4.3	4.1	47.6	26,818	24.9
12th White conservative	48.9	23.0	11.2	48,028	37.6
14th Latino/moderate white	28.6	15.4	27.7	17,512	27.7

Source: City Clerk, Election Division.

TABLE A.5
Los Angeles Times Exit Poll, 1993 Primary (percent)

	Riordan	*Wachs + Katz*	*Woo*	*% of votes*
White liberals	11	34	30	16
White moderates	42	32	11	24
White conservatives	78	11	2	19
Blacks	4	5	52	18
Latinos	20	19	30	8
Asian-Americans	21	11	60	4
Jews	21	52	14	16

Source: The *Los Angeles Times*.

was vibrantly high in the San Fernando Valley. The stakes were seen as much higher in Riordan territory than in Woo's strongest areas.

Woo's electoral weaknesses deepened in the battle for general election endorsements. J. Stanley Sanders, the leading Black candidate, shocked political experts by backing Riordan in the runoff. Riordan also claimed the endorsements of Wachs and Latino council member Richard Alatorre. Thus Riordan was supported by one political figure in each of the African-American, Jewish, and Latino communities. City Council president John Ferraro not only endorsed Riordan, but derided his council colleague Woo as "a snot-nosed kid" (*Los Angeles Times*, 18 May 1993).

Woo won the important endorsement of county supervisor Gloria Molina, but failed to gain the backing of U.S. Representative Maxine Waters, perhaps the city's most influential Black elected official. After heavy lobbying, Woo finally gained President Clinton's endorsement, but due to Riordan's close ties to the administration, the President's statement of support was tepid. Richard Katz and Zev Yaroslavsky, Jewish elected officials who could have helped Woo substantially, remained neutral.

In the June runoff, Riordan trounced Woo with 53.8 percent of the vote. He swept the Valley, where turnout was high, broke even among Jews and Latinos, and decisively lost only Blacks. Table A.6 displays the results in the key council districts.

Compared with longstanding patterns in Los Angeles, there were major changes in each of the four areas. The participation of the conservative Valley jumped dramatically. It had always been the most conservative, most anti-Bradley, most antitax area of the city, but now it was far above its usual levels of conservative support—a crest not seen since Yorty's 1969 defeat of Bradley. The long years of political marginality under the Bradley coalition had generated a furious, highly mobilized charge. For the first time in a generation, in both the primary and runoff elections, the

Valley conservatives had outmobilized the minority communities and their white liberal allies.

The Latino Fourteenth district had been a bastion of Bradley's political strength, but there Riordan ran nearly even with Woo. The district's councilman, Richard Alatorre, was a strong Riordan backer. The *Los Angeles Times* exit poll found that Riordan won 43 percent of Latino voters. Latinos represented 10 percent of all voters (10 June 1993). Although the Black percentage for Woo was very respectable—while less than Bradley usually received—the turnout was substantially lower than expected.

The most striking, indeed shocking, development was Riordan's victory in the heart of white liberalism, the Fifth council district. The Fifth is heavily Democratic, about one-third Jewish, and had long been the most reliable white liberal area in the city. In every mayoral election between 1965 and 1989 the Fifth backed the liberal candidate (Table A.7). It had always been very far from the Twelfth district's conservative position.

The loss of the Fifth doomed Woo's candidacy. Riordan's ability to carry that district, usually the highest turnout area in the city, undid the Bradley coalition at a crucial juncture.

The evidence thus far points to a major shift in mayoral coalition strength, as the conservative alliance of whites, some Jews, and some Latinos defeated the minority-liberal coalition of minorities and liberal whites, including Jews. Because the two candidates so neatly portrayed the left and right in Los Angeles, no new ground was carved out for a third type of coalition. It was a defeat of the liberal coalition by the conservative coalition rather than the creation of a new coalition.

In that sense, there was substantial continuity with the past. The white conservative area was the heart of the Riordan victory, and its preference was quite different from the white liberal area. Woo's polling showed persistent and large differences between Jews and white Gentiles (Maullin interview). Riordan's polling revealed a very large gap between Jews and

TABLE A.6
General Election in Key Council Districts (percent)

	Riordan	Woo	Votes (#)	Turnout
5th White liberal	57.0	43.0	66,016	45.8
8th African-American	14.1	85.9	34,669	34.4
12th White conservative	75.3	24.7	61.527	49.9
14th Latino/moderate white	46.3	53.7	23,607	39.2

Note: Riordan and Woo percentages are calculated as share of two-candidate vote; votes cast are all those who came to the polls including a small number who did not vote for mayor.
Source: City Clerk, Election Division.

TABLE A.7
Vote in the Fifth and Twelfth Council Districts for the Liberal Mayoral Candidate, 1965–1993 (percent)

	5th	12th
1965 James Roosevelt	48.0	19.5
1969 Tom Bradley	50.7	30.6
1973 Tom Bradley	58.0	44.0
1977 Tom Bradley	61.7	40.3
1981 Tom Bradley	68.7	44.3
1985 Tom Bradley	71.6	49.4
1989 Tom Bradley	51.8	39.1
1993 Michael Woo	43.0	24.7

Source: City Clerk, Election Division, various years.

white Protestants (Steinberg interview). The *Times* exit poll showed the same type of liberal-conservative split (Table A.8). There was a general shift rightward by everybody but African-Americans, who listlessly held up an unenthusiastic left end.

Table A.8 reveals that left-right differences among whites endured. Jews still were distinctive from other whites; Jews cast their votes in-between liberal and moderate ideology. Other studies indicate that Jews were divided geographically. More than two thirds of westside urban Jews voted for Woo; nearly the same proportion of Valley suburban Jews voted for Riordan (Meyerson 1993a). The overall range of Jewish voting still needs to be determined: the *Times* poll found an even split between Rior-

TABLE A.8
Ideological Differences among Whites (percent), 1993 Election

	General			Primary		
	Riordan	Woo	% of Voters	Riordan	Woo	% of Voters
White liberals	31	69	22	11	30	19
White moderates	75	25	31	42	11	28
White conservative	92	8	20	78	2	22
Jews	49	51	19	21	14	16
White Protestants	80	20	28	56	10	26
White Catholics	78	22	14	61	12	15

Source: Los Angeles Times exit polls.

dan and Woo, but Riordan's polling found Woo receiving nearly 60 percent of the Jewish vote by the end of the campaign. Riordan's polling also
showed that Jews were divided by gender, with men evenly split and Woo
carrying Jewish women by substantial margins (Steinberg interview).

The moderate white voter shifted dramatically to Riordan's side. One
study found that "ideological moderates held the balance of power in this
election, and it was their overwhelming vote for Riordan which ensured
his victory" (Kaufmann 1994). While I have closely examined the difference between white liberals and white conservatives in Los Angeles politics over the past thirty years in this book, white moderates have appeared
only rarely in the story. Ideological differences among whites are, however, a continuum rather than a contest with two separated sides. Bradley
could never have been elected, nor could he have maintained his coalition,
without the support of moderate whites. In 1993, that key pillar of urban
governance went to the right in the mayor's race. Without them, a dis-
pirited alliance of liberal white and minority voters could not prevail.

Nor did rainbow politics, a potential alternative to biracial coalitions,
prosper. Riordan's success in carrying a significant share of the Latino vote
was very much out of line with the steady support Bradley enjoyed among
Latinos since 1973. The only other non-Black minority group to vote
heavily for Woo were Asian-Americans, but that support most likely arose
from ethnic loyalty and might not have been available to a different liberal
candidate. Asian-Americans represented a key bloc of Woo's financial support, but a very small share of the total votes cast. Asian-Americans gave
Woo an estimated 69 percent of their votes, but cast only four percent of
all ballots (*Los Angeles Times* exit poll, 10 June 1993).

On the surface the Riordan coalition looked like the Yorty coalition that
won in 1969 (Pettigrew 1971; Hahn, Klingman, and Pachon 1976; Halley,
Acock, and Greene 1976; Maullin 1969). In that race Jews split and Latinos
strongly backed Yorty, together ensuring Bradley's defeat. Yorty's victory
was part of a major conservative backlash to liberal politics locally and
nationally. A number of ballot measures for public expenditures were defeated in the 1969 primary and school board races favored conservatives
(Chapter 6; Halley, Acock, and Greene 1976; Hahn, Klingman, and
Pachon 1976). So was 1993 really 1969 redux? The evidence suggests that
it was not.

Riordan's conservative victory in the mayoral race, striking as it is, appears more anomalous than Yorty's in 1969. For example, in June 1992—
only two months after the civil disturbance—city voters approved a very
strong police reform measure (Proposition F) with over 60 percent of the
vote. In November 1992, the city went for Bill Clinton with 62 percent of
the vote. On the same ballot, over 60% of the voters agreed to pay higher
property taxes to fund more police (Proposition N). In each case, the con-

TABLE A.9
Key Races in 1991, 1992 (percent)

	Prop F	Clinton	Prop N
5th White liberal	71.1	67.6	65.3
8th African-American	92.0	85.4	71.0
12th White conservative	46.3	43.8	52.4
14th Latino/moderate white	65.4	61.5	57.8

Sources: For Prop F: City Clerk, Election Division; For Clinton and Prop N: County of Los Angeles, Registrar-Recorder.

servative Valley was outvoted by an alliance of inner city and white liberal voters. Table A.9 shows the vote in the four key council districts, and it is a very familiar pattern in the history of the Los Angeles coalition.

Private polling (Fairbank, Maslin, and Maullin) revealed that support for Proposition F did not erode even after the civil unrest. Indeed, it remained completely stable throughout the year. Support for Proposition N was very solid, even though it fell short of the needed two-thirds majority.

By contrast, Woo never had a solid foundation. In a baseline survey taken for Woo in January 1993, 33 percent of voters said they would definitely vote against him, and another 18 percent said they probably would. Only 32 percent said they would vote for him. Riordan's polling showed Woo with a 25 percent negative rating at the start of the campaign. Riordan's pollster Arnold Steinberg noted, "It was really remarkable to run against a candidate who had so many people who from the start would not vote for him" (interview). As Hollywood's councilman, Woo had made many enemies during battles over the area's redevelopment.

In other words, there were a lot of people in Los Angeles who backed Bill Clinton for president, voted for police reform in the face of conservative and police opposition, supported higher taxes for public services— and then went out and voted for Riordan over Woo. That was quite a bit different from what happened in 1969.

Even if the Riordan election was a sort of ideological anomaly, it was nonetheless very important. It marked a powerful shift at city hall from a westside-minority coalition to a Valley-centered regime with limited minority power. A feature of the Bradley years had been the dominance of city commissions by liberals from westside and minority areas (Chapter 9). Riordan was in a position to change the direction of the government and, more importantly, to establish the leadership credibility of the conservative side. Were he to succeed, he would place progressives in a weakened position for some time to come.

In the short run, however, there was not a fundamental shift to the right among the city's voters. While conservatives clearly and solidly defeated the liberals in the mayoral race, the city retained its moderately liberal political ideology. Underlying the Riordan victory were two other important factors that have been extensively discussed in this book: interest conflicts among the city's groups and the quality of leadership in various communities.

Interest

By 1993 the public's perception of life in Los Angeles had reached critical lows, moved along steadily by fear of crime and disorder, and then exponentially by the civil unrest of 1992. Los Angeles was a very unhappy city, not just in the inner city where unhappiness was well documented, but in the mid-city areas and certainly in suburban San Fernando Valley. White disaffection with the status quo was less visible than the discontent of minorities and the poor but, with the white dominance of the voter rolls, it carried a much greater electoral punch. The immigration issue carried subterranean weight. Kaufmann (1994) found that, among white liberals, voting for Riordan was connected more closely with the immigration issue than with race.

Interminority conflict had also been growing for a number of years. As the city became more crowded, grittier, and more crime ridden, groups contended over spaces that had previously been separate. Approximately 400,000 more people lived in Los Angeles than a decade before. Because the engine driving the population increase was immigration—mostly by Latinos and Asians—the immigration issue suddenly became explosive.

All this took place in the midst of a blistering recession that hit Los Angeles and all of California extremely hard. A significant proportion of national job losses were in California, particularly in Southern California. The devastating job exodus set the stage for anti-immigrant rhetoric and intergroup hostility.

South Central Los Angeles, once a Black bastion, is now contested by Blacks, Latinos, and Korean-American storekeepers (Oliver and Johnson 1984). Koreatown is divided between Korean-Americans and Latinos. The near San Fernando Valley, once all white, is heavily Latino.

The notion that Los Angeles was living a charmed urban life immune from the difficulties of other big cities was destroyed in the violence of April 1992. Before and after the civil disturbance, Blacks and Korean-Americans fought bitterly over liquor stores in South Central Los Angeles—literally a life and death struggle (Sonenshein and Davis 1993). Blacks and Latinos fought over construction jobs in the rebuilding after the civil unrest, and the immigration issue was never far from the surface. These were truly conflicts of interest.

Some Latinos, such as Councilman Richard Alatorre, were amenable to Riordan's blandishments. Would Asian-Americans, increasingly concerned about the problems of Korean-American storeowners, have voted so heavily for the liberal candidate if he had not been Asian-American? Did some non-Asians vote against Michael Woo because he was an Asian-American in a city ambivalent about its increasing diversity?

Numerous criminal trials—the LaTasha Harlins, Rodney King, and Reginald Denny cases—raised sensitivities to a high pitch. The increasingly crowded city was becoming more intense and uncomfortable. There was no escape from gunfire, whether in the neighborhood or on the evening news, and gang graffiti sprang up everywhere. The line between real fear and symbolic issues became obscured as local television news programs were saturated with crime stories.

The *Los Angeles Times* conducts regular polls to assess the condition of the city. They provide a useful measure of the emotional climate. Subtle differences between African-Americans and other groups emerge. Table A.10 presents this question at three crucial moments: shortly after the Rodney King controversy erupted in 1991, immediately after the civil unrest of 1992, and just before the 1993 general election. By the election, only 21 percent said that things were going well; 76 percent said things were not going well. The negative attitude was remarkably multiracial; 79 percent of whites, 78 percent of Blacks, and 76 percent of Latinos picked the negative view.

Table A.10 suggests that the civil unrest had a huge impact on citywide perceptions of the state of the city in a way that the Rodney King case itself did not. After the King beating, African-Americans were more negative about the city's condition than other groups. The biggest shift toward the negative came *after* the civil unrest, first from whites, then from Latinos, two groups whose ambivalence cost Woo severely. In other words, the King beating did not lead a majority to see the whole city going down, but the civil unrest did. Even a year after the violence, the negative results had barely improved on the eve of the mayoral election—bad news for the liberal candidate to succeed the incumbent progressive regime.

The civil unrest added to the feeling of despair and threat. Unlike the geographically confined Watts uprising of 1965, the 1992 violence spread wildly, and news reports suggested that there were no real barriers to its expansion. Self-protection became a major concern in a city threatened and insecure.

Ironically, this feeling of general threat coexisted with a more progressive set of attitudes than in 1965. After the Watts uprising, Police Chief William Parker received overwhelming support from whites and Latinos, and almost total dislike from Blacks (Sears and McConahay 1973). By contrast, few in any group felt that the acquittal of the police officers in Simi Valley had been justified, and Chief Gates was widely disliked citywide. Near the end of his tenure his disapproval rating reached 81 percent in the *Los Angeles Times* poll (15 May 1992).

TABLE A.10
How Do You Feel Things Are Going in Los Angeles These Days? (percent)

	March 1991 After King Beating		May 1992 After Riots		May 1993 During Campaign		Change in Well
	Well	Badly	Well	Badly	Well	Badly	
All	40	55	13	85	21	76	−19
Whites	44	51	11	88	18	79	−26
Blacks	28	66	11	88	21	78	−7
Latinos	39	56	19	79	19	76	−20

Source: Los Angeles Times polls #247, #281, #311.

Jews were particularly ambivalent about the violence. There were significant efforts within the Jewish community to provide aid to South Central Los Angeles after the violence (Rubin 1993). Jews had been among the strongest opponents of Daryl Gates from the start, and were very strong supporters of police reform. But the plight of Korean-American storeowners raised unavoidable parallels with an earlier generation of Jewish shopkeepers burned out in 1965, and the shock of civil violence, the fear of street crime, and public reports of African-American anti-Semitism severely shook the Jewish community.

Latinos were also ambivalent. While much was made of the "rainbow riot," the main Latino community on the east side was not a part of the uprising. Its leaders were careful to make that known within the city. The great attention paid to South Central after the civil disorder detracted from the problems of the east side, and opened up further possibilities for conflict.

In the aftermath of the civil disturbances of 1992, there was a greater possibility for conflicts of interest among potential allies. Conflicts among African-Americans, Latinos, and Asian-Americans were widely discussed, but few were aware of the growing alienation of the group most able to make it count at the ballot box, namely whites. At the same time, the city was ideologically more progressive than it had been in the past. To maintain a progressive coalition, leaders would need to bridge these interest conflicts, to elicit ideological affinities, and to offer reassurance and practical solutions. In the troubled Los Angeles of 1993, such leadership was hard to find.

Leadership

The 1993 mayoral election coincided with the sudden disappearance of a whole generation of leaders. Within a very short span, Mayor Bradley, Police Chief Gates, District Attorney Ira Reiner, and county supervisor Kenneth Hahn left office. Those who remained in power were either too raw and new or too tied to their own communities to build coalitions. Others joined with Riordan. Few who would lead at the grass roots had the clout or the interest to build citywide coalitions. Never in the thirty-year span of biracial politics had there been so few well-known people trying to do this work. The most widely known leader in the city was probably the new police chief from Philadelphia, Willie Williams.

Beyond the fall of established leaders was the loss of confidence created by the devastating violence of 1992. The Watts uprising of 1965 brought confidence to progressives. They were out of power and could view the violence as a failure of the conservatives in power (Chapter 5). No such view could be credible in 1992, after nearly twenty years of liberal biracial rule. The fiasco of turning over the reconstruction of South Central to businessman Peter Ueberroth and the organization Rebuild L.A. bespoke a sense of weakened legitimacy at city hall. And would that not indirectly be an argument for the election of a businessman like Riordan a year later?

The loss of power and confidence by citywide leaders allowed others more attuned to confrontation to take center stage. Xavier Hermosillo of NEWS for America, a conservative Latino political organization, generated publicity with comments that offended many African-Americans. Danny Bakewell played a similar role in the African-American community, forcing contractors to replace Latino workers with Blacks after the civil unrest.

During the hegemonic years of the Bradley coalition such ethnocentric leaders tended to be left in obscurity, but now there was nothing to impede their messages. In this empty space, the question of leadership came down to the choices presented to the voters in the runoff election in June.

Surprisingly, Riordan was not a great campaigner. He had a personal fortune but commissioned television commercials that were at best silly and at worst embarrassing. He was a Princeton graduate, a lawyer, and by all accounts a bright and inquisitive man. But as a public speaker he was turgid and uninspired. His staff had little confidence in his ability to answer questions and shielded him from the press. He had numerous liabilities, including building a fortune in association with financier Michael Milken, giving money to prolife groups, and a series of drunk driving arrests that nearly derailed him at the end. He had a tendency to issue blanket denials of all charges, some of which later had to be admitted.

But his strengths were more than enough to win the election. He had business experience, an open and friendly manner, vast sums of money to produce and deliver a wave of first-rate direct mail, an outstanding absentee-ballot effort, and a simple slogan that dominated his campaign: "Tough Enough to Turn L.A. Around." The slogan was spectacular in its reflection of a city on the wrong track and in its suggestion that Riordan would be as tough as needed, but not tough for its own sake. The message of firmness, but within limits, was perfectly calibrated to appeal to white moderates, and even to some white liberals.

Riordan's long experience in Los Angeles politics gave him a legion of political friends, including a number of city council members and a raft of liberal Democrats to whom he had given campaign money. He was user friendly in a city that would be reluctant to back a right-wing ideologue. Even in inner-city neighborhoods where he would win few votes, Riordan had built ties over the years through gifts of computers to local schools.

In his own awkward and choppy way, Riordan spoke to people's real and media-induced fears—of being a crime victim, of random violence, of communities out of control. In one debate he recited a list of urban fears, all of which seemed to come from a summary of the local TV news: drive-by shootings, gang violence, ATM murders, drugs in the schools. It was a very effective recitation.

But unlike Yorty, Riordan did not cast the choice ideologically or as an assault on liberal policies; he aimed his attacks at city hall bureaucracy, not at liberalism. His slogan provided an ideologically neutral connection to the alienation so many felt from the condition of Los Angeles. He gave people a way to vote for him to turn the city around without turning themselves around ideologically. While some of his ideas were unlikely to be implemented, such as leasing the airport to hire more police, the focus on proposed policies contrasted with Yorty's cavalier disdain for government when all he needed was demagoguery.

The conservative victory was made possible in no small part by the problems of the liberal candidate. Arnold Steinberg, Riordan's pollster, commented that "we were blessed to be running against Michael Woo . . . anyone else would have been more difficult" (interview). One journalist noted that the Woo campaign "can establish an institute on how not to run for mayor" (Meyerson 1993a). Among other sins, Woo failed to expend all of his campaign money by election day (ibid.).

Riordan's personal fortune offered tremendous flexibility in financing his campaign. He outspent Woo, one of the city's leading political fund-raisers, by nearly a two-to-one margin. In fact, Riordan personally donated $6 million, more than Woo's entire $5.5 million campaign budget, and Riordan's campaign spent a total of approximately $10 million (*Los Angeles Times*, 4 August 1993).

The decision by local television stations to provide only the barest coverage of the mayoral election greatly helped Riordan against Woo. There were several reasons for the limited television attention. Local politics have never been as salient to the Los Angeles viewing audience as, for example, in New York City or Chicago. In addition, with the patchwork of communities that comprise Los Angeles County, there were millions of viewers of local television news who did not live in the city of Los Angeles. In the bitterly competitive Los Angeles local news market, it would be uneconomical to focus heavily on Los Angeles city politics.

Woo could not get air time to make charges against Riordan, and could not break the momentum of the well-funded Riordan campaign. Campaign debates received only marginal television coverage, reducing Woo's opportunities to strike dramatic blows or raise new doubts about his opponent. Most importantly, the regular coverage of crime that dominated local television news (*Los Angeles Times*, 8 June 1993) practically became campaign commercials for Riordan. With the news agenda focused on crime, voters were easily primed to evaluate the two candidates principally on that issue (Iyengar and Kinder 1987).

Woo lost the edge of racial harmony by his lackluster attempts to appeal to white voters. He was well regarded among Jews, but he failed to match Riordan's warm concern for that community (Marks 1993). Few in Woo's campaign had a sense of Jews as a community separate from other whites. Caught up in the rainbow model of progressive politics, Woo's campaigners were much less effective than Riordan's at massaging subtle and crucial differences among whites.

The Woo campaign's late May tracking poll found some very disturbing results. On many key measures of leadership, Riordan was swamping Woo (Table A.11). Woo was not far behind in voter preference, but he was in a weaker position than the "horse race" indicated. These results suggested that many people were sticking with Woo out of liberal habit, without feeling very confident about his leadership ability.

Woo's key appeal was that he could hold the city together, but on the issue of group harmony he reached only a virtual tie with Riordan. The only place where Woo might have made progress was by tying himself to working people, but middle-class people dominated the electorate. This

TABLE A.11
Selected Leadership Indicators (percent)

	Woo	Riordan
Looks and acts like a mayor	20	43
Will divide L.A.	30	33
Tough on crime	21	46
Attract jobs/industry	25	46
Good for my community	36	35
Will get things done	28	42
Will expand LAPD	21	40
Out of touch with working people	21	37
Overall preference	36	41

Source: Woo campaign poll, 30–31 May 1993.

may help explain why Woo's campaign devolved into declaring Riordan unacceptable.

At every opportunity, Woo painted Riordan as a right-wing Reagan clone with a weak commitment to abortion rights. He portrayed Riordan's shifting answers on his drunk driving record as evidence of dishonesty and argued that Riordan had made his fortune shutting down American factories and destroying American jobs. Riordan had some difficult moments on the drunk-driving issue until his supporters in the police union decided to accept his explanations; the issue soon faded away.

In a nervous city, only a durable appeal to a center-left coalition built around interracial politics offered hope for a progressive victory. A big bloc of whites had to be split off from the wave of conservative reaction; otherwise, there was no chance. Impressed by the demographics rather than by voter-registration figures, Woo's campaign spokesman uttered perhaps the truest expression of the campaign's sloppy underlying assumption: "Los Angeles isn't about to elect an old, rich, white Republican." It was as close to a slogan as Woo ever came, and the campaign's most appropriate epitaph. In an editorial, the *Daily News*, the principal newspaper in the San Fernando Valley, contrasted Woo's approach to whites to that of Bradley: "In strong contrast to the genuine inclusiveness practiced by Tom Bradley when he was in his political prime, Woo seems willing to write off people like Riordan (or people who like Riordan) in the belief that he can do without them" (25 April 1993).

An intangible aspect of Woo's campaign was the poor impression he made in public. I attended a public hearing during the primary sponsored by Representative Maxine Waters, primarily aimed at the African-American community. While this should have been Woo territory, he faced numerous hostile questions without any change of expression or variation of his voice. Later I heard him at a debate in the Jewish community where he used numerous opportunities to make personal attacks on Riordan. These charges, while effective, made him look petty and harsh in comparison to the calm, mature, avuncular Riordan.

Even for those who shared his philosophy, Woo was not an easy candidate to enjoy. He was either too passive or too aggressive and the best sides of his personality—well known to many in the city—did not materialize in the campaign. Riordan's pollster found

> when I went to parties and did not tell people I was polling for Richard, I would ask liberal Democrats about the election. They had a lot of negative feelings for Riordan, but they had a very high discomfort level with Woo as well. They often said they didn't like the way he talked. . . . His chemistry didn't work" (interview)

To make matters worse for Woo, he was shadowed from debate to debate by a group of phenomenally angry activists from his council district.

These people seemed to have a loathing for Woo that went beyond the normal bounds of politics, and they could be relied upon to address a steady stream of harsh questions at all forums. Their rage was intimidating and allowed Riordan to seem above the assault on Woo. At one campaign debate the audience question period consisted of one anti-Woo tirade after another; no one else had a chance to reach the microphone.

It was a very tough year to run as a liberal in a tense and nervous Los Angeles. Even a terrific campaign from the left, without a base in the center, was doomed to failure. As a coalition builder, Woo was extraordinarily successful in bridging serious conflicts between African-Americans and Korean-Americans, two pillars of his campaign. These efforts bore some fruit in the liquor store rebuilding controversy (Sonenshein and Davis 1993), and he deserves major credit for brokering some agreements between these highly opposed groups. In a conflict in which there seemed to be no middle ground, Woo helped push through city hall funding for the conversion of some liquor stores to laundromats.

But the crucial Black-Korean conflict was only one element in coalition politics, and fell far short of creating a citywide majority. Woo needed two other groups with whom he was much less successful: Latinos and Jews. The narrowness of seeing coalitions as settling inner-city minority conflicts failed to reach the heart of success: cross-racial citywide coalition building.

For progressives to have prevailed in post-violence 1993, they would have needed a different sort of approach, with a greater appeal to the center. Both Woo and Riordan preferred to run against the other, fearing most of all a moderate centrist. Riordan's pollster said that the ideal person to beat Riordan would have "a Valley base, be Jewish, a Democrat, moderate and for the death penalty" (Steinberg interview). He perceived both Wachs and Katz to be serious threats. The only minority candidate he felt could have beaten Riordan was maverick county supervisor Gloria Molina because of her crossover appeal as a reformer (interview). In each case, a liberal-moderate coalition would have challenged the emerging conservative base.

Centrist candidates, however, failed to capitalize on their opportunity. Wachs and Katz neutralized each other, and neither could set forth a powerful identity. Katz held back his campaign spending until after Riordan had already established his own name recognition. According to Woo's polltaker, as a result of "this major strategic blunder," Katz could not then gain similar recognition (Maullin interview).

On the progressive leadership front, then, two things were happening. Those leaders with experience at building citywide crossracial coalitions—people like Bradley, Ira Reiner, and James K. Hahn—either left the scene or stayed out of the race. Dynamic candidates like Gloria

Molina and Zev Yaroslavsky who could have learned to do so stayed out. The candidates who remained looked great on paper but did not campaign effectively. For many voters who might well have stayed in the moderately progressive camp, there was no choice from the progressive side that appealed to them. Many voted for Woo out of ideological loyalty, others went over to Riordan, and many others stayed home.

The Riordan Administration

As mayor of Los Angeles, Riordan has been something of a surprise. After a rocky start, he has generally taken a moderate stance and has largely been the pragmatic centrist that he said he was. He has built a close alliance with the Clinton administration and with Democratic members of Congress. He has strongly supported the new African-American police chief, Willie Williams. Despite the eerie similarity of their electoral bases, he has not at all seemed to be the reincarnation of Sam Yorty.

Riordan's first weeks in office were confusing and inconsistent. One of his first appointments was Bill Violante, head of the police union, as a deputy mayor and liaison to the Police Department. Chief Williams, fresh from bitter struggles with the union, was enraged. One of Riordan's first Latino appointees, Alfred Villalobos, eventually resigned as a deputy mayor after a long record of financial irregularities emerged (*Los Angeles Times*, 16 December 1993). Riordan approved a hugely generous settlement with the employees of the Department of Water and Power, thereby engendering great resentment from police officers who had been working for years without a contract. In 1994, a heavy majority of police turned down a city wage offer that fell short of the DWP deal (*Los Angeles Times*, 21 May 1994). By June, they had won a rich contract of their own.

But Riordan also placed a number of progressive people into key commission posts along with his conservative white and Latino allies. Shortly after his election, he marched in the annual gay-rights parade and was photographed hugging a participant. When California Governor Pete Wilson launched a demagogic attack on immigrants, Riordan spoke up in favor of maintaining services even for undocumented immigrants. He built a strong base on the powerful city council and brought potential foes like Yaroslavsky into the budget process at a high level. Despite the crowing of national Republicans over his victory, Riordan went to Washington to jog with President Clinton, and he met with Democratic Congressional leaders. He has been virtually invisible in Republican circles. Irritated that Riodan's key aides are Democrats, some Republican party activists sported RINO (Republican In Name Only) buttons at a Riordan speech (*Los Angeles Times*, 16 May 1994).

After his shaky beginning, Riordan began to apply his business-oriented approach to the city government. An indicator of the Riordan stance could be found in his budgetary policies. Shortly after his inauguration, Riordan appointed a committee of financial leaders to assess the city's fiscal direction. Their report, issued on February 24, 1994, proposed a number of ways to raise revenue without increasing taxes. Some were extremely difficult, such as leasing the airport, but others seemed feasible. Most strikingly, the report strongly supported the retention of key city services and called for greater attention to the city's physical infrastructure (*Los Angeles Times*, 25 February 1994).

In April 1994 Riordan formally proposed his city budget. He called for an end to cuts in libraries and parks, and proposed the consolidation of several city departments. Through restructuring of police operations, he proposed to take a step toward his campaign promise of placing three thousand more officers on the streets without imposing new taxes. The *Los Angeles Times* praised Riordan's wisdom in slowing the push toward privatization that he had introduced in his campaign (*Los Angeles Times*, 22 April 1994). The budget largely followed the guidelines of his planning report, and was praised by Yaroslavsky, the council's key budget specialist, who commented: "He has pulled off something I didn't think he could pull off. The guts of this thing are sound and compelling, although there may be some questions around the periphery" (*Los Angeles Times*, 21 April 1994).

While Riordan has generally received positive reviews for his administration, he is likely to have difficulties in two key areas: relations with the African-American community and reliance on a business model for governing a multiracial, multiclass city. He does not yet have a rapport with the African-American community, now out of power in the mayor's office for the first time in twenty years. During the campaign, he drew derisive laughs at a Black church when he tried to decide what to label the violence of 1992. He needlessly provoked a council revolt when he tried to appoint Latino conservative Xavier Hermosillo, who had made anti-Black comments, to the important Fire Commission (Kayden 1993). When the shockingly lenient federal sentence given to the police officers in the Rodney King case outraged the Black community, he said the justice system had worked and that healing should begin. His relations with key Black council members Mark Ridley-Thomas and Rita Walters have been uncomfortable. But there is no comparison to the hateful, vitriolic anti-Black words of Mayor Yorty or Police Chief Parker in the 1960s (see pp. 80–81).

Riordan's reliance on his connections to the business world may help produce an effective, coherent budget, but he will also have to consider the needs of a city most of whose residents are not wealthy. Although his financial plan was a thoughtful response to Los Angeles's broad crisis, it may have perpetuated the idea, discredited by Rebuild L.A., that a group of business executives can best respond to the community's needs. For example, Riordan has been urged to make a stronger commitment to bus services for working families, rather than solely aiming to create a business-friendly atmosphere in the area of transportation (Kayden 1994).

A small group of council liberals will continue to challenge Riordan to incorporate the concerns of minorities and low-income and working families, even if they were not key components of his election coalition. Newly elected Thirteenth district council member Jackie Goldberg, the city's first openly gay elected official, African-American Mark Ridley-Thomas (Eighth district), and Mike Hernandez of the Latino First district, have generally comprised the challenging, multiethnic, progressive coalition.

Overall, however, Riordan has been surprisingly flexible and pragmatic. In its moderation, his approach presents a challenge for Los Angeles progressives that Yorty did not. Yorty was a clear enemy, and even though he won in 1969, the progressive forces could hardly wait to get at him in 1973. He excluded the minority and progressive forces very effectively, helping to build their morale and unity for another battle and, eventually, for governing.

If Riordan succeeds in making the city work better without polarizing the electorate, he could actually make progressive politics more successful in the long run. Progressives do poorly when the public feels that government itself is unable to address and resolve problems. But with African-Americans out of power, and Jews and Latinos not so fully shut out, strains are likely to arise within the progressive coalition.

In the longer run, the leadership gap in Los Angeles coalition politics may be filled not only by politicians but by people at the grass-roots level: union activists organizing janitors in Century City; African-Americans trying to reach agreements with Korean-Americans to limit liquor stores in South Central; ministers and rabbis seeking to build cross-racial understanding; college students meeting in small groups to puncture stereotypes and build more positive images of each other; Latinos seeking to advance citizenship and political mobilization within their community. Perhaps the next stage for Los Angeles's urban progressives is not just to win elections, but to solve community problems.

Such meetings are going on all around the city, and their very obscurity provides a ray of hope; perhaps people will feel less bound to take confrontational stances if they are not publicly appealing to their own constituencies. Xandra Kayden has called these people "translators," and notes that while they cannot yet deliver their communities, "they are L.A.'s best—maybe only—hope." (Kayden 1993). These leaders will have to work through the pros and cons of rainbow and biracial coalitions, as well as the best balance between human relations and conflict resolution.

Riordan's election was a powerful defeat for progressive politics in Los Angeles. Already fading as the new decade came in, the ruling biracial coalition lost its way completely after the civil unrest of 1992. With its leaders aging or leaving office, with an electorate disenchanted with government policies and with the state of their city, circumstances favored the conservative outsider with seemingly limitless funds and a simple message.

But the meaning of the election was much more complex than a shift to the right. The ideological basis of coalition politics survived, and in that sense the moderation of the Riordan administration represented an accommodation to the moderately progressive nature of the city's voters. That ideological potential also counted for less than in the past, now that the city was filled with interest conflicts and uncertain leadership.

New York City and Los Angeles

Throughout this book I have explored the differing evolution of biracial politics in New York City and Los Angeles. For decades the two great metropolises have been out of step with each other. As John V. Lindsay embarked on his liberal biracial regime in 1965, conservative Sam Yorty won the mayoralty in Los Angeles. As Tom Bradley conquered city hall for the first time in 1973, the Lindsay regime was moving off to the sidelines. As Bradley's coalition declined in the late 1980s, New York City elected its first African-American mayor, David Dinkins, in 1989. Only in 1993 did the patterns coincide, as white conservatives took over from Black incumbent mayors in both cities.

The elections of Richard Riordan and Rudolph Giuliani indeed had much in common. Both Dinkins and Woo were liberal politicians with multiracial bases. Each was supported by an overwhelming majority of African-American voters but had trouble recruiting enough Jews and Latinos to turn the tides in their uphill battles. The winning candidate's electoral coalition was overwhelmingly white in each case and the communities were racially polarized.

Like Riordan, Giuliani avoided old-fashioned appeals to racial feelings. He won endorsements from enough groups to start isolating the African-American community. Herman Badillo and other Democrats gave Giuliani a centrist edge that he had lacked when he lost to Dinkins in 1989. And, of course, the Crown Heights violence placed Dinkins's leadership credentials at serious risk. Dinkins's Jewish support, already less than Bradley enjoyed in Los Angeles, was in jeopardy.

Exit polling in New York City showed that, as in Los Angeles, there were significant gaps among whites (Table A.12). The persisting difference between Jews and other whites is truly remarkable, since there are few settings in America in which Black-Jewish tensions have been more intense than the period leading up to the 1993 New York City mayoral election. Clearly, both Dinkins and Woo lost badly among white moder-

TABLE A.12
New York City Mayoral Race—Divisions
among Whites (percent)

	Dinkins	Giuliani
Jews	32	68
White Protestants	17	81
White Catholics	12	86
White liberals	50	48
White moderates	15	84
White conservatives	2	95

Source: Voter Research and Surveys exit polls, *New York Times*, 4 November 1993.

ates; even a decent showing among these voters would have made victory inevitable for Dinkins and possible for Woo.

A second area of similarity between the two elections was the intensity of white conservative voting. Staten Island was Giuliani's version of the northwest San Fernando Valley. Spurred by a nonbinding referendum on whether the Island should secede from New York City, Giuliani's voters turned out in very large numbers (*New York Times*, 4 November 1993). As in Los Angeles, the Black turnout was down from four years before. In both cities, white conservative voters returned with a vengeance and were met by depressed and unmobilized minority communities.

But the differences between the two cities remain. While the electoral bases of the winning candidates were similar—white mobilization with a share of minority votes—their styles of leadership have been different. Giuliani has been a more confrontational mayor and partisan Republican than Riordan.

These mayoral differences are indicated by their respective attitudes toward the Clinton administration. Riordan and Clinton have formed a close working relationship, the groundwork for which was laid by the numerous Riordan allies in the administration. With Clinton's close attention to California, and his partisan rivalry with Republican Governor Pete Wilson, the pragmatic Riordan has appeared as a godsend to the administration. Riordan has worked closely and supportively with Clinton and has represented no partisan threat. By contrast, Giuliani snubbed Clinton when the president visited New York City—an action sure to impress Republican leaders but unlikely to help the city's relations with Washington.

Riordan has worked closely and collegially with the powerful city council. Although Giuliani began in a similar manner, he entered a bitter and fruitless confrontation with the chancellor of the city schools. In so doing, Giuliani eroded his support on the heavily Democratic city council. While both mayors presented budgets meant to strengthen their police departments, Riordan protected social services to a greater degree. Giuliani, by contrast, completely exempted the police and fire departments from any budget cuts and proposed major reductions in social services (*Newsday*, 23 May 1994). In tone, the two mayors represent different approaches. Riordan has been largely conciliatory; Giuliani has mixed conciliation with a prosecutorial assertiveness that led to political disaster in his battle with the schools chief (*New York Times*, 8 April 1994).

But even with these differences, both Riordan and Giuliani have offered the new style of white-led urban coalitions. They reach beyond the hard racism of the white coalitions of earlier days and focus on their ability to act decisively in the face of the varied interests of the big city. They are likely to be far more acceptable to a large majority of white voters—and to some minorities—than earlier, openly polarizing white mayors. And they are both part of the larger centrist movement that calls for reinventing local government. That movement appears likely to have a successful run at the top of America's cities.

In both cities, progressive candidates in tense cities were unable to bridge the gap between the aspirations of minorities and the fears of whites. It is never an easy task in tough times, but it is a struggle that must continue. If progressives concede the bulk of the white vote to the conservatives and confine their minority appeals to the rainbow ideology, then they will be facing defeat for a long time to come. By contrast to the biracial model, the rainbow approach is by itself too narrow to be successful. Candidates must approach Latinos and Asian-Americans on their own terms, not simply as shades of the rainbow. Their interests are unique and their concerns must be taken seriously. Jews should not be marginalized in progressive coalitions; they still represent the single greatest link between minority communities and whites. It is crucial to build crosstown coalitions, rather than simply building an inner-city alliance against everybody else.

National Implications

Do the developments of the last several years mark the end of the era of minority politics and biracial coalition? Urban progressives need to be concerned that urban conservatives have been threatening to take hold of the center—an area thought long gone in urban politics. Successful urban progressivism requires the rebuilding of center-left coalitions.

To hold power, progressives need to realize that the other side is more formidable than in the past. Conservatives have gone beyond trashy demagoguery—or they do not need to prime the pump anymore—and are arguing that they can govern. This approach makes them a devastating threat to take control of the center. The center matters again in urban politics; if progressives want justice, and conservatives want peace, the balance of power increasingly rests with those who want both justice *and* peace.

Nowadays against a minority candidate, a white candidate will have the conservative vote already locked up. White conservative or moderate candidates are freer to spend their time courting Latinos, white moderates, and even white liberals. They preach harmony and reach out to leaders of these swing groups. They present themselves, as Black mayoral candidates once did, as models of competence and efficiency. They go after two selling points of Black mayoral candidates against old-fashioned white demagogues, managerial capability and healing, while resting comfortably on the crime and disorder issues.

It is possible that the era of Black mayors and the biracial coalitions that sustained them is drawing to a close after a twenty-five-year run, just as their rise marked the end of the old-style political machines. If that is so, then minority politics will once again be at a major turning point and the subject of coalition politics must be regenerated.

This new stage will begin with a continuation of the debate over the value of the urban movement for minority empowerment. An accurate analysis of the period that is now drawing to a close is crucial. The tendency to downgrade its achievements in light of its limitations—as has occurred in recent years with the earlier civil rights movement—would be a mistake. A balanced view of what was achieved and what remains to be done is essential.

If the movement for minority empowerment in American cities represents the second stage of the modern struggle for equality—with the civil rights movement as the first stage—then what is the next stage? Just as the civil-rights movement continued to exist even after its main era ended, the struggle to win political power in minority and mixed-group constituencies is likely to continue indefinitely. But it will not again have the enthusiastic energy of insurgency that it developed from the mid-1960s until the late 1980s. The issues of equality are likely to be confronted with new tactics in new settings. It is possible that it may be too limiting to see politics as only the search for local power in the next era of the struggle for equality.

Progressive multiracial coalitions must once again search for influence in national political coalitions and find ways to revive grass-roots activism outside city hall. The precarious national coalition behind President Clinton represents both an opportunity and a challenge to progressives. It does not promise the levels of urban funding that the Great Society offered, but it does suggest a majoritarian model for progressive action on a wide range of social issues. (For a discussion of the implications of the Clinton coalition for minority politics, see Browning and Tabb 1994.)

The multiracial politics of the 1990s must go beyond taking and holding urban power. It must begin to challenge the influential ideas that persuade Americans that certain policies fit their values and that other policies do not—the world of political symbols. In other words, interracial political communication is likely to play a crucial role in the shape of the national struggle for equality. The question then would not only be, as in the civil-rights movement, "What are the legal rights of minorities?" and not only the question of empowerment ("Who makes the decisions?") but the extremely difficult one, "Who can win the persuasive battle to create majority support for an agenda for society?"

Bill Clinton's success in ending the long Democratic drought at the presidential level depended on new definitions of issues that had haunted progressives for years. In the 1993 local elections, those liabilities continued to lead to progressive defeat. Jobs and crime were the principal issues of the 1993 Los Angeles election, and progressives were not part of the conversation.

The crime issue need not isolate the inner city nor be the exclusive property of conservatives. It is a crisis for people all over the city and nation and a problem that requires new ideas beyond fear mongering. Jobs still dominate the minds of the voters—not just unemployment in the inner city but the wider insecurity of a restructuring economy.

Finding a way to cross racial lines and to reestablish the frayed connections between poor and middle-class people must be the first steps in rebuilding not just urban progressive politics, but a national politics of change. It will be difficult to get there without restoring the interracial and multiracial bridges that have eroded in recent years.

In order to rebuild coalitions, the need for a new contract for interracial politics is paramount (Chapter 16). Coalitions must be built across racial lines that address the beliefs and interests of each participating group. Past relationships must be renewed, perhaps on a new basis, and with additional partners. Settings for political action based on equal status can help forge new bonds of trust. The balance between ideology and interest must be respected. New majorities can be built.

In the broadest sense, the 1993 Los Angeles election shows the importance of the debate over interracial political coalitions. In the long run, the cost of unexamined assumptions on this question may be profound—the rollback of hard-won minority political gains. Or, more hopefully, developing a new contract for biracial or multiracial politics may bring the struggle for equality aggressively and effectively into the next century. To apply the lessons of biracial coalition politics to a new generation of multiracial progressives is the most important task for the years to come.

References

Browning, Rufus, and David H. Tabb. 1994. Protest vs. Politics: What is Necessary? What is Enough? Revision of a paper presented at the annual meeting of the National Conference of Black Political Scientists, Oakland, CA. March 10–13, 1993.

Iyengar, Shanto, and Donald Kinder. 1987. *News That Matters: Television and American Opinion.* Chicago: University of Chicago Press.

Kaufmann, Karen. 1994. Us versus Them: A Group Conflict Analysis of the 1993 Los Angeles Mayoral Election. Paper presented at the annual meeting of the Western Political Science Association, March 10–12.

Kayden, Xandra. 1993. In Rejecting Hermosillo, the City Council Defines What Leadership Is. *Los Angeles Times.* Commentary, 29 August.

_____. 1994. Subsidize the Poor, not the Well Off; An MTA Budget Crisis Threatens to Cut Bus Service Urgently Needed by Lower-Income Urban Users. *Los Angeles Times.* Commentary, 28 April.

Lemann, Nicholas. 1993. Race, Reform and Urban Voters. *New York Times,* Commentary, 4 November.

Marks, Marlene Adler. 1993. Jewish Voters Will Not Be Forgotten. *Los Angeles Times.* Commentary, 23 April.

Maullin, Richard. Polltaker for the Woo campaign. Interview.

Meyerson, Harold. 1993a. The Word on Woo. *L.A. Weekly.* June 18–24: 12.

_____. 1993b. The End of Urban Liberalism? *L.A. Weekly,* November 12–18.

Pactech. 1992. Materials prepared for the Los Angeles city council redistricting process.

Rubin, Susan E. 1993. The Jewish Response to the Los Angeles Riots. *Western States Jewish History* 25 (April): 195–208.

Sleeper, Jim. 1993. The End of the Rainbow? The Changing Politics of America's Cities. *The New Republic,* November 1, 20–25.

Sonenshein, Raphael J., and Corecia J. Davis. 1993. The Battle over Liquor Stores in South Central Los Angeles. Paper presented at the annual meeting of the Western Political Science Association, March 18–20.

Steinberg, Arnold. Polltaker for the Riordan campaign. Interview.

The research for this Afterword was supported by a grant from the John Randolph Haynes and Dora Haynes Foundation, and benefited from the thoughtful advice of Rufus Browning and Alan Saltzstein.

REFERENCES

Adrian, Charles R. 1959. A Typology for Nonpartisan Elections. *Western Political Quarterly* 12:449–58.

Ainsworth, Ed. 1966. *Maverick Mayor: A Biography of Sam Yorty of Los Angeles*. Garden City, NY: Doubleday.

Anderson, E. Frederick. 1980. The Development of Leadership and Organization Building in the Black Community of Los Angeles from 1900 through World War II. Saratoga, CA: Century 21 Publishing.

Banfield, Edward C., and James Q. Wilson. 1963. *City Politics*. Cambridge, MA: Harvard University Press.

Bayor, Ronald H. 1978. *Neighbors in Conflict: The Irish, Germans, Jews and Italians of New York City, 1929–1941*. Baltimore: Johns Hopkins University Press.

Bellush, Jewel, and Stephen M. David, eds. 1971. *Race and Politics in New York City*. New York: Praeger.

Bollens, John C., and Grant B. Geyer. 1973. *Yorty: The Politics of a Constant Candidate*. Pacific Palisades, CA.: Palisades Publishers.

Bond, J. Max. 1936. The Negro in Los Angeles. Ph.D. diss., University of Southern California. Reprint. San Francisco: R & E Press, 1972.

Boyarsky, Bill. 1988. Westside Crude. *Los Angeles Times Magazine*, September 25, 9–23.

Browne, Eric C., and John Dreijaminis, eds. 1982. *Government Coalitions in Western Democracies*. New York: Longman.

Browning, Rufus P., Dale Rogers Marshall, and David Tabb. 1984. *Protest Is Not Enough: The Struggle of Blacks and Hispanics for Equality in City Politics*. Berkeley: University of California Press.

———, eds. 1990. *Racial Politics in American Cities*. New York: Longman.

Bullock, Charles S., III, and Bruce A. Campbell. 1984. Racist or Racial Voting in the 1981 Atlanta Municipal Elections. *Urban Affairs Quarterly* 20:149–64.

Bureau of Governmental Research. 1961. *BGR Observer*, November. University of California, Los Angeles.

Caditz, Judith. 1976. *White Liberals in Transition: Current Dilemmas of Ethnic Integration*. Holliswood, NY: Spectrum Publications.

Cain, Bruce E., D. Roderick Kiewiet, and Carole Uhlaner. 1986. The Political Impact of California's Minorities. Paper presented at the annual meeting of the Western Political Science Association.

Caper, Gene, and Norton B. Stern. 1984. First Jewish President of the Los Angeles City Council. *Western States Jewish History* 17 (October): 63–76.

Carmichael, Stokely, and Charles V. Hamilton. 1967. *Black Power: The Politics of Liberation in America*. New York: Random House.

Carmines, Edward G., and James A. Stimson. 1982. Racial Issues and the Structure of Mass Belief Systems. *Journal of Politics* 44:2–20.

———. 1989. *Issue Evolution: Race and the Transformation of American Politics*. Princeton, NJ: Princeton University Press.

Carney, Francis. 1964. The Decentralized Politics of Los Angeles. *Annals of the American Academy of Political and Social Sciences* 353 (May): 107–21.

City of Los Angeles. 1991. Comprehensive Housing Affordability Strategy. Housing Preservation and Production Department.

Clark, Peter B., and James Q. Wilson. 1961. Incentive Systems: A Theory of Organizations. *Administrative Science Quarterly* 6:219–66.

Cole, Leonard A. 1974. Electing Blacks to Municipal Office: Structural and Social Determinants. *Urban Affairs Quarterly* 10 (September): 17–39.

————. 1976 *Blacks in Power: A Comparative Study of Black and White Elected Officials.* Princeton NJ: Princeton University Press.

Collins, Keith E. 1980. Black Los Angeles: The Maturing of the Ghetto, 1940–1950. Saratoga, CA: Century 21 Publishing.

Conot, Robert E. 1967. *Rivers of Blood, Years of Darkness.* Toronto and New York: Bantam Books.

Dalfiume, Richard M. 1968. The "Forgotten Years" of the Negro Revolution. *Journal of American History* 55:90–106.

Davidson, Chandler. 1972. *Biracial Politics: Conflict and Coalition in the Metropolitan South.* Baton Rouge: Louisiana State University Press.

Davis, Mike. 1991. *City of Quartz: Excavating the Future in Los Angeles.* London: Haymarket Press.

Dawidowicz, Lucy S., and Leon J. Goldstein. 1963. *Politics in a Pluralist Democracy: Studies of Voting in the 1960 Election.* New York: Institute of Human Relations Press.

DeGraaf, Lawrence B. 1967. Interview with Tom Bradley. California State University, Fullerton, Oral History Program.

————. 1970. The City of Black Angels: Emergence of the Los Angeles Ghetto, 1890–1930. *Pacific Historical Review* 39:323–52.

DeLeon, Richard E., and Sandra S. Powell. 1989. Growth Control and Electoral Politics: The Triumph of Urban Populism in San Francisco. *Western Political Quarterly* 42 (June): 307–33.

Downs, Anthony. 1957. *An Economic Theory of Democracy.* New York: Harper and Row.

Dykstra, Clarence A. 1925. Los Angeles Returns to the Ward System. *National Municipal Review* 14 (May): 210–12.

Edsall, Thomas B., and Mary D. Edsall. 1991. *Chain Reaction: The Impact of Race, Rights and Taxes on American Politics.* New York: W. W. Norton.

Eisinger, Peter K. 1976. *Patterns of Interracial Politics: Conflict or Cooperation in the City.* New York: Academic Press.

————. 1982. Black Employment in Municipal Jobs: The Impact of Black Political Power. *American Political Science Review* 76 (June): 380–92.

————. 1983. Black Mayors and the Politics of Racial Economic Advancement. In William McCready, ed., *Culture, Ethnicity, and Identity: Current Issues in Research,* 95–109. New York: Academic Press.

Elkin, Stephen L. 1987. *City and Regime in the American Republic.* Chicago: University of Chicago Press.

Erie, Steven P. 1980. Two Faces of Ethnic Power: Comparing the Irish and Black Experiences. *Polity* 13 (Winter): 261–84.

Erie, Steven P., Harold Brackman, and James Warren Ingram III. 1992. *Paths to*

Political Incorporation for California's Newer Minorities. California Policy Seminar Research Report, University of California.

Fairbank, Maullin, and Associates. Various years. Private opinion surveys. Santa Monica, CA.

Fisher, Alan M. 1979. Realignment of the Jewish Vote? *Political Science Quarterly* 94:97–116.

Fisher, Alan M., and Curtis K. Tanaka. 1986. California Jews: Data from the Field Polls. *American Jewish Yearbook* 86:196–218.

Fogelson, Robert. 1967. *The Fragmented Metropolis: Los Angeles, 1850–1930.* Cambridge, MA: Harvard University Press.

Galm, Bernard. 1984. *The Impossible Dream: Thomas Bradley.* An oral history conducted under the auspices of the Oral History Program, University of California, Los Angeles.

Gelfand, Mitchell B. 1979a. Progress and Prosperity: Jewish Social Mobility in Los Angeles in the Booming Eighties. *American Jewish History* 68 (June):408–33.

———. 1979b. Jewish Economic and Residential Mobility in Early Los Angeles. *Western States Jewish Historical Quarterly* 11 (July): 332–47.

———. 1981. Chutzpah in El Dorado: Social Mobility of Jews in Los Angeles, 1900–1920. Ph.D. diss., Carnegie-Mellon University.

Giles, Micheal W., and Arthur Evans. 1986. The Power Approach to Intergroup Hostility. *Journal of Conflict Resolution* 30:469–86.

Giles, Micheal W., and Douglas S. Gatlin. 1980. Mass-Level Compliance with Public Policy: The Case of School Desegregation. *Journal of Politics* 42:722–46.

Gittel, Marilyn. 1971. Education: The Decentralization-Community Control Controversy. In Bellush, Jewel, and Stephen M. David, eds., *Race and Politics in New York City,* 134–163. New York: Praeger.

Glazer, Nathan, and Daniel Patrick Moynihan. 1970a. *Beyond the Melting Pot: The Negroes, Puerto Ricans, Jews, Italians, and Irish of New York City.* 2d ed. Cambridge, MA: MIT Press.

———. 1970b. How the Catholics Lost Out to the Jews in New York Politics. *New York* 3:38–49.

Governor's Commission on the Los Angeles Riots (McCone Commission). 1965. *Violence in the City—an End or a Beginning?* Los Angeles.

Greenstein, Fred I. 1982. *The Hidden-Hand Presidency: Eisenhower as Leader.* New York: Basic Books.

Greenstone, J. David, and Paul E. Peterson. 1973. *Race and Authority in Urban Politics: Community Participation in the War on Poverty.* New York: Russell Sage Foundation.

Guerra, Fernando J. 1987. Ethnic Officeholders in Los Angeles County. *Sociology and Social Research* 71:89–94.

Hahn, Harlan, and Timothy Almy. 1971. Ethnic Politics and Racial Issues: Voting in Los Angeles. *Western Political Quarterly* 24:719–30.

Hahn, Harlan, David Klingman, and Harry Pachon. 1976. Cleavages, Coalitions and the Black Candidate: The Los Angeles Mayoralty Elections of 1969 and 1973. *Western Political Quarterly* 29:521–30.

Halley, Robert M. 1974. An Analysis of Ethnic Voting Patterns in the 1973 Los Angeles Municipal Elections. M.A. thesis, University of Southern California.

Halley, Robert M., Alan C. Acock, and Thomas Greene. 1976. Ethnicity and Social Class: Voting in the Los Angeles Municipal Elections. *Western Political Quarterly* 29:507–20.

Hamilton, Charles V. 1977. De-Racialization: Examination of a Political Strategy. *First World* 1:3–5.

———. 1979. The Patron-Recipient Relationship and Minority Politics in New York City. *Political Science Quarterly* 94 (Summer): 211-28.

Hardy, Leroy. 1955. The California Reapportionment of 1951. Ph.D. diss., University of California, Los Angeles.

Harris, Louis, and Bert E. Swanson. 1970. *Black-Jewish Relations in New York City.* New York: Praeger.

Henry, Charles P. 1980. Black-Chicano Coalitions: Possibilities and Problems. *Western Journal of Black Studies* 4:202–32.

Hinckley, Barbara. 1981. *Coalitions and Politics.* New York: Harcourt Brace Jovanovich.

Holloway, Harry. 1968. Negro Political Strategy: Coalition or Independent Power Politics? *Social Science Quarterly* 49:534–47.

Independent Commission on the Los Angeles Police Department (Christopher Commission). 1991. *Report.*

Jackson, Byran O. 1987. The Effects of Racial Group Consciousness on Political Mobilization in American Cities. *Western Political Quarterly* 40 (December): 631–46.

———. 1988. Ethnic Cleavages and Voting Patterns in U.S. Cities: An Analysis of the Asian, Black and Hispanic Communities of Los Angeles. Paper presented at the Conference on Comparative Ethnicity, University of California, Los Angeles.

Jackson, Byran O., and Melvin L. Oliver. 1988. Race and Politics in the Advanced Industrial City: A Critical Assessment of Mayor Tom Bradley's Job Performance. Paper presented at the annual meeting of the American Political Science Association.

Jeffries, Vincent, and H. E. Ransford. 1969. Interracial Social Contact and Middle-Class White Reactions to the Watts Riot. *Social Problems* 16:312–24.

———. 1972. Ideology, Social Structure, and the Yorty-Bradley Mayoral Election. *Social Problems* 19 (Winter):358–72.

Jennings, James. 1982. Race, Class, and Politics in the Black Community of Boston. *Review of Black Political Economy* 12 (Fall): 47–63.

Johnson, James, Jr., and Melvin Oliver. 1989. Interethnic Minority Conflict in Urban America: The Effects of Economic and Social Dislocations. *Urban Geography* 10 (September/October): 449–63.

Johnson, Paula B., David O. Sears, and John B. McConahay. 1971. Black Invisibility, the Press and the Los Angeles Riot. *American Journal of Sociology* 76:698–721.

Jones, Mack H. 1978. Black Political Empowerment in Atlanta: Myth and Reality. *Annals of the American Academy of Political and Social Sciences*, 439 (September): 90-117.

Jones, William B. 1962. CDC and the Negro Community. *CDC Bulletin* 1:4–5.

Keiser, Richard A. 1990. The Rise of a Biracial Coalition in Philadelphia. In Rufus Browning, Dale Rogers Marshall, and David Tabb, eds., *Racial Politics in American Cities*, 49–74. New York: Longman.

Kinder, Donald R., and Lynn M. Sanders. 1987. Pluralistic Foundations of American Opinion on Race. Paper presented at the annual meeting of the American Political Science Association.

Kinder, Donald R., and David O. Sears. 1981. Prejudice and Politics: Symbolic Racism versus Racial Threats to the Good Life. *Journal of Personality and Social Psychology* 40:414–31.

Klein, Norman M., and Martin J. Schiesl, eds. 1990. *20th Century Los Angeles: Power, Promotion and Social Conflict*. Claremont, CA: Regina Books.

Kleppner, Paul. 1985. *Chicago Divided: The Making of a Black Mayor*. DeKalb: Northern Illinois University Press.

Krikorian, Greg. 1983. Caution: Spies at Work. *California Journal* 14 (November): 415–17.

Levine, Charles H. 1974. *Racial Conflict and the American Mayor*. Lexington, MA: Lexington Books.

Lewinson, Edwin P. 1974. *Black Politics in New York City*. NY: Twayne Publishers.

Lieske, Joel, and Jan William Hillard. 1984. The Racial Factor in Urban Elections. *Western Political Quarterly* 37:545–63.

Littwin, Susan. 1976. How Waxman and Berman Run the Bagel Boroughs. *California Journal* 7 (September): 299–301.

———. 1981. Inside Tom Bradley: The Making of a Mayor, 1981 and of a Governor, 1982. *New West* 6:85–89.

Los Angeles Headquarters City Association. 1992. *Los Angeles: At an Economic Crossroads*. Planning Institute, School of Urban and Regional Planning, University of Southern California.

Maller, Allen S. 1977. Class Factors in the Jewish Vote. *Jewish Social Studies* 39:159–62.

Maullin, Richard. 1971. Los Angeles Liberalism. *Trans-Action* 8:40–50.

Mayo, Charles G. 1964. The 1961 Mayoralty Election in Los Angeles: The Political Party in a Nonpartisan Election. *Western Political Quarterly* 17:325–37.

McClain, Paula D., and Albert Karnig. 1989. Black and Hispanic Socioeconomic and Political Competition. *American Political Science Review* 83 (March):165–92.

McPhail, I.R. 1971. The Vote for Mayor of Los Angeles in 1969. *Annals of the Association of American Geographers* 6 (December): 744–58.

Meyerson, Harold. 1991. After Rodney King, the Deluge. *L.A. Weekly*, May 3–9, 12, 16–17.

Miranda, Gloria E. 1990. The Mexican Immigrant Family: Economic and Cultural Survival in Los Angeles, 1900–1945. In Norman M. Klein and Martin J. Schiesl, eds., *20th Century Los Angeles: Power, Promotion and Social Conflict*, 39–60. Claremont, CA: Regina Books.

Modell, John. 1977. *The Economics and Politics of Racial Accommodation: The Japanese of Los Angeles, 1900–1942*. Urbana: University of Illinois Press.

Mollenkopf, John. 1990a. New York: The Great Anomaly. In Rufus Browning, Dale Rogers Marshall, and David Tabb, eds., *Racial Politics in American Cities*, 75–87. New York: Longman.

———. 1990b. The Dinkins Victory. *Urban Politics and Urban Policy Section Newsletter* 3 (Winter): 10–12.

Morris, Richard T., and Vincent Jeffries. 1970. The White Reaction Study. In

Nathan Cohen, ed., *The Los Angeles Riots: A Socio-Psychological Study*, 480—681. New York: Praeger.

Munoz, Carlos, Jr., and Charles P. Henry. 1990. Coalition Politics in San Antonio and Denver: The Cisneros and Peña Mayoral Campaigns. In Rufus Browning, Dale Rogers Marshall, and David Tabb, eds., *Racial Politics in American Cities*, 179–92. New York: Longman.

Murray, Richard, and Arnold Vedlitz. 1978. Racial Voting Patterns in the South: An Analysis of Major Elections from 1960 to 1977 in Five Cities. *Annals of the American Academy of Political and Social Sciences* 439:29–39.

Nakanishi, Don T. 1986. *UCLA Asian Pacific Voter Registration Study.* Los Angeles: Asian Pacific American Legal Center.

———. 1990. The Next Swing Vote? Asian Pacific Americans and California Politics. In Bryon O. Jackson and Michael B. Preston, eds., *Racial and Ethnic Politics in California*, 25–54. Berkeley, CA: Institute for Governmental Studies.

Nelson, William. 1987. The Rise and Fall of Black Politics in Cleveland. In Michael Preston. Lenneal J. Henderson, Jr., and Paul L. Puryear, eds., *The New Black Politics: The Search for Political Power*, 2nd ed., 172–99. New York: Longman.

Norvell, Nancy, and Stephen Worchel. 1981. A Reexamination of the Relation between Equal Status Contact and Intergroup Attraction. *Journal of Personality and Social Psychology* 41:902–8.

O'Laughlin, John, and Dale E. Berg. 1977. The Election of Black Mayors, 1969 and 1973. *Annals of the Association of American Geographers* 67 (June): 223–38.

Oliver, Melvin L. 1986. *Beyond the Neighborhood: The Spatial Distribution of Social Ties in Three Urban Black Communities.* ISSR Working Papers in the Social Sciences, vol. 2. University of California, Los Angeles.

Oliver, Melvin L., and James H. Johnson, Jr. 1984. Inter-ethnic Conflict in an Urban Ghetto: The Case of Blacks and Latinos in Los Angeles. In *Research in Social Movements, Conflict and Change*, vol. 6, 57-94. JAI Press.

Oxnam, G. Bromley. 1920. *The Mexican in Los Angeles.* Interchurch World Movement of North America. Reprint. San Francisco: R & E Research Associates, 1970.

Pachon, Harry. 1990. Latino Participation in California Politics. In Bryan O. Jackson and Michael B. Preston, eds., *Racial and Ethnic Politics in California*, 71—88. Berkeley, CA: Institute for Governmental Studies.

Parent, Wayne, and Paul Stekler. 1985. The Political Implications of Economic Stratification in the Black Community. *Western Political Quarterly* 38 (December): 521–37.

Patterson, Beeman. 1967. The Politics of Recognition: Negro Politics in Los Angeles, 1960–1963. Ph.D. diss., University of California, Los Angeles.

———. 1969. Political Action of Negroes in Los Angeles: A Case Study in the Attainment of Councilmanic Representation. *Phylon* 30:170–83.

Payne, J. Gregory, and Scott C. Ratzan. 1986. *Tom Bradley: The Impossible Dream.* Santa Monica, CA: Roundtable Press.

Petrocik, John R., and Dennis P. Patterson. 1986. *Party Coalitions and Ethnic Divisions in a Multi-Ethnic City.* ISSR Working Papers in the Social Sciences, vol. 2. University of California, Los Angeles.

REFERENCES **319**

Pettigrew, Thomas F. 1971. When a Black Candidate Runs for Mayor: Race and Voting Behavior. In Harlan Hahn, ed., *People and Politics in Urban Society*, 99–105. Beverly Hills, CA: Sage Publications.
Pettigrew, Thomas F., and Denise A. Alston. 1988. *Tom Bradley's Campaigns for Governor: The Dilemma of Race and Political Strategies*. Washington, DC: Joint Center for Political Studies.
Piven, Frances, and Richard A. Cloward. 1971. *Regulating the Poor: The Functions of Public Welfare*. New York: Vintage.
Plissner, Martin, and Warren Mitofsky. 1988. The Changing Jackson Voter. *Public Opinion* 11 (July/August): 56–57.
Poulson, Norris. 1966. *Who Would Have Ever Dreamed?* Oral History Program of the University of California, Los Angeles.
Preston, Michael B. 1990. Black Mayors: An Overview. *National Political Science Review* 2:131–37.
Ransom, Bruce. 1987. Black Independent Electoral Politics in Philadelphia: The Election of Mayor W. Wilson Goode. In Michael B. Preston, Lenneal J. Henderson, Jr., and Paul L. Puryear, eds., *The New Black Politics: The Search for Political Power*, 2d ed., 256–89. New York and London: Longman.
Reed, Adolph, Jr. 1986. *The Jesse Jackson Phenomenon*. New Haven: Yale University Press.
Regalado, James A. 1988a. Interview with Congressman Edward Roybal.
———. 1988b. Latino Representation in Los Angeles. In Roberto E. Villareal, Norma G. Hernandez, and Howard D. Neighbor, eds., *Latino Empowerment: Progress, Problems, and Prospects*, 91–104. New York: Greenwood Press.
———. 1991. Organized Labor and Los Angeles City Politics: An Assessment in the Bradley Years, 1973–1989. *Urban Affairs Quarterly* 27(September):87–108.
———. 1992. Political Representation, Economic Development Policymaking, and Social Crisis in Los Angeles, 1973–1992. In Gerry Riposa and Carolyn Dersch, eds., *City of Angels*, 160–79. Dubuque, IA: Kendall-Hunt.
Rieff, David. 1991. *Los Angeles: Capital of the Third World*. New York: Simon and Schuster.
Riker, William. 1961. *The Theory of Political Coalitions*. New Haven: Yale University Press.
Robinson, James Lee. 1976. Tom Bradley: Los Angeles' First Black Mayor. Ph.D diss., University of California, Los Angeles.
Romo, Ricardo. 1977. Work and Restlessness: Occupational and Spatial Mobility among Mexicanos in Los Angeles, 1918–1928. *Pacific Historical Review* 46:157–80.
Ross, Ruth. 1980. *The Impact of Federal Grants on the City of Los Angeles*. Federal Aid Case Studies Series, paper no. 8. Washington, DC: Brookings Institution.
Saltzstein, Alan, Raphe Sonenshein, and Irving Ostrow. 1986. Federal Aid to the City of Los Angeles: Implementing a More Centralized Local Political System. In Terry Clark, ed., *Research in Urban Policy*, vol. 2, 55–76. Greenwich, CT: JAI Press.
Saltzstein, Grace Hall. 1989. Black Mayors and Police Policies. *Journal of Politics* 51(August):525–44.
Sandberg, Neil C. 1986. *Jewish Life in Los Angeles: A Window to Tomorrow*. Lanham, MD: University Press of America.

Sandoval, Sally Jane. 1973. Ghetto Growing Pains: The Impact of Negro Migration on the City of Los Angeles, 1940–1960. M.A. thesis, California State University, Fullerton.

Scoble, Harry M. 1967. *Negro Politics in Los Angeles: The Quest for Power*. Los Angeles: Institute of Government and Public Affairs, University of California.

Sears, David O., and Donald R. Kinder. 1971. Racial Tensions and Voting in Los Angeles. In Werner Z. Hirsch, ed., *Los Angeles: Viability and Prospects for Metropolitan Leadership*, 51–88. New York: Praeger.

Sears, David O., and John B. McConahay. 1973. *The Politics of Violence: The New Urban Blacks and the Watts Riot*. Boston: Houghton Mifflin.

Shefter, Martin. 1983. Regional Receptivity to Reform. *Political Science Quarterly* 98 (Fall): 459–84.

Shingles, Richard D. 1989. Class, Status and Support for Governmental Aid to Disadvantaged Groups. *Journal of Politics* 51 (November): 933–64.

Singleton, Gregory H. 1979. *Religion in the City of the Angels: American Protestant Culture and Urbanization, Los Angeles, 1850–1930*. Ann Arbor, MI: UMI Research Press.

Sleeper, Jim. 1990. *The Closest of Strangers: Liberalism and the Politics of Race in New York*. New York: W. W. Norton.

Smith, Alonzo Nelson. 1978. Black Employment in the Los Angeles Area, 1938–1948. Ph.D. diss., University of California, Los Angeles.

Smith, J. Owens, 1987. *The Politics of Racial Inequality*. Westport, CT: Greenwood Press.

Sonenshein, Raphael J. 1971. Mayor Kenneth Gibson's Newark. B.A. thesis, Princeton University.

———. 1984. Bradley's People: Functions of the Candidate Organization. Ph.D. diss., Yale University.

———. 1990. Can Black Candidates Win Statewide Elections? *Political Science Quarterly* 105 (Summer): 219–41.

———. 1992. The Rodney King Case and Los Angeles Coalition Politics. Paper presented at the annual meeting of the American Political Science Association.

Stacey, William A. 1972. *Black Home Ownership: A Sociological Case Study of Metropolitan Jacksonville*. New York: Praeger.

Starks, Robert T., and Michael B. Preston. 1990. Harold Washington and the Politics of Reform in Chicago: 1983–1987. In Rufus Browning, Dale Rogers Marshall, and David Tabb, eds., *Racial Politics in American Cities*, 88–107. New York: Longman.

Stern, Norton B. 1976. Jews in the 1870 Census of Los Angeles. *Western States Jewish Historical Quarterly* 9 (October): 71–86.

———. 1980. The First Jew to Run for Mayor of Los Angeles. *Western States Jewish Historical Quarterly* 12 (April): 246–59.

———. 1981. Los Angeles Jewish Voters during Grant's First Presidential Race. *Western States Jewish Historical Quarterly* 13 (January): 179–85.

Stone, Clarence. 1989. *Regime Politics: Governing Atlanta, 1946–1988*. Lawrence, KS: University of Kansas Press.

Thompson, J. Phillip. 1990. David Dinkins' Victory in New York City: The Decline of the Democratic Party Organization and the Strengthening of Black Politics. *PS* 23 (June): 145–47.

Tryman, Mfanya D. 1974. Black Mayoralty Campaigns: Running the "Race". *Phylon*, 35 (winter): 346–358

Tuttle, Frederick B., Jr. 1975. The California Democrats, 1953–1966. Ph.D. diss., University of California, Los Angeles.

Uhlaner, Carole. 1991. Perceived Prejudice and the Coalition Prospects of Blacks, Latinos and Asian-Americans. In Byran O. Jackson and Michael B. Preston, eds., *Ethnic and Racial Politics in California*, 339–72. Berkeley, CA: Institute for Governmental Studies.

Uhlaner, Carole J., Bruce E. Cain, and D. Roderick Kiewiet. 1989. Political Participation of Ethnic Minorities in the 1980's. *Political Behavior* 11 (September): 195–232.

Unrau, Harlan Dale. 1971. The Double V Movement in Los Angeles during the Second World War: A Study in Negro Protest. M.A. thesis, California State University, Fullerton.

Vorspan, Max. 1969. Patterns of Jewish Voting, 1968. *Midstream* 15:39–42.

Vorspan, Max, and Lloyd P. Gartner. 1970. *History of the Jews of Los Angeles*. San Marino, CA: The Huntington Library.

Weiss, Edward J. 1985. The Waxman-Berman Organization. Senior honors thesis, University of California, Berkeley.

Welch, Susan, and Michael W. Combs. 1985. Intra-Racial Differences in Attitudes of Blacks: Class Cleavages or Consensus? *Phylon* 66 (Summer): 91–97.

Wilburn, James R. 1971. Social and Economic Aspects of the Aircraft Industry in Metropolitan Los Angeles during World War II. Ph.D. diss., University of California, Los Angeles.

Willens, Michele. 1980. The Sudden Rise of the Jewish Politician. *California Journal* 11:146–48.

Wilson, James Q. 1960. *Negro Politics: The Search for Leadership*. New York: Free Press.

―――. 1962. *The Amateur Democrat: Club Politics in Three Cities*. Chicago: University of Chicago Press.

Wilson, James Q., and Harold R. Wilde. 1969. The Urban Mood. *Commentary* 48:52–61.

Wilson, William Julius. 1978. *The Declining Significance of Race*. Chicago: University of Chicago Press.

Wolfinger, Raymond W., and Fred I. Greenstein. 1968. The Repeal of Fair Housing in California: An Analysis of Referendum Voting. *American Political Science Review* 62 (September): 753–59.

Woods, Joseph Gerald. 1973. The Progressives and the Police: Urban Reform and the Professionalization of the Los Angeles Police. Ph.D. diss., University of California, Los Angeles.

Yorty, Sam. Collection. Los Angeles City Archives.

NEWSPAPERS

California Eagle
Herald Dispatch-Watts Star Review
Los Angeles Herald-Examiner

Los Angeles Newsletter
Los Angeles Sentinel
Los Angeles Times
New York Times

PERSONAL PAPERS

Robert Farrell
Richard Giesberg
Carol Plotkin
Sam Yorty Collection

INTERVIEWS

Tom Bradley
Jesse Brewer
Anton Calleia
David Cunningham
Willis Edwards
Robert Farrell
Richard Giesberg
Maureen Kindel
Bob Kholos
Wanda Moore
Willard Murray
Irving Ostrow
Max Palevsky
Carol Plotkin
Don Rothenberg
Leslie Song-Winner
Tom Sullivan
Rick Taylor
Frank Terry
Maurice Weiner
Roderick Wright

CO-INTERVIEWS WITH ALAN SALTZSTEIN

Keith Comrie
Grace Davis
John S. Gibson, Jr.
Emma McFarlin
Fred Roberts
Ted Rogers
Grieg Smith

INDEX